FLORIDA STATE
UNIVERSITY LIBRARIES

NOV 6 1996

TALLAHASSEE, FLORIDA

Hunters between East and West
The Paleolithic of Moravia

INTERDISCIPLINARY CONTRIBUTIONS TO ARCHAEOLOGY

Series Editor: Michael Jochim, *University of California, Santa Barbara*
Founding Editor: Roy S. Dickens, Jr., *Late of University of North Carolina, Chapel Hill*

Current Volumes in This Series:

THE ARCHAEOLOGY OF WEALTH
Consumer Behavior in English America
James G. Gibb

CASE STUDIES IN ENVIRONMENTAL ARCHAEOLOGY
Edited by Elizabeth J. Reitz, Lee A. Newsom, and Sylvia J. Scudder

CHESAPEAKE PREHISTORY
Old Traditions, New Directions
Richard J. Dent, Jr.

DARWINIAN ARCHAEOLOGIES
Edited by Herbert Donald Graham Maschner

HUMANS AT THE END OF THE ICE AGE
The Archaeology of the Pleistocene–Holocene Transition
Edited by Lawrence Guy Straus, Berit Valentin Eriksen, Jon M. Erlandson, and David R. Yesner

HUNTERS BETWEEN EAST AND WEST
The Paleolithic of Moravia
Jiří Svoboda, Vojen Ložek, and Emanuel Vlček

PREHISTORIC CULTURAL ECOLOGY AND EVOLUTION
Insights from Southern Jordan
Donald O. Henry

STATISTICS FOR ARCHAEOLOGISTS
A Commonsense Approach
Robert D. Drennan

STONE TOOLS
Theoretical Insights into Human Prehistory
Edited by George H. Odell

VILLAGERS OF THE MAROS
A Portrait of an Early Bronze Age Society
John M. O'Shea

A Chronological Listing of Volumes in this series appears at the back of this volume.

A Continuation Order Plan is available for this series. A continuation order will bring delivery of each new volume immediately upon publication. Volumes are billed only upon actual shipment. For further information please contact the publisher.

Hunters between East and West
The Paleolithic of Moravia

JIŘÍ SVOBODA
*Academy of Sciences
Brno-Dolní Věstonice, Czech Republic*

VOJEN LOŽEK
*Academy of Sciences
Prague, Czech Republic*

and

EMANUEL VLČEK
*National Museum
Prague, Czech Republic*

PLENUM PRESS • NEW YORK AND LONDON

Library of Congress Cataloging-in-Publication Data

Svoboda, Jiří.
　　Hunters between East and West : the Paleolithic of Moravia / Jiří
Svoboda, Vojen Ložek, and Emanuel Vlček.
　　　p.　cm. -- (Interdisciplinary contributions to archaeology)
　　Includes bibliographical references (p.　　　) and index.
　　ISBN 0-306-45250-2
　　1. Paleolithic period--Czech Republic--Moravia. 2. Moravia (Czech
Republic)--Antiquities.　I. Ložek, Vojen. II. Vlček, Emanuel.
III. Title. IV. Series.
GN772.22.C94S96　1996
943.7'02--dc20
　　　　　　　　　　　　　　　　　　　　　　　　　　　　　96-31102
　　　　　　　　　　　　　　　　　　　　　　　　　　　　　　CIP

ISBN 0-306-45250-2

© 1996 Plenum Press, New York
A Division of Plenum Publishing Corporation
233 Spring Street, New York, N. Y. 10013

10 9 8 7 6 5 4 3 2 1

All rights reserved

No part of this book may be reproduced, stored in a retrieval system, or transmitted in any
form or by any means, electronic, mechanical, photocopying, microfilming, recording, or
otherwise, without written permission from the Publisher

Printed in the United States of America

IN MEMORIAM

The Paleolithic People of Moravia

Foreword

At first glance, the archaeological record of Moravia has been quite visible in the Anglophone world. Bits and pieces of this record have repeatedly made headlines in both the general and the specialized press for close to a century. First, it was the discovery of a mass grave of some 21 individuals found at the Upper Paleolithic site of Předmostí, then the oldest evidence for ceramic technology reported in the first quarter of this century in the *Illustrated London News*. Later on, the site of Petřkovice, dating some 23,000 B.P., produced evidence for the oldest burning of coal for fuel, while more recently the *New York Times* informed us that imprints in clay at Pavlov I attest to the oldest evidence for the making and use of textiles. This list of cultural innovations documented from Moravia can be expanded to include the use of ground stone technology to make stone pendants (e.g., at Předmostí), of large ground-stone rings whose use remains enigmatic (e.g., at Brno II, Předmostí, and Pavlov I)—but which if found in more recent contexts would pass as querns—as well as of possible needles (again at Předmostí). These exciting finds came from equally spectacular contexts: sites with numerous complex features including kilns (Dolní Věstonice I), boiling pits (Dolní Věstonice II), dwellings curbed with mammoth bones (Dolní Věstonice I and Milovice), bone dumps containing remains of up to 1000 mammoths (Předmostí, smaller numbers found at Dolní Věstonice I), and singular as well as multiple internments, some of which were accompanied by the richest of burial inventories (Brno II, for example).

This spectacular record has inspired artists and writers to offer us their versions of life in Paleolithic Moravia (e.g., the paintings of Burian or Auel's *Plains of Passage*). Furthermore, especially in the last 20 years or so, the Moravian Paleolithic record has also been incorporated into our introductory textbooks on prehistory. These inclusions have, however, been very patchy and opportunistic—incorporating some Moravian data to compare and contrast to evidence from other parts of the Paleolithic world. Nor has this database fared better in the archaeological literature. When acknowledged, it has generally been used highly selectively and anecdotally: bits of data have been cited when supportive, and the data have been ignored when they undermine the arguments being made. Such episodic and often acontextual use of the Moravian record, a use designed to titillate rather than explain, came about for a variety of reasons, and the result is that the sum total of this record and its significance are poorly known to scholars outside Moravia. Yet this is a record, coming as it does from the very center of Europe, which clearly needs to be known if we are to document fully the range of variability in Pleistocene adaptations and to explain satisfactorily the culture change during the Paleolithic.

There are a number of reasons why we know so little about the Moravian record. First, in contrast to the coverage of both Western and Eastern Europe, until recently there has never been a synthetic work—either in Czech or in any other language—presenting the sum total of the archaeological and paleontological evidence available. This book represents the first such monograph in English, an earlier version, *Paleolit Moravy a Slezska*, having come out in the Czech Republic in Czech in 1994. Second, although scholars working in Moravia (where, as Jiří Svoboda documents, Paleolithic research has a tradition that is more than 100 years old) did regularly publish their research findings, these publications were usually in languages poorly known by a large number of specialists, especially Anglophone ones: Czech and German. In addition, these findings were often published in regional journals and almanacs which were, and continue to be, very difficult to obtain. Furthermore, scholars working in Moravia, a region lying "betwixt and between" the west and the east of Europe, were affected not only by prehistoric research traditions, but also by the political turbulences of the day. These realities led to viewing (presenting) the Moravian record first in the light of that from France and then, a short time later, in the light of data from points further east.

Happily, in the appropriately and poignantly titled *Hunters between East and West: The Paleolithic of Moravia*, this unfortunate tendency has now been brought to a halt and English-language readers are offered a firsthand look at this important record "as is." This book goes a long way toward reducing our extant information gap. It is a rich and a multifaceted contribution to the literature written by three preeminent Czech specialists: an archaeologist (Svoboda), a geologist (Ložek), and a paleoanthropologist (Vlček). Their combined expertise is skillfully blended to produce an authoritative synthesis of the pertinent Moravian data. The book begins with a thorough review of the history of Paleolithic research in Moravia, an exposition which contextualizes both the questions asked and what is known within specific research traditions and historical times. The Pleistocene environments extant in Moravia at various points in time are next examined by Ložek, with an eye both to delimiting their different characteristics during glacial versus interglacial times and to outlining the challenges they posed for successful human occupation. In Chapter 3, Vlček discusses the fossil record of Moravia and its neighbors and offers his interpretations of the significance of population replacements versus *in situ* developments there. The following four chapters present the Moravian archaeological record for the different periods of Pleistocene time, offering quantified data not only on traditional technotypologies but on the use of raw materials and their procurement. In the concluding chapter, Svoboda notes that regional surveys have had a long history in Moravia and concludes that the record on hand today probably faithfully mirrors what has been preserved. He then goes on to discuss the regional pattern in the distribution of the sites and the changes in their location through time.

These eight chapters rightfully contain many provocative hypotheses about human evolution, adaptations, and behavior during the Pleistocene. Some of these will find easy acceptance among Anglophone specialists, while others will undoubtedly generate debate. What is equally significant and most laudable is that all of the chapters also present a myriad of quantified primary data in narrative, tabular, and figurative form on such things as the hominid fossil remains, lithic inventories, and radiocarbon dates. This emphasis on presenting as much of the database as possible is further augmented by two extremely useful appendixes, one of which catalogs all of the important Pleistocene sites in Moravia and the other of which lists the sites and pertinent references to the published literature on them. The exemplary format of this volume thus not only informs but also encourages interested readers either to use these data in their own research or to verify the interpretations offered by the authors of this book.

Hunters between East and West: The Paleolithic of Moravia is a most important addition to our literature about Paleolithic Europe. Our current literature on Paleolithic adaptations in Europe makes many claims. These, too often, are based on data gathered in one part of the world—usually Western Europe—extended and writ large to blanket the rest. By closing the extant "information gap," Svoboda, Ložek, and Vlček challenge scholars working in the field to include these data in their continent-wide constructs. Testing such constructs against this "new" database will eliminate some ideas, strengthen others, and permit us a richer and more catholic understanding of our distant past.

OLGA SOFFER
University of Illinois
Urbana, Illinois

Preface

In 1867 Dr. J. Wankel, from the small town of Blansko in the Moravian Karst, opened the first Paleolithic excavation in the former Austrian–Hungarian Empire: the Býčí skála Cave. Since that time, a number of other excavated caves, such as Pekárna, Šipka, Mladeč, and Kůlna, together with open-air loess sites like Předmostí, Dolní Věstonice, and Pavlov have completed the Paleolithic record of Moravia. The past was rich in fieldwork and splendid discoveries, but today more emphasis should be placed on resuming and interpreting the record. Even if part of this material—namely, some human fossils—was destroyed at the end of World War II, institutions like the Anthropos Department of the Moravian Museum (Brno), the Paleolithic and Paleo-ethnology Department of the Institute of Archaeology, the Academy of Sciences (Dolní Věstonice), other large museums (Olomouc, Opava), a network of regional museums, and, outside Moravia, the Natural History Museum (Vienna) have been able to concentrate important Paleolithic collections.

The regional record of Moravia may contribute to a number of more general questions. Traditionally, the Pleistocene deposits of Central Europe—namely, the loess—are used to create the stratigraphic and chronological framework of the period and to reconstruct past climates. Second, the archaeological record documents complex social development in a zone connecting, in fact, the east and west of Paleolithic Europe; Moravia and the adjacent part of Lower Austria create the most important system of lowland passages open to mammal herd migrations, human settlement systems, and lithic raw-material imports. Third, this territory may contribute, from its regional perspective, to hotly debated topics like the dispersal of modern humans and the development of the Upper Paleolithic. It has yielded a few fragmented Neanderthal fossils, several early modern fossils from the Aurignacian context, and a population sample—the largest of its kind and age—from the Gravettian. Archaeology completes this evidence by increasingly documenting the complexity of behavioral patterns: changing attitudes toward landscape, resource exploitation, technologies, and rituals.

In the literature, the west and east of Europe have hitherto received considerably more attention. The present efforts in defining the role of the center and describing its prehistory may therefore change the scope with which we tend to see the past of the continent. For the last several years, our small group—centered on the newly created Department of Paleolithic and Paleoethnology in Dolní Věstonice—has aimed to evaluate the large database stored there, to promote new fieldwork using modern techniques of excavation and recording, and to publish systematically the results in a series entitled The Dolní Věstonice Studies. Naturally, this research would be unthinkable without an interdisciplinary approach. The appearance of this book in the series Interdisciplinary Contributions to Archaeology is due to the continuous understanding and collaboration of several geologists, paleontologists, and physical anthropologists.

In reviewing the state of knowledge, this book, in fact, is an introduction. Anthropology and archaeology have become truly international sciences, and newly emerging projects may radically change the theoretical approaches and methodological insights to be used in the future. One of the significant phenomena in the present state of research is the change from descriptive to functional analysis, as reflected simultaneously in physical anthropology and archaeology. In consequence, the future research will primarily be concerned with the processes that were responsible for the emergence of various biocultural adaptations, rather than with further description of the ancestor–descendant relationships of cultural traditions and human lineages.

Contents

Chapter 1 • Central Europe, Moravia, and Past Paleolithic Research   1

Geographic Introduction 1
Past Research in Moravia 4
The Present State of Research 13

Chapter 2 • Pleistocene Paleoenvironments 15

Vojen Ložek

The Moravian Pleistocene in the European Context 15
The Development of Pleistocene Sediments 15
The Quarternary Climatic Cycle and Its Products 16
Warm Periods: Interglacials, or Thermomeres 19
Cold Periods: Glacials, or Cryomeres 21
The Upper Pleistocene Sequence 20
The Fluctuation of Pleistocene Climates and Their Characteristics 33

Chapter 3 • Patterns of Human Evolution 37

Emanuel Vlček

The Problem of Fossil Human Existence during the Lower Pleistocene 37
The Middle Pleistocene Record 38
The Upper Pleistocene Record 46
The Upper Paleolithic Humans of Central Europe 56

Chapter 4 • Lower and Middle Paleolithic Background 75

Stratigraphy 77
Cultural Development and Variability 80
Early Human Adaptations in Central Europe 88

Chapter 5 • **The Beginning of the Upper Paleolithic: The Bohunicians, Szeletians, and Aurignacians** 99

The Environmental and Stratigraphic Background 103
Cultural Patterns of the Middle to Upper Paleolithic Transition 107
The Upper Paleolithic Adaptations 118

Chapter 6 • **The Culmination and Decline of the Upper Paleolithic: The Gravettians and Epigravettians** 131

Stratigraphic Background 133
Environment 135
Techo/typological Interactions through Time 138
The Gravettian Adaptations 140

Chapter 7 • **Western Invasion: The Magdalenians and Epimagdalenians** 171

Stratigraphy and Environment 173
Cultural Patterns 176
The Late Glacial Adaptations 179

Chapter 8 • **Creating Settlement Networks** 195

Macroregional View: Central Europe 195
Microregional Focus: Moravia 197

Appendix A • **Catalog of Principal Sites** 205

Appendix B • **List of Sites** 239

References 253

Index 297

Chapter **1**

Central Europe, Moravia, and Past Paleolithic Research

GEOGRAPHIC INTRODUCTION

More than 10 years ago, Soffer (1985:1)—in her splendid review of the Upper Paleolithic of the Central Russian Plain—stated that "future generations of archaeologists will wonder why we, their predecessors, viewed the Upper Paleolithic prehistory of Europe, a continent over 10,000,000 km^2 in area, primarily as an extension of the territory of the Périgord region of France, an area that measures under 10,000 km^2." Since that time, a shift toward the documentation of regional diversity, or the "Pleistocene polyphony," is observed (e.g., Soffer and Gamble, 1990). The hunter–gatherer adaptation was dynamic in time and space, and the detailing of variability on a regional scale contributes to a more contextualized understanding of the Eurasian Paleolithic record. Actually, this general trend is supported by a series of publications in English and French focusing on the Central and Eastern European Paleolithic. This book centers on an interdisciplinary study of the Paleolithic of central Europe with a particular attention to Moravia, a region offering archaeological evidence from periods covering minimally the last half-million years, but particularly rich in evidence from the last 40,000 years.

Seen from the continental perspective, Central Europe (the Northcentral region of Gamble, 1986) makes a part of the loessic zone connecting the west and the east of the continent (Figure 1.1). Two glaciations, the Fennoscandinavian in the north and the Alpine in the south, expanded periodically over parts of this area, always, however, leaving an open and passable corridor in the center. Such a territory plays a key role in overcontinental cultural adaptations as represented by the Acheulean, Mousterian, or Aurignacian, but throughout the various states of Paleolithic evolution, certain parallels link Central Europe more concretely to cultures and technologies of the Near East as in the Bohunician, of the Eurasian steppic zones in the Gravettian and Epigravet-

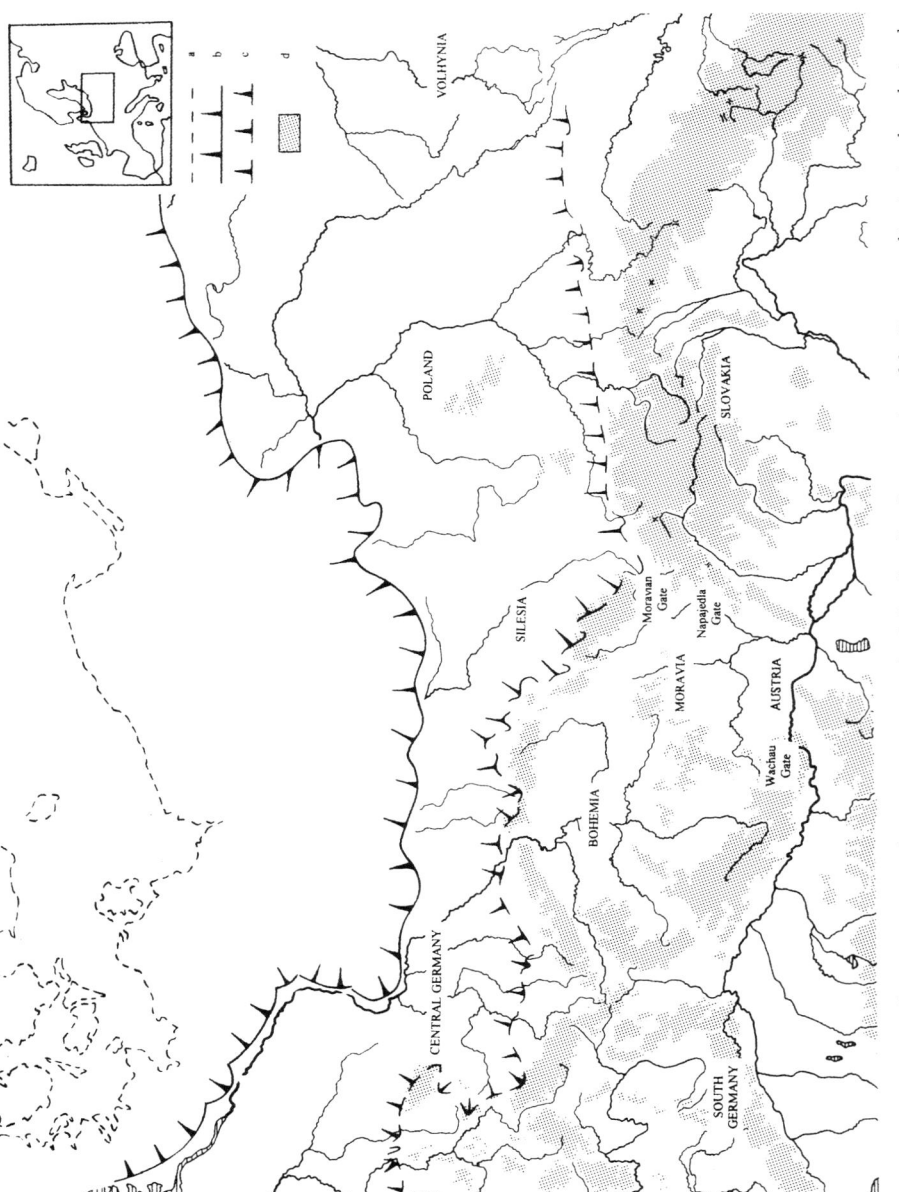

Figure 1.1. Location of Moravia in Central Europe: a—present-day Baltic shoreline; b—extension of the Fennoscandinavian ice sheet during the last glacial maximum (20,000–18,000 B.P.); c—maximal extension of the Fennoscandinavian ice sheet during the Middle Pleistocene; d—highlands.

tian, and of the western Francocantabrian zone in the Magdalenian. However, Central Europe is also the place of origin of region-specific cultures such as the Szeletian and, most probably, the Gravettian.

From a more regional perspective, the geomorphology of Moravia (the Czech Republic) creates here the most important system of lowland passages between the Bohemian Massif and the western Carpathians, connecting the Northern European Plain in the north (present Poland) and the Danube valley in the south (Austria). The Moravian Gate, a narrow corridor of tectonic origin between the two montanous systems, separates the historical land of Moravia from the Czech part of Silesia in the north. In central Moravia, the passage route divides into the Vyškov Gate and the Napajedla Gate. In the southern plains opened toward Lower Austria, the isolated chain of the Pavlovské Hills emerges as a marked orientation point (Figure 1.2). Finally, the Wachau Gate cut by the Danube River delimits the Moravian–Lower Austrian area in the southwest. The connecting function of this territory is reflected in both the archaeological and the paleontological records (Chapter 2).

As a result of the geographic setting, the Paleolithic occupation of Moravia is directly related to that of Lower Austria (Neugebauer-Maresch, 1993), southern Poland (Chmielewski, Schild, and Wieckowska, 1975; Kozlowski, 1986; Ginter, Kozlowski, and Sobczyk, 1987), and partly western Slovakia (Bárta, 1980, 1987). Further to the west, Lower Austria was connected with southern Germany by a chain

Figure 1.2. General view of the Pavlovské Hills dominating the South Moravian plains.

of sites along the upper Danube, while from southern Poland the route opened toward the Eastern European Plains. Slightly different cultural pattern are observed in basins and plains separated by low mountain ridges like Bohemia (Svoboda, 1984a), central Germany (Mania, 1984), and the territories further to the west (Chapter 8).

Favorable natural conditions during the Pleistocene and geomorphology predestined Moravia to be a meeting place of various traditions and technologies, a territory characterized by intergroup competition, and a melting pot creating specific behavior innovations. Even today, in interpreting the rich Paleolithic record from this area, archaeologists—more-or-less limited by modern international boundaries and language barriers—are influenced by the various intellectual traditions from European and world archaeology, starting with German and French, and continuing to Russian and Anglo-American.

PAST RESEARCH IN MORAVIA

The extremely ample evidence of the Palaeolithic in Moravia (including the Czech part of Silesia in the north), the archaeological material, and the contextual information have been assembled during systematic studies made over a period of more than 120 years (Absolon, 1926; Skutil, 1940c; Klíma, 1969c; Valoch, 1969c, 1978b, 1993a; Svoboda, 1984a; Svoboda, Czudek, Havlíček, Ložek, Macoun, Přichystal, Svobodová, and Vlček, 1994). Several generations of scientists have contributed to the long history of research with interpretations and concepts subsequently modified and refined. From today's viewpoint, the conclusions based on these interpretations carry more or less weight, especially if the material was discovered accidentally or comes from surface collections. Most important are the results of complex professional excavation projects; however, the present attempt at synthesis requires an assessment of the entire assemblage of data so far obtained that will make it fit a uniform pattern.

From 1867 to 1918

Paleolithic studies in Moravia were initiated in caves, that is, in locations that show the most complex stratigraphies. A dramatic advance during the last three decades of the 19th century was first evoked by uncontrolled exploitation of bones for industrial purposes and ultimately led to attainment of the professional level by the first generation of amateur archaeologists, seeking to bring themselves up to the European scientific standard (Table 1.1). No doubt a marked stimulus to these studies was given by J. Wankel (1871b, 1882, 1892). He still had difficulty in applying Thomsen's three-stage division of prehistoric times, as well as in separating Holocene and Pleistocene strata in caves. On the other hand, using the paleontological material and experience gained in France by E. Lartet, he was able to distinguish periods dominated by bears, mammoths, and reindeer and hence to point the way to future work (Wankel, 1884). Later, with the work of K. J. Maška, the level of research quickly became competitive with that of Western Europe.

Table 1.1. Important Fieldwork between 1867 and 1918

Býčí skála Cave, Habrůvka, distr. Blansko: 1867–1868, 1870–1871 J. Wankel; 1874 A. Makowsky; 1879 J. Knies; 1892 M. Kříž; 1914–1924 R. Czižek and others.
Výpustek Cave, Březina, distr. Blansko: 1870 J. Wankel; 1879 J. Szombathy; 1885 M. Kříž
Jaroslavice, distr. Znojmo: 1871 G. Wurmbrand
Šipka and Čertova díra Caves, Štramberk, distr. Nový Jičín: 1879–1883 K. J. Maška
Pekárna Cave, Mokrá, distr. Brno-venkov: 1880 J. Wankel, J. Szombathy, A. Makowsky, and F. Koudelka; 1884–1885, 1898 M. Kříž
Předmostí, distr. Přerov: 1880–1882, 1884, 1886 J. Wankel; 1882–1884, 1889–1895 K. J. Maška; 1895 M. Kříž; 1895–1898 J. Liška
Kůlna Cave, Sloup, distr. Blansko: 1881 J. Wankel; 1881–1886 M. Kříž; 1887, 1892, 1909–1913 J. Knies
Mladečské Caves, Mladeč, distr. Olomouc: 1881–1882 and later J. Szomathy; 1903–1911 J. Knies
Žitného Cave, Březina, distr. Blansko: 1883 J. Szombathy
Švédův stůl Cave, Ochoz, distr. Brno-venkov: 1886–1887, 1908 M. Kříž; 1905 K. Kubásek
Brno, Francouzská Street, distr. Brno-město: 1891 A. Makowsky
Křížova Cave, Ochoz, distr. Brno-venkov: 1893–1894 R. Trampler
Adlerova Cave, Ochoz, distr. Brno-venkov: 1893 R. Trampler
Balcarova Cave, Ostrov, distr. Blansko: 1898–1900 J. Knies
Ondratice, distr. Prostějov: 1907 I. L. Červinka
Kolíbky Caves, Jedovnice, distr. Blansko: 1907 J. Knies
Stránská skála I, Slatina, distr. Brno-město: 1910 J. Woldřich, later J. Knies
Verunčina Cave, Vilémovice, distr. Blansko: 1912 J. Knies

Maška's monograph *The Diluvial Man in Moravia* (1886) gives a useful account of the results of this first investigational stage. After describing 12 sites under study, particularly caves, he distinguished four stages, of which only the last one, the Paleolithic–Neolithic boundary, now seems questionable. The preceding three stages became a firm basis for further studies. Like Wankel, Maška relied on comparable evidence from France, but although influenced by the Mortillets system, he described the Moravian materials without strictly adopting foreign terms such as Chellean, Acheulean, Mousterian, Solutrean, and Magdalenian.

His first stage, comparable to the former Cave Bear Age and the site of Le Moustier, is marked by the presence of roughly shaped lithic and a problematic bone industry from Šipka and Čertova díra caves at Štramberk. The region-specific second stage (the former Mammoth Age) is represented especially by the open-air loess sites at Předmostí and Jaroslavice, the upper layers of the Šipka and Čertova díra caves, and the Kůlna and Poustevna Caves in the Moravian karst. The third stage, the Reindeer Age, corresponds to the material of La Madeleine in France and is evidenced especially by the Pekárna and some other caves in the Moravian karst.

Maška's historical concept was soon confronted with the simplified view of M. Kříž, presented in his book on two caves sites *Kůlna and Kostelík* (1891), and repeated later in a monograph *Contributions to Knowledge of the Quaternary Period in Moravia* (1903). By emphasizing for the first time the contextual information to the objects alone, Kříž assembled a large amount of geological information, particularly on the site of Předmostí and in the caves of the Moravian karst. It is unfortunate that he failed to subdivide the Quaternary period—attaining, in his view, its maximum in a single glaciation—and human prehistory, corresponding to a single stage and a single human race. The dispute that arose about the division of the Moravian Paleolithic was not the only topic discussed at that time, nor was it likely to be of fundamental importance. Researchers needed basic evidence that humans were contemporary with the mammoth and the rhinoceros (Wurmbrand, 1873; Maška, 1894; Makowsky, 1897, 1899a,b; Kříž, 1891, 1894), and that they witnessed the loess deposition (Wurmbrand, 1878). Particularly baffling was the supposed occurrence of "Pleistocene pottery" or even iron (Wankel, 1881). To 19th-century researchers, these were timely topics. Today theories suggesting that humans extracted fossil mammoth remains from earlier beds (Steenstrup, 1890; Wankel, 1890) and made underground shelters in loess, similar to those of the modern Chinese (Much, 1878), seem bizarre.

The materials collected by the founding researchers were still concentrated in several private collections, and only some of them reached large museums, such as the Natural History Museum in Vienna and the museum in Olomouc.

From 1918 to 1945

The foundation of the Czechoslovak Republic in 1918 was not immediately followed by changes in the amateur character of Paleolithic research in Moravia. The situation changed gradually by systematic efforts made by K. Absolon to attract the attention both of the public and of political personalities, including President Masaryk (Table 1.2).

In the first half of the 1920s, two synthesizing views from outside, by foreign researchers, brought new ideas. Abbé Breuil, in his *Remarks on a Paleolithic Trip to Central Europe* (1925), recognized evidence of the Acheulean and Mousterian in the Kůlna and Pekárna Caves and confirmed the Mousterian attribution to the Šipka and Čertova díra Caves. He concurred with Maška, Szombathy, and Bayer in assigning the Mladeč Caves to the Aurignacian as defined by himself. He was still uncertain about the age of Ondratice, from which numerous new material had been assembled, and

Table 1.2. Important Fieldwork between 1918 and 1945

Stránská skála I, Slatina, distr. Brno-město: 1925 K. Schirmeisen; 1929–1939 K. Absolon and F. Krumpholz
Mladečské Caves, Mladeč, distr. Olomouc: 1922 J. Smyčka
Dolní Věstonice I, distr. Břeclav: 1924–1938 K. Absolon; 1939–1942 A. Bohmers
Předmostí, distr. Přerov: 1923 and after J. Knies; 1924–1935 K. Absolon et al.; 1943 H. Schwabedissen
Petřkovice, distr. Ostrava: 1926–1929 J. Folprecht and K. Absolon
Žabovřesky, distr. Brno-město: 1927 K. Absolon
Brno, Kamenná Street: 1929 J. Skutil
Pekárna Cave, Mokrá, distr. Brno-venkov: early 1920s F. Čupik; 1925–1930 K. Absolon and R. Czižek
Býčí skála Cave, Habrůvka, distr. Blansko: 1914–1924 R. Czižek and others; 1936–1938 K. Absolon
Žitného Cave, Březina, distr. Blansko: early 1920s F. Čupik
Rytířská Cave, Lažánky, distr. Blansko: 1939 K. B. Absolon
Ondratice, distr. Prostějov: 1928 K. Absolon, 1942 H. Schwabedissen

tended to regard it as representing an intermediate between the Mousterian and Solutrean with Aurignacian features. Nor was the place of Předmostí easy to determine in view of French experience. Breuil concluded that it was attributable to the last Aurignacian stage affected by Solutrean from the Carpathian Basin. The Magdalenian, on the other hand, left the French visitor in no doubt, for it was fully comparable with the material found in his own country.

J. Bayer, a Viennese archaeologist, gave an overview, *The Early Stone Age in the Sudeta Lands* (1925), of his own classification system of three-stage Paleolithic development. He used certain distinctive terms such as *Faustkeilkultur*, *Handspitzenkultur*, and *Klingenkultur* for the Lower, Middle, and Upper Paleolithic, respectively. Besides following other scientists' view on the Paleolithic concept, Bayer was the first to attempt to compare the climatic history of the Pleistocene period with that of the Paleolithic cultures. With the data then available, he correctly rejected the existence of the hand-axe culture (Acheulean) in Moravia. The Middle Paleolithic, which he related to unfavorable climatic conditions (the Mousterian impact), was documented in six caves, of which only two are questionable today. The Aurignacian period of the Upper Paleolithic was believed to have coincided with a warmer climatic oscillation and a partial expansion of forest cover, later replaced by another peak of cold climate (the Solutrean impact). Viewed from the cultural viewpoint, 13 open-air sites and 5 caves can be attributed to the Aurignacian–Solutrean period. Bayer also anticipated the break in the following settlement and assumed that the population of Moravia had been completely replaced by another before the onset of the Magdalenian. Because the first discoveries at Dolní Věstonice were made at the time of the writing of the two synthesizing papers mentioned above, Breuil and Bayer were not able to incorporate the new evidence into the concepts they proposed.

Local literature was represented by J. Knies in a brief *Outline of the Moravian Paleolithic* (1925). Although Knies assigned Čertova díra to the Chellean, he did not essentially depart from the then existing views in the other aspects, particularly the views advanced by Bayer. Moreover, he provided new data from his own explorations, especially in the caves. In his view, two cold (glacial) periods correlated with the Mousterian (the Šipka type) and the Magdalenian (the Pekárna type, known from as many as 23 sites). The Mladeč type (Aurignacian) and the Předmostí type (Aurignacio-Solutrean) were regarded as "interglacial," in agreement with views generally held at that time. It is interesting that Knies made an attempt to refine the Předmostí-type material by subdividing it into the Ondratice, Předmostí, and Věstonice stages. This subdivision clearly shows a high sensibility to the morphological development of lithic industries.

I. L. Červinka was outstanding in his attempts to synthetize the new data and to address broader public. In this book *Moravia in Prehistoric Times* (1902), Červinka had already given support to Maška's chronology against Kříž's simplified concept. His later work, entitled *Prehistory of the Czech Lands* (1927), was clearly influenced by foreign authorities such as Breuil and Bayer, but it also echoed the latest discoveries made at Dolní Věstonice and Pekárna by Absolon. The main development in his work was not only the addition and determination of further surface sites, but also his introduction of the term *Szeletian* and his rejection of its cultural relationship to the Solutrean of France.

Červinka's work was immediately followed by the first geographically conceived paper on the Moravian Paleolithic by J. Skutil (1936). It contains no more discussion on Paleolithic history and subdivisions, but it supplied a valuable map. Subsequent papers by the same author (e.g., 1937a), focusing on new minor sites rather than on large excavations led by others, follow the same pattern.

The pre–World War II period culminated, both literally and in fieldwork, in the person of K. Absolon. He was responsible for concentrating private collections then available in the Department of Diluvium of the Moravian Museum (Absolon, 1926, 1937). Whereas previous investigators had aimed to cover the whole field of Pleistocene studies personally, Absolon was the first one to introduce interdisciplinary team collaboration (Absolon, Zapletal, Skutil, and Stehlík, 1933). In the field, Absolon introduced the method of opening larger areas in long parallel zones and of mapping them. Arising from these activities was a specific evolutionary concept strenuously disputed with Bayer. In principle, the Lower and Middle-Paleolithic should have been lacking in Moravia, the earliest culture being the Šipkian, equated with a pre-Aurignacian (Absolon, 1935a). Following is the Aurignacian, expanding from the east. It is divided into two or three stages, one of them including leaf-points. This evolutionary scheme is terminated by the Magdalenian, known from the caves only. Parts of this concept can be found only in topical monographs, since it has never been published more extensively. Nevertheless, it found expression in the *Review of the Czechoslovak Paleolithic* by Skutil (1940c). Differences in opinion between the two authors lie especially in the leaf-point problem: according to Skutil, they are not an integral part of the Aurignacian but were induced by the Solutrean expansion from the Carpathian Basin.

A review of the Moravian Paleolithic, published during the war years by the German investigator H. Schwabedissen (1943), reflects his endeavor to get his own way in a foreign situation and his doubts about the validity of Absolon's evolutionary concept. Further experience with Moravian materials—namely, the introduction of a more analytical view of large sites such as Předmostí—was published after the war by German archaeologists L. Zotz and G. Freund (1951). However, the postwar period witnessed one disastrous event: a large part of the Paleolithic and paleoanthropological collections of the Moravian Museum was destroyed by fire at Mikulov Castle.

From 1945 to 1989

The immediate atmosphere of the postwar period was optimistic. The appearance of a new generation of professional archaeologists and geologists, represented by B. Klíma, F. Prošek, K. Žebera, and K. Valoch, was related to the exciting growth of field research (Table 1.3), especially at Dolní Věstonice and in the Moravian karst. Another new feature was that the Paleolithic concept was based on a modern geochronological system. Studies of loess sequences were carried out over the whole territory of reestablished Czechoslovakia, under the scope of the Penck-Zeuners

Table 1.3. Important Fieldwork between 1945–1989

Stránská skála I, Slatina, distr. Brno-město: 1956–1972 R. Musil
Stránská skála II-IV, Slatina, distr. Brno-město: 1982–1989 J. Svoboda; 1982 K. Valoch
Šipka Cave, Štramberk, distr. Nový Jičín: 1950 F. Prošek
Švédův stůl Cave, Ochoz, distr. Brno-venkov: 1953–1955 B. Klíma
Kůlna Cave, Sloup, distr. Blansko: 1961–1976 K. Valoch
Bohunice, distr. Brno-město: 1969–1972, 1982 K. Valoch
Vedrovice V, distr. Znojmo: 1982–1983, 1987 K. Valoch
Dolní Věstonice I, distr. Břeclav: 1945–1946 K. Žebera: 1947–1952, 1966, 1971–1979 B. Klíma
Dolní Věstonice II, distr. Břeclav: 1959–1960 B. Klíma; 1985–1988 B. Klíma, J. Svoboda
Pavlov I, distr. Břeclav: 1952–1965, 1971–1972 B. Klíma
Pavlov II, distr. Břeclav: 1966–1967 B. Klíma
Milovice, distr. Břeclav: 1986–1991 M. Oliva
Předmostí, distr. Přerov: 1952–1954 K. Žebera; 1971–1973; 1975–1976, 1981–1983 B. Klíma; 1989 J. Svoboda
Petřkovice, distr. Ostrava: 1952–1953 B. Klíma
Boršice, distr. Uherské Hradiště: 1964 B. Klíma
Jarošov, distr. Uherské Hradiště: 1979 R. Procházka; 1980 K. Valoch
Zlín-Louky, distr. Zlín: 1950, 1953 B. Klíma
Brno, Koněvova Street, distr. Brno-město: 1972 K. Valoch
Pekárna Cave, Mokrá, distr. Brno-venkov: 1954, 1961–1965 B. Klíma; 1986–1987 J. Svoboda
Hadí Cave, Mokrá, distr. Brno-venkov: 1954, 1958 B. Klíma
Křížova Cave, Ochoz, distr. Brno-venkov: 1949–1950 B. Klíma
Adlerova Cave, Ochoz, distr. Brno-venkov: 1951 B. Klíma
Ochozská Cave, Ochoz, distr. Brno-venkov: 1953 B. Klíma
Pod vyhlídkou Cave, Ochoz, distr. Brno-venkov: 1957–1958 B. Klíma
Liščí Cave, Ochoz, distr. Brno-venkov: 1959 B. Klíma
Barová Cave, Habrůvka, distr. Blansko: 1983–1985 J. Svoboda, L. Seitl
Žitného Cave, Březina, distr. Blansko: 1955 K. Valoch
Nová Drátenická Cave, Březina, distr. Blansko: 1947–1948 B. Klíma
Kolíbky Caves, Jedovnice, distr. Blansko: 1982–1984 J. Svoboda
Rytířská Cave, Lažánky, distr. Blansko: 1960–1962 J. Skutil
Kateřinská Cave, Vavřinec, distr. Blansko: 1981, 1983 J. Svoboda, L. Seitl
Cave No. 184, Vavřinec, distr. Blansko: 1981 J. Svoboda
Pod hradem Cave, Vavřinec, distr. Blansko: 1956–1958 K. Valoch, R. Musil
Verunčina Cave, Vilémovice, distr. Blansko: 1960 J. Skutil
Srnčí Cave, Vilémovice, distr. Blansko: 1960–1962 J. Skutil
Záblatí, distr. Karviná: 1976–1979 J. Svoboda, P. Wodecki
Tišnov, distr. Brno-venkov: 1967 O. Kos
Staré Město, distr. Uherské Hradiště: 1949 and later V. Hrubý
Horní Věstonice-soutěska, distr. Břeclav: 1970 V. Ložek
Maršovice, distr. Znojmo: 1985 K. Valoch
Velké Pavlovice, distr. Břeclav: 1988 J. Svoboda

system of four glaciations (Günz, Mindel, Riss, and Würm). The last (Würm) glaciation was subdivided into three cold climatic fluctuations, numbered W 1–3. Attempts were made to correlate new evidence from Bohemia and Slovakia with the already classic territory of Moravia.

In 1953, the State Archaeological Institute was incorporated into the newly created Czechoslovak Academy of Sciences. Since Paleolithic research did not contradict historical-materialist doctrine, it was included in scientific programs, and a cooperative network of the Geological Survey and the museums was established. The Department of Diluvium in the Moravian Museum, a former center of Paleolithic research in the country, changed gradually into the specialized Anthropos Institute and Exhibition. The years of team collaboration between archaeologists and natural scientists are best reflected in the subsequent volumes of a new journal, *Anthropozoikum*, edited by K. Žebera.

In the international field, personal contacts with Russian archaeologists such as Efimenko and Boriskovskij helped in the application of methods of large-area excavation, enabling detections of dwellings and other features. In addition, new light was thrown on the cultural relationships between Dolní Věstonice and sites of the Central Russian Plain. It was surprising and unfortunate that this collaboration was quite soon broken for formal reasons, almost until today, when we are trying to reestablish it in a completely different political climate.

The first synthesizing paper based on new concepts, entitled *Stratigraphical Problems of the Czechoslovak Paleolithic*, was presented by Prošek and Ložek (1954). Evidence of the Lower Paleolithic as then conceived of was provided through an examination of loess sections at Modřice in Moravia, and the Middle Paleolithic was reconfirmed by a new trench in Šipka Cave. The Szeletian was newly defined and dated, together with the Aurignacian, to the Würm 1–2 and Würm 2 periods. A newly proposed term, *Gravettian*, was considered, instead of the former *Upper Aurignacian*. Further synthesizing papers were later published by Klíma (1957a) and Valoch (1959), both in the German journal *Quartär*. Finally, Žebera's book, *Czechoslovakia during the Old Stone Age* (1958), is an example of how an author's own geological approach may be applied to Paleolithic history.

Besides studies focused mainly on stratigraphic problems foundations were laid of a uniform typological classification of the lithics. Influenced by the terminology of D. de Sonneville-Bordes, J. Perrot, and F. Bordes, B. Klíma (1956b) and K. Valoch (1965c) presented Czech mutations of the typological lists of the Upper and Middle Paleolithic, respectively. The uniform nomenclature, further developed with regard to the specific character of local industries, became a standard work of reference for comparison purposes and for assessments to be made of the Moravian Paleolithic. Subsequently, a stress on typology became one of the characteristic features of Paleolithic research in our territory, to an extent where it was criticized especially by our Anglo-American colleagues. Typology plays a key role in basic cultural diagnosis, but it cannot substitute for stratigraphic and radiometric dating methods. Studies centered on adaptation, behavior, and social relations were missing during this period.

It would be worthwhile to do a special analysis of why the Paleolithic research did not stay in line with the quantitative growth of Czech archaeology during the 1960s and 1970s. Nevertheless, field excavations continued, especially in the classic areas of Dolní Věstonice-Pavlov and the Moravian karst, while surface surveys spread into new territories of Moravia. Simultaneously, the geochronological system was linked with the first C-14 datings and with widely comparable typological observations by authors of the new generalizing papers (Klíma, 1961c, 1969c; Valoch, 1961c, 1969c, 1978b). Klíma's paper (1961c), based on new excavation results, deals with the contemporaneity of and the relationship between the Aurignacian and the Szeletian. The Gravettian was clearly being separated from the Aurignacian, and a new term, the *Pavlovian*, was being introduced for its Moravian or Central European branch.

Consequently, doubts were initially expressed about the validity of the four-glaciations system. The climatic development of the Quaternary period, while studied by new dating and analytical methods by Kukla, Ložek, and others, began to appear much more complex than had been previously thought. Similarly, the concept of three cold peaks in the last glaciation failed to maintain validity. Instead, the scheme of two stages of glacial maxima, the lower and the upper pleniglacial, with a milder interpleniglacial period between, was applied to Moravian stratigraphies. Some of these questions are reflected in a new survey entitled *The Chronological Frame and Evolutionary Tendencies in the Czechoslovak Paleolithic* (Svoboda, 1984a).

Since the 1970s, another new feature has been the increased interest in the technological aspects of the lithics, along with attempts to make technological definitions competitive with the earlier advanced typological studies. Starting with studies of lithic outcrops (Štelcl and Malina, 1975; Valoch, 1975c; Přichystal, 1979; Svoboda, 1983; Oliva, 1984c), the technological systems evolved from a dynamic analysis of the reduction sequences in the sense of R. Schild (Svoboda, 1980, 1987d) to the new approach of core reconstructions by refittings (Svoboda and Škrdla, 1995; Škrdla, 1996).

During the 1980s, the reopened field research returned to the key areas of the Upper Paleolithic settlement in order to gain more stratigraphic and chronological evidence (Figure 1.3). Excavations were made in the Brno Basin and Krumlovský les areas to obtain new data on the Early Upper Paleolithic (Stránská skála, Vedrovice), in the Pavlovské Hills on the Gravettian (Dolní Věstonice, Milovice), and in the Moravian karst on the Magdalenian (Barová, Kolíbky). Simultaneously, the typological concept of Paleolithic research was tested in first, and vivid, critical discussions, centered on the reliability of surface collections for chronology, on the role of human behavior in the morphology of lithic industries, on the lithic exploitation areas concept, and, as a case study, on the newly defined Bohunician culture (Svoboda, 1983, 1984b; Oliva, 1981a, 1987c; Valoch, 1982c, 1984b).

Visits of Western scholars were limited, in the beginning, to informative trips to study local materials or to incorporating them into global syntheses (Delporte, 1959; Marshack, 1972). During this period, however, short visits changed to longer stays for specialized studies of Central European problems (Allsworth-Jones, 1986; Soffer, 1989, 1993; Vandiver, Soffer, Klíma, and Svoboda, 1990; Soffer, Vandiver, Klíma, and

O 18 Stage	Pedocomplex	Pleistocene	Alpine Glaciation	Continental Glac.	Paleolithic	Cultural units
2		UPPER	würm	weichsel (visla)	UPPER	12, 13, 14
3	PK I					11
4	PK II					7, 8, 9, 10
5	PK III		R/W	eem	MIDDLE	5, 6
6			riss	warthe		4
7	PK IV			treene		3
8				saale		
9	PK V	MIDDLE	M/R	elster-saale / holstein		2
10						
11	PK VI					
12			mindel	elster	LOWER	
13	PK VII					
	PK VIII					
	PK IX					
	PK X	LW	G/M	cromer		1

Table 1.4. Recent Excavations

Dolní Věstonice I, distr. Břeclav: 1990, 1993 J. Svoboda
Dolní Věstonice II, distr. Břeclav: 1991 J. Svoboda
Dolní Věstonice III, distr. Břeclav: 1993–1995 J. Svoboda, P. Škrdla
Mokrá, distr. Brno-venkov: 1994–1995 P. Škrdla
Petřkovice, distr. Ostrava: 1994–1995 J. Svoboda, L. Jarošová
Předmostí, distr. Přerov: 1990–1992 J. Svoboda
Vedrovice I, distr. Znojmo: 1992–1995 M. Oliva

Svoboda, 1993). Such collaborations, naturally, contributed widely to the exchange of ideas and prepared the way for future international projects.

THE PRESENT STATE OF RESEARCH

After the political change in 1989, the system of grants and problem-oriented projects has been introduced into Czech archaeology (Svoboda, Klíma, and Škrdla, 1995). With this new perspective, the most urgent task was a complex and interdisciplinary analysis of the sites hitherto excavated, as well as creating a meaningful chronological and spatial frameworks, rather than new fieldwork (Table 1.4). New syntheses of the Paleolithic in Moravia were published, entitled *In the Light of Fires of Early Hunters* (Valoch, 1993a) and *The Paleolithic of Moravia and Silesia* (Svoboda et al., 1994). The change in political orientation helped to establish a network of international cooperation, the results of which are already reflected in several publications by American authors (Blades, 1993; Gargett, 1994; Soffer and Vandiver, 1994; Tomášková, 1994), and further joint projects are in preparation. In Spring 1995, on the occasion of the 70th anniversary of Bohuslav Klíma, we organized a meeting of Paleolithic archaeologists from the Middle Danube area, now separated into four states (the Czech Republic, Austria, Slovakia, and Hungary), at Dolní Věstonice. This small event which, in fact, was the first specialized meeting on Paleolithic archaeology organized in the Czech Republic, summarized the results of recent field research in the four countries. The second one, in the autumn of the same year, was organized in Dolní Věstonice by the European Science Foundation, and dedicated to the period 30,000–20,000 B.P., where most of the sites are dated.

One of the most important topics was a multidisciplinary analysis of selected parts of the Gravettian site Pavlov I (Svoboda, 1994a; further volumes in preparation). Pavlov I is now being compared with other Gravettian sites of Moravia (Dolní Věstonice I–II, Předmostí), Silesia (Petřkovice), and Austria (Willendorf, Grubgraben). In order to control the extension of settled zones at these sites, review their

←

Figure 1.3. Correlation of the Pleistocene stratigraphy and the Paleolithic in Moravia. 1—undifferentiated Lower Paleolithic; 2—Acheulean; 3—Early Mousterian; 4—Taubachian; 5—Later Mousterian; 6—Micoquian; 7—Bohunician; 8—Szeletian; 9—Aurignacian; 10—Gravettian; 11—Epigravettian; 12—Magdalenian; 13—Epimagdalenian; 14—Tišnovian.

stratigraphic sections, and apply more precise methods of documentation and geological and environmental studies, limited fieldwork is being carried out simultaneously. The regional surface surveys are more problem-oriented as well, special attention being paid to the strategic locations ("gates") within the Moravian territory (Svoboda, 1994c). Therefore the project has several levels of analysis, starting with segments of sites, and continuing over microregions to a complex view of the Paleolithic landscape (Chapter 8).

In 1991, the former Czechoslovak Academy of Sciences awarded a grant for the processing of the first segment of the Pavlov I site: the 1952–1953 excavation area. In 1992, the L. S. B. Leakey Foundation awarded a parallel grant, to cover the expenses of further fieldwork. Since 1993, the Grant Agency of the Czech Republic has sponsored another grant, entitled The Gravettian in South Moravia. We would like to acknowledge support of all the mentioned agencies.

Chapter 2

Pleistocene Paleoenvironments

VOJEN LOŽEK

THE MORAVIAN PLEISTOCENE IN THE EUROPEAN CONTEXT

Moravia is an important crossroads demonstrating the interplay of influences from the oceanic west and the continental east, as well as from the cool north and the warm south, which supported migrations of fauna, flora, and prehistoric humans. The Fennoscandinavian glaciation twice penetrated the Moravian Gate, meeting its extreme limit at the continental divide between the Baltic and Black Sea drainage areas, that is, between the catchment areas of the Odra and Bečva Rivers. For this reason, the Moravian Gate is one of the few places in Europe in which Pleistocene sequences forming the context between the Scandinavian and Alpine glaciations can be continuously traced.

The aim of this chapter is to present a reconstruction of the environmental conditions in individual phases of the Pleistocene climatic cycle in various periods of time, particularly during the last interglacial and the last glacial. This time span has provided the richest evidence, so that it serves as a general guide for older cycles. It also includes the great majority of stratigraphically fixed archaeological finds.

THE DEVELOPMENT OF PLEISTOCENE SEDIMENTS

Well-differentiated depositional sequences developed in Moravian basins as well as in the adjacent warm uplands, where in protected areas mighty complexes covering several cycles have been preserved. More favorable conditions occur at the margin of the Bohemian Massif because of the predominance of solid rocks, which have been better protected from erosion than the less resistant rocks forming the outer Carpathians. Among Pleistocene deposits, the loess series are dominant. They are formed by individual loess covers separated by complexes of fossil soils and slope sediments, in regular sequences called *pedocomplexes* (PK). By their structure, the loess series reflect all phases of the Pleistocene climatic cycle, which are represented by specific types of fossiliferous sediments and soils. Some sections, particularly at Červený kopec near Brno, belong to the most complete Pleistocene sequences in Europe (Fink and Kukla, 1977; Smolíková, 1982). Other kinds of sediments correspond only to certain phases of the climatic cycle and do not form continuous cycle sequences. Of prime importance among them are fluvial sediments developed as terrace steps which can be correlated with overlying loess series and, in the north, also with products of the glaciation. Of minor importance are slope sediments and travertines, which correspond only to shorter time spans of the cycle or occur only in a small number of sites.

Of particular interest are Pleistocene sediments in karst areas, especially the fills of caves and rock shelters (abris). Although the extent of Moravian karstlands is very restricted, there are large numbers of sites with well-differentiated sequences rich in fauna and generally also in archaeological objects. The most favorable conditions occur in areas where loess series extend into the karstlands, as for instance at the foot of the Pavlovské Hills or in the southern part of the Moravian karst.

In the northern part of the Moravian Gate, as well as at the northern margin of the Carpathians and the Sudetes, mighty glacigenic deposits developed. These include intercalations of lake and marsh sediments from warm phases which have provided a rich local flora. However, terrestrial deposits are here developed as lime-deficient dust loams (staublehm), which used to be paleontologically sterile (Macoun, Šibrava, Tyráček, and Kneblová-Vodičková, 1965). This region is also rather poor in archaeological finds and thus has only minor importance in paleoenvironmental reconstructions.

THE QUATERNARY CLIMATIC CYCLE AND ITS PRODUCTS

As pointed out before, the cycle of climatic changes can be best traced in the loess series of southern and part of middle Moravia, which are well differentiated and fully developed, and which provide sedimentological, pedological, and paleontological evidence (Figure 2.1; Ložek, 1965a,b). The course of certain phases of the cycle is reflected in detail by cave and slope deposits in karst areas or by tufa deposits.

Moravia is situated in the periglacial belt, where single climatic oscillations are expressed in full intensity, and where even intervals of a lower order can be clearly distinguished (Figure 2.2; Soergel, 1925:135). Interglacials and glacials, in the strict sense, represent only extreme phases of the climatic cycle. Whereas the culmination phases of interglacials were at least as warm and damp as the present local climate, the culminations of the glacials are comparable to conditions in cold areas of northern Asia. Both extremes are linked by a sequence of transition phases, and the warm periods can be subdivided into a sequence of minor phases corresponding to those of the postglacial.

It should be stressed that the great majority of records have come from warm, dry areas, which differ considerably from those located at higher elevations (Ložek, 1976).

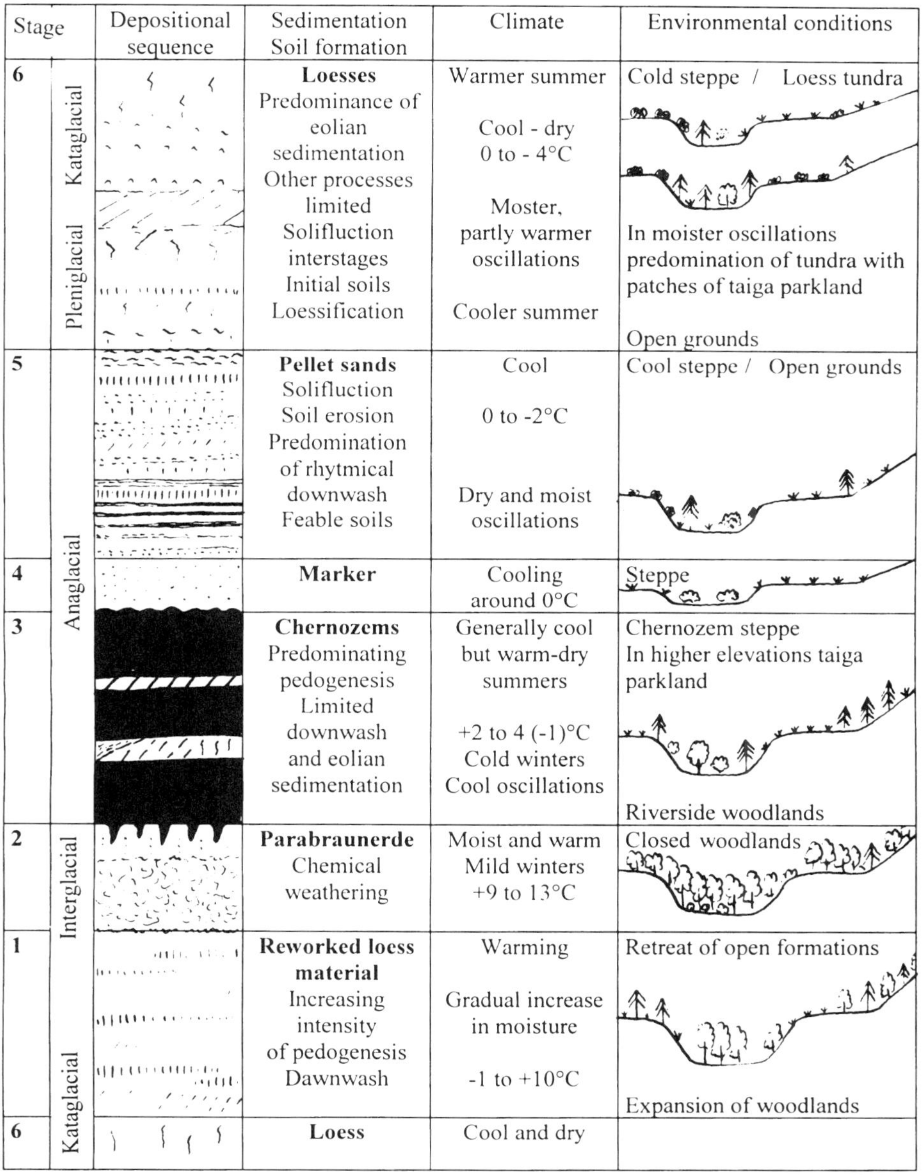

PLEISTOCENE PALEOENVIRONMENTS

Stage		Depositional sequence	Sedimentation Soil formation	Climate	Environmental conditions
6	Plenigacial / Kataglacial		**Loesses** Predominance of eolian sedimentation Other processes limited Solifluction interstages Initial soils Loessification	Warmer summer Cool - dry 0 to - 4°C Moster, partly warmer oscillations Cooler summer	Cold steppe / Loess tundra In moister oscillations predominance of tundra with patches of taiga parkland Open grounds
5	Anaglacial		**Pellet sands** Solifluction Soil erosion Predomination of rhytmical downwash Feable soils	Cool 0 to -2°C Dry and moist oscillations	Cool steppe / Open grounds
4			**Marker**	Cooling around 0°C	Steppe
3			**Chernozems** Predominating pedogenesis Limited downwash and eolian sedimentation	Generally cool but warm-dry summers +2 to 4 (-1)°C Cold winters Cool oscillations	Chernozem steppe In higher elevations taiga parkland Riverside woodlands
2	Interglacial		**Parabraunerde** Chemical weathering	Moist and warm Mild winters +9 to 13°C	Closed woodlands
1	Kataglacial		**Reworked loess material** Increasing intensity of pedogenesis Dawnwash	Warming Gradual increase in moisture -1 to +10°C	Retreat of open formations Expansion of woodlands
6			**Loess**	Cool and dry	

Figure 2.1. Diagram of the Upper Pleistocene climatic cycle in the environment of the dry loess region of southern Moravia.

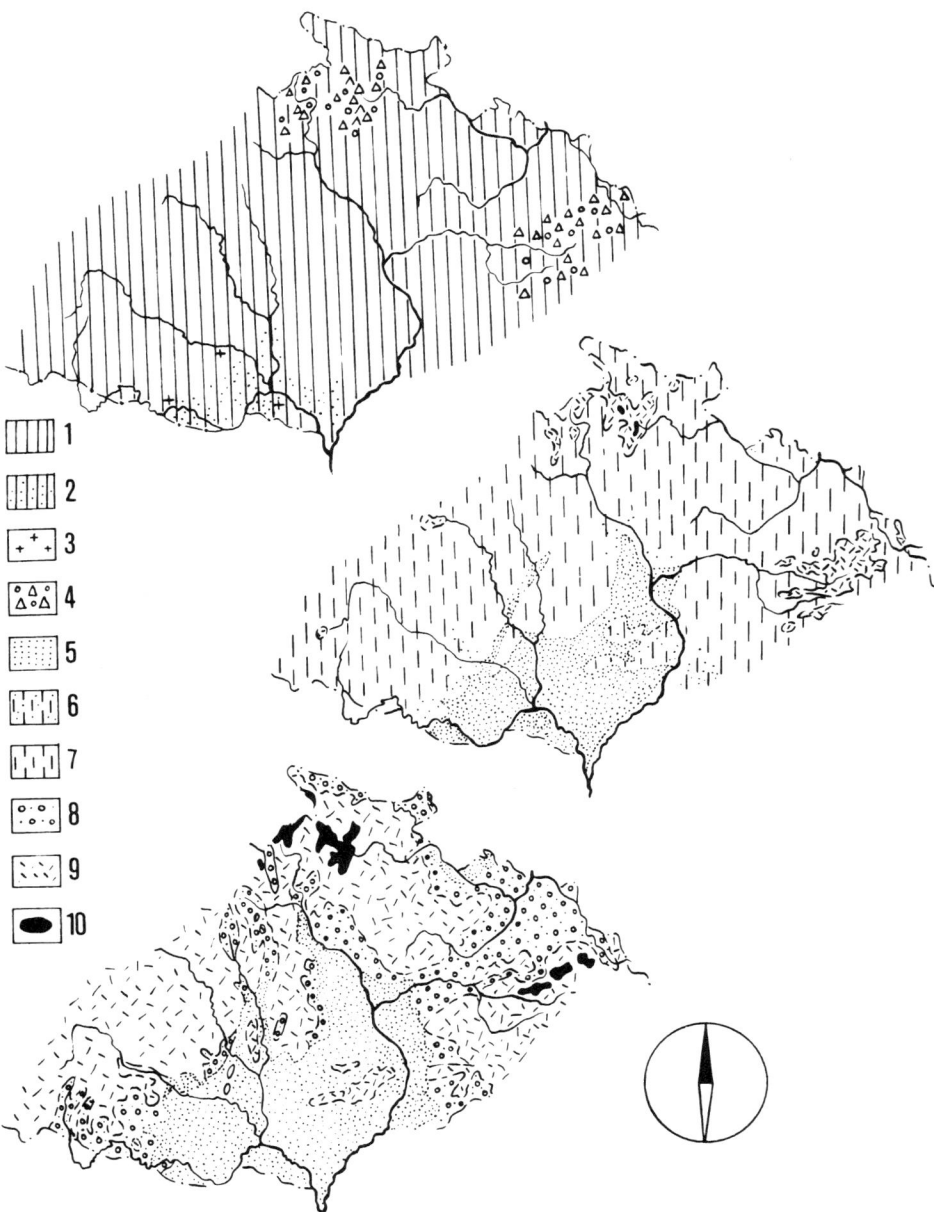

Figure 2.2. Ecozones in Moravia during the full interglacial (above), during the Lower Würmian interstadials (middle), and during the loess stage of the pleniglacial (below). 1—temperate mixed deciduous forest; 2—forest with small steppic patches; 3—rock steppe; 4—mixed mountain forest; 5—loess steppe; 6—forest steppe; 7—steppified taiga parkland; 8—loess tundra; 9–mountain stony tundra; 10—frost desert.

PLEISTOCENE PALEOENVIRONMENTS 19

However, in Moravia, there are no records from sites in higher-altitude zones which would provide suitable evidence for environmental reconstructions.

Because the Pleistocene climate had a cyclic development, corresponding phases of different age were often characterized by nearly identical environments, even when they were separated by a long time span. For this reason, in the following text, the characteristics of warm and cold time periods—interglacials and glacials, or thermomeres and cryomeres—are presented in general, with additional comments on their chronology and selected dates on single important records.

WARM PERIODS: INTERGLACIALS, OR THERMOMERES

The most reliable evidence of interglacials is the records of characteristic faunas and floras in certain kinds of sediments. Within the loess sequences (Figure 2.3), such records come generally from the calcareous base of pedocomplexes. These records are mostly of markedly hygrophilous and thermophilous molluscan faunas corresponding to the early phase of the climatic optimum, whereas later phases are represented by strongly weathered basal soils (parabraunerde, braunlehm) without fossils. Flora remains are very sparse; only the stones of *Celtis* occurring in older interglacials provide valuable evidence of a climate which was warmer than the present climate. A higher number of minor climatic phases is distinguishable in travertines, for instance, at Tučín, where a sequence from the final glacial to the culminating climatic optimum

Figure 2.3. Červený kopec: Stratigraphic section showing Middle Pleistocene loess and interglacial paleosoils.

has been recorded. The complete course of a thermomere from the final phase of the preceding glacial to the start of the succeeding cryomere has been recorded only rarely; an example is the sequence of slope deposits at the foot of the Stránská skála rock (site I), which is comparable to analogous postglacial sequences.

In general, the culmination of thermomeres (the climatic optimum) was somewhat warmer (1.5°C–3°C) and mainly moister than the climate of the same area at the present time. In a number of cases, the mean annual rainfall was more than 100% higher than now, for instance, in the Pavlovské Hills area up to 1000 mm instead of the present 500–550 mm. The result was the absolute predominance of mesic closed forest on decalcified brown soils of parabraunerde or brown plastosol types (braunlehm), which were rubified during the oldest thermomeres (Smolíková, 1967). This is also true of areas now dominated by chernozem soils and xerothermic steppe vegetation of low, open submediterranean woodland (Corni-Querceta). Major open areas have not been recorded. Although it has not been possible to document paleontologically all interglacials represented by characteristic fossil soils within the loess series, the records available show that the interglacials differed from one another in various details:

The Cromerian interglacial, which came before the first large glaciation in northern Moravia, is well documented by the footslope deposits at Stránská skála I. Its early climatic optimum is characterized by *Granaria frumentum* (Drap.) in high numbers, which suggest a considerable extent of semiopen thermophilous woodland with steppe patches. The same situation has also been recorded in this thermomere in Bohemia (Únětice-Holý vrch, Zlatý kůň), as well as in the Slovakian karst. The climate of this interglacial was thus rather dry (at least in the earlier climatic optimum), similar to the present but warmer.

The earliest phase of the Middle Pleistocene is represented by the interglacial which is documented by rich faunas discovered in the Mladeč Caves and in the Liščí díra Caves in the Moravian karst. By contrast to the Cromerian interglacial, it is dominated by purely forest snail assemblages, including Atlantic elements such as *Azeca goodalli* (Fér.) and *Cepaea nemoralis* (L.), as well as by several species extremely rare in the Pleistocene thermomeres of Central Europe, for example, *Oxychilus glaber* (Rssm.) and *Alinda biplicata* (Mtg.); the alpine element *Fusulus interruptus* (C.Pfr) is probably its index species. Also some extinct species, such as *Aegopis klemmi* (Lžk. and Schl.) and *Acicula diluviana* (Hocker), may be mentioned. These suggest a mild, humid climate. Of particular interest is also the light red color of the soils. As yet, no evidence is available about which PK of the loess series this interglacial corresponds to (PK VII or VIII; i.e., OIS 13 or 15); however, there is no doubt that it is older than the pedocomplexes with well-developed chernozems, that is, older than PK VI (OIS 11).

The Holstein interglacial (OIS 9–11) *sensu lato* is probably represented by the antepenultimate thermomere documented in the loess series, for instance, in the brickyard at Dolní Kounice (Ložek, 1966). It has a woodland malacofauna rich in species and the last occurrences of some later extinct ones, particularly *Aegopis klemmi* (Lžk. and Schl.). Also, the interglacial recorded at the top of the Turold Hill (Pavlovské Hills) may be attributed to this phase. Besides *Celtis* stones, it is characterized by a rich snail assemblage documenting a mesic forest even at this site, which is markedly xerothermic at present. This observation suggests a rainfall at least 100% higher than at present.

The penultimate interglacial associated with PK IV (OIS 7) of the loess series has been recorded in several stratigraphically important sections, such as the Dolní Věstonice brickyard, Dolní Kounice, Červený kopec, and Předmostí II. Its malacofauna considerably differs from that of other interglacials, whose assemblages are rich in species (25–50 species) and include southern elements that are extinct in Central Europe at present. The malacofauna associated with PK IV generally consists only of a few species indicating a warm, dry, deciduous woodland to shrub parkland with a high proportion of marginal ecotones. Characteristic snail species are *Helix pomatia* (L.), *Fruticicola fruticum* (Mull.) and *Euomphalia strigella* (Drap.), locally also *Monachoides incarnatus* (Mull.). The warm character is documented by the admixture of such elements as *Discus perspectivus* (Muhl.) and particularly by the occurrence of *Celtis* stones, type *neopleistocenica* (Dohnal, 1961). Unlike other interglacials, this thermomere is thus markedly dry, even though no evidence of more extensive steppe formations is available. It may be mentioned that this interglacial is also represented by the famous travertine of Ehringsdorf in Central Germany, where southern snail species that are actually extinct in Central Europe are also absent, while the flora includes several exotic elements.

The last interglacial—Eemian or Riss/Würm—is reliably documented by sparse finds from the brickyard of Dolní Věstonice. However, of prime importance in deducing its characteristics is the malacofauna from Pavlov (Ložek, 1961), which shows an extraordinary richness in species corresponding to damp warm forest even in this very xerothermic area. This richness agrees well with observations from Bohemia. It is the last phase in which southern European elements appeared in Central Europe and when open grounds were reduced to a minimum.

In summary, it is apparent that the interglacials had a wholly woodland character even in the driest and warmest regions of Moravia. Of importance is their gradation of intensity, which is expressed in their soils. Thermomeres before PK IV show a higher degree of soil maturity than the later ones. They are characterized by brown plastosols (braunlehm), often markedly rubified in the oldest periods. It may be assumed that, in karstlands, terra rossa covered by dwarf xerothermic semiopen woodland occurred on extensive areas. Such habitats were also characterized by *Celtis*, however, of a different type from the penultimate interglacial (type *cromerica*; Dohnal, 1961). It will be obvious from the foregoing that, during the Pleistocene, the intensity of climatic optima gradually decreased from submediterranean conditions in the Cromerian interglacial to those comparable to the present-day climate of the southern part of Central Europe. An exception represents the penultimate interglacial, its malacofauna indicating a light, comparatively dry deciduous woodland.

COLD PERIODS: GLACIALS, OR CRYOMERES

The general characteristics of a glacial are more complicated than those of an interglacial, since an interglacial consists of a sequence of rather different phases, whose mean annual temperature is, however, considerably lower than that of the present. Species that demand higher temperatures and humidity are lacking, and elements tolerant of open, treeless areas predominate.

Here the characteristics only of the culminating glacial (pleniglacial, full glacial) will be given, that is, the characteristics of the phase which largely coincides with the main period of the loess formation from which very rich faunas of the oldest cycles are available. From the last glaciation, the Early Glacial (Eoglacial), with its variety of climatic oscillations, as well as the decline of the glacial (late glacial, tardiglacial) associated with the decline of loess formation, will be described in detail because this period offers the richest available paleontological evidence.

A very rich literature exists about loess and environmental conditions during the formation of the last glaciation. This is also true of our territory (Ložek, 1965a,b, 1991), where these aspects have been analzyed in detail, so that we can restrict our description to general data which apply both to loesses underlying the Cromer interglacial (e.g., at Stránská skála I) and to the youngest ones, and thus to a time span of more than 750,000 years! The loess is both eolian sediment, as documented by its depositional conditions and its granular and mineral composition, and a peculiar synsedimentary soil type, as shown by its fabric, by its form of $CaCO_3$, and iron hydroxides, and, above all, by the incorporated fauna and pollen flora. The environment where eolian dust was sedimented and simultaneously converted into loess by specific pedogenic processes was the loess steppe, a peculiar type of xeric habitat with ecologically specialized vegetation and fauna. This steppe had an enormous extent, covering a large belt south of the southern margin of the glaciation from the Atlantic shore of Normandy to inner Asia. Local differences in composition and faunal content in the European part can be considered unimportant. The climate was predominantly cold and markedly dry, except for a short vegetation period, which was sufficiently humid and rather warm. A comparison of these environments with those of the present subpolar zone is thus not appropriate in the light of faunal evidence. It is evident that the loess steppe, whose extent is documented by the present range of loess, had very peculiar and uniform environments. It is certain that, during the loess formation, most of the other processes were greatly reduced: the caves were dry, karstification did not take place, and the movement of slope scree was extremely restricted, as documented by deposits of pure loess at the foot of steep rocky slopes, where the loess is covered by coarse screes formed during later warm phases (Ložek, 1988). This pattern can be observed in the Cromer interglacial (Stránská skála I) as well as in the postglacial (Pavlovské Hills-Soutěska, Martinka, Barová Cave, etc.). In uplands, at the margins of the loess zone, the loess grades locally into fine clastic sediments called *grèzes litées* in the French literature. In Moravia, these are classically developed on the eastern slopes of the Pavlovské Hills, and in a less typical facies, they occur in cave entrances in the northern part of the Moravian karst (Pustožlebská Zazděná Cave).

The loess dust was deposited not only in wind-shadow drifts in valleys or at the foot of hills, but also in regions of no relief, where moister phases induced the formation of ephemeral swamps in which swamp loesses with very rich aquatic malacofauna accumulated. These occurred also in the landslide area at the foot of the Pavlovské Hills near Dolní Věstonice in the context of the Gravettian settlement.

However, the loess steppe did not cover the whole area of the loess zone. In the valleys of water streams, it graded into extensive gravelly and sandy floodplains of braided rivers with stands of climatically resistant trees and shrubs (willows, poplars, *Hippophae*); in floodplains of small streams, which, during the loess phase, were often ephemeral, it graded into mesic grassland comparable to present meadows. The steep rocky slopes had a character of desert rocky steppes.

An important problem of the reconstruction of hunter-gatherers' environments is the state of biocenoses at the margin of the loess zone (i.e., in uplands and foothill regions), where loesses occurred only as local accumulations and graded into coarser clastic slope sediments. Paleontological evidence comes in Moravia particularly from karstlands, such as the Moravian karst or the Pavlovské Hills. Whereas in the southern part of the Moravian pure karst loess still occurs, the northern part is dominated by fine cryoclastic sediments (*grèzes litées*) that are very poor in fossils (Srnčí Cave, Pustožlebská Zazděná Cave, etc.). At the foot of the Pavlovské Hills cliffs, the loess grades into talus deposits consisting of small limestone fragments. These include a poor fauna resembling that of the alpine zone of high mountains, however, in a very dry environment. At that time, even some alpine elements penetrated this area, for instance, the snail *Chilostoma achates* (Rssm.), recorded in the fill of the crevasse Velký Špunt in the Martinka cliffs (Horáček and Ložek, 1990) and in the Barová Cave (Seitl, Svoboda, Ložek, Přichystal, and Svobodová, 1986). Hilly countries at the margin of the loess steppe must obviously have had a less monotonous vegetation, with patches of resistant trees such as pines (*Pinus silvestris* and *P. cembra*) or larch. Environmental diversity was here higher than in the loess landscape. The most diversified environments occurred in the contact areas of various formations, for instance, on the slopes of the Pavlovské Hills, where the following zonation can be reconstructed: at the foot of limestone cliffs, subalpine formations with open woodland patches, a lower downslope zone of the loess steppe (with the Gravettian settlements), and, along the Dyje River, an extensive floodplain with swamps, riverside stands of moisture-loving trees (willow, poplar), gravel banks and sandbanks, and oxbow lakes. The situation in higher altitudinal zones can only be estimated on the basis of observations from high limestone Carpathians, where relevant records are available (e.g., from the Mažarná Cave at an elevation of 830 m; Ložek, 1980c). The mountain slopes were covered by alpine tundras and meadows, and in protected places, with dwarf woodland patches, which at elevations of 1000 m and over graded into frost deserts with local glaciers or firn fields. The mountain glaciation, however, was poorly developed in Moravia and Silesia. A small glacier formed the cirque of Velká Kotlina in the Hrubý Jeseník Mountains, while in other places only firm basins or boulder screes with ice matrix occurred.

The environmental conditions described above are characteristic of the loess phase, which corresponds to the middle and late part of the pleniglacial as shown by the structure of well-differentiated loess series. The early pleniglacial is characterized by slope erosion, mass movements of coarse clastics and cryogenic processes, such as gelifluction, congelifraction, and various soil deformations due to frost action. It was a period of intensified erosional and sedimentation dynamics, of downcutting in a certain phase, replaced later by fluvial accumulation. Further characteristic processes are the removal of cave and rock shelter fills, a slope retreat associated with the retreat of cave entrances, and the dismantling of bedrock on large areas (Ložek, 1980b). It is likely that, at that time, most of the characteristic periglacial features were formed (frost cliffs, cryoplanation terraces, cryopediments, etc.). All these phenomena were developed mainly in areas with stronger relief at higher elevations. In the dry loess zone, they occur in considerably moderated forms and are expressed by the formation of pellet sands (lehmbrockelsand), impure loess with coarser clasts, loess reworked by solifluction, and so on. In many areas, these processes affected the vegetation and the fauna, but in protected areas, they supported the existence of more diversified biocenoses because of higher humidity. In general, the environmental conditions can be considered rather severe, but the diversity of biota was somewhat higher than that of the full loess phase. More details cannot be presented because of restricted paleontological evidence.

While the Alpine glaciation extended as far as the mountainous south of Lower Austria, the continental glaciation extended into the northern marginal area of Moravia and the Czech part of Silesia (Macoun et al., 1965). The later region where glacial deposits covered extensive areas and locally attained a considerable thickness (more than 100 m) has been called the Ostrava Glacial Basin. It is connected with the Moravian Gate, whose northeastern part was equally glaciated. The ice sheet covered this area in both of the great glaciations of the Middle Pleistocene: the Elster and the Saale. The Elster glaciation sensu lato can be subdivided into two phases: the older Opava and the younger Kravaře glaciations. The first one did not obviously penetrate as far as the Odra Gate (tributary of the Moravian Gate), but its meltwaters were drained by the Bečva River to the Danube. Deposits of the Kravaře glaciation occur both in the Odra Gate and in the foothills of the Beskydy Mountains. Both glaciation phases were probably separated by a marked warm oscillation. The following Saale glaciation can also be subdivided into two phases: the Palhanec and the Oldřišov glaciations. In the first one, the meltwaters were also drained by the Bečva River across the main European watershed in the center of the Moravian Gate. In the comparatively long time span between the Elster and the Saale glaciations, the Holstein interglacial is placed, whose environments are documented by the rich flora of the fossil Stonava lake (Kneblová, 1960).

Environmental conditions in warmer oscillations separating the individual ice advances are poorly known because of very sparse fossil evidence. Their paleosoils show a different development from those in the dry loess zones, because of the lime-deficient substrate and the humid climate, so that a stratigraphic correlation based on pedology remains rather obscure. On the basis of the terrace levels of the Bečva River, J. Macoun (1982) correlated the older members of the loess series exposed at Předmostí with the above glaciations. Besides soil relics from the last interglacial, the loess series of Předmostí includes two older interglacials associated with PK IV and PK V, well documented by molluscan faunas and *Celtis* stones. Of prime importance is the finding that the PK IV was of post-Saalian date, which means that, after the Saalian glaciation, two true interglacials can be distinguished.

The above-described environmental conditions are characteristic of fully developed glacials, that is, of their pleniglacial phases. The early glacial has as a whole a more favorable climate, since it includes warmer intervals: the interstadials, during which even woodland formation and chernozem steppes expanded. This is also true of the late glacial, however, to a reduced extent. Particular problems are associated with warmer oscillations within the pleniglacial (interstadials, or, more exactly, the interpleniglacial), which are best known from the last glacial period.

In general, the glacials can be characterized as phases with a severe, predominantly continental climate which hindered the expansion of woodland. A number of substages, particularly the main time of loess formation, were markedly treeless, and a continuous steppe zone was developed in the middle latitudes throughout the whole of Eurasia. It was interrupted only by mountain ranges, where the loess steppe graded into mountain steppe and alpine meadows. The loess phases were characterized by a very low habitat diversity, but their species richness was much higher than that of the present subpolar zone. This is particularly true of the fauna of warm-blooded vertebrates; however, even the molluscan fauna includes a number of species which do not now occur in northern regions, for example, *Helicopsis striata* (Mull.), *Pupilla* species, and a number of elements restricted to certain areas, such as *Vestia turgida* (Rssm.) in the periphery of the Carpathians or *Neostyriaca corynodes* (Held) at the foot of the Alps.

Little is known about the time span separating the main phase of the loess formation from the early glacial, that is, about the early pleniglacial, which differed from the preceding and following phases in its more intensive depositional and erosional dynamics and its maximum impact of cryogenic processes.

Even though the environmental conditions of the glacials were much more monotonous than those of the warm phases, the biota and soils were moderately differentiated, according to altitudinal zones. The loess steppe was interrupted by river floodplains with specific biocenoses, while the adjacent uplands and foothill areas were characterized by different ecosystems. The highest habitat, as well as the most species diversity, occurred at the boundary of different zones, that is, in contact zones with a concentration of ecotones. Without doubt, these areas were important both for biota and for the hunters-gatherers, who found here their most favorable life conditions. In Moravia, such areas are concentrated at the margins of the Bohemian Massif from Znojmo over Brno to Mohelnice, in the Pavlovské Hills region, and in the Moravian Gate, particularly in its southwestern part. Whatever differences in site selection strategies distinguished the individual Upper Paleolithic cultures (Chapter 8), the great majority of the sites are concentrated in these regions. Particular environments characterized the karstlands where the most favorable conditions occurred in contact with the loess zone, as in the southern part of the Moravian karst or in the karst areas of Mladeč or Hranice.

THE UPPER PLEISTOCENE SEQUENCE

The last interglacial and the following glacial are well known from a number of well-differentiated depositional sequences in the dry loess landscape of southern

Figure 2.4. Dolní Věstonice: Stratigraphic section of the Upper Pleistocene showing paleosoil of the last interglacial (below) and of the last glacial oscillations.

Moravia (Figure 2.4). Their sections show a uniform stratigraphic pattern corresponding to that in Lower Austria as well as in the dry region of middle and northwestern Bohemia (Ložek, 1968). The typical site is the brickyard of Dolní Věstonice II (Klíma, Kukla, Ložek, and de Vries, 1962; Havlíček, 1991). The basal member of the Upper Pleistocene sequence is a complex of fossil soils consisting of the basal parabraunerde (luvisol, brown-gray podzolic soil) overlaid by three chernozems separated by thin interlayers of light loessified slope sediments. In Lower Austria, this soil sequence has been described as the Stillfried Complex (according to the section at Stillfried an der March), called, for short, Stillfried A (Fink, 1956). Because the interlayer separating the lower and middle chernozems is, in most of the sites, markedly thicker and includes even a horizon of pure loess, the sequence has been subdivided into two pedocomplexes: lower PK III, consisting of the basal parabraunerde covered by the lower chernozem, and upper PK II, formed by both upper chernozems, which are mostly separated only by a thin brownish gray interlayer. The sequence described in detail from Dolní Věstonice has been recorded in a number of other Moravian sites, such as Modřice, Lechovice, Znojmo, Bulhary, Velké Pavlovice, and Ždánice, as well as from sites in inner Bohemia (Sedlec and Letky on Vltava river, Jenerálka, Litoměřice I, and II, Kutná Hora, etc; Ložek, 1968).

At many sites, the upper chernozem is covered by a thin band of fine loess described as marker (Kukla, 1961). This is generally overlaid by a complex of soil sediments consisting of rhythmically bedded crumbs of eroded soils described as pellet sands. These grade rhythmically into the overlying thick loess sequence, which is divided into two loess covers by a pale brown soil (or soil complex) mostly affected by solifluction. In Lower Austria, this horizon is called Stillfried B and, in Czech literature, PK I. Whereas the soils of PK III + II are comparable with current postglacial soil types, the soils of PK I have no recent equivalent. They differ from the loess mainly by decalcification. PK I is overlaid by the youngest loess with several initial pseudogley horizons at the basis (Klíma, 1958a). This loess is capped by postglacial soils, in the dry loess landscape of chernozem type. Late glacial sediments mostly cannot be recorded in the loess sections because they have been overprinted by postglacial pedogenic processes.

Important evidence additional to that from the above loess sequences is provided by cave fills in the southern part of the Moravian karst, where loess also occurs. However, only the youngest loess is here developed as typical loess, while older horizons occur as screes, with a loesslike matrix in the upper parts grading into moderately humic gray or brownish gray loams in the lower horizons. Marked equivalents of the chernozems of PK III and PK II are not developed in caves, where they may be correlated only with a complex of humic stony loams of slope character. On the top of the youngest loess, a loamy horizon with numerous fine fragments can be distinguished in most caves. It corresponds to the late glacial (Weichselian Tardiglacial) and includes Magdalenian artifacts (Barová, Srnčí, and Pekárna Caves). Concerning the question of PK III + II equivalents, it should be stressed that the Moravian karst is situated out of the dry loess zone, that is, in the moister peripheral belt where, even in surface loess sequences, the chernozems in question are not developed.

The Last Interglacial

As already mentioned, the last interglacial in Moravia has been documented so far only in comparatively sparse fossil records, even though its soils (parabraunerde) are known from numerous sites. In addition to its characteristics, it is worth mentioning that the appearance of highly demanding and very species-rich fauna in its initial phase are very rapid—it may be said abrupt. Its subdivision into individual climatic phases has not been recorded in Moravian sites so far. Within the loess series, this whole time span is represented by strongly developed parabraunerde soils, which are paleontologically sterile (Ložek, 1976). However, the fossil evidence available shows with certainty that the last interglacial represented a very warm and moist period, when closed forest covered most of the territory in question. Forest steppe enclaves characterized in the postglacial by chernozem soils were not developed in the last interglacial (Ložek, 1966a).

The Early Glacial

The early Würmian (Weichselian) glacial covered a comparatively long time span. The cooling of the climate was considerable compared to that in the preceding interglacial (or in the present), but the extent of continental glaciation was reduced, so that the climatic regime characteristic of the Ice Age was not fully developed. In the loess sequence, this phase is represented by the chernozems of PK III + II, including the light interlayers.

From the whole complex, rather complete malacological evidence is available. The chernozems contain characteristic assemblages of flower-rich steppes, the index species being *Chondrula tridens* (Mull.) associated with *Helicopsis striata* (Mull.), *Vallonia costata* (Mull.), *Pupilla muscorum* (L.), *Cochlicopa lubricella* (Pr.), *Truncatellina cylindrica* (Fér.), and, locally, also xerothermic elements such as *Granaria frumentum* (Drap.) and *Pupilla triplicata* (Stud.) in smaller amounts.

The humus-deficient or slightly humic interlayers are characterized by loess assemblages of warmer type. The index species is *Helicopsis striata* (Mull.) associated with *Pupilla muscorum* (L.), *P. triplicata* (Stud.), and *Vallonia costata* (Mull.)—an assemblage which resembles that of the chernozems but is poorer in species. Arctic-alpine and subpolar elements do not occur. All early glacial snail species are represented by races identical to those of the present fauna. For instance, the *Pupilla muscorum* (L.) represented is indistinguishable from present-day populations.

Light interlayers separating individual soils generally consist of reworked loess material, mostly with an admixture of humic sediments. Locally, pure loess forms a thin horizon within the interlayer between PK III and PK II, which is in most sites markedly thicker than the interlayers separating the soils of both PK III and PK II. Within this interlayer a thin horizon of initial chernozem is often also developed. The basal chernozem of PK II commonly has a basal brown zone resembling a Bv-horizon. Locally it includes less tolerant species, indicating a relatively warm parkland—*Fruticicola fruticum* (Mull.) and *Euomphalia strigella* (Drap.)—and represents the warmest and moistest phase of the whole early glacial sequence.

Of prime importance in environmental reconstructions within this time span are the finds of malacofauna from the brickyard of Ždánice, where the sequence in question grades into floodplain deposits, so that it is partly developed in swamp facies, including even lenses of loose tufa. This fact, together with a species-rich snail fauna, indicates the existence of open floodplain woodland and mesic to moist meadows, but even here no demanding elements have been recorded. Another important locality is the brickyard in Bulhary near the Pavlovské Hills, where a rich snail and vertebrate fauna was found in burrow fills situated within the PK II. There occurs not only a steppe fauna, with *Chondrula tridens* (Mull.), but also aquatic species transported from the near floodplain of the Dyje River by a predator. Like the fauna from Ždánice, this assemblage suggests a rather favorable parkland with a number of aquatic and marshy habitats.

Our data demonstrate that the early Würmian was characterized by an alternating occurrence of cool steppes and chernozem steppes or parklands in a continental climate with rather warm summers. At the beginning of the formation of PK II, the parkland became warm for a short interval. Nevertheless no species have been recorded which might indicate a warm and rather damp climate comparable to that of today. On the other hand, alpine, arctic-alpine, subpolar, and inner Asiatic elements characteristic of typical loess are also lacking.

This period shows a marked altitudinal zonation documented by the limited occurrence of chernozem soils, which are developed only within a dry landscape, that is, in approximately the same area as in the postglacial or at present. At higher elevations and in more humid areas, the chernozems are lacking, and the soil horizons are poorly differentiated. In most cases, their equivalent is only a complex of slope sediments. In their marginal zone, the chernozems are generally brown-spotted (spotted soils) or largely converted to brown soils.

In caves, this whole period is represented by medium-coarse screes with a loamy matrix, which is generally dark and slightly humic. At higher elevations (i.e., in altitudinal zones corresponding to present submontane and higher belts), the equivalents of early glacial sequences have not been identified so far.

From the standpoint of broad stratigraphic correlations, it is likely that oscillations represented by the early glacial chernozems correspond to the Amersfoort, Brörup, and Odderade interstadials described from the area of North European glaciation. Their paleontological correlation, as well as their absolute chronology, still remain problematic, since this time span lies out of the range of C-14 dating.

Concerning the environmental conditions of the hunters-gatherers, this time span is highly important, since it provided favorable life conditions: easily penetrable landscape, where steppes alternated with open woodland of taiga and temporarily even of a warmer character, which extended into the submontane belt. A relatively luxuriant vegetation with species-rich biocenoses covered the valley floors, where eutrophic wetlands were often found.

According to faunal evidence, the climatic conditions, particularly during the warmer intervals, were comparable to those in the extreme east of Europe (i.e., at the foot of the Ural Mountains); the winters were long and severe, but there was a relatively warm vegetation period.

The Culminating Glacial (Pleniglacial)

The culminating glacial (pleniglacial) in the loess series of the dry region is separated from that of early glacial by the band of the marker. This is overlaid by the basal member of pleniglacial sequence called *pellet sands*. These represent a very characteristic soil sediment consisting of rhythmically bedded crumbs of eroded underlying soils and partly also of older loess or even of weathered bedrock (Kukla and Ložek, 1961). Recent analogies suggest that pellet sands become established in areas higher upslope, where the surface is formed by bare soils which are intensively eroded during torrential rains after longer periods of dryness and are transported downslope. At the foot of slopes, they are accumulated in the form of pellet sands. At present, this process occurs because of the erosion of soils affected by ploughing; however, the characteristic texture of recent pellet sand is rapidly changed by the activities of soil organisms, particularly earthworms.

The environments of pellet sand formation thus consist partly of erosion areas corresponding to desert steppes without continuous herb cover, and partly of accumulation areas where bioturbation is reduced to a minimum. This situation raises a question concerning the analyses of fossil assemblages, since the pellet sands contain shells not only of species living in their accumulation area, but also of species which lived in the erosion areas and of fossils reworked from the eroded layers. For this reason, the pellet sands include predominantly assemblages with *Helicopsis striata* (Mull.), resembling those of the early glacial warm loesses (an autochthonous component), with a variable admixture of shells coming from eroded early glacial and interglacial sediments or soils (an allochthonous component). Thus, at a number of sites, the pellet sands have provided records of interglacial faunas in secondary position. Typical pellet sands occur only the dry loess landscape. At higher elevations or in moister areas, they are replaced by coarser clastic slope sediments with a loamy matrix. One stratigraphic equivalent of pellet sands is sandy gravels sedimented by water streams, as documented by several records of malacofauna (Ložek and Šibrava, 1968).

Toward the top, the pellet sands rhythmically grade into basal layers of the main body of loess. These loesses are often impure, including interlayers of coarser material, traces of solifluction, and other disturbances. They contain malacofaunas mostly poor not only in the number of species but also in the number of individuals. That is, they contain mostly monotonous assemblages dominated by *Pupilla* species, the so-called *Pupilla* faunas indicating severe loess steppe environments. Stratigraphic analyses of numerous depositional sequences on the slopes of karst uplands and highlands have demonstrated that, at higher elevations, an intensive slope erosion leading to the retreat of slopes and cave entrances took place at that time (Ložek, 1980b). In areas of moderate uplift, as, for instance, in the Bohemian Massif, this process was immediately preceded by a marked phase of downcutting (Ložek, 1981). In Moravia, at the boundary between the Carpathians and the Bohemian Highlands, the situation was more complicated, however, because of recent tectonic movements. In karst uplands, and in general at the periphery of the loess belt, this older loess phase is mostly represented by coarser clastic sedimentation with a loesslike matrix.

These data suggest that the time span in question had a severe and rather unbalanced climate which supported the slope erosion and various cryogenic processes. This complicated interaction of erosional and depositional processes gradually declined and was replaced by the formation of increasingly purer loess, which indicated the establishing of typical loess steppe. This loess deposition was interrupted by climatic oscillations which were moister and more balanced, but not warmer. Interpleniglacial intervals, which could be correlated with such oscillations as, for instance, Hengelo, have not been identified more precisely in this area of Moravia so far (Ložek, 1980a).

By contrast, the interval represented by the soils of PK I corresponds, without doubt, to the Stillfried B in Austria,[1] which can be correlated with the interstadials of Arcy and Maisières in France or of Denekamp in North Europe. An open problem is

---

[1] The term *Paudorf* or *Paudorf interstadial*, currently used may be outdated because, at the eponymous site of Paudorf, the soils in question represent a solifluidal disturbed relic of last interglacial soils as documented by the incorporated malacofauna.

the lower boundary of PK I, since PK I may also belong to the interval described as Hengelo (Chapter 5).

PK I is known from many sites as an important horizon separating the youngest loess complex into two parts and bearing on its surface the Gravettian artifacts. Its paleoenvironmental interpretation is difficult, since it has no pedological analogies among modern European soils (on loess) and only in rare cases occurs in an autochthonous position, being mostly affected by solifluction. Therefore it mostly includes admixtures from various older layers eroded higher upslope. As a well-developed soil complex, it was recorded, for instance, in the brickyard of Ždánice. The soils of PK I are poorly weathered, but generally decalcified, and thus paleontologically sterile. If fossil records are available, they come from calcareous interlayers introduced into the PK I by solifluction. Nevertheless some basic facts may be mentioned: PK I is generally parallel to the present surface of loess deposits, but it is discordant with PK III + II, a fact suggesting erosional events before its formation. It never grades into footslope deposits or fills of various depressions which could provide suitable fossils and could thus throw light on the development of PK I. It has never provided faunal remains indicating a warming of climate which is inconsistent with paleobotanical data (Frenzel, 1964; Svobodová, 1991a,b). The reconstruction of environmental conditions controlling the soil formation of PK I must remain open. It may only be inferred that the climate was markedly moister than that during loess formation, and that the temperature did not reach the heights associated with interstadials of the early glacial. It may be assumed that the vegetation was more luxuriant and included a considerably higher admixture of some tolerant wood plants, from which the charcoals in the Paleolithic hearts are derived (Opravil, 1994; Mason, Hather, and Hillman, 1994).

Toward higher elevations and moister areas, the horizon of PK I loses its character of soil separating two loess covers and becomes simply a boundary between the youngest loess, which keeps its loess properties (e.g., in the cave entrances in the Moravian karst, Průchodnice Caves), whereas the loess underlying PK I is replaced by screes consisting of fine fragments with a loesslike matrix. Such a boundary is currently affected by cryoturbation, and a distinct fossil soil cannot be distinguished.

In basal layers of the loess overlying PK I, pale grayish horizons of initial pseudogleys are locally developed (Klíma, 1958a). In this lowest part of the youngest loess, a rich cold-climate malacofauna occurs. It is characterized by a high number of subpolar (*Vertigo parcedentata*, A. Br.), arcto-alpine (*Vertigo modesta*, Say; *Columella columella*, Mart.), and inner Asiatic elements (*Vallonia tenuilabris*, A. Br.; *Vertigo pseudosubstriata*, Lžk.; *Pupilla loessica*, Lžk.) associated with further, more frequent species of the loess malacofauna. However, *Helicopsis striata* (Mull.) is absent from this horizon, whereas *Trichia hispida* (L.) and *Arianta arbustorum* (L.) are abundant, the latter in a dwarf form corresponding to that now found in high mountains (*A. arbustorum alpicola*, Fér.). This assemblage shows the most hygrophilous character among the malacocenoses of the last glacial loess and thus corresponds more to the herb formations of the tundra or the alpine meadow than to those of the loess steppe. In sites where the youngest loess is developed in full thickness, several horizons in its higher layers can be distinguished. These are differentiated by color and structure and may include a more xerophilous malacofauna in *Helicopsis striata* (Mull.). Such horizons are, however, less distinct and occur only locally (Pavlov), while in other places the loess in question seems to be homogeneous.

An important character of the youngest loess is its large range. It is developed as pure loess even at the periphery of the loess zone, where lower loess covers are replaced by slope sediments. This is particularly true of the caves in the Moravian karst.

As already noted, the formation of this loess was associated with a standstill phase in slope sedimentation and erosion, which is documented by the occurrences of pure loess layers at the foot of rock walls or steep rocky slopes, where other members of depositional sequences are developed as screes, often consisting of coarse fragments. This is particularly true of the covering of Holocene deposits. Examples of such a sedimentation pattern are deposits at the foot of the Soutěska Cliff at Pavlovské Hills and several sites in the Moravian karst (Barová Cave).

During the formation of the youngest loess, the loess steppe reached its farthest extent. It met its farthest limits in the valleys of uplands, for instance, in the Dyje Canyon between Vranov and Znojmo and in the gorges of the Moravian karst. While earlier, by the time of the Gravettian occupation, it was moister, later its dry steppe character was fully manifested. It seems that the loess areas were not settled at this time.

Late Glacial

The final phase of the Pleistocene, usually called the *late glacial*, cannot now be found in the dry loess landscape, since the eolian accumulation of loess was replaced by a limited slope sedimentation which in most cases, consisted of small amounts of reworked loess. Such thin horizons were later modified by the pedogenic processes forming recent soils.

Late glacial deposits remained better preserved at the foot of steep slopes or rocks, as well as in the entrances of caves and rock shelters, where the slope material accumulated in large amounts and the possibilities of preserving them were more favorable. For this reason, the late glacial in terrestrial facies is best documented in the karstlands (Chapter 7).

Data from lake and wetland environments, particularly in North Europe, show that the late glacial included warmer intervals called the Bölling and the Alleröd, which differed from the cold Dryas phases particularly in the expansion of tolerant woodlands (pine, birch). It is to be expected that, in the warm region of southern Moravia (Rybníčková and Rybníček, 1972; Svobodová, 1991c), these oscillations were poorly expressed, since the woodland could here survive the cold phases, namely the Upper Dryas—the final state of the Pleistocene. Terrestrial deposits of minor thickness are poorly differentiated, so that it is appropriate to give only a general description of the environmental development of the late glacial in comparison with the preceding pleniglacial.

The late glacial is characterized by a marked change in fauna due to higher habitat diversity, which includes an increase in species number and a differentiation of zoocenoses. Besides steppe communities still including a number of loess elements (e.g., *Vallonia tenuilabris*, A. Br.; *Dicrostonyx*; *Microtus gregalis*; and *Columella columella*, Mart.), more mesic assemblages appeared, corresponding somewhat to meadow habitats (e.g., *Conchlicopa lubrica*, Mull.; *Perpolita*; *Punctum*; *Arianta*; and *Vitrea crystallina*, Mull.), as well as to a wide range of wetland and small water habitats. The vertebrate fauna is characterized by the regular incidence of *Microtus oeconomus*, *Arvicola terrestris*, *Sicista* cf. *subtilis*, *Crocidura* and *Cricetus cricetus*. Characteristic woodland and thermophilous species are, however, mostly absent, although in the eastern part of the Carpathian Basin first demanding elements, such as *Pipistrellus*, *Muscardinus*, and *Glis*, appeared.

It will be obvious from the foregoing that environmental conditions during the late glacial became much more differentiated than those of the preceding pleniglacial. Wetlands and small water bodies were numerous; besides the steppes, which during this period gradually change from loess to chernozem steppes, mesic grasslands occurred, and tolerant woodland dominated by pine and birch expanded. This development was diversified in accordance with local conditions: in damp areas, woodland became dominant, although still semiopen and thus enabling the survival of a number of open-country elements. In dry areas, the above-mentioned development of the steppes occurred. Also, the floodplains were affected by changes resulting from the gradual transition of braided rivers into meandering streams. Little is known about the occurrence of demanding species, although several lines of evidence indicate that, at that time, the area in question was already occupied by such snail species as *Fruticola fruticum* (Mull.) and *Euomphalia strigella* (Drap.), as well as by more demanding trees, such as hazel or oak.

The first stage of the Holocene, the Preboreal, had a fauna and vegetation similar to those of the late glacial, but with an increasing admixture of thermophilous species. This development culminated in the following Boreal, when the rapid increase in temperature and later also in humidity induced a change from late glacial conditions to an overall dominance of formations characteristic of warm periods.

THE FLUCTUATION OF PLEISTOCENE CLIMATES AND THEIR CHARACTERISTICS

Climatic shifts largely controlled the environment of hunters–gatherers, and, at the same time, they provided a basis for a detailed subdivision of the Pleistocene. Because these fluctuations are often unsufficiently defined, so that the result may be discrepancies in stratigraphic conclusions or in environmental reconstructions, it is appropriate to give their exact characteristics.

Quaternary climatic fluctuations considerably varied in intensity and duration, and thus fluctuations of different order have to be distinguished. Fluctuations of the first order are represented by interglacials, whose characteristic products are brown weathered soils, and by glacials, or more exactly by their pleniglacial phases, reflected in loess formation. As fluctuations of the second order, warm intervals within the early glacial are represented in chernozem soils within the loess series in the dry loess landscape. Fluctuations of the third order are moister phases with a more balanced climate, whose products are pale brown feeble soils in pleniglacial complexes, for instance, the soils of PK I or of warm late glacial intervals (particularly the Alleröd). For both categories, the term *interstadial* has been used; however, the difference is considerable. Fluctuations of the third order within the pleniglacial, often specified by the term *interpleniglacial* used more recently, were much cooler than the early glacial warm oscillations, being quite comparable to the cold phases of the early glacial complexes. This character is reflected also by their occurrence in various regions. For instance, the pleniglacial loess complexes in moister areas of Western Europe are more differentiated than those in the dry loess landscapes of Central Europe (Schonhals, Rohdenburg, and Semmel, 1964). The individual developmental phases of Pleistocene thermomeres, as well as those of the postglacial, could be considered fluctuations of the fourth order. In climatically different regions, these fluctuations may show a different intensity. Such is the case of the final cold phase of the Pleistocene: the Upper Dryas, which was obviously expressed more in the northern European region (i.e., near the margin of the glaciation) than in warm, dry areas of Central Europe, to which most of the Moravian lowlands and dry uplands belong.

A definition of individual categories of climatic fluctuations can be only relative; that is, it must be based on a comparison with the present local climates reflected by the indicators used in paleoclimatic reconstruction (fauna, flora, paleosoils). Just as the recent thermomere, the Holocene, is characterized by very different environments at the foot of the Pavlovské Hills, at the northern foot of the Beskydy Mountains, or even in the High Sudetes, so, too, analogous differences existed in the past. For this reason, it is impossible to establish an absolute, uniform definition, which might characterize climatic and environmental conditions in all the mentioned regions. In the following, definitions of fluctuations of the first to third orders are given:

Interglacial is a phase whose fauna and flora, in comparison with the present, have similar or higher temperature and moisture requirements; it also has a comparable species richness in the local area in question, and its soils show a comparable or higher developmental intensity. This definition is clear; however, when the interglacial is represented only by a relict (e.g., by its initial phase) its character cannot be proved, and it may be confused with fluctuations of a lower order. By contrast, a relict of characteristic soil with sparse fragments of index species can be considered interglacial (Svoboda, Ložek, Svobodová, and Škrdla, 1994). In contrast to the definition of interglacial, it is much more difficult to characterize the glacial as a whole, including its warmer intervals.

Glacial is a phase whose fauna and flora consist predominantly of tolerant species which are able to live under severe temperature conditions in open grounds and do not include the warmth- and moisture-loving elements of the closed woodlands; the species richness of its phytocenoses and molluscan communities, compared to those of the present, is markedly lower, and its soils do not reach the stage of weathered brown forest soils.

In both definitions, the comparison with the present must be based on a reconstructed natural state in the area in question, which is particularly true of the fauna and flora, since these are easily changed by cultivation of the landscape. For instance, the present-day malacofauna of steppified agricultural landscapes may greatly resemble the assemblages of the early glacial warm phases. It differs only in the occurrence of so-called modern elements, that is, elements of species which invaded Central Europe during the postglacial and which were unknown in the Pleistocene (Ložek, 1982).

Early glacial warm phases, represented by chernozems as well as the pleniglacial period, particularly the part of this period characterized by pure loess, are rather well distinguishable by their malacofauna:

Early glacial interstadials have a malacofauna consisting of eurythermic steppe and indifferent species, with an admixture, in certain areas and cases, of further tolerance elements which are able to live in dry, semiopen woodland or grassland–woodland ecotones. Warmth- and moisture-loving inhabitants of closed forests, as well as typical loess elements, are absent.

The pleniglacial is characterized by malacocenoses which are poor in species, but generally rich in individuals. They consist of elements that are able to live in open habitats in a severely cold climate with great temperature and moisture extremes. Of importance is the occurrence of arctoalpine, subpolar, and inner Asiatic steppe elements, whereas woodland species are totally lacking. In broad terms, this characteristic is also true of the vegetation, which, however, cannot be recorded in such detail as the malacofauna.

It is hardly possible to give a general definition of the oscillations of the third and fourth orders, whose characteristics must be based on various local differences, on the comparative composition of the biocenoses, on the appearance or disappearance of individual species, on their relative and absolute abundance, and, if possible, on the occurrence of certain index species, in comparison with records from the underlying and overlying strata. Of major importance are statistical analyses of fossil assemblages represented graphically by diagrams or histograms (pollen diagrams, histograms of malacofauna). The basic postulation is of a profound knowledge of the ecology of individual species as well as of whole assemblages, for instance, of the difference between the soil climate in a closed woodland and that in an open grassland.

In this context, it is worth noting that the term *interstadial* is often used in cases where the evaluation of a certain record remains obscure. This is particularly true of depositional sequences in caves and of slope sediments which do not include well-preserved soil horizons. However, an interstadial is documented only in cases where it represents an oscillation reflected by a characteristic sediment, soil, fauna, and flora associated with an interlayer within sediments, whose development and fossil content clearly indicate a colder climate. A typical example is the soils of PK I within the complex of pleniglacial loesses.

Therefore, in considering the natural environments of the hunters-gatherers, all the records available must be taken into account, including not only the properties of the sediments and soils providing archaeological finds and the associated fauna and flora, but also the position of the site in both a local and a regional landscape context (Chapter 8)—means in relation to areas or slopes, summits and valleys, water streams and rivers, wetlands, rock forms, and so on, since it may be assumed that various ecosystems were settled differently throughout the Pleistocene.

Chapter 3

Patterns of Human Evolution

EMANUEL VLČEK

Fossil human remains from Central Europe (former Czechoslovakia and its immediate vicinity) date to several larger geological and biostratigraphic periods. Their dating is based on a stratigraphic system, as expounded in the previous chapter.

The biological development of humans during the Middle Pleistocene of Central Europe is characterized by a gradual, but not linear or straightforward, pattern from the erectoid to the archaic sapient forms. During the Upper Pleistocene, the continuity in the development of humans is documented in the rich finds of modern humans, concentrated especially in Moravia.

Therefore, the overview given here summarizes the finds of fossil hominids from Central European territory generally, but with a focal point on Moravia, including finds from the new field excavations. As for the older finds, the data are based on the results of previous revised surveys and detailed paleoanthropological investigations. All these facts will be highlighted. Furthermore, this text is aimed at specifying and complementing the version of the latest edition of the *Catalogue of Fossil Hominids* (Oakley, Campbell, and Molleson, 1971).

THE PROBLEM OF FOSSIL HUMAN EXISTENCE DURING THE LOWER PLEISTOCENE

Dating from the end of the Lower Pleistocene, or to the Cromerian interglacials corresponding with PK X, several localities are recorded from Central Europe, such as Bečov, Suchdol, and Přezletice (Fridrich, 1976a, 1982), but no fossil human remains have been discovered thus far.

Special mention should be made of the Zlatý kopec locality near Přezletice in Central Bohemia (Fridrich, 1989). A Lower Paleolithic settlement was situated on the former riverbank of the Elbe's inundation zone. In addition to fauna, stone and possibly bone tools, and, possibly, even remnants of a settlement feature, a tiny fragment of a human molar has been described (Fejfar, 1969, 1976). Unfortunately, a detailed histological study of the fragment showed that it does not belong to the species *Homo* and has to be regarded as a bear's tooth (Vlček, 1978a; Vlček and Kysela, 1979; Königswald, 1987).

For the sake of completeness, mention should also be made of the lost human skull discovered in the travertines of Dreveník Hill near Spišské Podhradie in East Slovakia. A human skeleton (J. J., 1937) was discovered there in D. Grünapfel's quarry at a depth of 4 m in 1936 during a blasting of compact travertines. Judging by the fauna (antilope, determined by O. Fejfar) and imprints of flora containing Tertiary relics (determined by F. Němejc and V. Kneblová-Vodičková), the stratigraphic position belonged to the dividing line between the Tertiary and the Quaternary. The owner of the quarry kept, from the whole find, only the skull filled with travertine. According to eyewitness accounts (Dančo, 1966), the skull had considerably formed supraorbital parts and a receding forehead. The skull had no temporal parts.

At the beginning of World War II, Grünapfel was sent to a Nazi concentration camp. Throughout the war, the skull was kept in the safe of a government emissary at Spišská Nová Ves. During following consultations with Austrian and Hungarian anthropologists, the exceptional significance of the find was emphasized. The skull was photographed by E. Franc, but the photographs are lost. At the end of the war, the find was returned to its owner. After 1948, the owner of the quarry died, and the skull has been missing ever since. This has caused a considerable loss to science (Bárta, 1987).

We have to conclude, therefore, that no fossil remains of Lower Pleistocene humans have been found in Central Europe so far.

THE MIDDLE PLEISTOCENE RECORD

The Middle Pleistocene has already yielded several fragmentary finds of fossil hominids within the wider environs of our territory. These finds can be divided in two morphological groups: the forms still bearing erectoid features and the already typically archaic *sapiens* forms.

"Advanced" *Erectus*

Central Europe's oldest finds so far come from the Vértesszölös locality in Hungary. This is an open settlement in a travertine quarry near the village of Vértesszölös, some 50 km west of Budapest. During a systematic survey, carried out between 1963 and 1968, small-dimensional tools (Kretzoi and Vértes, 1965) were unearthed in an archaeological context in a layer corresponding with Upper Biharian (inter-Mindel), and in 1964 and 1965, modest human remains were also found: three milk molars of a seven-year-old child and fragment of a permanent molar, which were designated as Vértesszölös 1, and in the stratigraphically younger horizon, a fragment of an occipital bone of an adult male (Vértes, 1965; Thoma, 1966, 1967, 1969). Thoma

(1966) classified these finds taxonomically as *Homo* (*erectus seu sapiens*) *palaeohungaricus*.

Further finds come from Bilzingsleben in Central Germany (the former German Democratic Republic), from an open settlement in travertines in the "Steinrinne" site, 35 kilometers north of Erfurt. During a systematic survey of the area on the bank of a stream flowing out of a mineral spring crater, deliberately crushed human skulls and isolated teeth have been found repeatedly since 1971, both in the settlement area and in the sediments of the adjacent brook. The locality is dated to the younger phase of the Holstein interglacial *sensu lato* (stage 9, about 350,000–420,000 B.P.). Small-dimensional tools are accompanied by Middle Pleistocene fauna and thermophile flora (Mania, Toepfer, and Vlček, 1980; Mania and Weber, 1986; Mania and Vlček, 1981, 1987; Vlček, 1978b, 1979, 1983, 1986a, 1987, 1989a).

Since the first find of a human skull fragment in 1972, remains of at least three individuals, two of adult age and one child, have been discovered so far. In morphological terms, the finds from Vértesszölös and Bilzingsleben are close to the human forms from Arago near Tautavel in France (de Lumley, 1982) and to the find from Petralona in Greece (Stringer, Howell, and Melentis, 1979; Murrill, 1980, 1981). While the settlements in Vértesszölös and Bilzingsleben were located near flowing openings of mineral springs (i.e., in travertines), the finds from Arago and from Petralona were made in caves, which causes various difficulties in dating such finds more precisely. Dating has not yet been definitely established, but the age of these finds corresponds to the periods of the antepenultimate and penultimate glaciations. The new dating of the find from Petralona is in the range of 240,000–160,000 B.P. (Xirotiris and Vlček, 1982).

In morphological terms, the above-mentioned finds represent a group in which numerous erectoid aspects of *Homo erectus* are still present. In addition, it is possible to assign to this group the find of a mandible from Mauer near Heidelberg, whose assumed age corresponds with PK VII. The find was, however, made in a secondary position in a sandpit. The original position of the fossil has not been unequivocally determined even after repeated attempts.

The morphology of this group is best represented by a partial reconstruction of the neurocranium of the man from Bilzingsleben, first in the individual No. 1 (Figure 3.1). As for the forehead, the most conspicuous feature is the huge torus supraorbitalis, which is not interrupted in the glabella area. Its size is remarkable. Between the glabella and the crista frontalis, the frontal bone is 25 mm thick, and in the nasion point torus, it is 21 mm high. The supraorbital torus is medium thick. The front surface of the torus was frontally flattened. The eye sockets had a horizontal position. The sulcus supraorbitalis is not formed, but a broad and smooth depressio glabellae is clearly noticeable. The pars ossis nasalis constitutes another group of features. The root of the nose is massive and broad. The squama frontalis documents an oblique course of the frontal squama without a trace of the formation of a tuber frontale. The linea temporalis is angular and doubled. The sinus frontales are formed only in the massif of torus supraorbitalis. Their shape is cauliflower-like, made up of two chambers which are not separated by other septa. The postorbital strangulation of

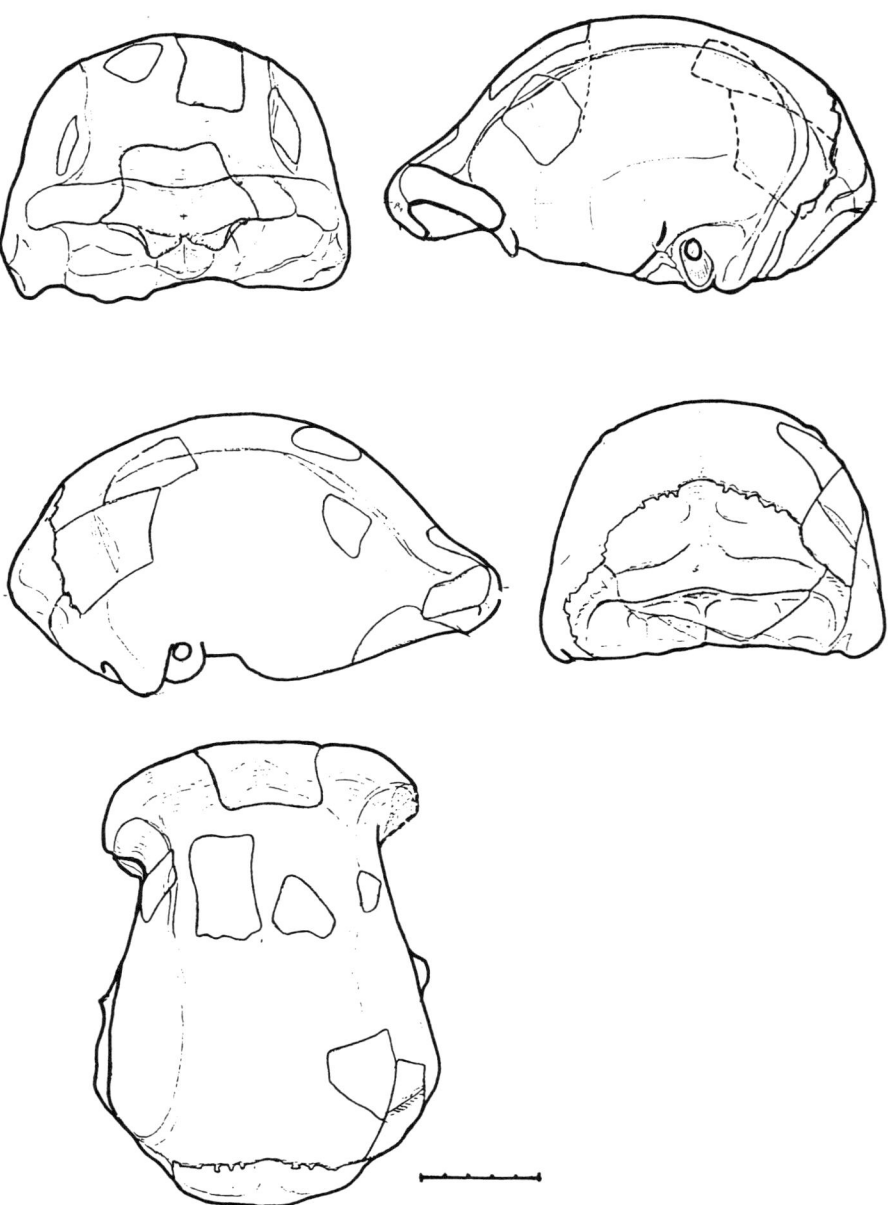

Figure 3.1. Bilzingsleben 1: Fragments of skull No. 1 compared to the Olduvai Hominid 9 specimen (orig. E. Vlček).

the skull's vertical outline is only slightly stressed. A fragment of the os parietale dx displays in section L 3 of the lambda seam a marked thickening of the bone into the shape of the torus angularis.

The occipital bone of the Bilzingsleben man has a torus occipitalis which sits typically saddlelike (astraddle) on the edge of the occipital bone notching. In the central section, the torus is not divided but is laterally outlined through the linea nuchae superior. Then, it continues by a laterally uplifted edge up to the asterion area. The planum occipitale is low, and the l-i-o angle measures a mere 108 degrees. The planum nuchea is flattened but even and is not, therefore, concavely deepened. The thickness of the bones is striking, primarily in the section of the sutura occipito-mastoidea, where it reaches 17 mm. The opistocranion matches the inion point. Hence, the maximum length of the skull corresponds to the length g-i. The sutura lambdoidea is thickened and extends into the torus angularis described together with the parietal bone.

Further discoveries made between 1986 and 1993 (Mania, Mania, and Vlček, 1994) provide a much more accurate picture of the neurocranium of the Bilzingsleben man. It was possible to reconstruct the brain box of the second individual (Bilzingsleben 2; Figure 3.2). Fragments of the frontal bone B 4 and B 7 demonstrate the development of a massive torus supraorbitalis but also determine the breadth of the frontal area in the section of postorbital narrowing. Furthermore, they confirm the creation of an angular linea temporalis. The parietal parts of the skull, pieced together from several fragments, give an idea of the length and arching of both ossa parietale. The preserved fragments of the left os parietale (B 4 and D 3) prove that, in the Bilzingsleben 2 individual, the ossa interparietalia were formed in lambda just as in the finds from Arago and Petralona. As regards the Vértesszölös find, the situation in this particular area is not clear because of the incomplete state of preservation.

The find of a fragment of the right temple bone G 1 was a groundbreaking discovery, informing us about the formation of the auricular area, processus mastoideus and part of squama ossis temporalis. Last but not least, another fragment of the occipital bone A 3 confirms the occipital notching and the formation of a typical toruslike torus occipitalia which is more accentuated than in the Bilzingsleben 2 individual.

Thanks to the greater number of fragments of the right and left parts of the skull of the Bilzingsleben 2 individual, it is possible to complete the missing parts in a mirror fashion, thus substantially contributing to the picture of the original shape of the skull of the Bilzingsleben hominid.

Very important features are recorded in the endocranium morphology. Particularly typical is the developed *bec encephalique*. The rostrum orbitale is narrow and high, just as in the finds from Arago and Sinanthropus (Xirotiris and Vlček, 1982).

The neurocranium of the Bilzingsleben man was long, low, and broad (Vlček, 1989a). Absolutely exact identities in terms of the shape and size of the occipital parts were discovered in Sinanthropus III (with an accuracy of 1 mm). However, the frontal parts of the Bilzingsleben hominid are more robust. Further surprising correspondences are visible between the fragments of a calvarium from Bilzingsleben and the

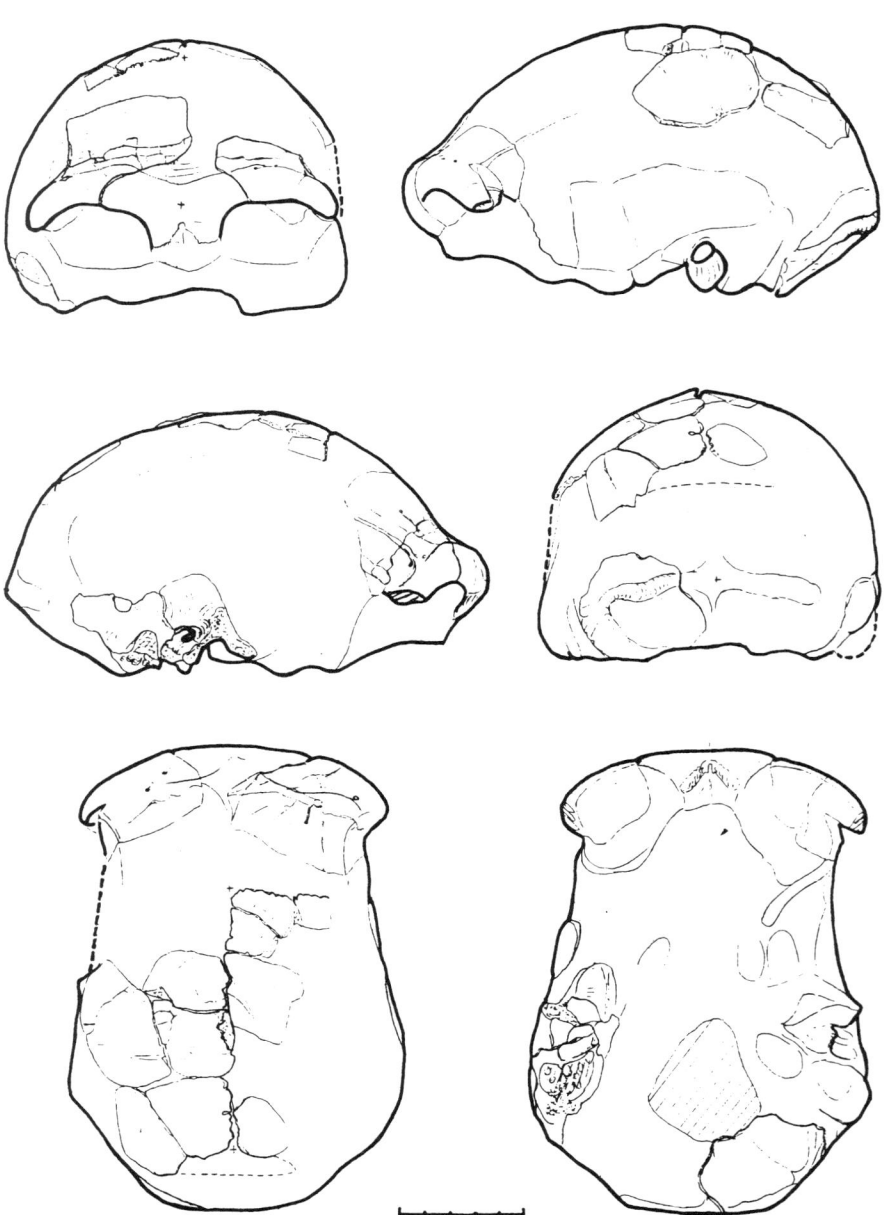

Figure 3.2. Bilzingsleben 2: Neurocranial reconstruction of the individual No. 2 (after Vlček).

considerably older find Olduvai OH 9, both in size and—more important—in the shape of the glabellal and occipital areas. However, the frontal part of OH 9 is, on the whole, narrower. The find was compared to the skull from Petralona as well. Striking morphological similarities have been determined in the morphology and size of the frontal area; on the other hand, dissimilarities in size have been detected in occipital parts. The skull of the Petralona individual was larger in absolute terms. Utter correspondence in the formation of the occipital parts of the Vértésszölös find can be seen precisely in the skull from Petralona.

The described characteristics of the neurocranium of the Bilzingsleben man correspond with erectoid human forms. Comparative studies (Vlček, 1986a, 1989a,b) show that, on a European scale, the find from Bilzingsleben stands closer to finds from Arago—Vértésszölös 2—Petralona. There is no clear-cut notion yet concerning the splanchnocranium of the Bilzingsleben finds.

"Archaic" *Sapiens*

Our attention will now be focused on the second group of finds in Europe, which are represented by the discoveries at Swanscombe, Steinheim, and Ehringsdorf (Clark Le Gros and Morant, 1938; Berckhemmer, 1933, 1936; Weinert, 1936; Breitinger, 1955). The finds from Swanscombe and Steinheim are generally dated to the Holstein period, but we do not know whether to its earlier or later stages.

In the territory under review, we should concentrate on the earlier series of finds from Ehringsdorf near Weimar, Central Germany, which belong to the warm Rügen period, between 250,000 and 100,000 years (Schwarcz) or 244,000–102,000 years (Brunnacker). The finds were made between 1908 and 1925 in an open-air settlement during travertine quarrying in several localities. The cultural association is Early Mousterian (Chapter 4). There is an extensive literature, which is summarized primarily in the most recent studies on the cultural layers and their dating, fauna, and present flora (Behm-Blancke, 1960; Feustel, 1983).

As regards the available anthropological material, this includes a crushed skull of an adult individual (H) and fragments of parietal bones of another four adults (A,B,C,D). Out of the splanchnocranium, a mandibula of an adult (F) was discovered, as well as a femur fragment (E) representing the postcranial skeleton. In addition to remains of adults, there are also fragments of a child's skeleton (G). This important body of material has been studied on a number of occasions, and the skull H was reconstructed (Linding, 1934; Weidenreich, 1928; Kleinschmidt, 1931). The latest thorough revision of the material was presented by E. Vlček (1985, 1993a).

Since the majority of information about the morphology of this group is being supplied by the Ehringsdorf find, the whole group may be characterized by the skull from Weimar-Ehringsdorf H (Vlček, 1985, 1993a). The H skull is long, narrow, and lower, bearing a well-formed torus supraorbitalis, which is well separated from the frontal squama. In the glabella area, the torus is arched wavily but is not divided. The thickness of the torus is even from the glabella as far as the processus zygomaticus frontalis. On the frontal bone, the linea temporalis is formed in a crestlike manner but does not extend into the parietal bones. There is no postorbital narrowing of the skull at all. The squama ossis frontalis is steep, and the forehead is bomb-shaped, with maximum rounding in the metopion area. This arching in the middle of the frontal squama is clearly delineated so that a tuber frontale was formed.

The parietal parts are well arched, and the occipital parts are raised backward but rounded. There is no notching on the occiput. The opistocranion is found 20 mm above the inion. The planum occipitale is also rounded and bomb-shaped. The linea nuchea superior is well formed, separating the planum occipitale from the planum nuchae. The torus occipitale is indistinct. The tubera parietali are well formed on the parietal bones. Viewed from the back, the walls of the skull's outline are positioned in parallel, creating the characteristic "Hausform Typus" of the skull. The os temporale is relatively small, with a slightly developed processus mastoideus. The porus acusticus is small, and the edge of the os tympanicum is not thickened. Similarly, other fragments of parietal bones attest to the modern architecture of the brain box of the Ehringsdorf man, which is morphologically closer to modern sapiens than to the Neanderthal forms.

Considerable similarities to the find from Ehringsdorf are also displayed by older finds from Steinheim and Swanscombe. In these, too, the maximum width of the skull is found in the norma occipitalis in the upper half of the norm's outline, and because of its overall formation, it is reminiscent, primarily in Steinheim, of the Hausform Typus brain box. The torus angularis, or thickening in the sutura lambdoidea, is not formed. Basic differences between both groups are borne out by medisagittal and transveral CT cuts of the Steinheim skull in comparison with the skull from Petralona.

Two Populations during the Holstein Period

During the Holstein period, we can therefore follow two parallel population groups in Central Europe (Vlček, 1986a, 1989b): first and foremost, the group which still displays erectoid features in the structure of the brain box, the so-called advanced *erectus*, and another kind, which may be assigned to the typical ancient sapient forms, archaic *sapiens*. Such a distinction is similarly attested to in the archaeological record, where the first group is related to the small-dimensional industries and the second, instead, to the Acheulian and Early Mousterian (Svoboda, 1987a, 1989b). The basic morphological differences in the structure of the brain box between the two groups are given in Table 3.1.

When reviewing the phylogenetic trends in development of the Middle Pleistocene hominids in Central Europe, the question arises how far it is necessary to ascribe finds bearing erectoid features solely to sapient forms. We believe that the "advanced" *erectus* forms are not identical with the "archaic" *sapiens* ones, and that they belong to independent cultural contexts. The differences identified in the structure of the neurocranium reach beyond the frame of a single subspecies. That was the main reason for distinguishing, within the Middle Pleistocene in Europe, two phylogenetic subspecies: one in the frame of the *Homo erectus* species, and the other in *Homo sapiens*.

Table 3.1. Chief Differences in the Shape of the Neurocranium between the Advanced *Erectus* and Archaic *Sapiens* Forms

	Homo erectus bilzinglebensis		Homo sapiens steinheimensis	
	Male	Female	Male	Female
Max. skull length	Cca 210	Less than 200	Cca 200	184–210
Skull capacity	1200 ccm	1100–1160	1400	1200–1300
Torus supraorbitalis	Frontally flattened	Frontally flattened	—	Rounded
Squama frontalis	Flat Slanting	Flat Slanting	—	Tuber centrale
Linea temporalis	Doubled	Doubled	—	Simple
Postorbital narrowing	Clearly formed	Clearly formed	—	Weak
Occiput	Broken	Broken	Rounded	Rounded
Max. length	i = op	i = op	i under op	i under op
Torus occipitalis	Above edge of curving	Saddlelike on the edge of curving	Below op	Below op
Planum occipitale	Low to medium high	Low	High	High
Norma occipitalis	Low, broad, max. width in the lower third	Low, broad, max. width in the lower third	High, max. width in center of lower third	High, Hausform
Norma occipitalis	Parietalia saddlelike	Parietalia saddlelike	Parietalia saddlelike	Parietalia saddlelike
Planum nuchae	Flat, convex	Flat	Convex	Convex
Torus angularis	+	+	—	—
Os interparietale	+	+	—	—
Bone thickness	Thick	Thick	Thin	Thin
Rostrum orbitale	++ pointed	++ pointed	+? low	+? low

For the archaic *sapiens* form, the subspecies *Homo sapiens steinheimensis* (Berckhemmer, 1936) was already established. For the advanced *erectus* forms, the most easily datable and adequately morphologically definable find from Bilzingsleben is selected as a reference specimen and named *Homo erectus bilzingslebensis* (Vlček, 1978b). The new finds from Bilzingsleben confirm the viability and justifiability of the proposed taxonomy.

In both phylogenetic subspecies, we observe, as their development progressed, the pattern of individual features. One observation is quite noteworthy: the changes in the shape of the neurocranium are retarded compared to the development of the brain. Therefore, the study of the brain development, hence the endocranium, is perceived as decisive in the evaluation of the finds. In the old archaic finds from Olduvai OH 9, Arago, and Bilzingsleben, a certain balance is discernible in the development of a small and primitive endocranium and a primitively shaped neurocranium. For instance, the frontal part of the endocranium of the aforementioned finds is on a lower level of development and is comparable with *Sinanthropus*. But within the same erectoid group, the finds from Petralona have shown that the primitively shaped neurocranium did contain a considerably developed brain, corresponding, in terms of development, with the Neanderthal forms. The same applies to the Vértésszölös 2 find. It follows that the development of individual components proceeds not evenly, but in a mosaiclike fashion, and that the decisive impetus for further changes is given by the development of the brain: the endocranium.

THE UPPER PLEISTOCENE RECORD

Fossil Human Finds of the Last Interglacial

A new stage of the development of Central European Paleolithic populations is evidenced during the last (Eemian) interglacial, which corresponds to PK III. The finds from that period include an important specimen from a travertine site at Gánovce and an isolated tooth discovered in a cultural layer in travertines at Taubach.

Gánovce

During a blasting in a quarry at an open settlement in the "Hrádok" travertine knob at Gánovce, 3 km from the town of Poprad, Slovakia, a human skull fragment filled with natural travertine casting (Vlček, 1949, 1953, 1955) was discovered. During a revisory research at the locality carried out between 1955 and 1960 by E. Vlček and F. Prošek, imprints of a human radium and fibula were recovered (Vlček, 1958a,b).

In stratigraphic terms, the layer of the finds belongs to the latter half of the Eemian interglacial, more precisely to the end of the period with *Quercetum mixtum* and to the arrival of conifers (100,000–90,000 years B.P.). Together with interglacial fauna and rich flora, Taubachian industries were discovered in four positions. The settlement was situated around a circular basin of a warm mineral spring at the top of a travertine knob.

The find consisted of an almost complete natural travertine endocranium to which fragments of the ossa parietalia, the left os temporale, and part of the squama occipitalis were attached. At the base of the casting are preserved bony bases and, on the endocranium's frontal poles, fragments of os frontale. The endocranium is perfectly cast, with well-imprinted foramen magnum, sinuses, and imprints of arteries and gyrifications on the occipital, temporal, and frontal lobes of the endocranium. The remains probably belong to a woman of mature age. The capacity of the skull was 1,320 ccm. The maximum width was measured in the middle of the endocranium. Its frontal parts are flat, with a reduced content and with a triad of morphological features (concave arching of the frontal edges of casts, a massive rostrum orbitale, and a large protrusion in the opercular area of the cast, the so-called cap). The cast is conspicuously flat in the lateral norm, as corroborated by the height measured above the Kappers horizontal. The endocranium's occipital parts are noteworthy for conspicuously raised occipital poles and flattened cerebellum parts.

A small angle of the kyfosis of the skull base and rounding of the parietal torus of the skull, found in the remains of the bony calva, which becomes evident in the section b-ast-ba (Sergi), attest to a low neurocranium of the Gánovce hominid. At CT sections, sinus frontalis were detected in the remains of the frontal bone, formed solely in the torus supraorbitalis massif because the sinus roof does not rise into the frontal squama (Vlček, 1988).

The above-mentioned features of the Gánovce find suggest a low and broad brain box, an originally well-formed torus supraorbitalis, and raised occipital parts of the skull. The root of the nose was broad, and the round eye sockets were set far apart. The skull base was considerably flat. Morphological and metric comparisons with a whole number of human development forms establish the Gánovce find as a pre-Neanderthal form which displays the most similarities to the find from Broken Hill, Gibraltar, and Krapina. The taxonomic classification of the Gánovce find is *Homo sapiens neanderthalensis* (Vlček, 1953, 1969).

Taubach (Central Germany)

At Taubach in 1887, in an open-air settlement in H. Sonnrein's travertine quarry, the owner discovered in a cultural layer the first lower molar tooth of a 12- to 14-year-old child (Nehring, 1895a; Virchow, 1917; Adloff, 1911, 1920). The dating of the cultural layer corresponds to the Eemian interglacial and to the Taubachian culture, while the fauna includes *Palaeoloxodon antiquus* (Behm-Blancke, 1960). Another tooth, a milk molar, was recovered in Mehlhorn's quarry by A. Weis in 1892 (Nehring, 1895b). In morphological terms, both teeth can be assigned to Neanderthals.

In conclusion, the existence of Neanderthal humans, culturally belonging to the Taubachian (Valoch, 1984a; Svoboda, 1989b), has been proved in Central Europe during the last interglacial. Remarkably enough, travertine localities in particular have yielded the most complete evidence of human settlement.

Early Glacial Neanderthals

Another stage in the development of fossil hominids dates to the early phase of the Last Glacial corresponding with PK II. The available finds suggest most probably a continuity to the development of Middle Pleistocene populations of *Homo sapiens steinheimensis*.

The oldest find from Königsaue, Central Germany (the former German Democratic Republic), is dated to the Brörup interstadial. No human bone remains have been recovered there, only imprints of human papillary lines preserved on a fragment of resin binder. Another discovery of a frontal bone from Šala nad Váhom, Slovakia, comes from river sediments. The accompanying fauna dates the find, with a high degree of probability, to the Early Glacial period.

The other finds of fossil hominids are from caves. During a systematic research in Kůlna Cave in the Moravian karst, fragments of a maxilla, os parietale, and free teeth were found. Furthermore, dating to this period are the Moravian finds of a jawbone from Šipka Cave near Štramberk, fragments of a jawbone, a free molar tooth, and a fragment of os parietale and os temporale from Švédův stůl Cave near Ochoz, as well as the finds of two individuals from Subalyuk Cave in Hungary.

Königsaue

In the thick sediments of Aschersleben Lake in the capping of a brown coal basin near Köningsaue, 65 km from the town of Halle, a group of strata documenting 11 climatic oscillations of the Upper Pleistocene was uncovered, starting with the last interglacial and ending with the Holocene (Mania and Toepfer, 1973). A salvage archaeological research launched in 1970 discovered three Micoquien layers with fauna in the sediments of the Brörup interstadial (PK II) dated to about 55,800 B.P. In the oldest position, A, an exceptional discovery was made: two fragments of a resin binder attaching a retouched artifact to a wooden handle. The surface of the resin retains a plastic relief of human papillary lines. This is so far the oldest depiction of the surface of fossil human skin.

Šala nad Váhom

During river dredging in a sand island in the middle of the River Váh near the town of Šala, some 50 km north of Bratislava, V. Černianský discovered in 1961 a human frontal bone (Figure 3.3). Unearthed from the same position was the fauna with the species *Dicerorhinus hemitoechus*, *Megaloceros giganteus*, *Bos primigenius*, and *Elephas sp.*, which, together with the established position, dates the find of the frontal bone to the beginning of the last glaciation (Vlček, 1964, 1968b, 1969).

The os frontale, belonging to an adult individual (probably a female), is very well preserved. The squama ossis frontalis is low and receding, but slightly arched, forming a small ridge in the metopic line. Tubera frontalis are indicated. The torus supraorbitalis is massive, uninterrupted in the mediosagittal plane and laterally proceeding in a fluent and evenly thick torus as far as the processus zygomaticus of the frontal bone. The massif of the supraorbital torus is well separated from the frontal squama. The root of the nose in the Šala find is distinctly broad, displaying a primitive architecture of this area. According to the shape of the upper edges of the eye sockets, these were oval-shaped. The sinus frontalis is simple, taking up the entire root of the nose without jutting out into the frontal bone squama.

The cast of the frontal parts of the endocranium displays a lesser development of the rostrum orbitale compared to the classical Western European Neanderthals. When comparing the find, a precise analogy in shape and size was established with the find from Galilea-Zuttiyeh whose arching of the frontal squama and its receding and shape match precisely those from Šala. The only difference was found in the glabella section on the supraorbital torus, which is massive in Galilea, a fact which can be well explained by sexual dimorphism (Galilea male, Šala female). Other great similarities are displayed by the Šala find when compared with the series of discoveries from Skhul, placing it among the forms of the so-called intermediate Neanderthals.

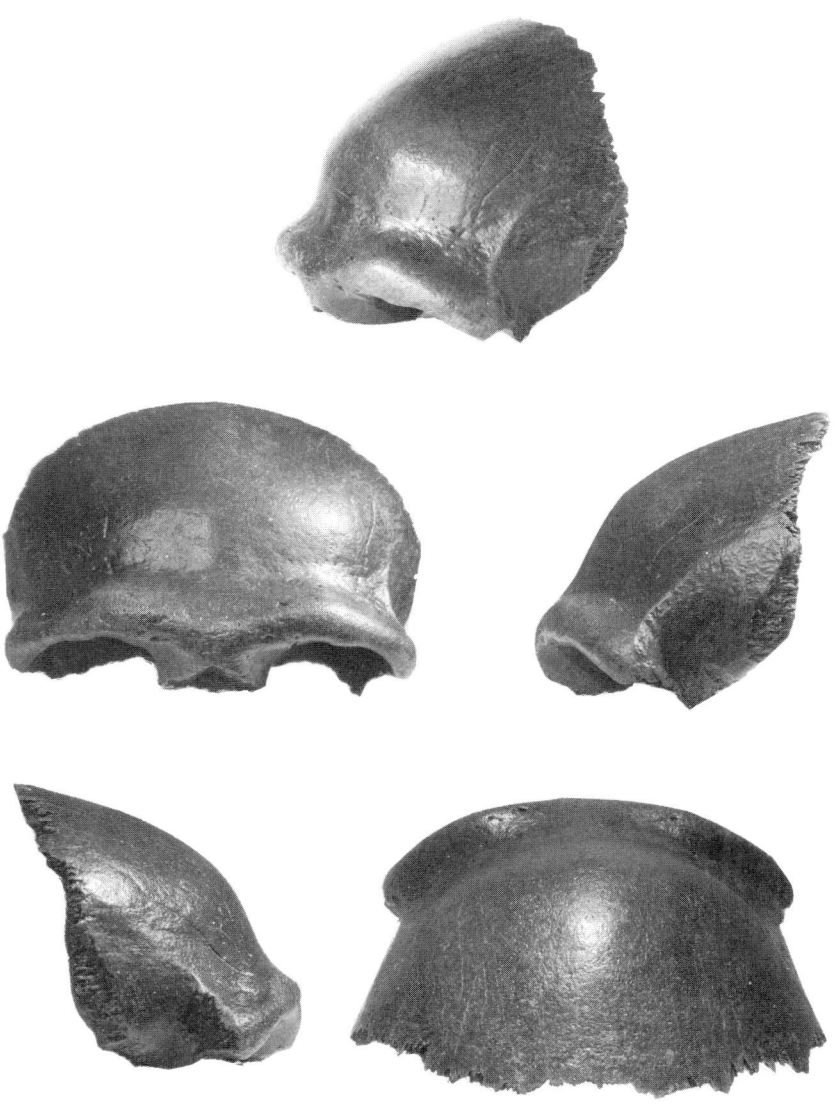

Figure 3.3. Šala nad Váhom: Neanderthal frontal bone.

Kůlna

Systematic archaeological research was carried out between 1961 and 1976 by K. Valoch (1988) in a cave near the village of Sloup in the Moravian karst, some 35 km north of Brno (Appendix A). The fieldwork uncovered a sequence of layers, starting with the final period of the penultimate (Riss) glacial and ending with the Holocene. Human fragments were discovered in the Early Würm layers together with Micoquian artifacts. In layer 7a, V. Gebauer discovered in 1965 a fragment of right maxilla, E. Dvořák recovered in 1970 a fragment of the right os parientale, and between 1966 and 1969, another three milk molars were found during the sieving of sediments of layer 7a (Figure 3.4; Jelínek, 1966, 1967, 1981). In absolute chronology, these finds date before 38,600–43,660 B.P. (minimal C-14 datings). The anthropological finds were comprehensively described by J. Jelínek (1988).

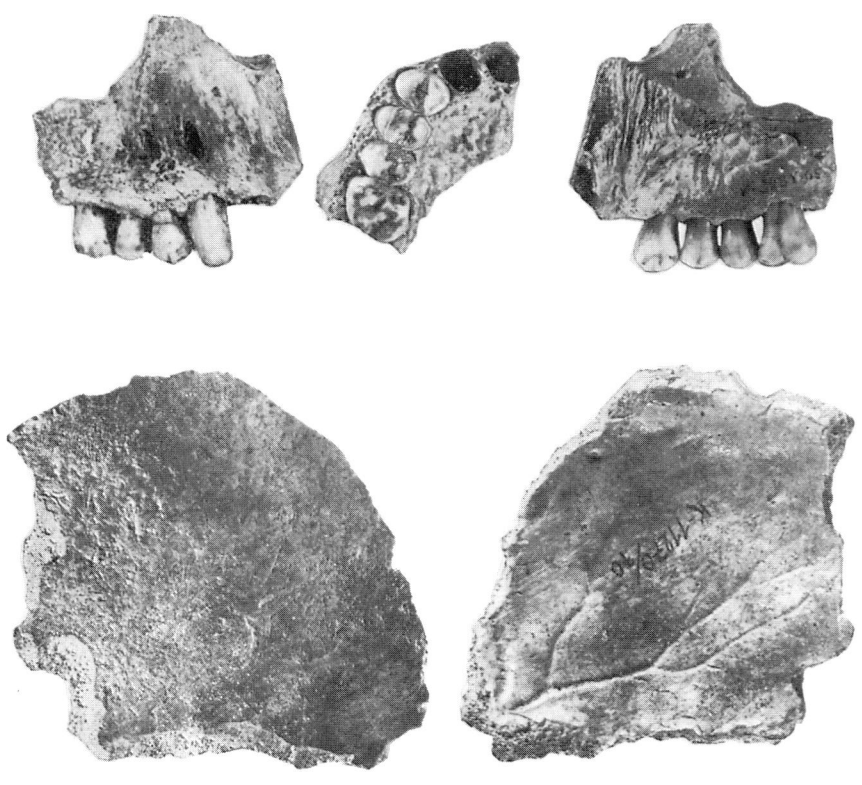

Figure 3.4. Kůlna: Fragments of a right maxilla and of a right parietal bone.

The fragment of right maxilla (Kůlna I) has a broken-off processus frontalis, processus zygomaticus, and tubera maxillae; part of the facies anterior; and the entire facies orbitalis. The processus alveoralis has been preserved in section I 1–M 1 with set teeth C–M 1. Also missing is part of the os palatini. The front wall of the corpus maxillae, wherever preserved, is smooth and without a fossa canina. Between the root of the canine and the second incisor tooth there is a deep sulcus, 7 mm wide and 21 mm high. Starting with the canine, the edges of the alveolus are thickened and receding high, so that the roots of the preserved teeth are exposed up to 4 mm. This may be regarded as a pathological feature. Still, on the palatinal side, the edge of the alveolus is lowered but not thickened. This pattern contrasts with the small abrasion on the occlusal surfaces of the preserved teeth.

The height of the jawbone pr-ns can be estimated at 31 mm. The lower part of the 19-mm-long incisura nasalis was preserved from the apertura piriformia. Its edge is thickened, measuring some 6 mm, with a sulcus praenasalis about 3 mm wide, in the frontal part defined by a sharp edge and at the back by a 2-mm-broad rounded torus formed inside. The spina nasalis anterior was originally doubled. The median wall of the canalis incisivus was broken off from the right half. A right-sided foramen canalis incisivi was formed on the rear torus behind the spina nasalis. The course of the groove can be traced on the wall of the sutura intermaxillaris. It leads out through a short groove into the foramen incisivum on the palatinal projection of the jawbone. Its bottom has been preserved behind the sinus maxillaris; the remaining walls are broken off.

The processus palatini is to the right, 20 mm broad (measured at the level of M 1). As a result, the hard palate of the Kůlna hominid was narrow, some 40 mm. The estimated length of the palate is about 56 mm. No trace has been found of the sutura incisiva. Because of their morphology, the preserved teeth fall within the variation range of the Neanderthal and *sapiens* forms. Only in M 1 was a marked crista obliqua formed, an implication of a fovea Carabelli, and a small fossa anterior, and the lingual surface of the crown is divided by a deep vertical groove which extends uninterrupted as far as the dental root. Taurodontism is only indicated. Morphological analogies are observed at Le Moustier and Krapina.

Of the right parietal bone (Kůlna II), only the central part has been preserved, in a fragment of trapezoid shape. In the extent of S 2–S 3, 48 mm of the margo sagittalis has been preserved. The margo occipitalis and the squamosus were broken as a result of blows from the inside and the margo frontalis with a strike to the angulus sphenoidalis. As for morphological details, the facies externa has a well-preserved central part of the linea temporalis superior and also a small portion of the linea temporalis inferior, at the level of which the lower section of the fragment ends. The ring between both lines is up to 16 mm wide. Bone thickness varies from 5 to 6 mm in the postbregmatic area and in the vicinity of the obelion, reaching up to 12 mm on the right parietal torus. The margo sagittalis is 8–10 mm thick.

As for the facies interna, there is a well-formed thickening of the margo sagittalis edge with half of the imprint of the sinus sagittalis superior. The edge of the seam is considerably damaged, so that it is impossible for us to venture an opinion as to the degree of obliteration of the arrow seam. Pacchionian granulations are also present. There is a well-preserved imprint of the section arteria meningea media, namely, an incomplete but wide-stem ramus anterior, which is traceable throughout the entire height of the fragment. Situated in the lower section of the angulus sphenoidalis area, running away from this stem of ramification, is the ramus medium, passing across beneath the parietal torus. In addition to branches, there are evident anastomoses leading to the ramus posterior, which is not depicted on the fragment. The adjustment and distance of the medial branch from the massive ramus anterior points to a pattern encountered in the Neanderthal. Because of a faulty position of the fragment of the bone, Saban (1982) and Jelínek (1988) regard the ramus anterior as the ramus posterior. Both described bone fragments can be ascribed to an adult individual, because of the small degree of abrasion of the preserved teeth and given considerable changes on the paradontium. Judging from the thickness of the parietal bone and the height of the jawbone, we can classify this individual as a male.

During the sieving of the sediment of layer 7a, crowns of an upper molar and two lower molars, coming from a temporary dentition, were discovered. The roots of the teeth had already been damaged by resorption, a fact suggesting that the teeth had fallen out physiologically during dental change. The morphology of the teeth is indistinct, corresponding with both the Neanderthal and sapient forms.

In conclusion, fragments discovered in Kůlna Cave can be assigned to at least two different individuals. Morphologically and typologically, they conform with the forms of intermediate Neanderthals, as encountered in Moravia, Slovakia, and the Near East.

Šipka

As early as in 1880, during a systematic exploration of sediments in the Šipka Cave, in the limestone Kotouč Hill, 1 km from the town of Štramberk, K. J. Maška discovered fragments of a lower jawbone of a child in connection with Mousterian artifacts and early glacial fauna (Figure 3.5; Appendix A; Maška, 1882, 1886). In 1950, F. Prošek carried out a revisory survey of the cave sediments which confirmed the original dating of the found human fragments, fauna, and tools to the Lower Würmian or PK II (Prošek and Ložek, 1954; Kukla, 1954). Between 1957 and 1961, K. Valoch (1965c) compiled the archaeological inventory accumulated during earlier surveys.

Old literature lists the well-known "Šipka jaw-bone," preserved as a fragment of a jawbone set with six teeth. Judging by the degree of mineralization of the teeth, the age of the individual can be estimated at between 9 and 10 years (Vlček, 1986b).

As for the fragment of a chlid's jawbone, the height and thickness of the body are conspicuous (30 and 14 mm, respectively). The planum alveolare is transverse, with a well-formed torus transversus superior and also a well-formed incurvation mandibulae anterior. On the inside of the jawbone's body, a horizontally positioned fossa mandibularis genioglossi is formed instead of a spina mentalis. On the basal surface of the body, a broad horizontal fossa digastrica is formed with a clearly defined tuber basale. A protuberantis mentalis is totally lacking on the mentum osseum.

Significant features were detected on the preserved teeth. The incisor teeth are

Figure 3.5. Šipka: Fragment of an infantile Neanderthal mandible.

very large, having thick roots with longitudinal grooves on their mesial and distal surfaces. All the teeth display a considerable degree of taurodontism, and the second premolar P2 shows a degree of molarization. All the teeth range well within the variation of the Neanderthals with close analogies to the finds from La Noulette, Malarnaud, Le Moustier, and Krapina (Jelínek, 1965; Vlček, 1958b, 1969).

Švédův stůl

In the lower layers of Švédův stůl Cave near the village of Ochoz, K. Kubásek discovered in 1905 a fragment of the mandibula of an adult individual together with a few Mousterian artifacts and fauna (Figure 3.6; Appendix A; Rzehak, 1906, 1909). Between 1953 and 1955, B. Klíma (1962a) carried out a revisory archaeological survey in the cave, which yielded further Mousterian artifacts accompanied by fauna identical with that unearthed in Šipka Cave, and dating to the Lower Würm period. This find helped to make precise the age of the human jawbone. In 1964, J. Vaňura (1965a,b) and his daughter discovered an isolated molar and two skull fragments in the residual sediments.

The "Ochoz jawbone" is preserved as a fragment, with a broken-off basal part of the body and both ramuses. The dentition is complete but considerably worn off. The jawbone belongs to an adult.

The body of the jawbone is formed by a massive torus transversus superior on a broad planum alveolare and an equally distinct curvatio mandibulae anterior. Once again, on the spot of the spina mentalis, there is a fossa mandibularis genioglossi. There is a well-developed tuber symphyseus on the front surface of the body.

Important features have also been identified on the teeth. The root area is similar in shape and size to the Subalyuk find, while the dental arch is reminiscent of the jawbones from Krapina, Skhul, and Circeo III. Taurodontism is found in all the teeth, in the molars in particular. Correspondences in shape and metric similarities are demonstrated between the Švédův stůl jawbone and those from Western Europe, as well as from the Near East. Generally, the jawbone features the forms of intermediate Neanderthals (Jelínek, 1962; Vlček, 1958b, 1969).

An isolated M3 right has five caruncles with a strongly formed hypoconuclide. The system of grooves on the occlusal surface of the crown matches the pattern of the typical Neanderthals. The root of the teeth is obtusely cylindrical with an open canalis dentis and is also taurodontic. This tooth belongs to another individual (Vlček, 1969).

The left squama ossis temporalis has a considerably thickened margo sphenoidalis, the same type encountered in the Galilea-Zuttiyeh find. The indentation of the sutura sphenosquamalis is rough and simple (Vaňura, 1965a,b; Vlček, 1969). The fragment of the os parietale is insufficient for typological diagnosis. In view of the different types of fossilization, the two neurocranium fragments probably belong to two different individuals.

Subalyuk

Very similar fossil remains, corresponding to the variation range of Neanderthal and intermediate Neanderthal forms, were discovered in Subalyuk Cave near the

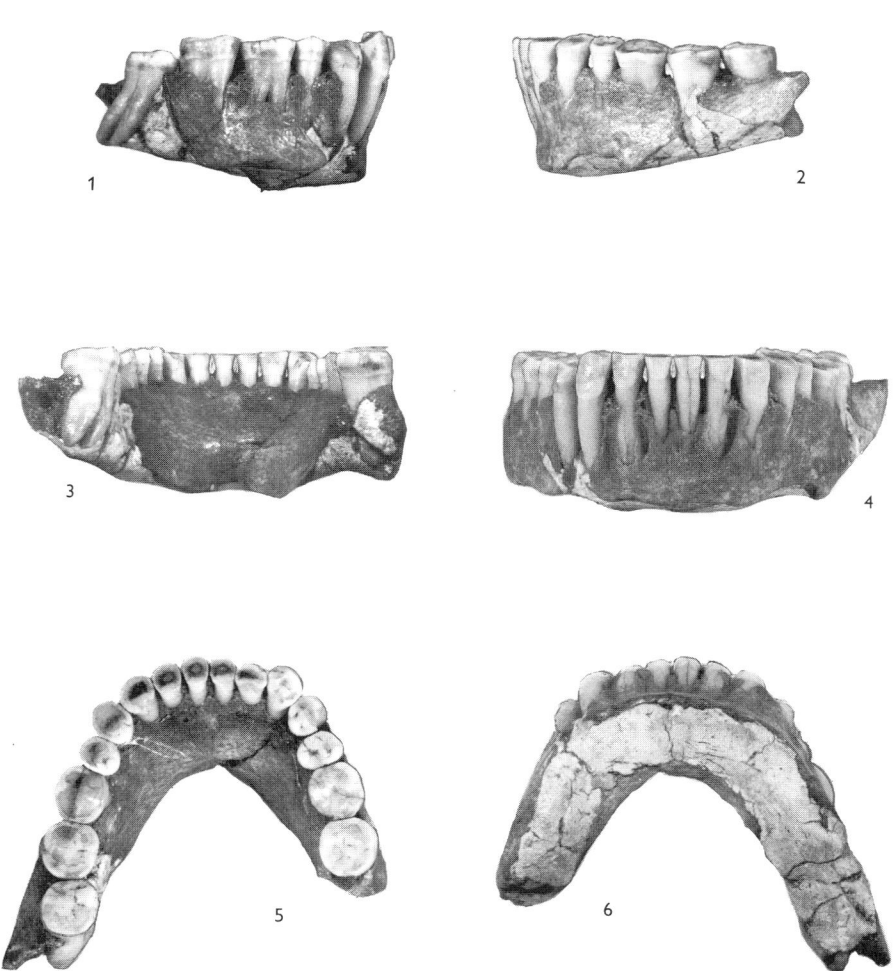

Figure 3.6. Švédův stůl: Fragment of a Neanderthal mandible.

village of Cserépfal in Hungary. The remains have been well covered in a monograph by Bartucz and Szabo (1940), and therefore the individual finds will not be described here. It is appropriate to note that they belong to two individuals: an adult female of mature age and a three- to four-year-old child.

THE UPPER PALEOLITHIC HUMANS OF CENTRAL EUROPE

The bulk of anthropological finds of Upper Paleolithic humans in Central Europe dates to the Würmian interpleniglacial, which corresponds to PK I. Generally, two chronological and cultural horizons have been established in the fossil record: the populations of the Aurignacian (and Szeletian) and the Gravettian.

The oldest forms of *Homo sapiens sapiens* in Central Europe were discovered in the cave system at Mladeč in Moravia, at two sites numbered Mladeč I and Mladeč II (Szombathy, 1925; Smyčka, 1922); at Koněprusy at Zlatý kůň in Bohemia (Vlček, 1952c, 1957a,c; Prošek, 1952); and at St. Prokop Cave in Prague (Vlček, 1951b). In all three cases, human remains were discovered in halls in cave systems, in debris cones beneath huge rock chimneys. It is possible to add to these finds the less significant discoveries from two more localities: Dzeravá skála Cave in Slovakia (Hillebrand, 1914) and Istállóskö Cave in Hungary (Malán, 1955).

As for dating, the above-mentioned localities can be assigned to the middle of the interpleniglacial, that is, to two time periods in the range of 35,000–30,000 B.P. The Mladeč I series of finds and the Istállóskö find belong culturally to the Aurignacian; the Mladeč II find, the one from Koněprusy Cave of Zlatý kůň, and possibly the find from St. Prokop Cave belong to an Upper Paleolithic Aurignacoid industry; and the Dzeravá skála find belongs to the Szeletian.

Last but not least, this group includes the find of a human tooth from the gorge of Silická Brezová in Slovakia (Vlček, 1957b) and the abri Tapolca find from Hungary (Thoma, 1957). Both finds are dated solely by the Würmian fauna.

The Earliest Modern Humans

Mladeč

The Mladeč I series of the Upper Paleolithic humans was discovered in the "Bočkova díra" cave system (Fürst-Johanns-Höhle), 4.5 km from the town of Litovel in northern Moravia (Figures 3.7 and 3.8; Appendix A).

In 1881, J. Szombathy carried out an exploratory trench, called a, in the D hall and described the section of the cave's sediments. In the trench, he discovered a Würmian fauna and a human skull (Mladeč I). In the following year, he worked on the same spot and opened another trench named b. Another human skull was discovered there (Mladeč II) and numerous bones of a human postcranial skeleton of an adult individual. In the middle of the D hall, a maxilla of another individual (Mladeč IIa), a child's skull (Mladeč II), and numerous other isolated bones of the remaining skeleton were recovered.

PATTERNS OF HUMAN EVOLUTION

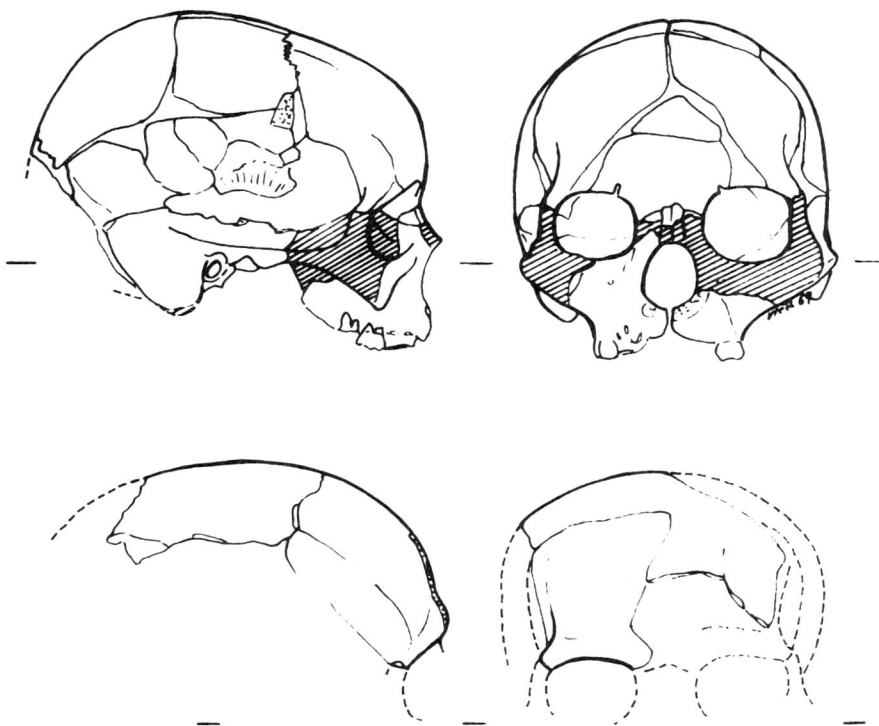

Figure 3.7. Reconstruction of skulls Mladeč II (above) and IV (below).

In 1903, J. Knies sunk another trench, called e, in the neighboring hall E and recovered a calvarium of a male individual (Mladeč IV) and other individual bones of the skull, the maxilla, the mandibula, and the skeleton (Szombathy, 1925; Figure 13). In 1922, during access-providing operations in the cave hall D, near the spot of Szombathy's original trench, other human remains were discovered, together with Würmian fauna (Smyčka, 1922), in sediments beneath the large rock chimney. All in all, five skull fragments and other bones of the postcranial skeleton, belonging to one male individual, a female individual, and three children (Fürst, 1922; Mladeč VIII, IX, X), were found there. These finds have never been thoroughly examined.

The second locality, Mladeč II, which was situated some 50 m west of the entrance to the "Bočkova díra" Cave, provided other major finds of fossil human remains in sediments of a small cave in a limestone quarry. Some of the finds were later deposited in the Litovel Museum and some in the Brno Museum (Smyčka, 1904). This body of material was anthropologically examined by J. Szombathy (1925), namely, the individuals Mladeč V (calotte, maxilla, mandibula), Mladeč VI (calotte, mandibula), and a series of bones from several individuals. The remains of a child (Mladeč VII)

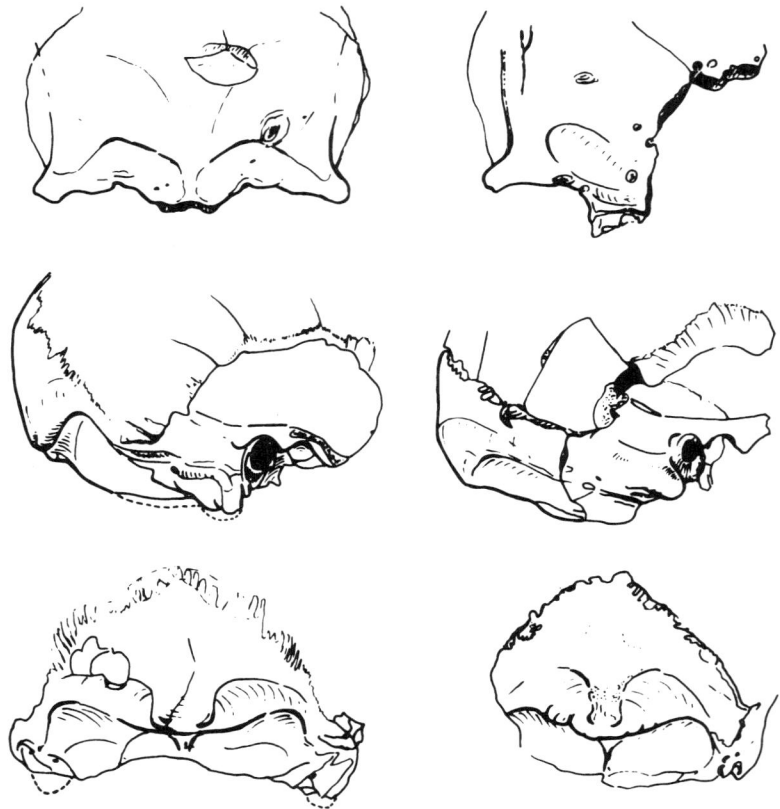

Figure 3.8. Comparison of the frontal and occipital parts of skulls Mladeč V (left) and Koněprusy I (right).

were only partially published by J. Kneis (1906). Regrettably many finds were destroyed by the end of the World War II.

Koněprusy-Zlatý kůň

The second locality, which yielded a corpus of Early Upper Paleolithic anthropological material, was again a large hall on the second floor of a cave system inside the Zlatý kůň Hill, situated some 500 m from the village of Koněprusy and 6 km from the town of Beroun in the Bohemian karst. These new caves were discovered during a blasting in a large limestone quarry in 1950. Occipital parts of a human skull (in the catalog listed as Zlatý kůň 1) were found at the foot of a huge debris cone on the central floor, in the so-called Prošek Hall (Figure 3.8). Consequently, the Archaeological Institute of the former Czechoslovak Academy of Sciences in Prague carried out systematic research of this hall under the leadership of F. Prošek (1952) between 1951 and 1953, recovering a further 12 fragments of the skeleton of an adult individual (Zlatý kůň 2; Vlček, 1952b,c, 1957a,c). Investigations of the finds deposited in the National Museum and in the Archaeological Institute of the former Czechoslovak Academy of Sciences showed that all the fragments (occipital parts and a newly discovered frontal part) belonged to one individual (a female of mature adult age). The skull of the woman has been gnawed away in the frontal part and on the left side of the facial skeleton, probably by a hyena or a wolf. Several vertebrae and three rib fragments have been preserved from the skeleton. The woman's personal belongings, probably stored in a leather pouch, were discovered near the remains, concentrated in a restricted area.

St. Prokop Cave in Prague

In the residues of a sinter breccia at the bottom of the original Cave of St. Prokop in St. Prokop's Valley in Prague, human remains were found in 1887, together with Würmian fauna and a bone tool (?) sintered in the loess position. Revision of the finds has shown that, with great probability, the fragment of the occipital bone and the head of the femur may be regarded as of Pleistocene age, while the other finds, in view of the degree of their fossilization, date back to the Holocene. The occipital parts display an arrangement of protuberantia occipitalis very similar to that of the Koněprusy specimen (Vlček, 1951b).

In terms of typology, the finds mentioned in this chapter can be classified as follows.

The finds from the Mladeč I Cave (Mladeč I, II, III, IV) correspond to the classical Cro-Magnon type as described from Dordogne. The finds from the second locality, Mladeč II (Mladeč V, VI, VII) and the finds from Koněprusy and from St. Prokop Cave still display a number of archaic features in the structure of the brain box, primarily in its frontal and occipital areas (Figures 3.7, 3.8). The relatively primitive formation of the child's jaw bone (Mladeč VII) is reminiscent of the forms of the intermediate Neanderthals. This applies to the presence of a groove in the course of the original symphysial seam (incisura mandibulae anterior) and a triangle-shaped depression above the trigonum basale. The development of the tuber mentale is indicated, as seen in Neanderthal children (Pech de l'Azé, Chateuneuf, La Chaise, Šipka etc.). Therefore these oldest modern Central European humans show certain relationships to the forms of the intermediate Neanderthals of Central Europe. Continued development of the aforementioned features can be traced, in a reduced form, to as late as some individuals of the earlier Gravettian populations in Moravia.

The other smaller finds, as listed above, do not make a considerable contribution to what we know about this population, and therefore no detailed account of them is given here.

The Gravettian Population

The most complete evidence of the populations of the Upper Paleolithic in Central Europe is provided by the slightly younger horizon of the interpleniglacial, dated radiometrically between 30,000 and 25,000 years B.P. In cultural terms, most of the finds are classified as Gravettian, or, more precisely, its earlier stage called Pavlovian (Chapter 6).

Stratigraphically, the oldest find of this group was made at Svitávka in Moravia (Vlček, 1968a). Also included in this group are two finds from Brno: Brno-Francouzská Street, in literature listed as Brno II (Makowsky, 1892; Jelínek, Pelíšek, and Valoch, 1959), and Brno-Žabovřesky, designated as Brno III (Absolon, 1929; Matiegka, 1929).

The most important and richest record of this population was found in the site of Předmostí I (Maška, 1895a,b; Matiegka, 1934, 1938), dated 27,000–26,000 B.P. The other large center of the settlement and burial sites was discovered beneath the Pavlovské Hills in southern Moravia, at Dolní Věstonice and at Pavlov. Dolní Věstonice I and II yielded graves and remains of as many as 29 individuals (Malý, 1939; Jelínek, 1953, 1954; Absolon, 1935b; Vlček, 1990) in several time horizons of the Pavlovian, ranging from 29,000 to 25,000 B.P. Similarly, the second locality at Pavlov (Vlček, 1961), where dating varies in the range 27,000–25,000 B.P., yielded another ritual burial site and a number of isolated human finds. All the remains can be included culturally in the Pavlovian. Their anthropological significance lies primarily in the number and complexity of the population, since Předmostí provides the remains of 25 individuals and Dolní Věstonice of a total of 29 individuals. Both series contain individuals of both sexes and various ages, including children.

Svitávka

During geological surveying in 1962, L. Smolíková discovered fossil human remains (Smolíková and Ložek, 1963) east of Svitávka, 50 km north of Brno, in the wall of a loess exposure. The following salvage excavation by B. Klíma and E. Vlček unearthed *in situ* a crushed skull and other skeleton bones. The skeleton originally lay on its back with crouched legs. In stratigraphic terms, the find belongs between two solifluction horizons, formed on the basis of the youngest fossil soil.

The facial bones could be reconstructed from the skull (Figure 3.9). As for the postcranial skeletal remains, the bones of the left upper arm, a fragment of pelvis, and a femur have been preserved. The exposed right side of the skeleton was destroyed in the wall of the brickyard by weather conditions. Several stones and pieces of charcoal were discovered next to the skeleton. The following archaeological research also uncovered Upper Paleolothic stone tools (Klíma, 1963c).

The skeleton belonged to a juvenile individual, probably a female. Unfortunately, out of the whole skull, only facial bones showing striking typological similarities to the find Brno III could be evaluated (Vlček, 1967).

Brno I

In a loess section at Červený kopec Hill in the western part of Brno (Appendix A), in 1885 A. Makowsky found (1888, 1890, 1899b) fragments of a skeleton of a young man, probably in the Würmain loess. Würmian fauna was discovered, but no tools

PATTERNS OF HUMAN EVOLUTION

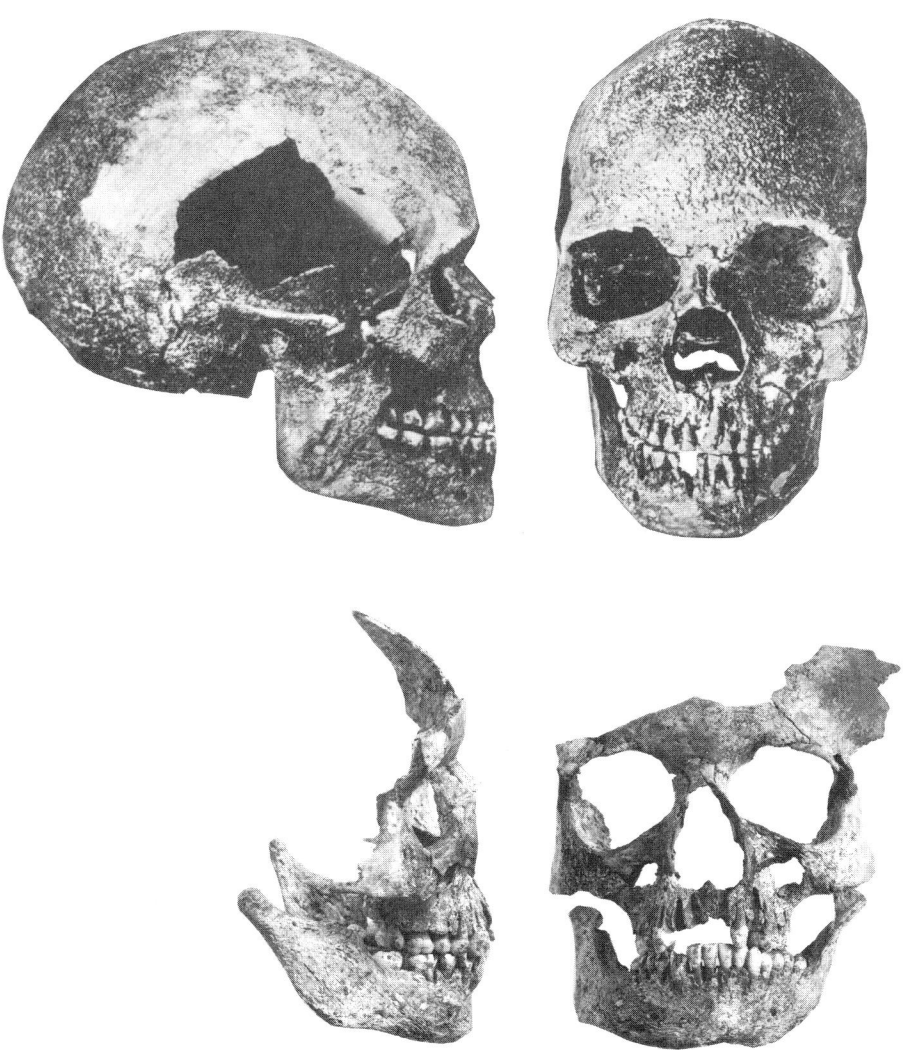

Figure 3.9. Skulls Brno III (female) and Svitávka (female).

Brno II

An Upper Paleolithic grave was disturbed at the base of the last loess during the construction of Brno's municipal sewage network in Francouzská Street in 1891 (Appendix A). Conservation and salvage research was carried out by A. Makowsky (1892). At the depth of 4.5 m, a crushed human skull was discovered beneath a mammoth bladebone and tusk. The skeleton was destroyed by the digging, so that only few fragments of long bones could be salvaged. The Brno find has received priority as the first ritual burial of the mammoth hunters in Moravia. The burial had rich artifactual content; the body of the deceased was strewn with ocher and covered by a mammoth scapula. In 1956 a revisory research was carried out near the original grave, however, the original layer was not reached (Jelínek et al., 1959).

The bone remains belong to a male of mature age, considerably robust and tall (Figure 3.10). In terms of typology, he differs from the Cro-Magnon type, and that is why a number of authors view him as a representative of independent Upper Paleolithic type: "the Brno type" (Jelínek et al., 1959; Vlček, 1967).

Brno III

Another Upper Paleolithic burial was discovered in Brno-Žabovřesky in 1927 (Appendix A). The grave, cut into the surface of the river terrace, was covered by loess earths and by redeposited Miocene silts. The cultural classification of the grave is based solely by the identification of rite: the skeleton was placed in a crouched position and covered with ocher. Tools and any other equipment were missing from the grave (Absolon, 1929).

In the grave numbered Brno III, the skeleton of a middle-aged female individual was discovered (Figure 3.9). The skull was described by J. Matiegka (1929), but the salvaged part of the skeleton has not been published. Unfortunately, the find was destroyed during World War II.

Předmostí

The first find of a fossil man at Předmostí was made by J. Wankel in 1884 (Předmostí XXI). In 1894 K. J. Maška launched his archaeological research, and on June 7, 1894, he uncovered a monumental mass grave containing 18 individuals (Předmostí–XVIII; Maška, 1895a,b). Remains of another two individuals were recovered (Př. XIX–XX) near the mass burial site (Appendix A). In the following year, M. Kříž added further finds (Př. XXII–XXV, XXVIII, and XXIX; Kříž, 1903). K. Absolon made new discoveries at Předmostí XXVII (Absolon, 1929) in 1928, and finally, J. Skutil (1940c) listed yet another find: Předmostí XXVI. Apart from the remains of fossil humans, rare anthropomorphic sculptures of pregnant women, the well-known

PATTERNS OF HUMAN EVOLUTION

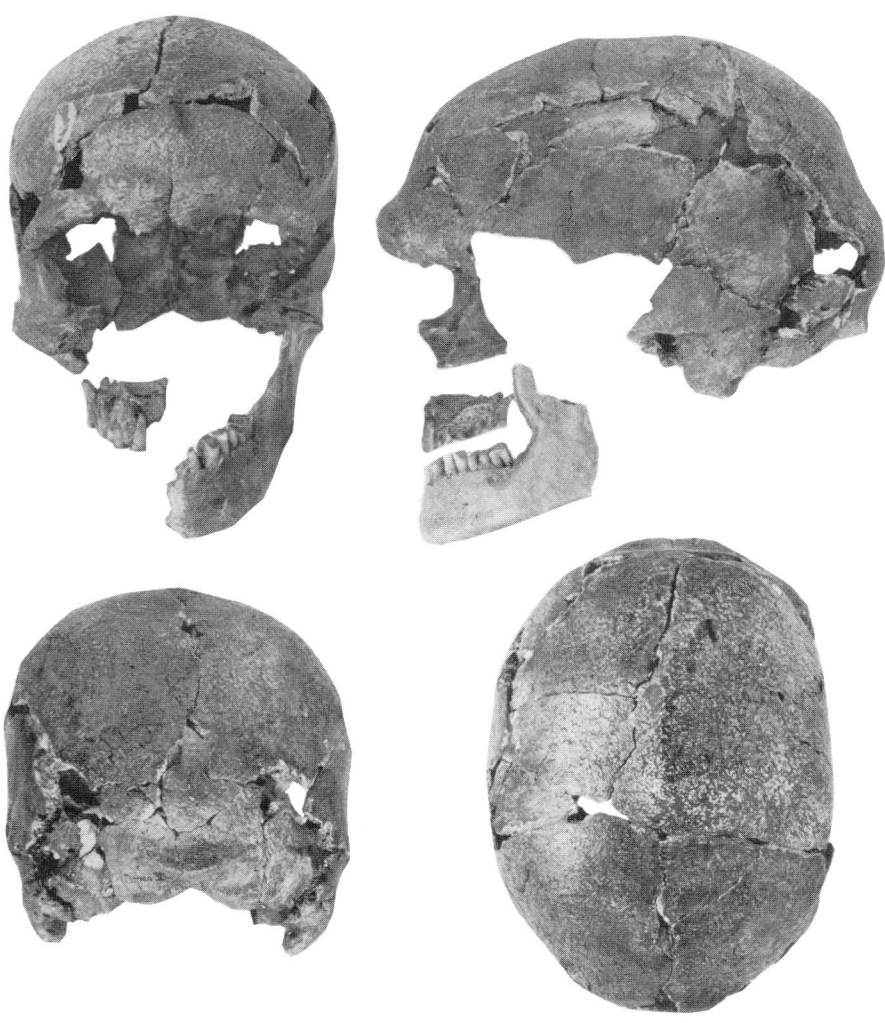

Figure 3.10. Male skulls Brno II (the Brno-type).

stylized engraving of a woman on a mammoth tusk, and so on complete the picture of the Gravettian population.

An anthropological evaluation of the aforementioned finds was made by J. Matiegka (1934, 1938). An additional revision of the evidence showed that remains of at least 25 individuals (men, women, and children of various ages) were found at

Předmostí. Regrettably, most of the finds were destroyed by fire at the end of the World War II.

Dolní Věstonice

The open-air Upper Paleolithic settlement of localities I and II, situated on the northern slopes of the Pavlovské Hills near the village of Dolní Věstonice in South Moravia (Appendix A), became a genuine treasury of knowledge about mammoth hunters, their culture, and their physical appearance.

As early as in 1924, at the beginning of his survey at the site I, K. Absolon recovered fragments of the skull of a young individual, of which one fragment was burnt (Dolní Věstonice XXVIII); a child's incisor tooth (DV XXIX); and another fragment of calvarium (DV XXX). In 1925 a calva which had disintegrated along the seams (DV I) and a fragment of frontal and occipital bone (DV V, VIa, VIb) were recovered. Finds made in 1927 included a partially burnt child's skeleton (DV IV), two isolated teeth (DV VII), and two fragments of a skull burnt to ashes (DV XXIII). In 1930 new acquisitions included another calva (DV II), while in the 1934 an incisor tooth bored through and arranged as a pendant (DV VIII) was found. In 1936 another two fragments of a calva (DV XXIV, XXV) were discovered. The calva DV I and II was anthropologically described by J. Malý (1939), and the pierced incisor tooth by K. Absolon (1935b).

After the war, the Archaeological Institute of the Czechoslovak Academy of Sciences at Brno continued its research at the site headed by B. Klíma. Apart from exceptional archaeological terrain discoveries, such as dwellings, hearths, and enormous accumulations of bones, other significant finds of fossil humans were made. In 1948 B. Klíma uncovered 2 isolated teeth (DV XXVI, XXVII; Klíma, 1963b) and, in the following years, 1949 and 1951, another three isolated teeth (DV IX, X; Klíma, 1963b). In 1949 a discovery was made of a female burial covered with ocher and with two mammoth shoulder-blades (DV III; Klíma, 1950a). The woman was buried in a strictly crouched position on her right side. The first anthropological investigation of the woman's skeleton was presented by J. Jelínek (1954).

Surveying a cultural layer belonging to the earlier phase of the settlement of the site's central part, B. Klíma discovered two molars in trench DE of partition profile A in 1974 (DV XXXI, XXXII; Klíma, 1981b).

These discoveries were followed by a long break, during which continued archaeological research yielded no new anthropological finds. As late as 1986, industrial loess exploitation in the upper part of the site Dolní Věstonice II disturbed a layer of settlement at a depth of 5 m beneath the present surface. On the settlement surface, an isolated calvarium of an adult individual (DV XI) was discovered and, several days later, a frontal bone fragment (DV XII). As it turned out, both skull fragments belong to one individual. Two months later, on August 13, 1986, a triple burial was unearthed with exceptionally well-preserved skeletons of three individuals (DV XIII, DV XIV, DV XV), covered by burnt spruce logs and branches. The exceptional find was announced by B. Klíma (e.g., 1987b). During the continuing quarrying, J. Svoboda

PATTERNS OF HUMAN EVOLUTION

discovered another burial of a male in a crouched position, lying on his right side near a hearth (DV XVI; Svoboda, 1989a; Svoboda and Vlček, 1991). Two burnt fragments of a parietal bone (burnt-burial? DV XVII) and other isolated parts of skeletons (DV XVIII–XXII) were discovered on the uncovered plane.

This rich body of anthropological material is now being investigated by a group of specialists headed by E. Vlček and E. Trinkaus (Figures 3.11–3.16). On burnt clay lumps, imprints of papillary lines were discovered (Vlček, 1951a, 1952a) which

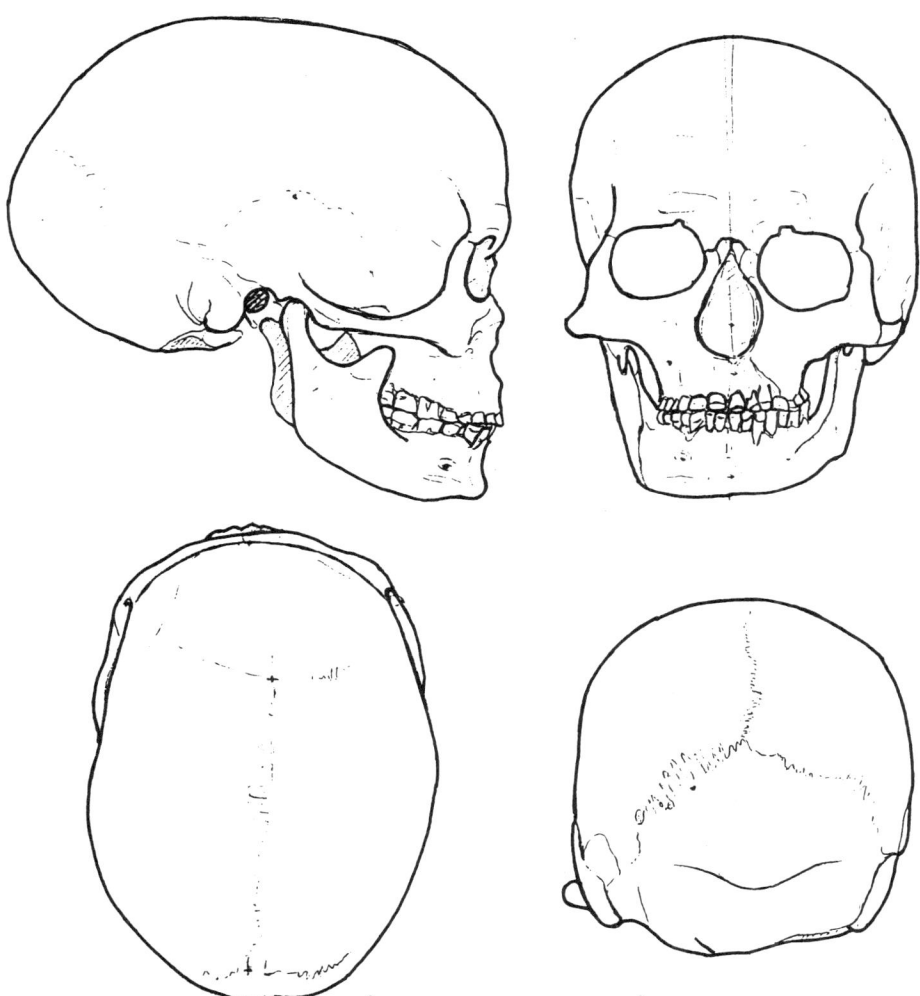

Figure 3.11. Skull Dolní Věstonice III (female).

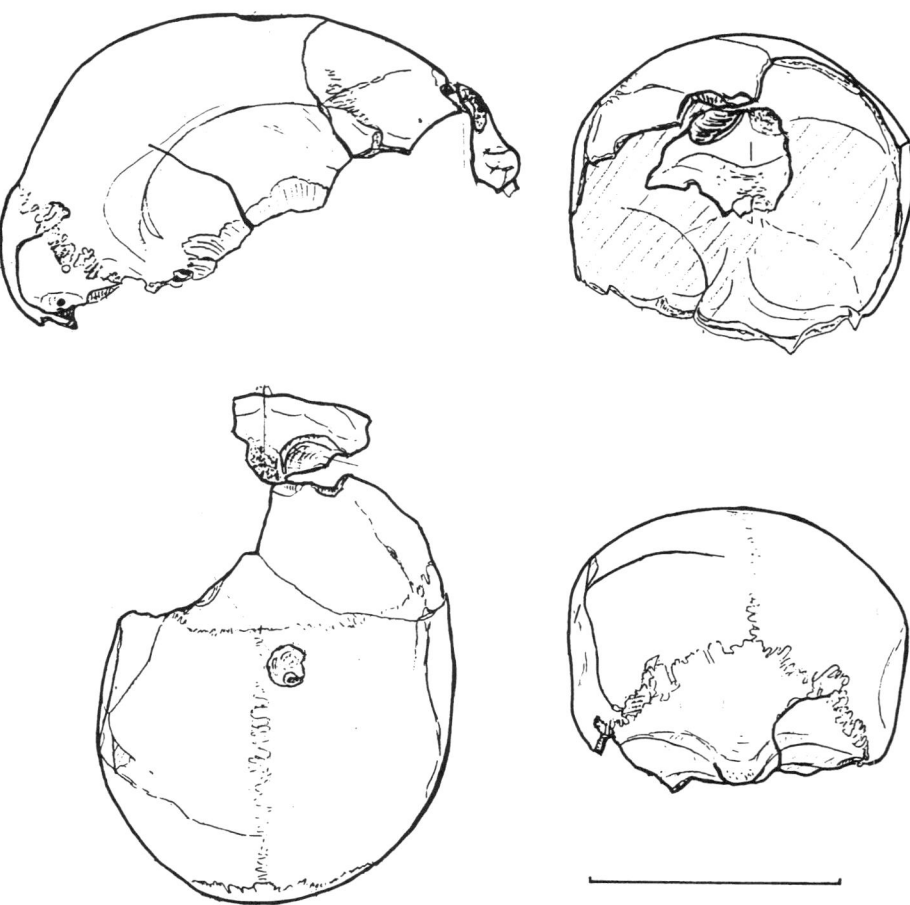

Figure 3.12. Skull DV XI and XII (male).

provided direct evidence about the surface of the body of fossil humans. Further evidence is supplied by the anthropomorphic sculptures showing a varying degree of stylization of the human body.

Pavlov

During a systematic survey of another settlement near the village of Pavlov, some 500 m east of the localities at Dolní Věstonice (Appendix A), B. Klíma discovered in 1957 a human burial, disturbed by solifluction movements. The man had originally been placed in a strongly crouched position and was covered by a mammoth scapula

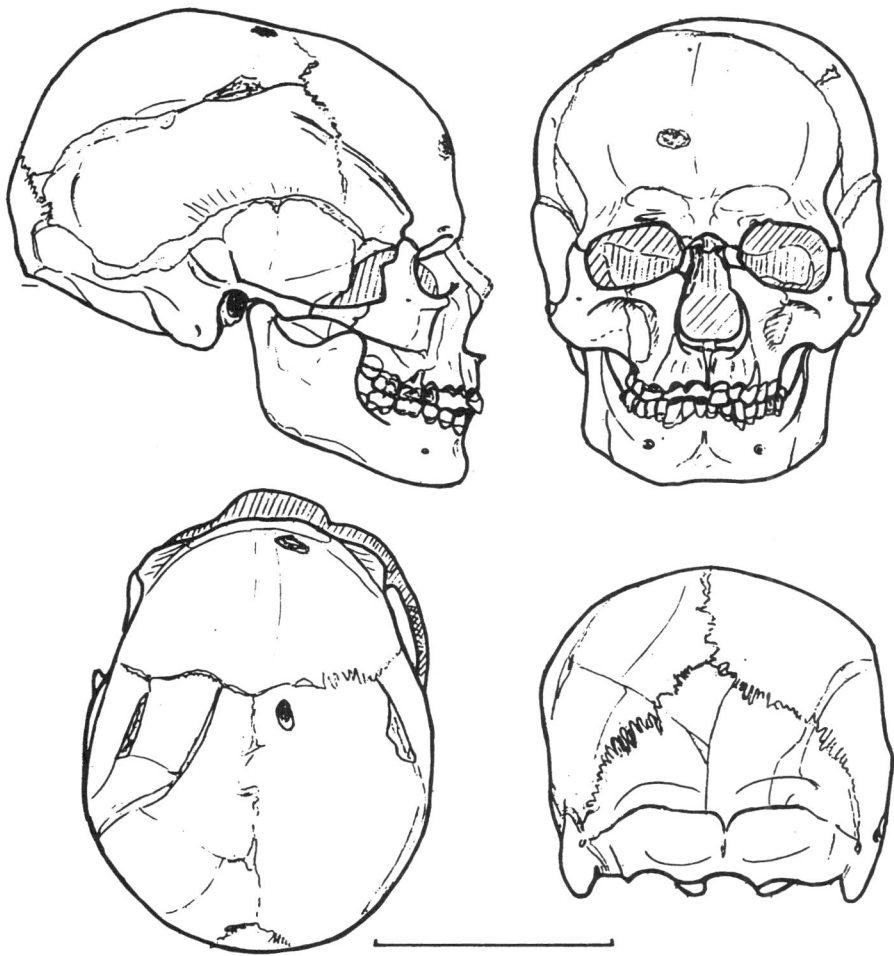

Figure 3.13. Skull DV XIII (male).

and several other bones (Pavlov I). The time and cultural dating of the find is relatively accurate (Klíma, 1959c). During the research, minor remains of other individuals (Pa II, III) were found in the immediate vicinity of the grave, and the cultural layer in other parts of the site yielded several isolated teeth of adults and particularly a series of child's milk teeth.

In anthropological terms, the remains of the buried male Pa I were published in preliminary reports (Figure 3.17; Vlček, 1961), and a new, complex presentation of the material has been prepared within the framework of the Gravettian Project. Apart from bone material, the locality yielded imprints of papillary lines on burnt clay lumps (Szilvássy, 1983) and, again, anthropomorphic sculptures.

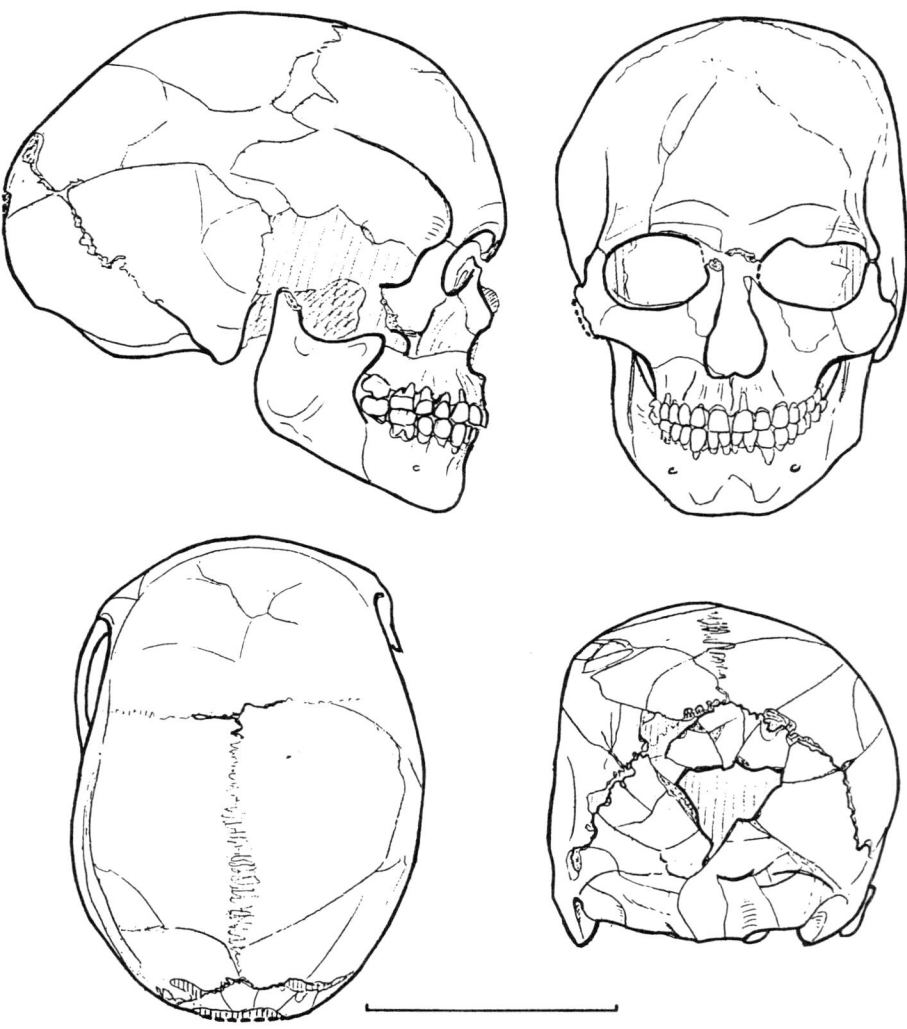

Figure 3.14. Skull DV XIV (male).

Willendorf

For the sake of completeness, mention should be made of the well-known locality discovered not far from the Krems-Mauthausen highway, 23 km north of Willendorf in Austria. The locality forms a sequence of strata, dated to the interpleniglacial and upper pleniglacial (Felgenhauer, 1959). A fragment of a mandible, free teeth, and part of a femur, possibly belonging to a young woman, were found

PATTERNS OF HUMAN EVOLUTION 69

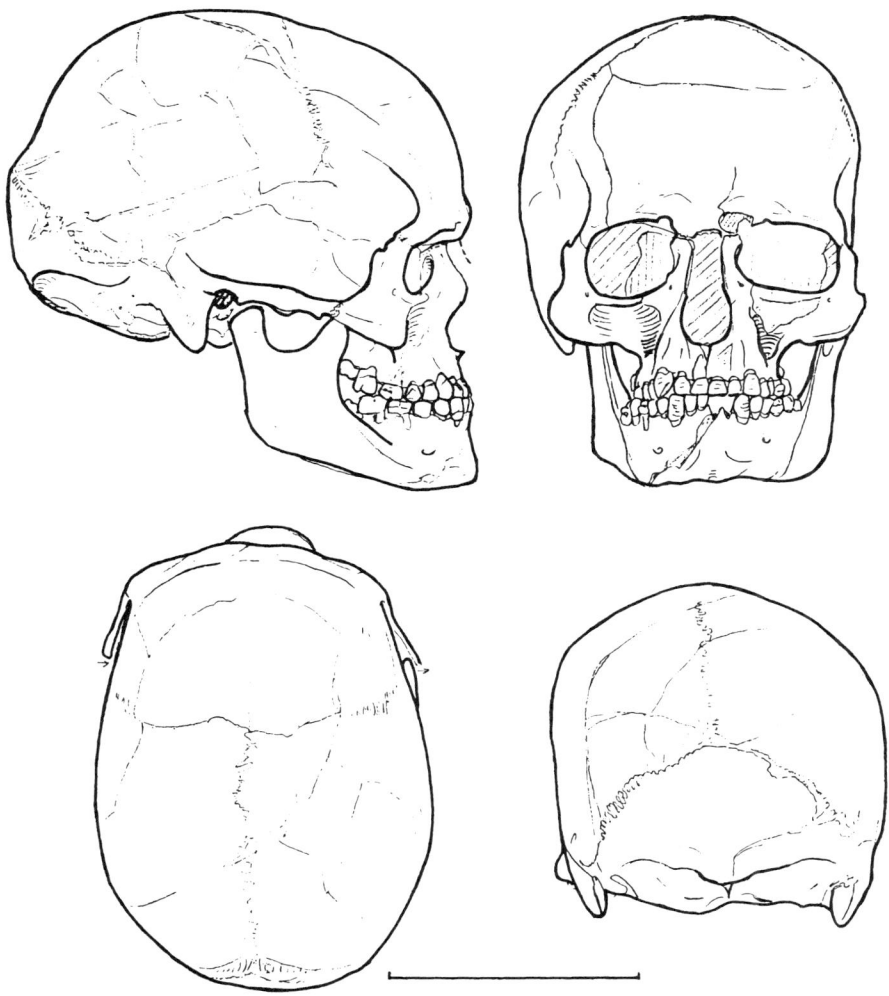

Figure 3.15. Skull DV XV (female).

there in 1908 (Szombathy, 1910; Ehgartner, 1959). This locality also yielded the world-famous "Willendorf Venus."

Balla

In 1909 and 1911, the remains of a child (Hillebrand, 1911) were discovered in Hungary's Balla Cave, not far from the village of Répáshuta near Miskolc. The horizon of the find is dated to the upper pleniglacial. A cranium, a mandible, and a number of long bones have been preserved from the skeleton of a one-year-old child.

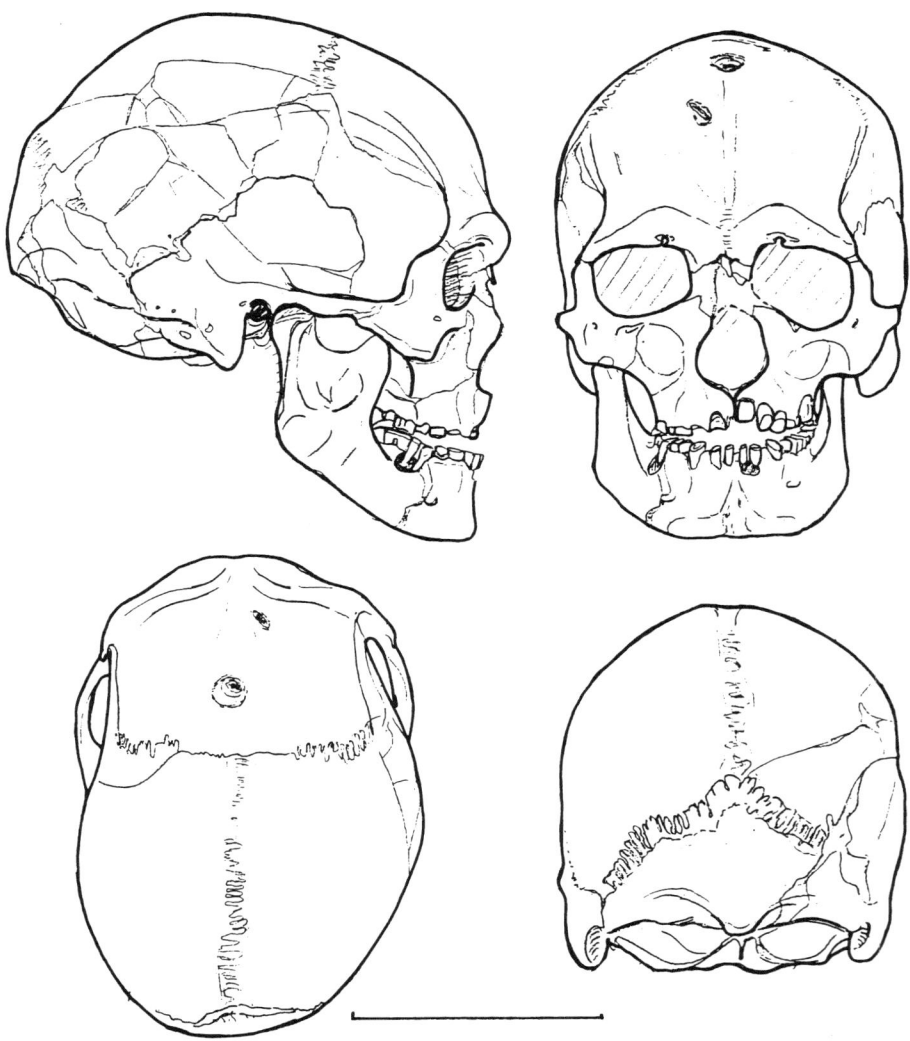

Figure 3.16. Skull DV XVI (male).

In conclusion, a typological classification of the Gravettian population should be suggested. For Předmostí, this problem has already been discussed by Matiegka (1934, 1938), so that we shall concentrate on the structure of the newly discovered population of South Moravia. In principle, the presence of two biological types, which may be morphologically and metrically delineated within a fairly broad variability of the Upper Paleolithic population of Central Europe, has been established.

PATTERNS OF HUMAN EVOLUTION

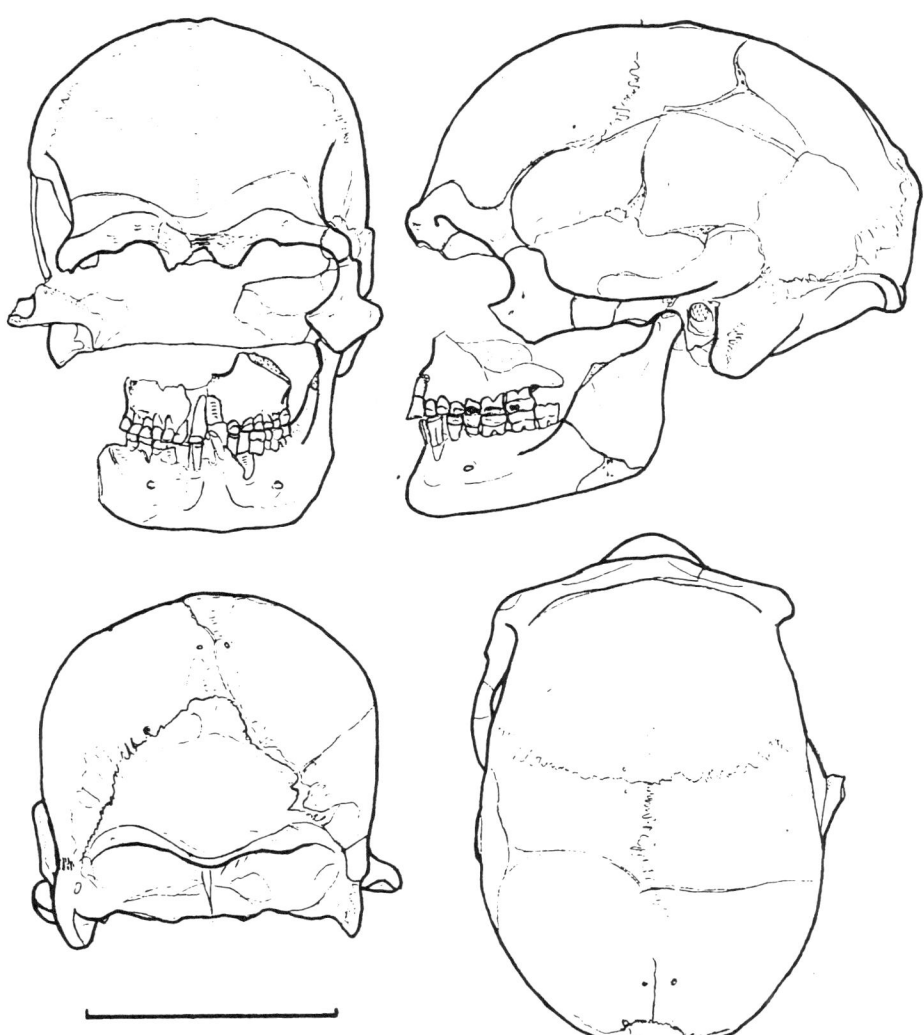

Figure 3.17. Skull Pavlov I (male).

First and foremost is the Brno type and its intermediate forms (Vlček, 1967, 1970). As far as male individuals are concerned, this type is characterized by a figure up to 180 cm tall, robust in structure, and having a powerful musculature. The skull is long and spacious, the face is medium high, and, similarly, the eye sockets and nose are of medium width. Medium robust jawbones carry rather weak teeth. In Dolní Věstonice, this type includes the individuals DV XVI, DV XI, and XII; the male from

Pavlov I; and primarily the type Brno II. Other individuals are present in the population from Předmostí and elsewhere in Eastern Europe, as in Kostenki and Sungir. The females are markedly slimmer than the males, their height averaging around 160 cm. The skull architecture is basically similar, but more delicately executed. This category includes women DV II, DV III, and Brno III and the girl from Svitávka. Sexual differences in the skeletal morphology of men and women are considerable.

Further finds from Dolní Věstonice contributed additional morphological elements to the type structure of the population. In this second type, the males reach only some 170 cm in height, and their skeletons show only a medium robustness. The skulls are long to medium long and display a low face, with low eye sockets and broad noses. The relatively strong jaw bones, in view of the more delicately built brain boxes, usually carry strong teeth. The forehead is arched to bomb-shaped. In Dolní Věstonice, this type is represented by the male DV XIII, and the young man DV XIV is very close to that type. Another very close analogy is offered by the young man from Sungir II. As for females, they differ from males in their smaller figures, only 160 cm tall, but the morphology of women's skulls is similar to the men's. As regards the female DV XV, the purity of the type is marred by a number of pathological features. Another find from Sungir Su III, again, corresponds well to this specimen. Sexual dimorphism in this type, is slight, including the typical features on the pelvis. In addition, it is possible to include here the find from Kostenki XIV–Markina Gora, where the face and its parts are even lower. We can therefore infer that, during this period, contacts must have been maintained between populations living in relatively distant geographic and hunting regions.

New research projects make it possible to study the whole populations primarily demographically, to search for family and tribal relationships, and to determine health patterns and nutritional records. Specific finds of bones of the Gravettian hunters provide a whole range of features which are covered by ethnography. These include the production and use of "beakers" made of human skulls; the healed wounds repeatedly found on frontal and parietal bones of the male skulls (initiation rites?); and the wearing off of dental enamel on the buccal sides of the crows of the teeth, probably caused by placing stones in the mouth (possibly as a means of increasing salivation to assuage thirst) etc.

Furthermore, this record enables us to examine not only skeletons, but also other body systems. Endocranial casts tell us about the degree of development of the brain and about the arrangement of blood supplies to the central nervous system, while imprints of papillary lines on fired lumps of clay provide some information concerning the skin surface.

Last but not least, this unique corpus of material makes it possible to study, together with the social sciences, the "archaeology of death" in the hunting societies. The origin of life was always associated with the cult of the mother and woman, as reflected in discoveries of the "Venuses" and related symbols. These symbols speak of the sexual ideas of these hunters, and finds of the Venuses contribute information on the ideal canon of female beauty. A counterpoint to these were ideas about death, an afterlife, the existence of a soul, and so on, as documented by the burial rituals. These complex issues require an interdisciplinary approach.

Fossil Man of the Late Glacial

The last stratigraphic horizon of the populations of Central Europe falls at the very end of the loess sedimentation, from the end of the upper pleniglacial to the late glacial. The most significant finds in Central Europe were made in the caves near Döbritz, at Ranis (both in the former German Democratic Republic), in Kůlna Cave and two other Moravian caves, and at an open-air settlement at Staré Město. Culturally, these finds belong to the Madgalenian and to the Late Paleolithic.

Döbritz

The caves near Döbritz are situated on the western slopes of Mount Tafelberg, 1 km to the north of the village of Döbritz, 40 km east of the town of Weimar. Between 1930 and 1938, R. M. Richter (1955) discovered a Magdalenian layer in sediments of the final Würmian. Judging by the fauna, the locality belongs to Dryas II, in absolute chronology to about 10,235 ± 90 B.P. (Feustel, 1971, 1974). Human remains were discovered in the Kniegrotte Cave and in the nearby Urdhöhle. These belong to four individuals. The most important find is the skull Döbritz I (Grimm and Ullrich, 1956; Bach, 1974). Traces of artificial operations are discernible on isolated bones of the skeleton. Typologically, the skull Döbritz I recalls the Upper Paleolithic finds from Dolní Věstonice, as well as the find from Kostěnki XIV. Further development of this type is traceable as late as the Lower Holocene.

Ranis

Working in the sediments of the Ilsenhöhle Cave beneath Ranis Castle, 40 km from the town of Weimar, W. Hülle (1939) discovered in 1934 a Magdalenian layer with fauna and the mandible of a child approximately one year old. The age of the individual was revised by Lorenz-Römer (1957), and Ullrich (1979) concentrated on the artificial damage observed on the jawbone.

Kůlna

During a systematic survey of Kůlna Cave (Appendix A) between 1961 and 1963, K. Valoch discovered in layer 3 two teeth of an adult man which date to the Epimagdalenian. Anthropologically, the find was described by J. Jelínek (1988). Previous research at the same locality by M. Kříž in 1913 has yielded a fragment of a mandible assigned by Jelínek (1988), on the basis of color and degree of fossilization, to layers 5 and 6, and thus to the Magdalenian.

Staré Město

In the open-air settlement "Na Valách" near Uherské Hradiště, 60 km northwest of Brno, V. Hrubý found in 1949 a damaged burial in the sand of the youngest terrace of the Morava River (Jelínek, 1956). A skull, long bones of the limbs, and short bones of the legs have been preserved from the skeleton of a young woman. In typological terms, this find comes well within the variation range of the Dolní Věstonice population.

Chapter 4

Lower and Middle Paleolithic Background

Certain Central European sites with complex evidence from systematic excavations, such as Přezletice in Bohemia, Vértésszölös in Hungary, or Bilzingsleben in Central Germany, play a key role in the current discussions about exactly when representatives of the *Homo erectus*/early *Homo sapiens* grade colonized this part of the Old World, as well as in understanding human adaptations in the high latitudes in general. However, Moravia, in spite of its central geographic location, was scarcely settled during these early periods (Figure 4.1).

Although basic definitions of the Middle Paleolithic (cave-bear period, Mousterian) in Moravia were postulated as early as the 19th century by Wankel and Maška, evidence of an earlier, Lower Paleolithic settlement was missing, and probably not even expected. In 1910, the geologist J. Woldřich excavated one of the small caves at the newly discovered paleontological site Stránská skála I and collected there an earlier Pleistocene fauna characterized by the presence of *Machairodus*. Some bone fragments from this context, still covered by charcoal, led Woldřich to suspect an early Paleolithic occupation in Moravia. The Stránská skála question, crucial to the topic and posed as early as beginning of the century (Woldřich, 1916), still remains unsolved today.

In 1926, K. Schirmeisen reopened the Stránská skála question by recalling the fragmentary state of preservation of some bones from Woldřich's excavation, suspected to be traces of cutting and chopping, and also some lithic artifacts. However, his ideas were immediately criticized by Skutil and others. A few years later, H. Mohr introduced the eolithic question raised in Western Europe by publishing obvious pseudoartifacts ("mohrolits") from the Svitava River terraces in Brno and evoked criticism by Professor Zotz from Germany. The evidence, as it stood, was controversial and archaeologists were not ready to accept it.

The later excavations by Absolon and Krumpholz at Stránská skála I yielded

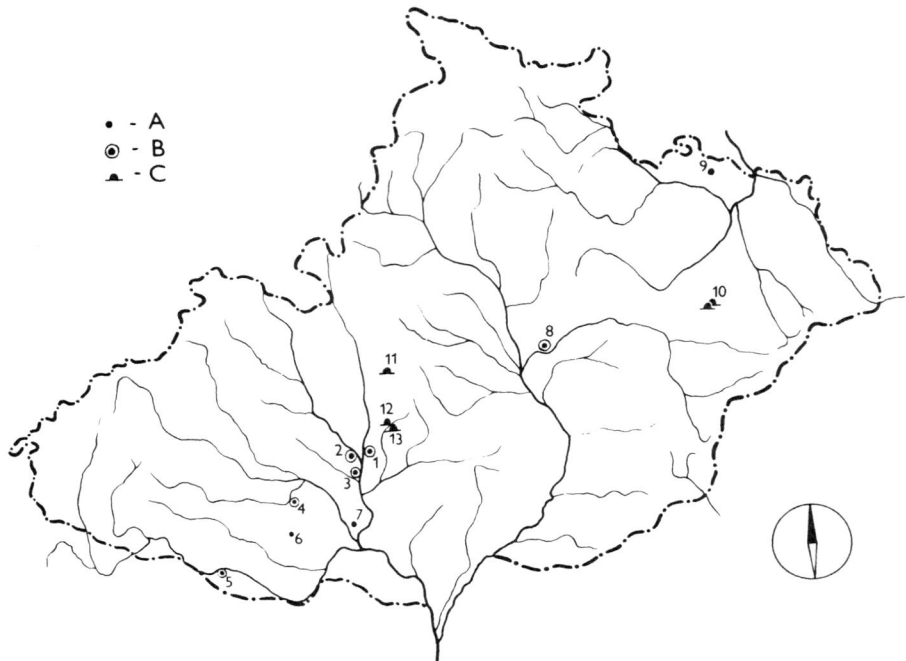

Figure 4.1. Map of important Lower and Middle Paleolithic sites. A—surface sites; B—stratified sites; C—caves. 1—Brno east (Stránská skála I, Růženin dvůr, Nová hora); 2—Brno west (Červený kopec); 3—Brno south (Modřice); 4—Moravský Krumlov; 5—Sedlešovice; 6—Miroslav-Kašenec; 7—Přibice and Ivaň; 8—Předmostí; 9—Bohuslavice; 10—Šipka and Čertova díra; 11—Kůlna; 12—Švédův stůl; 13–Pekárna.

some more promising objects, of both local chert and bone. However, because of Absolon's rejection of all Lower and Middle Paleolithic evidence from Moravia, they were not even mentioned at the time and were only much later reexamined by Valoch (1972). As a result of the dramatic change of attitude toward the Lower Paleolithic problem after World War II, the excavation reopened by Musil at this site paid special attention to the question of human presence (Musil and Valoch, 1968). During evaluation of the recovered material, Valoch's position gradually changed from objective criticism (Valoch, 1972) to near certainty (Valoch, 1987b).

It should be recalled that such a change of position, in fact, reflected an influx of new ideas into both Czech and world archaeology, such as the publications of Movius, Leakey, and Rust. In 1947, Prošek published a large flake from a pedocomplex of the penultimate warm period at Letky, Bohemia, and later added further artifacts from Horky and Karlštejn. In 1953, Žebera presented surface finds of archaic pebble industries from Mlazice and other sites in Bohemia and named them Heidelbergian (after Rust) and Bohemian. Once the ideal form of a Lower Paleolithic industry was determined in Bohemia, pebble tools were intensively searched for in Moravia (Valoch, 1982a) and Slovakia (Bárta, 1987) as well. Finally, a huge number of primitive-looking choppers and chopping tools has been collected, but the questions of their reliability and age are open.

Since the 1960s, larger excavations have been started of Lower Paleolithic (Přezletice: Fridrich, 1989), Lower and Middle Paleolithic (Bečov: Fridrich, 1982) and Middle Paleolithic sites (Kůlna: Valoch 1968a, 1988). However, the most complex evidence of Lower Paleolithic living floors, including fossil human remains, was given by the excavations at Vértésszölös, Hungary (Kretzoi and Vértés, 1965) and Bilzingsleben, Germany (Mania et al., 1980). Contrary to all previous predictions of large size and crude morphology in the pebble artifacts, both the Vértésszölös and Bilzingsleben industries were small-dimensional, and even microlithic. With the new evidence, it was generally accepted that the Paleolithic record in this part of Europe starts during the Cromerian, at the latest, and some finds (Beroun, Červený kopec, Bečov T: Fridrich, 1976a) are even earlier. In the following comparisons, however (Svoboda, 1989b), especially the sites of Vértésszölös and Bilzingsleben remain the largest, comprehensible, and solid evidence of the Lower Paleolithic (450,000–300,000 years old) in this part of Europe.

The latest trends in the interpretation of all records earlier than the two last-mentioned sites are critical (Roebroeks and van Kolfschoten, 1994): a review of the artifactual and chronological evidence, including all the surface sites and certain excavated sites such as Stránská skála and Přezletice, suggests that there should be no solid traces of hominid activities prior to 500,000 years ago. However, this "short chronology" curtain should not limit further research on earlier occupation traces and should not lead to an *a priori* negation of all possible indications.

STRATIGRAPHY

The classical framework of the Alpine chronology valid in south and central Moravia (Günz, Mindel, Riss, and Würm) and the Nordic chronology applicable to the glaciated parts of north Moravia and Silesia (Elster, Saale, Warthe, and Weichsel) have been criticized but have not yet been replaced by more precise systems of general value (Tables 4.1 and 4.2; Kukla, 1975). On the contrary, contemporary research is directed toward the elaboration of local stratigraphic systems rather than toward their correlation (Havlíček and Macoun, 1994; Macoun, 1985, 1989; Macoun et al., 1965; Zeman, 1983; Chapter 2).

In south Moravia, the stratigraphic system is based primarily on fluviatile sediments and loess sections. In the Brno Basin area, the fluviatile sediments were separated into several stratigraphic units (Zeman, 1982). The earliest level (the Líšeň terrace) has a minimal age of 2.5 million years (Kočí, 1982). At the next level is the older gravel and sand cover, including the Stránská skála terrace, and the younger gravel and sand cover, including five stratigraphic members. The loess sections are

Table 4.1. Stratigraphic Correlation of Lower and Middle Paleolithic Sites in Eastern Central Europe (former Czechoslovakia)

O 18 Stage	Pedocomplex	Bohemia	Moravia	Slovakia
4	Loess PK II	Bečov, Ládví	Kůlna 9-7a, Švédův stůl, Šipka	Prepoštská Cave
5	PK III	Bečov I A-III-3, B-III-1, Sedlec, Ládví	Předmostí, Červený kopec, Kůlna 11, Modřice	Gánovce, Bojnice (130–80,000), N. Mesto n. V.
6	Loess	Bečov I A-III-5, A-III-4	Předmostí, Kůlna 14, Modřice	
7	PK IV	Bečov I A-III-6, Sedlec, Letky		Vyšné Ružbachy (200,000), Behárovce (~207,000), N. Mesto n. V.
8	Loess	Bečov I B-III-4, Horky		
9	PK V	Sedlec, Horky II	Červený kopec, Růženin dvůr	
11	PK VI	Karlštejn	Růženin dvůr, Sedlešovice	
13	PK VII		Růženin Dvůr	
	PK X	Přezletice (660–590,000), Bečov IB	Stránská skála I (>730,000), Červený kopec	

interstratified by pedocomplexes numbered PK I to XII (Kukla, 1975; Smolíková, 1984), but there are earlier soil complexes below.

At the site of Brno-Červený kopec, the lower part of the younger gravel and sand cover is covered by a thick loess deposit with the most complete fossil soil sequence. The main stratigraphic boundary is the Matuyama/Brunhes inversion within the brown clay (Braunlehm) soil complex PK X (Cromerian), in association with Upper

Table 4.2. Th/U dating of Last Interglacial Sites in Kyr (after Hausmann and Brunnacker, 1986)

Sample	Site	Value
GH 01	Gánovce, Slovakia	83.5 + 3.3 − 3.1
GH 02	Gánovce, Slovakia	130.8 + 4.0 − 3.9
GH 03	Gánovce, Slovakia	104.5 + 10.4 − 9.4
TATA 01	Tata, Hungary	101 ± 10
TATA 13	Tata, Hungary	98 ± 8

LOWER AND MIDDLE PALEOLITHIC BACKGROUND

Biharian fauna (Musil, 1982). In the site of Brno-Růženin dvůr (Smolíková and Kovanda, 1983), the younger gravel and sand cover is overlaid by loess including the soils of PK V to PK X, in the frame of the positive polarity. The site of Stránská skála I is located in slope sediments and in small caves (Musil and Valoch, 1968; Valoch, 1987b). The Matuyama-Brunhes boundary was found within the slope sediments (layer 18), and the underlying strata go back to the Jaramillo event about 900,000 years ago; the fauna from the slope sediments and from the caves dates to the Upper Biharian (Musil, 1982). Possible artifacts or small assemblages from all the mentioned sites deserve reexamination and discussion.

In northern Moravia and Silesia, the chronology is based on the stratigraphy of glacial sediments (Macoun, 1985, 1989; Macoun et al., 1965). Again, various pseudo-artifacts of glacial flint were recovered from this context.

For the penultimate interglacial (PK IV, stage 7), as shown by evidence from soils in the loess sections at Červený kopec, Dolní Věstonice, Dolní Kounice, and other geologic sites, we may reconstruct a semiwoodland landscape, rather a xeric landscape, nevertheless very warm (Chapter 2). Despite the favorable conditions, we have no evidence of human occupation in Moravia during this period. In the loess section at Předmostí, the occupation probably starts later, by the end of the penultimate glaciation (Acheulean?), and continues to the last interglacial (Taubachian: Svoboda et al., 1994). Similarly, the earliest artifacts in the Kůlna Cave in the Moravian karst (Valoch, 1988) date from the penultimate glaciation (layer 14), although the more important archaeological horizons date later.

The last interglacial (PK III, stage 5) is marked by a full expansion of closed dumped forests because of higher temperature and humidity (Chapter 2). From the archaeological viewpoint, among the deposits, particular attention must be given to travertines adjacent to large springs with Taubachian occupations (Hungary, North Slovakia, Moravian Gate), while caves, as evidenced by the sinter formation, were mostly too humid for human occupation (the Kůlna Cave, layer 11, is an exception). In Moravia, the open-air sites either are in the vicinity of mineral springs (Předmostí) or are smaller assemblages and isolated artifacts in soils (parabraunerde) of the loess sections.

The beginning of the last glacial is marked by horizons of chernozems interbedded with highly typical deposits referred to as *pellet sands* and *loess* at the base of the sections, whereas the upper part contains an increasing number of pure loess interlayers reflecting an approach to a next stage. The Middle Paleolithic evolution is well evidenced from the interglacial to the early glacial, still in a relatively favorable climate showing irregular cooling, a humidity decrease, and gradual changes in the fauna and flora (coniferous forest). Only in the later part of this period are further cooling and decreasing humidity observed, leading to the first arctic phase of the pleniglacial. The Middle Paleolithic (Mousterian and Micoquian) human settlements in eastern Central Europe were mainly in large caves clearly because of the general decrease of moisture after the interglacial: the caves had now changed to favorable dry and sheltered places for habitation (Kůlna, layers 9–6a, Švédův stůl, Šipka, Pekárna; Figures 4.6–4.8, 7.5).

CULTURAL DEVELOPMENT AND VARIABILITY

The Problem of the Earliest Industries

The earliest specimens published as artifacts from Moravia are isolated pieces or collections dating to a period around the Matuyama/Brunhes boundary. Some of them are natural pieces; others require additional contextual evidence to prove their reliability and Lower Paleolithic age (Mušov and Ivaň: Valoch, 1982a; Dolní Kounice: Valoch, 1991; Přibice: Valoch, Smolí-Ková and Zeman, 1978).

Few specimens are from stratified positions in loess. At Červený kopec in Moravia, in the lower, reversed-polarity part of the section (several cycles below PK X), there was found a possible pointed chopperlike implement of quartz (Svoboda et al., 1994; Figure 27), in a level around the polarity reversion (PK X) a possible pebble core of quartz (Valoch, 1977a), and a few flakes from the soil numbered PK Va (Klíma, 1963a). At Růženin dvůr, the levels of the PK VII, PK VI, and PK V pedocomplexes yielded single artifacts (Valoch, 1977a). A quartz pebble core was found in the level of PK VI at Sedlešovice (Valoch, 1981c).

At Stránská skála I (Appendix A), the lithics under discussion are fragments of local chert which show no clear traces of working, except for a few possible flakes from the small Cave No. 8. Valoch (1987b) argues that some specimens are made of chert, which is slightly different from that available at the site, and of river pebbles, but transportation by natural processes must be excluded if we are to accept these lithics as proof of human activity (Svoboda, 1989b:38). Valoch's argument is also based on indications of burning on three bones and a piece of chert, and on some modified animal bones. More recently, the material has been revised by Roebroeks and van Kolfschoten (1994:497), who observed no clear traces of human workmanship on the material and tended to support Valoch's earlier doubts concerning the artifactual character of this assemblage.

Leaving aside the question of reliability, Bohemia seems to be generally more rich in indications of early settlements than Moravia, but it is impossible to quantify this difference more precisely. Larger assemblages have been found in Přezletice (Fridrich, 1989) and Bečov I-B. Both industries have a coarse character due to the local raw material (lydite at Přezletice and quartzite at Bečov), and some tend to fracture along natural fissures. Fridrich (1976a) estimated the presence of choppers, a few artifacts with bifacial retouches along the edges, polyhedrons, and various types of scraperlike retouches. In contrast to Stránská skála, Přezletice has a sequence of systematically excavated living floors offering contextual information (the pattern of faunal distribution and possible features) and thus opens up more possibilities to authoritative discussion.

The Small-Dimensional Industries

The earliest undisputable industrial complexes of Central Europe that are associated with sufficient contextual evidence are small-sized. They appear in a temperate climate with deciduous and other forest elements, at water sources, and, sometimes, in travertine formations, rather than in deposits of cold periods (loess). The mean width of the artifacts in these industries is smaller than 3 cm, and in the extremely small industries like those of Bilzingsleben and Vértésszölös, most of the artifact are less than 2 cm wide. Wood and bone probably served as supplementary raw materials (Mania, 1979). There has been considerable discussion about the meaning of this specialization in small tools: how far it was a result of adaptation (Svoboda, 1982) or of culturally induced limitations (the Early Taubachian: Valoch, 1976c).

At Vértésszölös I and III (Kretzoi and Vértés, 1965; Svoboda, 1987a), very small pebbles, mainly of quartz (with some limestone, radiolarite, and chert), were intentionally selected to be worked: these were smashed into debris and chips. The industry does have some heavy-duty components' but bigger tools are extremely rare. As noted by Kretzoi and Vértés, there is no standardization in reduction sequences, but only in terms of dimensional seriation. Sidescrapers are the dominant class (more than 50%) and are mostly straight or concave and often double and convergent. The second most important class is notches, including denticulates, convergent denticulates (Tayac points), and becs defined by two notches. Other tools include fine borers and endscrapers, both flat and thick. Microchoppers, microchopping tools, and an exceptional normal-sized chopper complete the toolkit.

The industry from Bilzingsleben (Mania et al., 1980) is more clearly divisible into heavy-duty tools made of large cobbles of coarse-grained rocks and light-duty (small-sized) tools made of flint. The flint nodules were still roughly trimmed or smashed rather than exploited systematically, but the quality of the material meant that flakes were produced rather than debris. Again, there are numerous scraperlike and denticulate retouches (convex, direct, concave, and converging to Tayac points). Other types include endscrapers and microendscrapers, becs, borers (some of them surprisingly fine), and rare burins. Some of the small pieces have a flat bifacial retouch, but it is still irregular and unstandardized. All these types may occur, associated in numerous combinations. The heavy-duty artifacts are large cobbles with traces of utilization, fragments of rocks, larger flakes, anvils, and a few typical choppers and chopping tools.

Recently, smaller sites of comparable character have been excavated in southern Poland (Trzebnica: Burdukiewicz, 1993). The lithic industry includes microcores, small flake tools (sidescrapers, denticulates, borers), and larger choppers. In Moravia, there is no solid evidence of a comparable nature (except perhaps for the few abovementioned artifacts from Růženin dvůr: Valoch, 1977a).

The Acheulean

The biased evidence now available does not permit a more concrete dating of the Acheulean appearance in Central Europe. The evolved Acheulean of Central Europe seems to be a steppe and tundra phenomenon, extending from the west toward the center of the continent during the antepenultimate and penultimate glaciations (stages 8 and 6). Under these steppic conditions, stone and bone (rather than wood) became the most important raw materials, and technological standardization developed more rapidly.

Evolved Acheulean technology, based on core preparation and the spread of

Levalloisian technology, is the earliest to involve specialized workshop assemblages at primary sources of quartzite, which document the entire process of lithic exploitation and use. The abundant material available at such sites in Germany and Bohemia has permitted the analysis of different techniques and the partial reconstruction of reduction sequences (Bosinski, 1967; Fridrich, 1982). Specialized blade technologies occur in this context for the first time, and they reach their culmination in industries such as the late Rissian blade industry of Piekary IIb in Poland (Morawski, 1992). Typologically, the assemblages include bifaces and Levalloisian points (which are more finely made on flint), very rare cleavers, numerous sidescrapers, notches and denticulates, and some Upper Paleolithic types.

Again, raw material heavily influenced the specific character of Acheulean assemblages. The flint-based Acheulean extended from Northern France onto the North European Plain (Hannover-Döhren, Lebenstedt, Markkleeberg, Hundisburg), with the easternmost occurrences in Czech Silesia (Bohuslavice, Polanka, and Odrou; Figure 4.2: Svoboda, Macoun, and Přichystal, 1991). We may consider the site of Markkleeberg, East Germany as the earliest and easternmost fairly typical example of the northern group (Baumann and Mania, 1983). The site dates to a warmer phase at the beginning of the Saalian cold period and is located near sources of high-quality flint, and the lithics are widely influenced by the local processing. The material indicates a high frequency of flat cores (some of them typically Levalloisian in form), numerous irregular cores, and some prismatic cores for production of blades, but the blades themselves are rare (10%–11%). The retouched tools are dominated by convex and straight scraper edges, sometimes converging to symmetrical points. Bifaces are relatively rare, but fair and typical.

To the south, Acheulean populations in the Central European highlands, from eastern France through Germany into Bohemia, specialized in the use of fine-grained quartzite and various cherts (Reutersruh, Weddersleben). The easternmost, typologically expressive assemblages of the southern group are in Northern Bohemia (Bečov, Stvolínky). Further to the east, as in Moravia, the Acheulean is mostly evidenced by isolated bifaces only (Kadov, Lednice, and Určice). Although some Acheulean-like bifaces were repeatedly reported as far as Ukraine and Balcans, a look at the geographic distribution of the typical Acheulean clearly demonstrates that Moravia lies at the eastern boundary of this culture in Europe.

The Early Mousterian

The Early Mousterian industries appear in various environments in the penultimate glaciation (stage 6) and the preceding warm period (stage 7). They are represented by three distinct assemblages: the Rheindahlen type (after Rheindahlen B-3: Bosinski, 1982b), the Bečov type (after Bečov I, location A-III-6: Fridrich, 1982), and the Ehringsdorf type (after the Lower Travertine: Behm-Blancke, 1960); again, the Early Mousterian assemblages seem to be absent in Moravia (with a possible exception at Kůlna, layer 14).

These assemblages lack handaxes, and the Levalloisian technique was less

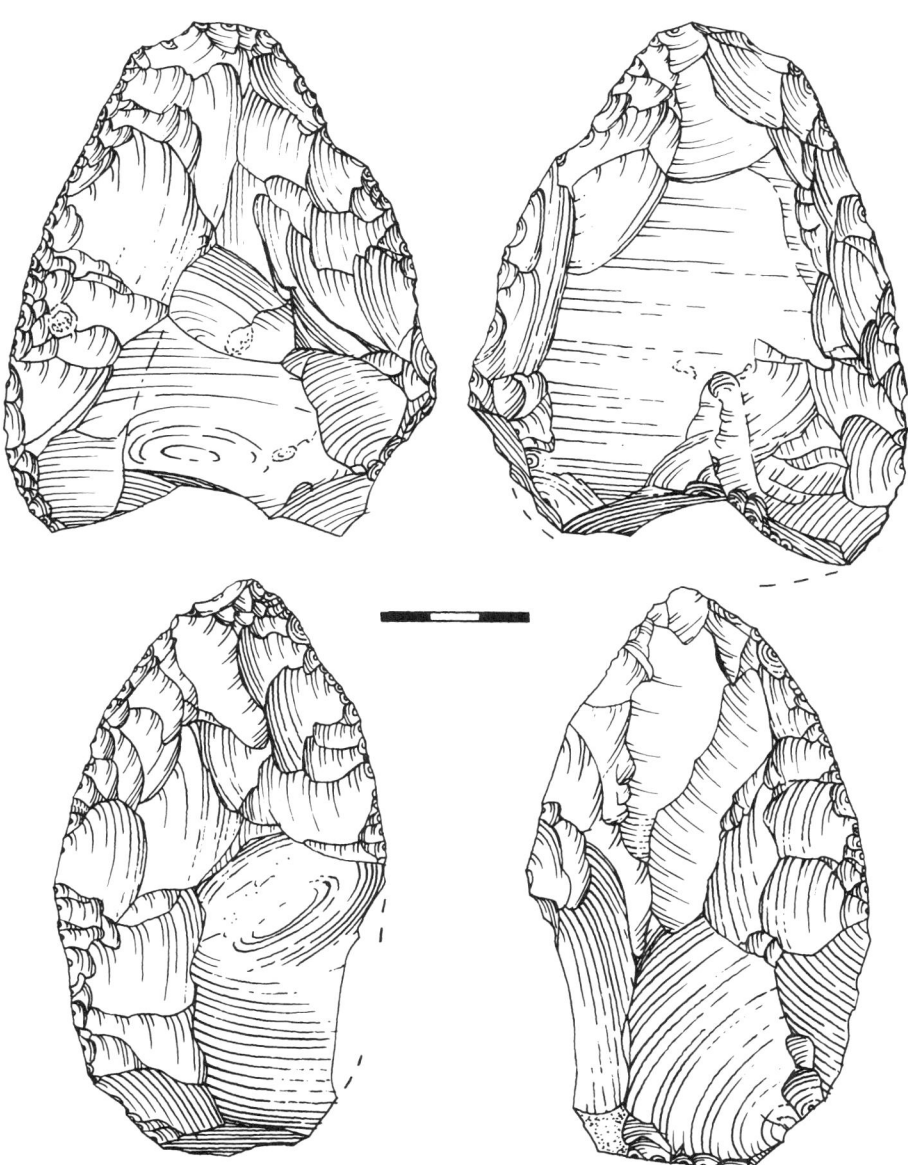

Figure 4.2. Middle Paleolithic bifaces: 1—Bohuslavice; 2—Polanka nad Odrou.

common than in the evolved Acheulean. The Rheindahlen type has been defined by the predominance of single and double sidescrapers, including Quina scrapers made on thick flakes, and by a series of characteristic points, including symmetrical and assymetrical types with convex edges (Bosinski, 1982b:167). The Bečov type is less distinctive but includes numerous sidescrapers and some Quinson-type points (Fridrich, 1982). The Ehringsdorf type is very characteristic: apart from typical sidescrapers and convergent points, it includes smaller leaf-shaped points and other bifacially worked specimens (Behm-Blancke, 1960).

The Taubachian

The reappearance of a variety of small-sized industries, sometimes stratified above each other, is an important phenomenon of the last interglacial and early glacial periods. Another important phenomenon is the concentration of living sites around warm, travertine-forming springs in Central Germany, Slovakia, and Hungary. In Moravia, sites of this cultural attribution represent the earliest more stable occupation (larger lithic assemblages with certain contextual information), but they do not lie directly embedded in travertines (Kůlna Cave, Předmostí). The common name for these assemblages, in the sense of the "shorter" concept of Valoch (1984a; cf. Valoch, 1976c, for the "longer" concept) is the Taubachian.

The assemblages are mainly composed of small debris and flakes produced from quartz, quartzite, flint, chert, and radiolarite. Several reduction techniques are observed in the various raw materials. First, the simple reduction of a pebble, beginning with cortical flakes, over partly cortical and noncortical flakes, and ending with flat core residuals (one- or multidirectional), showing a cortical back. The second approach recalls the Levalloisian technique: the reduction of small, prepared cores of flat shape. Prepared striking platforms, however, are very rare. While the first technique dominates in quartz, the latter is more frequently applied to quartize, radiolarite, or flint. Blades are unusual in the both cases.

The sites in eastern Slovakia, such as Gánovce, have industries made by the direct striking of debris from the raw material or by the exploitation of unprepared cores. Straight or convex scraperlike retouches predominate among the tools, but there are also pointed types, extremely rare borers, and massive endscrapers (Bánesz, 1991). In 1987, Kaminská reopened the excavation at another site, Ondrej-Horka, and revealed a sequence of stratified assemblages (Kaminská, Kovanda, Ložek, and Smolíková, 1993). In Hungary, the most important site is Tata. There are some regular flat cores, mostly exhausted, which were sometimes retouched and used as scrapers, and some of the flake platforms are prepared, especially those of radiolarite. The types of retouching are the same as those found at the other travertine sites, except for some Quina-like retouching and bifacial retouching.

In Moravia, the typological data from Kůlna Cave, layer 11 (Appendix A; Valoch, 1988) indicate the predominance of scraperlike retouching including straight, convex, and concave forms and few bifacially worked specimens. Notches and denticulates are also present, as well as some Upper Paleolithic types (burins). There are typical becs and microendscrapers, defined by two notches, and quite fine borers. The various points include some Tayac points. The coarse component of the industry consists of only a few unstandardized artifacts, which would seem to be chunks of raw material rather than shaped tools.

Within the interglacial sequence at Předmostí, layers 9 and 8 (Figure 4.3; Appendix A; Svoboda et al., 1994), the edges with notches and denticulates are more frequent than continuously retouched edges (sidescrapers). Lateral retouches are marginal, scalariform, or flat. More rarely, the whole surface is covered by flat retouching, unifacially or bifacially. The most typical artifact of this kind is a fragment of fine flint leaf-point, the earliest of this kind in Moravia. Among the other tool types, there are splintered pieces, some endscrapers, and a few burins. A typical association, appearing repeatedly in the lower layer, is sidescrapers combined with splintered edges. Small assemblages or comparable artifacts come from the Sklep Cave (Valoch, 1977a) and from Nová Hora (Svoboda, 1991d).

The Micoquian

The name *Micoquian* has been traditionally used in Central Europe (Bosinski, 1967), but in another sense than in the West. The paradox has often been criticized, but there is actually no other common term that can replace it.

In Moravia, the stratigraphy of Micoquian (in the Central European sense) is based on the section of Kůlna Cave, layers 9b–6a (Valoch, 1988; Appendix A). It appears in several stratigraphic positions, with a culmination during a Lower Würmian interstadial, possibly Brörup (layer 7c), then interrupted by a thick sterile layer (7b), and another culmination in layer 7a. This last-mentioned layer, in which Neanderthal fossil remains have been found, is dated by C-14, but these datings are minimal and lie at the very limits of this method.

Micoquian industries (Figure 4.4) are characterized by non-Levalloisian techniques of flake production and by a dominance of sidescrapers (48% in Kůlna 7a), some of them with characteristic flat retouching and Quina retouching. Furthermore, Kůlna is typical in its flat-retouched bifacial tools (knives, bifacial points, leaf-shaped points). The relative frequencies of blades (9% in layer 7a) and of Upper Paleolithic tool types (3% in the same layer) are low. These frequencies increase only in the uppermost Micoquian layer 6a. If this assemblage was not created by mechanical contamination with an Upper Paleolithic industry, it may reflect an evolutionary tendency toward the Szeletian.

In three other caves of the Moravian karst, possible Micoquian occupation is evidenced by only a few artifacts (Pekárna, Drátenická, Výpustek Caves). In the open air, a number of Micoquian-like implements appear among the EUP surface collections, especially from the Bořitov and Krumlovský les exploitation areas (Oliva, 1979a, 1987b,c, 1991a; for comments, see Svoboda, 1983). With respect to the supposed gradual evolution from the Micoquian to the Szeletian, and to the seemingly "archaic" appearance of some implements from primary workshops, separating the two cultures in the surface records seems a very difficult task.

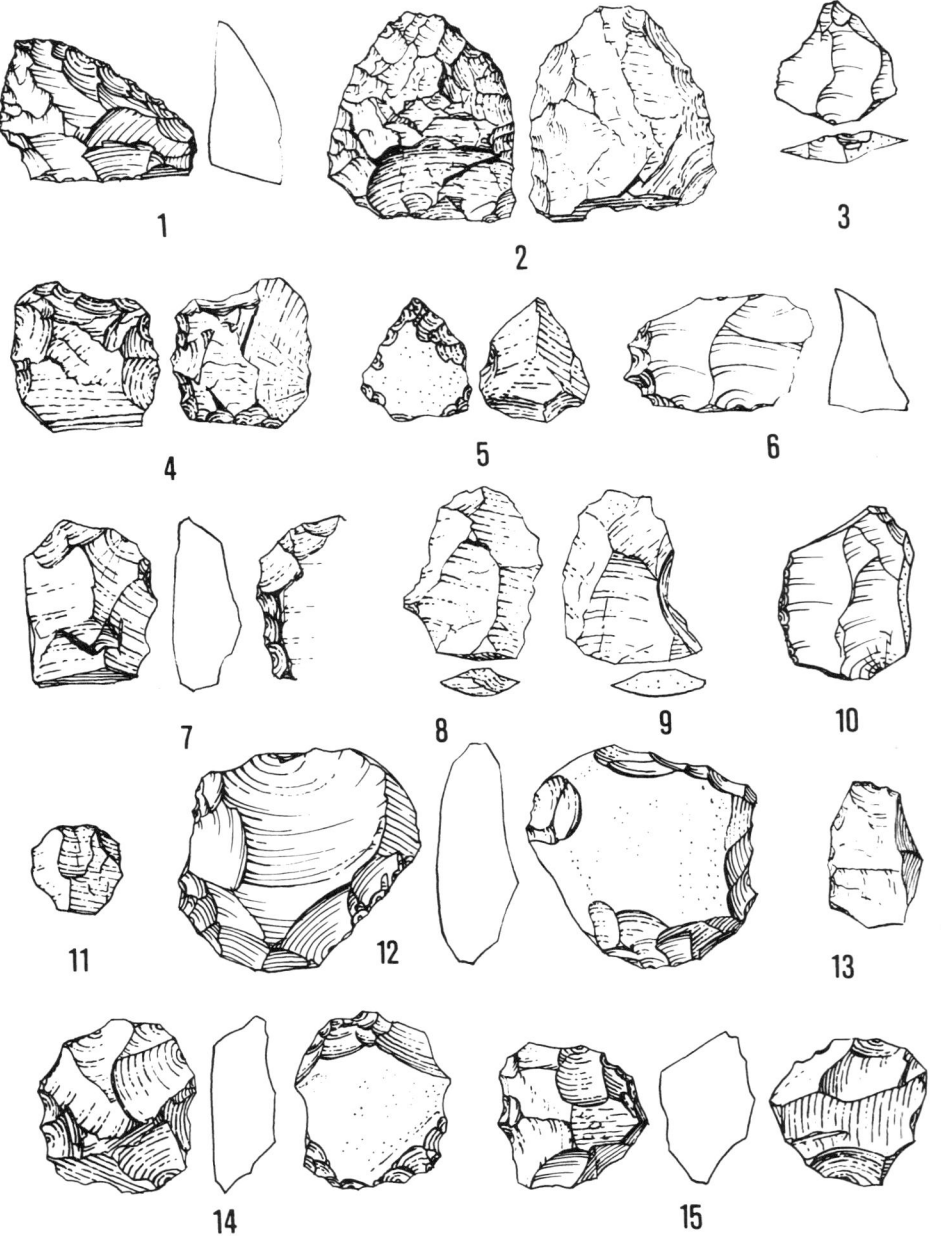

Figure 4.3. Taubachian industry: Předmostí, layer 8.

LOWER AND MIDDLE PALEOLITHIC BACKGROUND

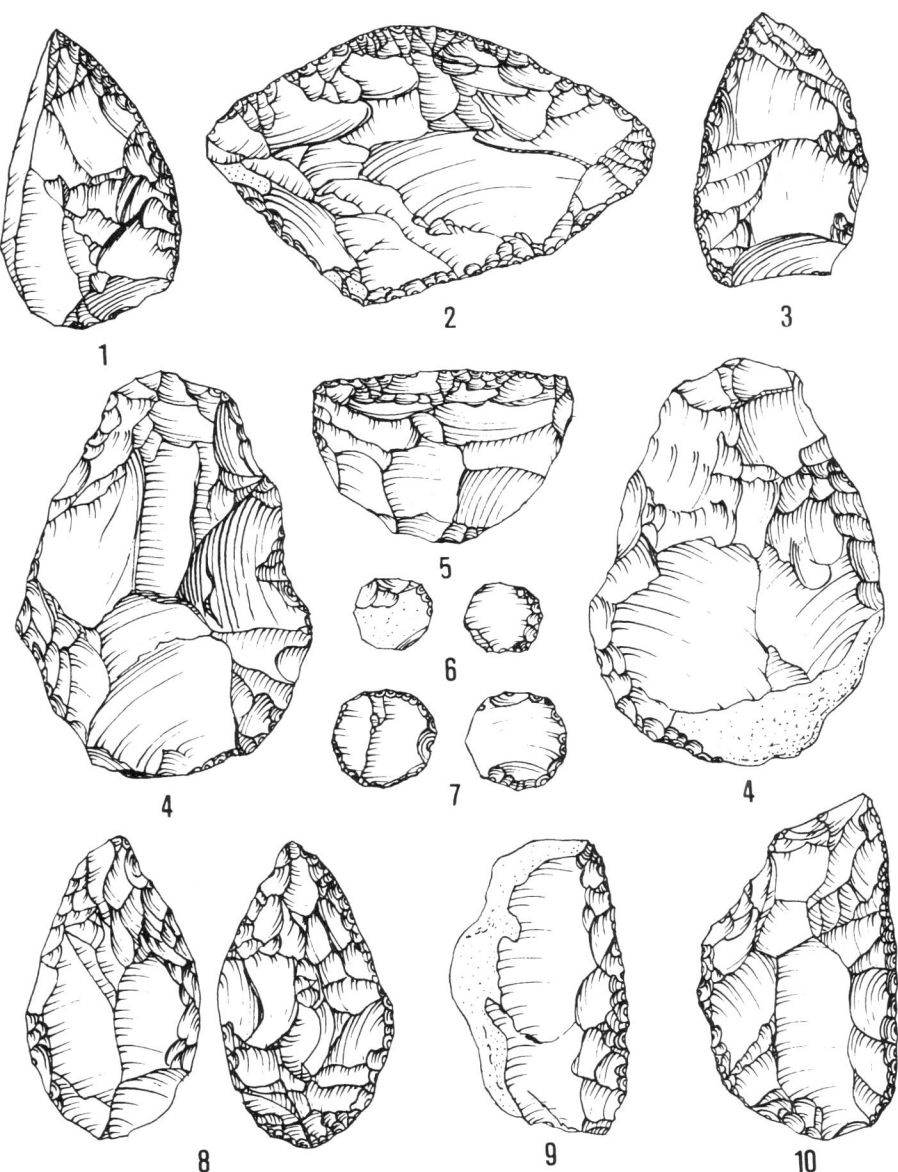

Figure 4.4. Micoquian industry: Kůlna, layer 7a.

The Late Mousterian

To establish the stratigraphy of the Mousterian occupation in Moravia, it is necessary to evaluate correctly the position of humus layers containing the industries of Neanderthal fossil remains, which are below the last Würmian loess in the caves of Šipka and Švédův stůl (Appendix A; Valoch, 1965c; Klíma, 1962a). Paleontological evidence indicates that these portions of the sediments of both caves were deposited between the final Eemian and the climatically favorable episodes of the Lower Würmian. They may be compared with layers 9–7c of Kůlna Cave, or with the pedocomplex PK II in the open-air loess deposits (Amersfoort and Brörup). The Mousterian settlement is concentrated in the upper parts of the humus layers.

The Mousterian industries (Figure 4.5) were made by flake technology but show an increase in the relative proportion of blades (15% at Šipka) and have some elements of Levalloisian technology. The most frequent tool types are simple sidescrapers. Furthermore, at Šipka, there is an observable increase in the proportion of Upper Paleolithic tool types (endscrapers and burins, 14%). Compared to the Micoquian, the use of flat and bifacial retouch is rather rare.

EARLY HUMAN ADAPTATIONS IN CENTRAL EUROPE

In contrast to the following Upper Paleolithic, the Lower and Middle Paleolithic are often portrayed as a period of stable and monotonous adaptations. This view is based on the nature of the archaeological record, which suggests a generally low level of technological specialization, and hardly allows us to separate distinct activity areas within regions and sites (among the exceptions are the few killing sites, or burial sites, which, however, do not occur in Central Europe). Another premise is to interpret the early human behavior in terms of environmental adaptation. However correct this idea may be, environmental variations and "stresses" do not operate in a organizational vacuum.

In view of these presuppositions, the following text examines the available evidence on settlement patterns, resource exploitation, and possible symbolic behavior in order to determine how far behavioral and technological development occurred. The incompleteness of the archaeological record given by postdepositional processes, and the limitations in compatibility with the Upper Paleolithic contained in the very nature of this evidence, are among the major obstacles to a direct approach to the presumed social, symbolic, and ritual frameworks that lie beyond these adaptations.

Settlement Pattern

Small foraging groups have left their "visiting cards" (sites, bones, and artifacts) all over Central Europe. The fact that a region of key geographic importance like Moravia was scarcely settled during the Lower (and even Middle) Paleolithic (Figure 4.1) suggests that these early hominids preferred kinds of environments other than

LOWER AND MIDDLE PALEOLITHIC BACKGROUND

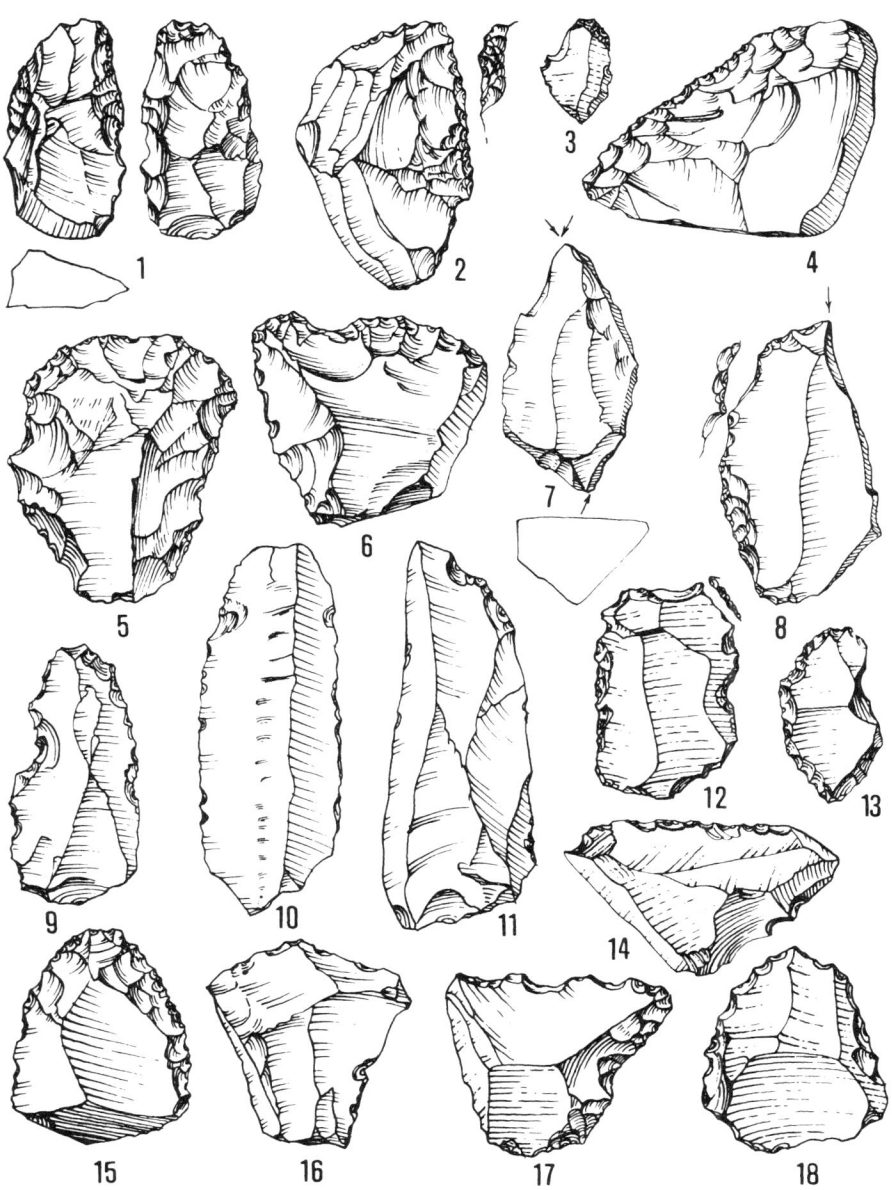

Figure 4.5. Mousterian industry: Šipka.

this territory may have offered and that they migrated less systematically through strategic passes typical for the region, than their Upper Paleolithic successors.

The majority of the earliest Lower Paleolithic sites in eastern Central Europe lie in deposits of warm periods, such as travertines, paleosoils, and limnic sediments (the so-called small-dimensional industries and the pebble industries: Kretzoi and Vértés, 1965; Šibrava, 1979; Mania et al., 1980). These situations enable a complex analysis of the sites, including their environmental context, but the wide time scale, the lack of more precise intersite correlations, and later changes in the landscape geomorphology make it impossible to explore whether or how far the individual site locations form a meaningful settlement system within the landscape. It seems that the location of Lower Paleolithic settlements was determined by sources of water and lithic material, while the role of natural shelters (caves and rock shelters) and of strategic hunting posts is difficult to evaluate since the landscape and the cave fillings have often been profoundly altered by geologic processes. Artifacts in cold-period deposits, especially in the loess, are not found until the Lower–Middle Paleolithic boundary (the Acheulean: Baumann and Mania, 1983). Thus, with the Central European evidence, adaptation to a cold climate and an open landscape seems to be an important phenomenon related to the beginning of the Middle Paleolithic.

Relatively high moisture and the expansion of forest during the last interglacial are clearly related to an increase in the number of sites throughout the eastern part of Central Europe, including Moravia (the small-dimensional industries or Taubachian: Behm-Blancke, 1960; Valoch, 1988; Svoboda et al., 1994; Vértés, 1964; Kaminská et al., 1993; Vlček, 1969). With this enlarged database, a more meaningful settlement pattern may be reconstructed. The open-air travertine sites show a relationship to warm-water sources and, probably, to more open patches within generally wooded environments. Even if the Předmostí habitation site lies in loess, the mineral springs of the Přerov area are located nearby. Caves (with the exception of Kůlna, Figure 4.6) were mostly avoided in the interglacial, probably because of the high moisture. However, with the climate cooling and the landscape opening at the beginning of the last glaciation, the Micoquian and Late Mousterian settlements mostly occurred in caves, now offering optimal, dry shelters (Figures 4.7 and 4.8). This behavioral change seems to have been an adaptive reaction to the climatic changes. Furthermore, the settlement pattern studies suggest that, after the Middle Paleolithic, the Moravian Gate started to be a communication axis in Central Europe (Svoboda et al., 1994).

In all the mentioned cases, the formation of settlement networks was influenced by important landmarks: springs, caves, and geographic corridors. Mountainous sites, like those in the Alpine region, are missing in our territory. Relationships to relief and to relatively constant altitudes suggest that the hunters consciously preferred locations where two environments (forest and open landscape) met. It seems, therefore, that the trends toward an optimal settlement pattern in the following Upper Paleolithic had a solid Middle Paleolithic background.

On the other hand, the variability of the environments settled by the pre-Neanderthal and Neanderthal populations of eastern Central Europe and their changing strategies in preferential site location (spring–open-air site–cave) document a

LOWER AND MIDDLE PALEOLITHIC BACKGROUND

Figure 4.6. Kůlna: Historical photograph of the cave.

Figure 4.7. Sipka: View of the cave.

Figure 4.8. Švédův stůl: View of the cave during excavations by B. Klíma.

relatively high adaptability to warmer and colder climates, and to forest and steppe landscapes. However, we still lack good evidence on Neanderthal persistence and adaptation during the cold peak of the Lower Würmian pleniglacial: this question seems crucial to establishing the hotly debated Upper Paleolithic origin in this region.

Besides the evidence on preferential settlement network formation, the means of artificial protection (dwellings) should be included in the analysis of adaptational processes. Lower and Middle Paleolithic dwelling reconstructions from eastern Central Europe are actually based only on the circular or oval features of larger objects and on traces of fire and are not yet confirmed by more detailed studies of small artifact scatters (*sensu* Stapert).

The earliest dwelling was supposedly at Přezletice (Fridrich, 1989). In the view of Fridrich, it lies inside the settlement area between the lake shore on the south and the side of a block of phthanite, several meters high, on the north. It presents itself as an oval structure on the surface of the ground, built of phthanite rocks and loam and measuring 4 by 3 m outside and 3 by 1.5–2 m inside. The opening seems to be toward the northwest. On the northern side near the entrance was a small hearth (about 30 cm in diameter), not dug into the ground. At Bilzingsleben, Mania (Mania et al., 1980) has discovered three features of larger bones and stones, two of them circular and one oval, which he interprets as dwellings as well. They are 3–4 m in diameter.

Accumulations of charcoal near the supposed entrances may indicate hearths. There were also localized bone-working areas in the vicinity. If we are to accept the authenticity of Přezletice, there are patterns common to both sites: all features open inland, rather than toward the shore, and the hearths are supposed to have been located at the entrances to, but outside, the sheltered areas. If the excavators' interpretations are correct, the hearths would have been used for cooking and other activities outside the dwellings, and perhaps for protecting the entrance, but not for heating the interior. This is an important difference in comparisons with later structures, which date to colder periods.

Fridrich (1976b) excavated such a type of dwelling at the base of section I A at Bečov (Early Mousterian location A-III-6). This was a fairly regular oval depression, measuring 6.60 by 4.25 m and dug to a depth of 0.75 m into the subsoil. He supposes that it was originally sheltered by a quartzite rock shelter on the north, while the eastern and western flanks were protected by small, stone-built walls. The entrance may have opened toward the south. There was a fireplace in the center with a large pile of pieces of red ocher.

Raw Material Acquisition and Technology

The lithic material transport was not frequent during the Lower and Middle Paleolithic, and the sources of favorable rocks, if fulfilling the other functions of an early hominid site, were directly settled. The Central European highlands supplied mainly coarse-structured rocks such as lydite, quartzite, limestone, and basalt, but sources of more amorphous rocks, such as various cherts, are present as well. Limestones of the Alps and the Carpathians yielded radiolarities, while the primary and secondary (glacial) sources of the North European Plain yielded various types of flint. River gravels and glacial deposits were exploited as easily accessible sources of pebbles of all the mentioned materials (Valoch, 1975c; Přichystal, 1994b).

Middle Paleolithic industries are made mostly of local lithic materials (Valoch, 1987d). At Kůlna 7a, for example, the materials are the Cretaceous chert (79%), accompanied by quartz, various other cherts, mostly from the Moravian karst, and, quite rarely, by some long-distance imports (flint and radiolarite). At Šipka, the cherts from local flysch sandstone were primarily used, only rarely accompanied by flint, radiolarite, and quartz, even if the sources of flint were accessible in the nearby glacial deposits. At Předmostí, the variability of raw materials corresponds well to the rocks available in the Bečva riverbed in the same vicinity. At Bečov, North Bohemia, local quartzites were intensively exploited throughout the Middle Paleolithic, forming, for the first time, the pattern of a "lithic exploitation area," but not yet that of a "lithic distribution area" (Svoboda, 1983; Chapter 5). These data suggest that the range of hominid activities in the vicinity of a site was limited, and that interactions with more distant environmental zones were rather random.

All the more noteworthy are the existing transport patterns, as followed and drawn by J. Feblot-Augustins (1993). Their limited occurrences reflect a well-defined and stabilized kind of Middle Paleolithic behavior, including operations outside the settled area. From the point of view of quantity, however, the amount of Middle Paleolithic transport cannot be compared with that of the Upper Paleolithic, and we cannot speculate whether the imports were due to random movement of the group over larger territories, or to the beginning of intergroup exchange networks.

Another question is the extent to which the size of the stone tools may reflect adaptation to various environments. In Central Europe, the so-called small-dimensional industries (including the Taubachian, as the most recent stage) always appear in interglacials. Researchers have suggested various explanations, ranging from the cultural-stylistic (K. Valoch, 1976c) to adaptive (V. Toepfer, J. Svoboda). These questions deserve further attention, as well as a critical examination with a broader comparative database than the region under study may offer (Svoboda, 1987a).

Finally, one of the most important questions is laying a base for future blade technologies during this period. In contrast to the early blade industries of Northwest Europe, in Central Europe tendencies toward blade production are more clearly observed at the beginning of the Middle Paleolithic (evolved Acheulean: Bosinski, 1967; Piekary II: Morawski, 1992) than at the end of this period.

Subsistence

Central European researchers traditionally conclude that the large mammalian fauna from the contexts of Middle Paleolithic archaeological sites represents the remains of hunting activities (e.g., Soergel, 1922; Kretzoi and Vértés, 1965; Šibrava, 1979; Mania, 1983). With the new approaches to faunal analyses (e.g., Binford, 1981), the hunting model calls for a critical revision in each particular case. This problem concerns the mineral springs which, during the last interglacial, served as spots of natural animal aggregation, and the caves that are the site of sediments including all sorts of associated faunal remains. Discussion has already been initiated; during the last glaciation, for example, Moravian caves were frequently occupied by cave bears (Musil, 1962; Gargett, 1994), but these remains tend to have accumulated in caves which were not continuously settled by humans (Sloupské Caves, Kateřinská Cave). Human presence alone does not prove specialized hunting of these animals, as has been suggested in the earlier literature.

The rich faunal assemblages from the early archaeological sites of Central Europe give a fairly standard picture. It may seem paradoxical that it was precisely the hunters of the biggest mammals—Proboscidea and Perissodactyla—who produced most of the small-sized industries. However, as experiments have shown, the effectiveness of small, sharp flakes in dismembering large carcasses is higher than would be thought. Judging from the associations, elephant and rhinoceros would seem to have been important prey of the early hunters. Their earliest appearance is at Přezletice, together with horse and bison (Šibrava, 1979). At Vértésszőlős, the animal bones (of horse, red deer, bison, and rhinoceros) were highly fragmented, and the variability of the mode of their association with the cultural layers only makes it all the more probable that they really are the remains of early hunting (Kretzoi and Vértés, 1965). There is a pattern of human selection in the species distribution of the animals at archaeological sites I and III, whereas the composition of the fauna at paleontological site II is closer to the natural proportions of herbivores and carnivores. At Bilzingsleben, especially in the shoreline zone, Mania (1983) observed a predominance of rhinoceros, red deer, beaver, bear, and elephant bones, including those of young and female animals. Bovids, horses, pigs, and other animals were also present. Analysis of the bones demonstrates that only certain parts of the heaviest animals (elephant, rhinoceros) were brought to the site, while the bovids, horses, and red deer were butchered, and their entire carcasses were brought in. The presence of bears, represented mainly by skulls and paws, suggests that, in this case, the hunters were interested in skins rather than in meat. The abundance of red-deer bones in the redeposited fluviatile sediments of the site is a result of natural transport. The bones show considerable evidence of pounding and smashing, indicating both how they were exploited and their subsequent use as tools.

The faunas from the travertine sites of Ehringsdorf and Taubach are composed of rhinoceros, elephant, and horse. Soergel (1922) compared elephant and rhinoceros bones from the two sites and noted a difference in age at death between the sites, with predominantly young animals (especially among the rhinos) at Taubach and an underrepresentation of young animals at Ehringsdorf. There are several ways in which human activity could explain this difference (Behm-Blancke, 1960). The faunal compositions at Gánovce and Tata are quite similar: a predominance of young elephants was observed at Tata. However, the rather fragmentary material from Kůlna, layer 11, included large numbers of horses, accompanied by rhinoceros.

For the beginning of the last glaciation, there are good faunal data from the above layers at Kůlna (Valoch, 1988). Musil (1988) observes that the horse dominates at the base of the Lower Würmian deposits (layer 9b) and was replaced by reindeer in layer 8a. At the top (layers 7d–6a) of the sequence, the most frequently hunted animals become mammoth and reindeer. At Šipka (lower humus layer), Musil (1965b) indicates the presence of cave bears, reindeer, wolves, bovids, rhinoceros, mammoths, horses, and other animals, while the upper humus layer is less rich in animal species. Judging from settlement geography, however, most of the caves are in separate valley locations within highlands that do not allow control over larger hunting territories (Gudenus in Lower Austria, Švédův stůl and Kůlna in Moravia), the only exception being Šipka, because of its location near the Moravian Gate. These data seem to be in accord with the lithic import data, suggesting operations within a frame of restricted territories.

Important evidence concerning early hunting activities is provided by killing sites at Lehringen (Thieme and Veil, 1985) and Neumark-Gröbern (Mania, Thomae, Litt, and Weber, 1990). At Lehringen, an elephant skeleton was associated with a wooden spear and a few stone artifacts. The hunters probably made use of the local landscape and drove the animal into a natural or artificial corral. In addition, some Middle Paleolithic sites in northern Central Europe show more specialized hunting: reindeer at Lebenstedt, North Germany (Tode, Preul, Richter, Selle, Pfaffenberg, Kleinschmidt, and Guenther, 1953), and horse at Zwolen, Poland (Schild and Sulgostowska, 1988). These cases reflect adaptation to environmental conditions and to site setting, and they also indicate an important behavioral pattern which is not observed again until the Upper Paleolithic.

Despite the doubts about the intentionality of the earliest faunal assemblages, the data indicate that, by the Middle Paleolithic at the latest, hominids were relatively efficient hunters of large game but were limited by the immediate vicinities of their home bases, and there is no evidence of more ambitious hunting strategies over the Moravian territory.

Symbols, Rituals, and Art?

The capability for symbolic behavior of the Lower and Middle Paleolithic populations is currently under discussion (e.g., Chase and Dibble, 1987; Marshack, 1988; Noble and Davidson, 1993). In the context of this debate, several objects from Lower and Middle Paleolithic sites in eastern Central Europe deserve attention and some of them have already been introduced into the debate. The pre–World War II excavations at Stránská skála I yielded an elephant vertebra scarred by three large recent lines but also incised with seven short engraved radiating lines (Valoch, 1972). Unfortunately, it remains possible that the short lines were engraved after the specimen had been excavated: this possibility would accord with the continued lack of any other solid evidence of early human presence at Stránská skála. Mania's later discoveries at Bilzingsleben of large mammal bones engraved with parallel lines may cast some light on this early find (Mania et al., 1980), since at Bilzingsleben, there is no doubt about the authenticity of the finds. Interpretations of the origin and function of these engravings, however, are the matter of discussion. According to the Central European authors, these finds are nonutilitarian and suggest that the first symbols were rhythmical rather than aesthetic.

There is indirect evidence of creative activities in the numerous chunks of local ocher and the quantities of powdered ocher found within the dwelling structure at Bečov I, A-III-6 (Fridrich, 1976b; Marshack, 1981). One of the pieces of red ocher has striations and abrasion marks on both faces, and a flat rubbing stone, with a granular crystalline surface, had been abraded in the center during the preparation of ocher powder. Roughly contemporaneous is an isolated piece of red ocher from the Lower Travertine at Ehringsdorf (Behm-Blancke, 1960).

Further evidence originates at Tata (Vértés, 1964): a "churinga" carved from a piece of elephant ivory and an amulet, supposedly inscribed with a cross, made on a polished nummulite fossil. Marshack (1988), who examined both the churinga and the nummulite, observed that one or both arms of the cross "engraved" on the nummulite are in fact natural fractures that penetrate through the stone. However, the ivory plaque appears to have been carefully separated from a compound molar tooth, shaped and beveled, and colored by rubbing with ocher. At the other Middle Paleolithic sites in Hungary, selection and even engraving of pebbles are documented: the nummulite of Tata (Vértés, 1964:141) and an engraved pebble of Erd (Gábori-Csánk 1968:158). At Předmostí, there were several intentionally selected flat pebbles, all from the lower layer (Svoboda, 1991d). Even if usage as small plates or ambosses is possible, no use or wear traces are observed on the surface, and only one pebble of this kind, found in the upper layer, possesses a denticulate retouching along one edge. The selection of these pebbles seems to have been an unusual behavior, rather symbolic than utilitarian.

Three Moravian sites—Šipka, Švédův stůl, and Kůlna—have yielded Neanderthal cranial remains in a fragmented state (Chapter 3). However, without precise contextual information about these discoveries (a hearth is being described from Šipka—see Appendix A—and a sort of charcoal lense from Kůlna—see Valoch, 1988), any speculation about funeral ritual behavior that would be related to these finds is excluded. Equally, the presumed cave-bear rituals, as described in earlier literature from the Alpine regions of Central Europe, are subject to serious criticism.

Chapter 5

The Beginning of the Upper Paleolithic
The Bohunicians, Szeletians, and Aurignacians

With the Upper Paleolithic, anatomically modern humans (*Homo sapiens sapiens*) appeared on the European scene. Correlations of the changes in biology and in behavior, as well as the search for behavioral differences between the moderns and the archaics, have been the subject of research for over a century (Mellars, 1989). The Central European record suggests that not all of the changes traditionally associated with the Upper Paleolithic, especially the technological ones, can be ascribed only to modern humans: some may have been earlier and some later (Svoboda, 1993c). On the other hand, the Early Upper Paleolithic (EUP) archaeological record is being enriched by the first sound evidence of symbolic behavior, as reflected in Aurignacian art (Hahn, 1986).

Changing interpretations in Central European archaeology—namely, of the role of migrations versus gradual evolution in one place—have widely influenced the controversy. Early Moravian researchers believed that Paleolithic hunters were highly mobile, and they saw migrations as causing cultural change and development. Wankel (1884:99), probably influenced by discoveries in Russia, believed that the mammoth hunters who replaced the bear hunters came from "far to the east." Knies (1925) suggested that, in the temperate period following the Neanderthals (*Homo mousteriensis Hauseri*), there were two waves of migration: one moving eastward from Africa across Spain, the other moving from the east westward. A meeting of these two nomadic streams would explain the variability in the physical characteristics of the modern Central European population and the diversity of the material culture at Upper Paleolithic sites.

Absolon (Absolon et al., 1933) believed that in fact premodern populations (*Homo primigenius*) never reached as far as Moravia. Taking into consideration the new discoveries in Eastern Europe and Siberia, he further developed Wankel's theory that

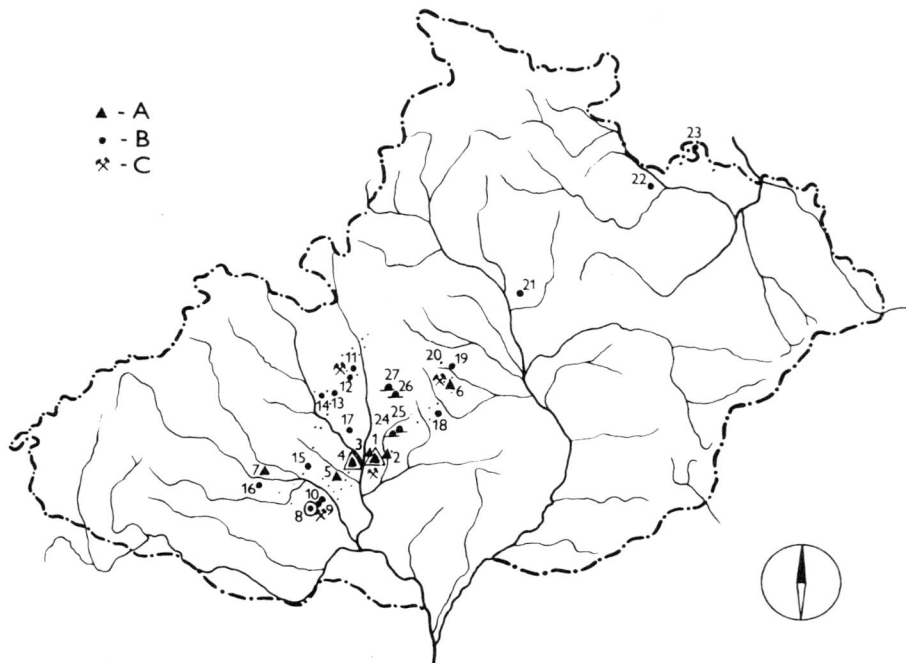

Figure 5.1. Map of important Bohunician (A) and Szeletian (B) sites; C: lithic exploitation areas. 1—Brno, Stránská skála II–III; 2—Brno, Líšeň; 3—Brno, Nová hora; 4—Brno, Bohunice; 5—Ořechov I–II; 6—Ondratice I; 7—Mohelno; 8—Vedrovice V; 9—Jezeřany; 10—Maršovice; 11—Bořitov; 12—Černá Hora; 13—Malhostovice and Nuzířov; 14—Hradčany; 15—Neslovice; 16—Dukovany; 17—Rozdrojovice; 18—Drnovice and Opatovice; 19—Vincencov; 20—Myslejovice; 21—Droždín; 22—Otice; 23—Třebom; 24—Pekárna Cave; 25—Křížova Cave; 26—Rytířská Cave; 27—Pod hradem Cave.

modern humans and Upper Paleolithic culture were brought in from the east. In consequence, all skeletal remains from Moravia, including the Šipka jaw, and all Middle Paleolithic and Aurignacian industries were ascribed to these immigrant populations. International scientists—for example, A. Keith, who visited Moravia at that time—supported Absolon's ideas, at least in attributing an Asian origin to modern humans, although Keith stressed the southwestern instead of the eastern part of Asia.

The picture so clearly drawn by Absolon was complicated not only by continuing discussions about the local Middle Paleolithic, but also by the presence of leaf-points in the EUP assemblages described as Solutrean or Szeletian (Červinka, 1927; Skutil, 1928a). If such an evolutionary line connecting the Middle and Upper Paleolithic stages existed, it would naturally throw doubt on any unequivocally migratory explanation. Since that time, the idea of continual evolution toward the Upper Paleolithic has been progressively developed by Czech archaeologists.

Lineages, as followed by physical anthropologists, provide another aspect of this

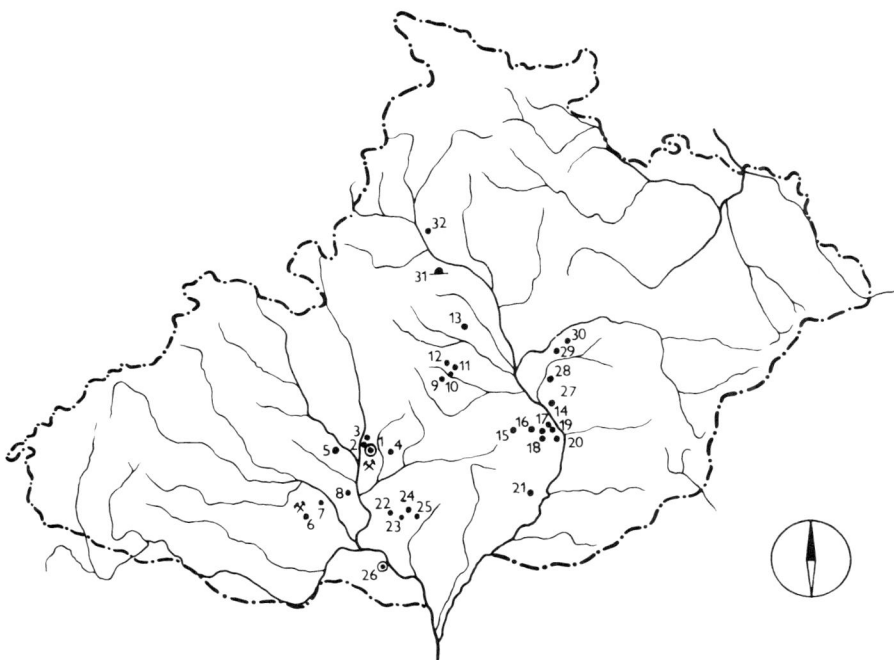

Figure 5.2. Map of important Aurignacian sites. 1—Brno, Stránská skála; 2—Brno, Maloměřice (Borky II); 3—Brno, Maloměřice (Občiny); 4—Tvarožná; 5—Brno, Kohoutovice; 6—Vedrovice I, II; 7—Kupařovice; 8—Vojkovice; 9—Ondratice II; 10—Brodek; 11—Dobrochov; 12—Určice; 13—Slatinice; 14—Kvasice; 15—Zdislavice; 16—Milovice (Kroměříž) and Lhotka; 17—Karolín; 18—Nová Dědina; 19—Bělov; 20—Žlutava; 21—Stříbrnice; 22—Křepice; 23—Diváky; 24—Klobouky and Krumvíř; 25—Brumovice; 26—Milovice (Břeclav); 27—Míškovice; 28—Přestavlky; 29—Pavlovice; 30—Lhota; 31—Mladeč Caves; 32—Dubicko.

Lineages, as followed by physical anthropologists, provide another aspect of this question. Although most of the skeletal material from Moravia had been destroyed in the Mikulov Castle by the end of the World War II, it was possible to present several comparative studies and syntheses based on the casts and newly excavated material (Chapter 3). According to Vlček (1969), all Middle Paleolithic specimens except Gánovce may be classified as transitional Neanderthals. They probably formed one of the bases for the appearance of the primitive but already sapient Brno-type population in Central Europe. In Moravia, sapient forms of the Brno type encountered the Western European Cro-Magnon race (Mladeč): a process that may have been followed by the polytypic population of Předmostí (Vlček, 1969:255). According to Jelínek (1969), the morphological variability of the skeletal material was determined by genetic factors and a degree of isolation rather than by migration currents. From his viewpoint, the appearance of *Homo sapiens sapiens* in the region could be even more clearly explained by local evolution. In 1982, the skeletal material of Central Europe was reconsidered by Smith, who observed a consistent pattern of change between "early" and "late" Neanderthals in the direction of early modern *Homo sapiens*, as well as Neanderthal-reminiscent features in the *Homo sapiens sapiens* specimens. Smith, like both Czech anthropologists, concluded that there is a sort of morphological continuum between *Homo sapiens neanderthalensis* and *Homo sapiens sapiens* in this region.

More recently, Stringer and Andrews (e.g., 1988) have underlined the absence of transitional Neanderthal–modern fossils both in Europe and in Southwest Asia. Furthermore, new discoveries and dating have suggested that modern *Homo sapiens* were present in Southwest Asia before Neanderthals, some 60,000 years prior to the last Neanderthals of Western Europe. Contrary to Smith, Stringer and Andrews observed no continuity of genuine regional features: the primitive characters and homoplasies of early modern humans are shared and found elsewhere.

There is a broad variety of opinions about the archaeological context in eastern Central Europe. After World War II, the Szeletian question was reconsidered. On the basis of newly excavated materials from west Slovakia, Prošek (1953) suggested a model of local development of the Szeletian from the Mousterian, influenced by the Aurignacian invading from the southeast. Subsequently, Klíma (1961c:88) accepted the model of Aurignacian–Szeletian influence but questioned whether the influence did not act in the opposite direction: from the local Szeletian to the infiltrating Aurignacian. With Valoch (e.g., 1966a, 1976a,b), there was a shift from migratory to local development models: in his view, both the Szeletian and the Aurignacian were of local origin.

The first C-14 dates (for Szeleta Cave in Hungary and Čertova pec Cave in Slovakia) suggested that transitional cultures, such as the Szeletian, appeared as early as 40,000 B.P. An important question, still unresolved, arose after Prošek's death: Was there any Aurignacian that existed at such an early date that it could have influenced the Szeletian? F. Bordes and some Central European scholars saw the Szeletian development as an independent process, a sort of local leptolithization trend parallel to the Chatelperronian of France. Still others (Žebera, 1958) defended a simple Mousterian–Szeletian–Aurignacian evolutionary scheme. Valoch and Oliva still debate whether the emergence of the Szeletian was due to an Aurignacian influence (Valoch, 1993b) or to a spontaneous development of the Micoquian (Oliva, 1991c).

The publication of EUP industries from Bohunice (Valoch, 1976a), Ondratice (Svoboda, 1980), and new excavations at Stránská skála (Svoboda, 1987d, 1988, 1991e) introduced the concept of another transitional culture, contemporary with or even earlier than the Szeletian: the Bohunician. This culture, with its Levalloisian–leptolithic technology, shows parallels to comparable industries in Southeastern Europe and Western and Central Asia. The definition of the name *Bohunician*, again, evoked hot debates, questioning the cultural homogeneity of the Bohunice site and the subsequent interpretations (Oliva, 1981a, 1984b, for comments see Valoch, 1982c, 1990b; Svoboda, 1984b; Svoboda and Svobodová, 1985; Allsworth-Jones, 1986, 1990).

Further disagreements concerned the question of Aurignacian origin. Valoch (1971, 1976a,b) and Oliva (1980, 1987a) searched for the roots of the Aurignacian in the so-called Krumlovian of south Moravia, consisting of surface collections around local chert outcrops. Because of the lack of stratified evidence and datings at that time (Valoch, 1985a), the danger existed that the "archaic" morphology and the larger size of the "transitional" industries may have been due to workshop activities in areas with raw material abundance, and that functional differences could be explained by age. Debates on EUP chronologies, including the newly defined lithic-exploitation-area concept (Svoboda, 1983), were centered on these points (Svoboda, 1984b; Valoch, 1984b; Oliva, 1987c; Allsworth-Jones, 1990). Recently, a new series of Aurignacian C-14 datings entered into this discussion: first, the dating of a specific transitional industry with Aurignacioid elements at Bačo Kiro, Bulgaria, to about 40,000 B.P., later followed by comparable data from northern Spain, and, most recently, by datings between 37,000–38,000 B.P. for the Aurignacian layer 3 at Willendorf (Haesaert, personal communication, 1995). In light of these early datings, it appears that, in a Europe dominated by transitional cultures, the Aurignacian dispersed quite rapidly over the continent and accelerated the Upper Paleolithic development processes, culminating in the Gravettian.

THE ENVIRONMENTAL AND STRATIGRAPHIC BACKGROUND

The Upper Paleolithic is generally viewed as a period of severe climatic conditions, but large parts of it were subject to climatic ameliorations called the *interpleniglacial* (Figure 5.3; Table 5.1). In the last decade, the excavations at Stránská skála (Figure 5.4; Appendix A; Czudek, Smolíková, and Svoboda, 1991; Svoboda, 1987d, 1991e) have yielded some evidence on the environmental context of the transition from the Middle to the Upper Paleolithic.

During a period before 40,000 B.P., which is not precisely dated, the impact of the Lower Würmian pleniglacial climate can be observed in sediments affected by cryogenic features such as solifluction and sorted-circles formation. T. Czudek estimated the mean annual temperatures to be $-12°C$ to $-8°C$ (a layer without human occupation) and $-8°C$ to $-3°C$ (the earliest Bohunician). Paleobotany suggests poor vegetation and, later, a cold *Salix*-dominated tundra landscape (Svobodová, 1987d). This evidence evokes questions about Neanderthal persistence over the most severe climatic episodes of the lower pleniglacial into the interpleniglacial. It should be repeated that, at present, we have no hard evidence in human fossils to support such a continuity. The numerous archaeological writings concerned with this question only try to follow ancestor–descendant relationships in cultural traditions and lithic technologies (namely, the Micoquian and the Szeletian) before and after the lower pleniglacial peak. The use of C-14 dating puts serious limitations on dating such early periods, so that the transitional cultures with a number of Middle Paleolithic elements (Szeletian and Bohunician) may have started well before we have believed until now.

With the beginning of the Würmian interpleniglacial, an increase in temperature

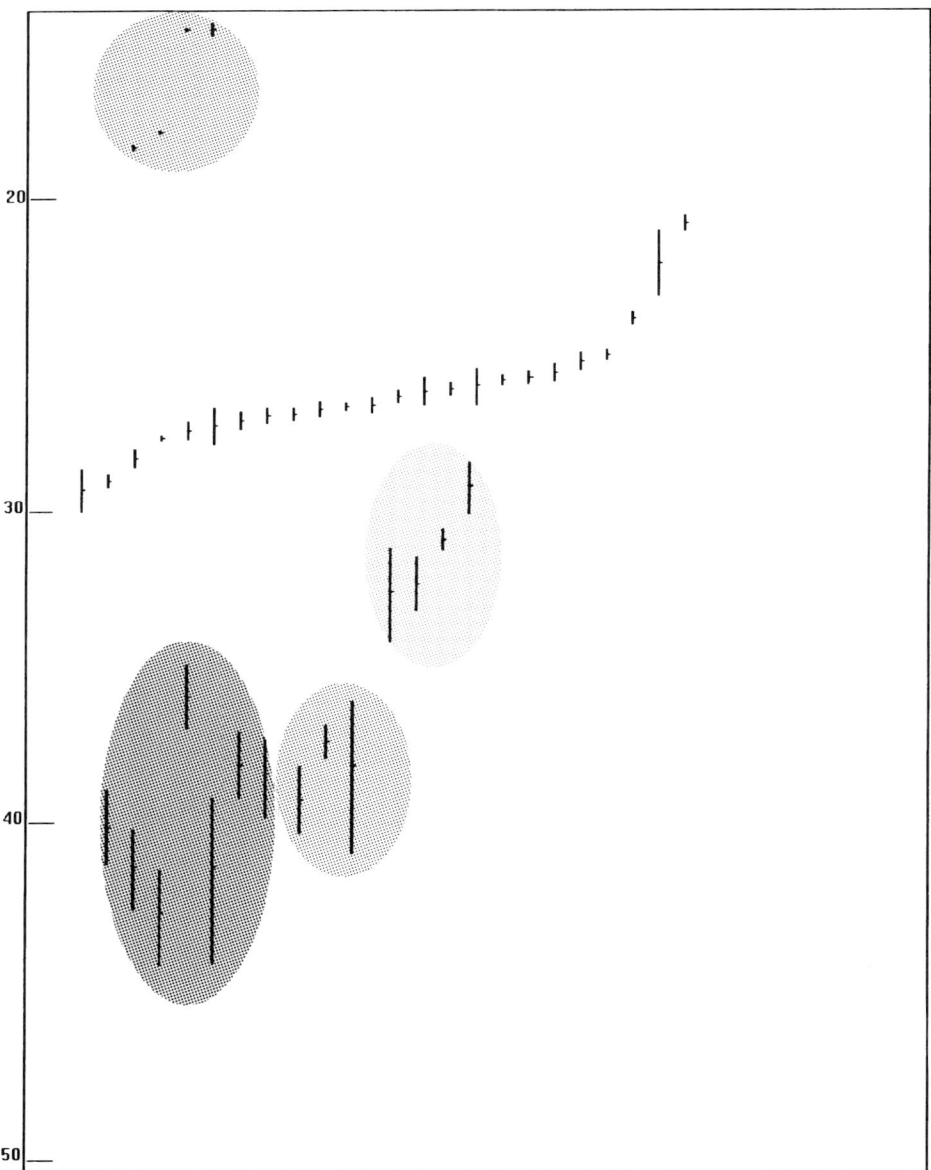

Figure 5.3. Diagram of Upper Paleolithic C-14 datings. From the base to the top: Bohunician, Szeletian, Aurignacian, Gravettian, and Epigravettian. The scale is given in thousands of years.

BEGINNING OF THE UPPER PALEOLITHIC

Table 5.1. Review of Early Upper Paleolithic Stratigraphy in Moravia

Period	Stratigraphy	Dating	Sites
Interpleniglacial	Last loess	After 30,000 B.P.	Stránská skála IIa-3, Vedrovice Ia (Aurignacian)
	Upper soil	30,000 B.P.	Stránská skála II, IIa-4, IIIa-3, IIIb-4, Milovice (Aurignacian)
	Lower soil	38,000–35,000 B.P.	Stránská skála III (Bohunician), Vedrovice V (Szeletian)
Lower pleniglacial	Solifluction	Before 40,000 B.P.	Stránská skála IIa-5, IIIa-4, Bohunice (Bohunician)

and humidity has been reconstructed, with the formation of steppe and shrub-steppe landscapes, accompanied by two more important soil formation processes and several initial soil horizons (complex PK I; see Chapter 2). These soils are usually separated by a short period of loess sedimentation. It is in this context of climatic amelioration that we observe an expansion of both transitional cultures: the Bohunician and the Szeletian (in the lower soil; see Tables 5.2 and 5.3) and subsequently the Aurignacian (mainly in the upper soil; see Table 5.4).

The lower soil formation, or the Bohunice soil (Haesaerts, 1990), documents a warmer and moister climate, with an extension of steppe and shrub-steppe environments (Opravil, 1976; Svobodová, 1987a). After Smolíková, this soil may be classified as a pseudogley with developmental tendencies toward arctic braunerde (Bohunice, Vedrovice V). The mean annual temperatures were certainly several degrees above 0°C. The dating of this soil, however, is still unclear. There are several datings around 38,000 B.P. from charcoal within the soil (Stránská skála III, Vedrovice V), as well as datings ranging between 36,000 and 43,000 B.P. from charcoal below the soil (Schwallenbach, Bohunice). Therefore, the exact chronological position of this soil and its correlation with the development in Northern Europe (Hengelo) remain unresolved.

The upper soil formation, or the Stránská skála soil (Svoboda, 1993b), is dated around 30,000 B.P. and may be compared to Denekamp-Arcy and Maisières. At Stránská skála, micromorphological investigation shows that this soil ranges typologically between the pararendzines and chernozems. The soil developed within a short time span, during repeated eolian sedimentation, redeposition, and solifluction. In the subsoil, we observed horizontal movements of loams (solifluction) and vertical movements of stones (the formation of sorted circles), both prior to the soil formation (Czudek et al., 1991). At Dolní Věstonice II, a stratigraphically identical soil has been classified as a weakly developed pararendzine, mixed with relics of earlier chernozem soils. Again, it evolved during a short time span, in a cold and relatively dry climate. The following moister oscillations were responsible for its pseudogleyfication. At the nearby site of Milovice, on a different substrate, this soil corresponds to a weakly developed pseudogley (Smolíková, 1991). At Willendorf II, a comparable

Figure 5.4. Stránská skála III: The position of the Bohunician (upper location) and Aurignacian (uppermost location) layers.

Table 5.2. C-14 Datings: The Bohunician in Moravia

GrN 6802	Bohunice-Kejbaly, layer 4a	41,400 + 1400–1200 B.P.
GrN 6165	Bohunice-brickyard, 4a	42,900 + 1700–1400 B.P.
GrN 16920	Bohunice-brickyard, 4a	36,000 ± 1100 B.P.
GrN 12606	Stránská skála IIIa	41,300 + 3100–2200 B.P.
GrN 12297	Stránská skála III, layer 5	38,200 ± 1100 B.P.
GrN 12298	Stránská skála III, 5	38,500 + 1400–1200 B.P.
Q 1044	Bohunice-Kejbaly, 4a	40,173 ± 1200 B.P.

horizon (layer 5) is represented by lenses of humus sediments (Haesaerts, 1990). Paleobotanical studies of this soil (Svobodová, 1987b, 1991a) suggest a steppic environment with a limited extension of trees.

CULTURAL PATTERNS OF THE MIDDLE TO UPPER PALEOLITHIC TRANSITION

After World War II, comparative typology, together with stratigraphic data, created a research tradition that still dominates Early Upper Paleolithic research in Moravia. Although more complex approaches have recently evolved, the traditional typology seems justified, at least as it concerns understanding and defining the surprisingly high degree of cultural variability in this period.

The Bohunician

Focusing on Southeastern and Central Europe at the critical time, around 40,000 B.P., we observe a mosaiclike pattern of several cultural units: the Bachokirian and other transitional industries of the Balkans; the Szeletian (Allsworth-Jones, 1986); a less distinctive industry from Willendorf II, layer 2 (Felgenhauer, 1959); and the Bohunician. All of them show well-determined Upper Paleolithic tool equipment, while the technologies, as if they were more "retarded," retained and modified various Middle Paleolithic traditions.

Table 5.3. C-14 Datings, Szeletian in Moravia and West Slovakia

GrN 12375	Vedrovice V	39,500 ± 1100 B.P.
GrN 12374	Vedrovice V	37,650 ± 550 B.P.
GrN 15514	Vedrovice V	37,600 ± 800 B.P.
GrN 15513	Vedrovice V	35,150 ± 650 B.P.
GrN 2438	Čertova Pec, Slovakia	38,400 + 2800–2100 B.P.

Table 5.4. C-14 Datings, Aurignacian in Moravia and Lower Austria

GrN 12605	Stránská skála IIIa, layer 3	30,980 ± 360 B.P.
GrN 14829	Stránská skála IIa, layer 4	32,350 ± 900 B.P.
GrN 16918	Stránská skála IIIb, layer 4	32,600 ± 1700–1400 B.P.
GrN 14826	Milovice	29,200 ± 950 B.P.
GrN 848	Pod hradem Cave	33,300 ± 1100 B.P.
GrN 1724	Pod hradem Cave	33,100 + 530 B.P.
GrN 16263	Grossweikersdorf, Austria	32,770 ± 240 B.P.
GrN 16244	Grossweikersdorf, Austria	31,630 ± 240 B.P.
GrN 15641	Stratzing, 1985, Austria	30,670 ± 600 B.P.
GrN 15642	Stratzing, 1985, Austria	31,190 ± 390 B.P.
GrN 15643	Stratzing, 1985, Austria	29,200 ± 1100 B.P.
GrN 16135	Stratzing, 1988, Austria	31,790 ± 280 B.P.
GrN 11192	Willendorf II, layer 3, Austria	34,100 + 1200–1000 B.P.
GrN 1273	Willendorf II, layer 4, Austria	32,060 ± 250 B.P.
H249/1276	Willendorf II, layer 4, Austria	31,700 ± 1800 B.P.
KN 654	Krems-Hundsteig	35,500 ± 2000 B.P.

The Bohunician introduced certain formal elements of Levalloisian technique with striking analogies not only in the Near East (Boker Tachtit) but also in North and Central Asia (Kara Bom and other sites) into the predominantly non-Levalloisian context of eastern Central Europe. The sites are widely dispersed and rare. In Southeast and Central Europe, certain comparable industries exist in Bulgarian caves (Samuilica, Temna), Romania (Ripiceni), and Volhynia (Kulychivka). However, their density cannot be compared to the more stabilized network of Szeletian sites, perhaps because of higher mobility and the more episodic character of settlement.

The appearance of the Bohunician technology in Moravia is clearly related to the exploitation areas and distribution of two raw materials: the Stránská skála cherts and the Ondratice quartzites (Figures 5.1, 5.12 and 5.13), with a higher density of sites around lithic exploitation areas. Technological analyses of both materials (Svoboda, 1980, 1987d; Allsworth-Jones, 1990), now attested to by refittings (Svoboda and Škrdla, 1995; Škrdla, 1996), present the Bohunician technology as an example of a conceptual fusion of the Upper Paleolithic technique, represented by the initial crested cores, and the Levalloisian technique, represented by the flat core residuals. Reconstructed flat cores clearly show that they were not intended for one or few final flakes, but for series. The original core shape was more voluminous than we expected, and a crest blade could open the reduction sequence similarly to the Upper Paleolithic technique (Figures 5.5, 5.16). With this progressive, "Levalloisian-leptolithic" reduction system, the relative proportion of blades increases rapidly to 20–45%.

The stratigraphic and environmental studies at Stránská and Bohunice enable us to separate the Bohunician into two stages by the date of 40,000 B.P. (Svoboda, 1987d, 1991e). The lower stage is found in the redeposited soil sediments, while the upper one lies in the lower soil horizon of the interpleniglacial. Typologically (Table 5.5;

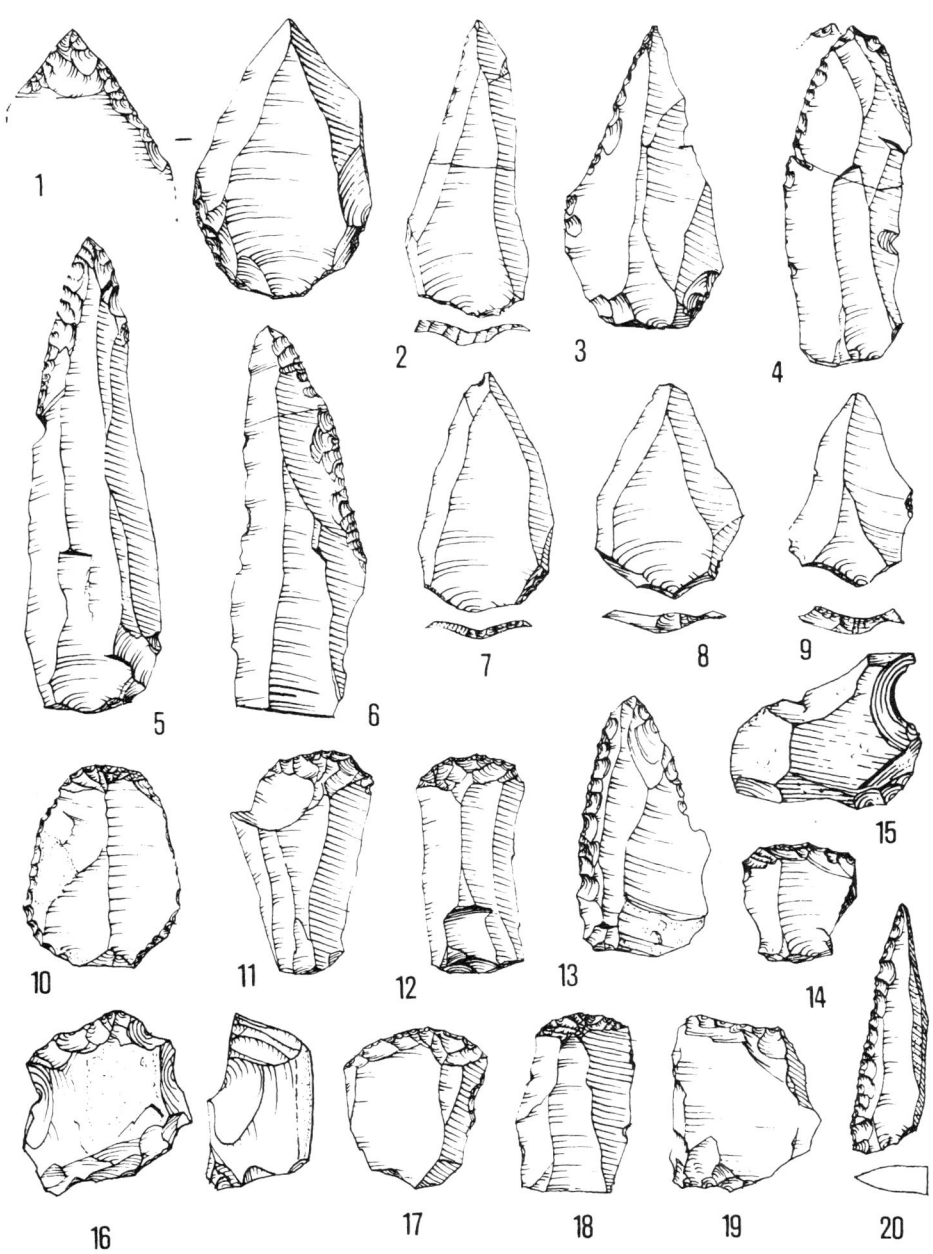

Figure 5.5. Bohunician industry (around 38,000 B.P.): Stránská skála III, layer 5.

Table 5.5. Bohunican Typology

	SS-III-5	SS-IIIa-4	Bohunice	Líšeň	Ondratice quartzites	Mohelno
Aurignacian endscrapers	2.5	8.6	0.9	4.5	3.2	1.4
Other endscrapers	37.8	24.5	12.0	38.1	23.4	15.9
Burins	0	5.2	14.1	5.5	8.2	5.8
Leaf-points	0	0	5.2	4.2	0.7	5.8
Ventroterminally retouched points	2.5	1.7	0	3.6	0	0
Retouched points	5.0	0	1.3	3.0	8.5	2.9
Other points	5.0	0	0.9	1.0	0.4	0
Sidescrapers	17.5	17.2	21.9	15.7	36.0	21.7
Notches and denticulates	7.5	27.6	34.7	11.0	7.9	13.0
Combinations	0	0	0.4	0.6	0.4	2.9
Others	22.2	15.5	8.6	12.8	11.3	30.4
Total tools	40	58	233	1391	946	59

Valoch, 1976a; Svoboda 1987d, 1990a), tool types of Upper Paleolithic character dominate in the both stages, mostly endscrapers (Stránská skála) and, less frequently, burins (Bohunice). At some sites, there are steep endscrapers of Aurignacian form, leaf-points, and other types more characteristic of the other EUP cultures. The Middle Paleolithic component is represented by some sidescrapers and Mousterian points, most typically at Ondratice (Svoboda, 1980).

The Szeletian

Szeletian is a typically local culture of southeast Central European origin (Allsworth-Jones, 1986), where it forms several regional clusters. One of them reaches from the Váh valley in western Slovakia over the western Carpathians to central and south Moravia (Figure 5.3), with surprisingly few traces in the adjacent lower Austria (Trnka, 1990). A smaller cluster lies in Silesia, with several surface sites in the Czech part, and the most important excavated site at Dzierzyslaw in Poland (probably superposed over an earlier Bohunician layer: Bluszcz, Kozlowski, and Foltyn, 1994).

In south and central Moravia, the industries are very numerous on the surface. They are made mainly of Moravian cherts, of which the Cretaceous chert and the Krumlovský les chert are the most common sorts. Around these two outcrops, again, we observe the formation of lithic exploitation areas (Figure 5.14 and 5.15, Svoboda, 1983). The share of quartzites is clearly related to distance from places of dense natural occurrences, because this material has not been imported from longer distances. Imports, such as the other Moravian cherts, flint, and radiolarite, show a higher frequency at some sites only (i.e., Stránská skála chert at Drnovice III).

The Szeletian technology of eastern Central Europe probably has its roots in the local Middle Paleolithic, as it develops its typical bifacial tool-making tradition. It is based on flake and blade production by non-Levalloisian methods. The proportion of blades is considerably higher than in the Micoquian, but slightly lower than at most of the Bohunician sites. Flat and bifacial retouches are typical and cover not only the surface of leaf-points, but also the surfaces of sidescrapers and other tool types. Sidescrapers are still among the most typical tool types (20% to 30%), followed by endscrapers (20%–30%), which are flat rather than steep in shape (Table 5.6; Figure 5.6). In addition, some sites yielded Mousterian points and pointed retouched blades (Želešice, Drnovice III, Opatovice I, II).

The earliest evidence of the Szeletian (before 40,000 B.P.) comes from Hungary (Svoboda and Simán, 1989). In Moravia, a single site—Vedrovice V—is precisely dated and stratified in the lower interpleniglacial soil (Hengelo), at around 38,000 B.P. (Appendix A; Valoch, 1993b), and a comparable date exists from the Radošiná Cave in western Slovakia (Bárta, 1980). Some Szeletian artifacts lie in the pure loess as well, so that we may infer that the Szeletian lasted longer than this single pedogenetic process. In addition, the thermoluminiscence datings of the Dzierzyslaw sequence (Bluszcz et al., 1994) supply a broad chronological frame to the Bohunician—Szeletian superposition expected to have existed at this site.

An effort to subdivide the Szeletian into three chronological stages, based on presumed developmental trends from the Middle Paleolithic (Micoquian) to the Upper Paleolithic, was published by Valoch (1973). Later, Svoboda (1983) suggested that the typology of the earliest stage sites (Jezeřany, but also Bořitov, which has not been classified Szeletian by Valoch) is, in fact, influenced by lithic exploitation and primary material-treatment functions, which could have increased the relative proportions of simple sidescrapers, notches, denticulates, and unfinished bifaces. Another atypical site, Vincencov, is quite extraordinary assemblage because of the smaller dimensions of the artifacts, the higher proportion of blades (including microblades), and the typological spectrum—with numerous burins, notches, and splittered pieces (Svoboda and Přichystal, 1987)—a composition that would suggest a character more evolved toward the Upper Paleolithic than all other Szeletian industries. However, we cannot be sure how well these morphological and stylistic differences correlate with real Upper Paleolithic chronology.

Since the late 1970s, O. Soudský, J. Svoboda, and M. Oliva have made various efforts to use the cluster analysis for more precise comparisons of EUP typological variability. Most recently, Weber (in Valoch, 1993b) used this method to compare certain Szeletian, Bohunician, and Micoquian assemblages. As a result, the groups of Bohunician industries (Stránská skála, Líšeň, and Ořechov, but not Bohunice) and of "Micoquioid" industries (Kůlna, Bořitov, and Jezeřany) were clearly separated from the remaining Szeletian stock. The interpretation of the both groups has undergone a vivid discussion in the recent literature: while Kůlna serves as a stratified example of a Micoquian industry (Valoch, 1988), Bořitov V, which differs in the presence of Upper Paleolithic tool types, has been explained either as the result of Micoquian-Aurignacian symbiosis (Valoch, 1978c, 1993b) or as Micoquian spontaneously developing toward the Upper Paleolithic (Oliva 1987c, 1991c), and a comparable industry from Jezeřany as the earliest Szeletian (Valoch, 1966a; Oliva, 1979a). Since the persistence of Middle Paleolithic (Micoquian) types in an Upper Paleolithic context

Table 5.6. Szeletian Typology

	Neslovice coll. MM	Vincencov	Drmovice site I	Drmovice site III	Opatovice site I	Želešice site I	Jezeřany site I	Bořitov site V
Aurignacian endscrapers	1.4	3.1	4.2	3.7	1.5	6.7	1.4	2.8
Other endscrapers	19.1	9.9	16.9	6.2	9.2	27.7	5.9	6.0
Burins	6.7	17.5	7.4	9.9	9.9	10.1	1.4	5.2
Leaf-points	12.4	9.4	5.3	3.7	3.8	5.9	11.5	2.0
Other bifaces	1.2	0.6	3.2	2.5	0	0	8.3	8.7
Ventroterminally retouched points	0.4	0.6	0	1.2	0	0	*	0.1
Retouched points	1.2	1.9	0	3.7	3.8	2.9	1.8	*
Other points	0	0.6	1.1	1.2	2.3	0	0.5	0.6
Sidescrapers	25.1	25.6	31.3	17.3	26.7	17.0	37.4	24.3
Notches and denticulates	8.7	2.5	6.3	17.3	12.2	7.6	6.4	34.9
Combinations	0.4	2.5	2.1	1.2	0.8	0.2	0.7	*
Others	23.4	25.8	22.2	32.1	29.8	21.9	*	*
Total tools	507	160	91	81	131	476	564	687

*Present but not calculated.

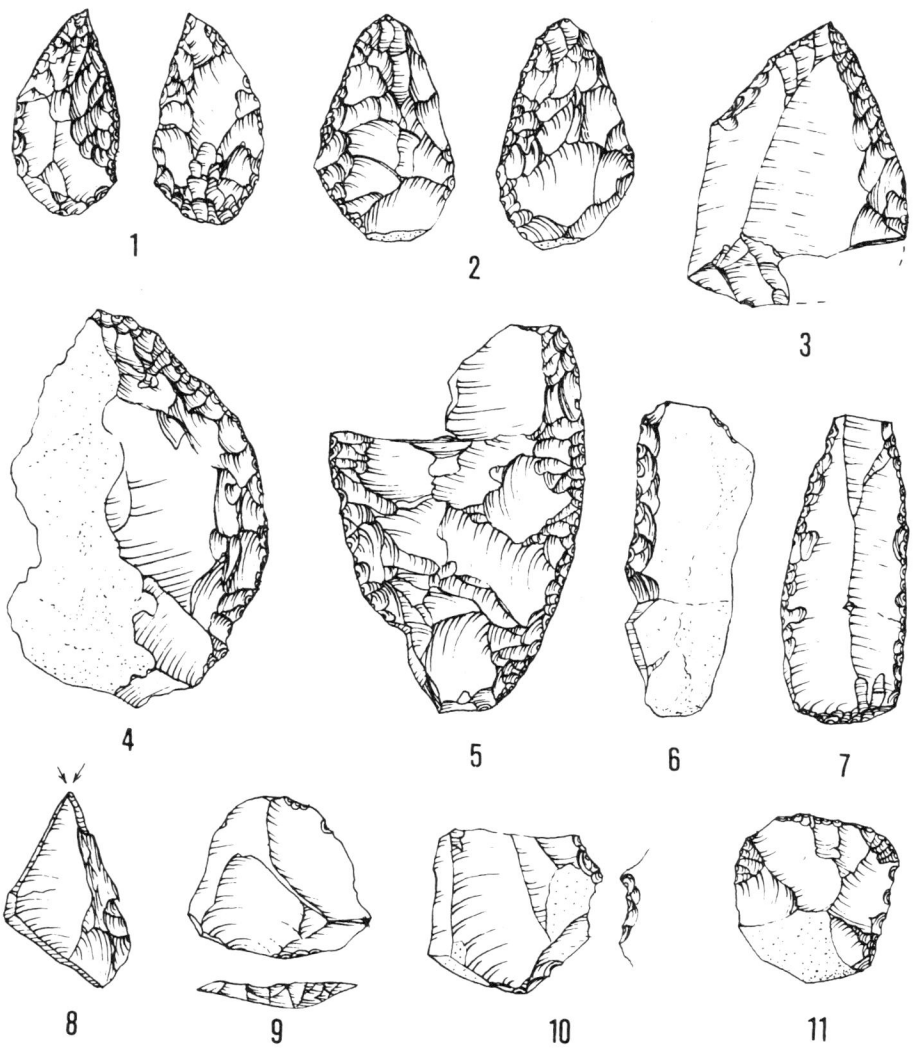

Figure 5.6. Szeletian industry (around 38,000 B.P.): Vedrovice V.

actually corresponds to what we define as the Szeletian, there seem to be no formal reason for separating Bořitov and Jezeřany into two distinct cultures.

The Jerzmanowician

In 1961, W. Chmielewski defined a new culture on the basis of laminar, ventroterminally retouched points in southern Polish caves. The identification of this culture subsequently underwent discussion, since similar points had been observed dispersed at considerable distances from each other over the North European Plain (cf. maps in Otte, 1990), as well as concentrated in some Bohunician territories of Moravia (Líšeň and Ondratice: Svoboda, 1987d:96–98). On the basis of the stratigraphy and the C-14 dating at Nietoperzowa Cave, southern Poland, the Jerzmanowician points—as a technological simplification of the bifacial leaf-point—are more recent than the Szeletian points (after 38,000 B.P.: Chmielewski et al., 1975). With the continuous simplification of retouching, the development of similar points continued in the Gravettian (Chapter 6).

The Aurignacian

Several times, it has been emphasized in the literature that the Lower Austrian–Moravian territory represents the densest cluster of Aurignacian sites in Europe east of France (Oliva, 1987a, 1993a), and focusing on the geography of our territory more explicitly, we observe that it is patterned in several smaller site clusters (Figure 5.2).

In Lower Austria, there are a number of important stratified assemblages (Willendorf II, layers 3–4: Felgenhauer, 1959; Langmannersdorf: Angeli, 1953). Some are currently under excavation (Stratzing: Neugebauer-Maresch, 1988), but some have not yet been published in detail (Senftenberg, Grossweikersdorf: Brandtner, personal communication, 1992; Neugebauer-Maresch, 1993). On the other hand, for the most part, the typical Moravian Aurignacian materials of central and southern Moravia have now been published, both the bulk of the materials originating from surface (Oliva, 1987d) and the excavated materials (Stránská skála II–III: Svoboda, 1987d, 1987f, 1991e, 1993a; Milovice: Oliva, 1989a). Excavations at Vedrovice I by M. Oliva (1993b) are still in progress.

Chronologically, the time span covered by the Aurignacian is surprisingly long. Leaving aside the radiocarbon dates around and before 40,000 B.P. at Willendorf II, layer 2, and at Istállóskö (there are serious doubts about the Aurignacian attribution of layer 2 at Willendorf and about the relationships of the samples to artifacts at Istállóskö: Haesaerts, 1990; Svoboda and Simán, 1989), we now have new datings for the typical Aurignacian layer 3 at Willendorf (37,000–38,000 B.P.: Haesaerts, personal communication, 1995) and for the Geissenklösterle Cave in adjacent southern Germany (36,500 B.P.: Hahn, 1987). Further early data come from Senftenberg, Lower Austria (Brandtner, personal communication, 1992), and Krems-Hundsteig, which, however, differ slightly from the typical Aurignacian (35,500 B.P.; Neugebauer-Maresch, 1993) and have been nominated "Kremsian" by Fridrich and Bánesz (cf. Fridrich, 1973).

The largest series of Aurignacian datings and stratigraphic observations from recent excavations in Lower Austria and Moravia is correlated with the upper soil of the interpleniglacial (Denekamp and Maisières) between 33,000 and 29,000 B.P.: this interval covers the sites of Stránská skála II, IIa, and IIIa (Svoboda, 1987d,f, 1991e, 1993a); Milovice (Oliva, 1989a); Willendorf II, layer 4; Stratzing; and Grossweikersdorf (Neugebauer-Maresch, 1988, 1993). All these sites are typically Aurignacian, with diagnostic endscrapers and burins made of short flakes, blades, and thick fragments (Figure 5.7); only the small Milovice assemblage retains more Szeletioid elements.

At Stránská skála IIa, layer 3, there is stratigraphic evidence for a later, Upper Aurignacian industry in the overlying loess. At the Lower Austrian sites, the late persistence of Aurignacian (or, rather, Epiaurignacian) sites is confirmed by C-14 datings: Langmannersdorf (Angeli, 1953) and Alberndorf (Trnka, 1992; Table 6.3); these sites, however, possess a number of Gravettian features.

Because in Moravia the stratified sites were not available until recently, the published chronologies have been based primarily on the typological relationships of the surface assemblages, namely, the percentages of burins, endscrapers, sidescrapers, and combinations (Valoch, 1976b; Oliva, 1980, 1987a). The comments on this system (Svoboda, 1983, 1984b) have argued that the earliest stage sites (Vedrovice II, Kupařovice) are located at the raw material sources and may have been influenced by working activities similar to those in the Szeletian. With the new data now in hand, the typological model of the hypothetical early Aurignacian in Moravia is not being confirmed. The evolved, "latest" sites (Epiaurignacian, after Oliva, 1987a), on the other hand, differ more sharply in the raw material composition (a higher share of flint and radiolarite), in the smaller dimensions of the artifacts, in a higher proportion of blades (including microblades), and in a typological spectrum with numerous burins, few backed microblades, and some leaf-points. Like Vincencov in the Szeletian, these sites seem to be of a more recent age and are probably contemporaneous with the Gravettian. It should be recalled that a number of Aurignacioid features are observed as late as the Epigravettian, after 20,000 B.P. (Chapter 6).

Another kind of diversity in the Aurignacian is evidenced by the geographic clustering of the Moravian sites (Figure 5.2; Table 5.7; Oliva, 1987a; Svoboda et al., 1994). Apart from the sites in the Krumlovian exploitation area, there are areas with a predominance of burins and small-dimensional artifacts (the Prostějov area), areas with a predominance of endscrapers (the Kroměříž area), and areas with a coexistence of both types (the Brno area). All these regions and sites, representing the typical Aurignacian, indicate an increase in the number of precores with a frontal crest, derived prismatic cores, and blades (up to 50% relative to flakes); in other words, the Upper Paleolithic technological system seems to have been established. The Szeletioid (atypical) Aurignacian of eastern Moravia is distributed mainly in the Moravian Gate area and continues along the Morava River as far south as the Ždánický les area; generally, the typical Aurignacian endscrapers and burins are present, but the assemblages retain more evidence of Middle Paleolithic techniques and tool types. Klíma (1978, 1979a) named such Aurignacian industries the "Morava River type," while Oliva (1990) preferred to name them the "Míškovice type" after one of the typical surface sites.

In addition to the lithics, the Aurignacian is the first culture to offer a distinctive bone and antler industry, especially the sagaies with an oval section: the Mladeč type (Figure 5.17). The Mladeč Caves, both sites I and II, yielded a series (Szombathy, 1925), and two more specimens come from nearby surface sites of the Prostějov area (Hluchov, Slatinice I). The Mladeč I site also provides pierced decorative objects

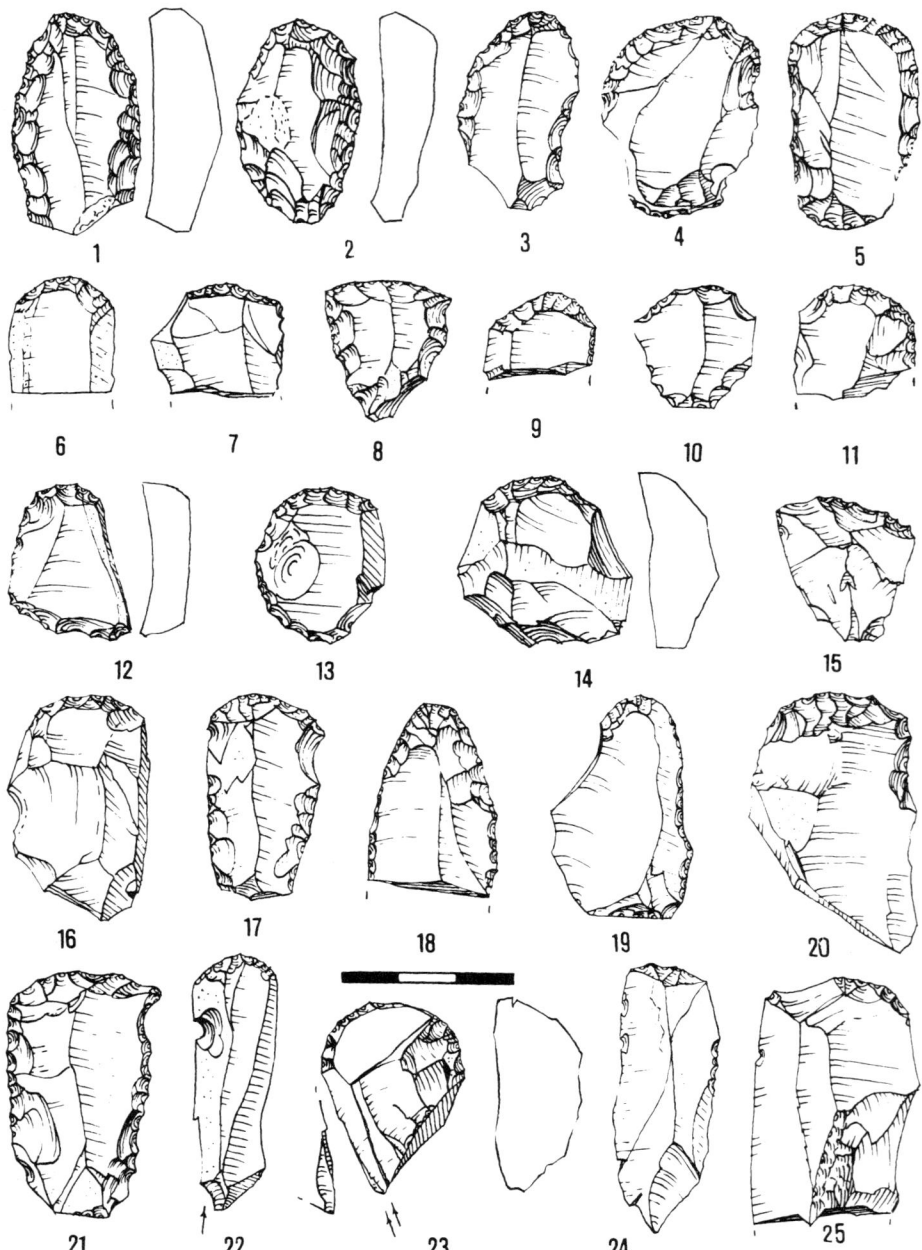

Figure 5.7. Aurignacian industry (around 31,000 B.P.): Stránská skála IIa, layer 4.

BEGINNING OF THE UPPER PALEOLITHIC

Table 5.7. Aurignacian Typology

	SS IIa-4	SS IIIa-3	Maloměřice Borky II	Tvarožná	Ondratice site II	Vedrovice site II	Kupařovice site I	Křepice	Dobrochov (silicites)
Aurignacian endscrapers	6.7	21.9	7.2	5.3	3.0	3.3	4.1	6.2	10.3
Other endscrapers	26.9	15.6	19.5	16.3	9.2	7.0	20.0	25.8	20.7
Aurignacian burins	0.7	3.1	9.8	19.6	15.0	5.5	2.2	0	0.9
Other burins	12.7	12.5	21.6	22.7	44.7	19.6	38.5	17.5	21.6
Leaf-points	0	0	0	0.3	2.3	0	1.5	4.2	0
Other points	0	0	0	0.3	0.9	3.4	0.4	1.0	4.3
Sidescrapers	7.4	12.5	7.9	5.1	3.4	24.4	14.1	5.2	13.8
Notches and denticulates	19.5	18.8	4.7	5.9	3.4	14.0	4.4	2.1	5.2
Combinations	2.7	0	2.2	5.6	2.3	0.4	3.0	1.0	1.7
Others	23.4	15.6	27.1	18.9	15.8	22.4	11.8	37.0	21.5
Total tools	149	32	277	1524	469	262	270	97	116

(Figure 5.18; White, 1993), and the Austrian and southern German sites even have the earliest representative art (Hahn, 1986; Neugebauer-Maresch, 1988).

THE UPPER PALEOLITHIC ADAPTATIONS

There is considerable debate over where the differences in Upper Paleolithic behavior lie. Actually, some authors have opposed the dichotomized view of the Middle and Upper Paleolithic and have emphasized instead a "mosaic" (Chase and Dibble, 1990) or "gradual" (Svoboda, 1993b:33) view of the transition. This approach calls for detailed argumentation that lies beyond the scope of this review.

The global evidence suggests that the most complex Upper Paleolithic adaptations appeared not in areas where modern humans presumably originated, such as Africa and the Near East, but in the contact zones with the Neanderthals, as in Europe. The Neanderthals were prepared to create transitional cultures with clear trends toward Upper Paleolithic technology (the Middle Paleolithic blade industries of northwestern Europe, or Chatelperronian), but representative art is ascribed to modern humans exclusively (Aurignacian and later). The transitional industries of Central Europe (Bohunician and Szeletian) combine the Middle and Upper Paleolithic technotypological elements, but an understanding of their nature and their association with a distinct human form is still restricted by the limited database. In the light of this evidence, the cultural diversity observed in Central Europe leads us to describe the Upper Paleolithic adaptations as a developmental process in an area of contact between various (at least two) populations.

The archaeological record from Moravia, though biased, suggests the existence of distinct activity areas, such as the lithic exploitation areas, small hunting posts in cave entrances, and possible ritual burial sites in deep caves. It may even be suggested that the higher level of spatial diversity is related to modern human behavior. Following this assumption in the archaeological record, however, we face the problem of the fusion of various activities in one single space (e.g., the vivid discussion of the lithic exploitation areas) or a total absence of traces of certain activities.

Settlement Patterns

Several authors have stressed the differences in the use of the landscape by Neanderthals and modern humans (Gamble, 1986; Lieberman and Shea, 1994) and the extent of their organization and planning (Binford, 1989).

For Moravia, some important data arise from studies of changes in landscape use. In site location, there is an important difference between the Late Middle Paleolithic and the EUP (cf. Figures 4.1, 5.1, 5.2): while most of the well-documented Late Middle Paleolithic sites, both Mousterian and Micoquian, were in caves and in karstic regions, the EUP settlements had moved to open landscape, with special attention to marginal highlands at 250–400 m above sea level, enabling the exploitation of a variety of altitudinal zones and environments and a better control over the movements of game herds in the adjacent lowlands (territorial type B, Chapter 8). At favorable sites, we observe superimposed reoccupation (Stránská skála). The loess deposits, however, were limited in such exposed areas, and, in consequence much of the evidence is now found on the surface.

The "out-of-the-caves" phenomenon observed at the beginning of the Upper Paleolithic in Moravia may find some parallels in Lower Austria and southern Poland, but hardly elsewhere in Europe. Therefore, the reasons for the move should be searched for in the specific geomorphological patterns of the area, and in its new functions in both resource control and interregional communication. With regard to the data in lithic raw-material imports, the move may also imply a change from the more radiating mobility pattern centered on a cave to a more circulating pattern over longer distances and in a free landscape (cf. Lieberman and Shea, 1994). Caves were visited occasionally, perhaps only seasonally (small assemblages and single artifacts at Pod hradem, Cave 184, Křížova Cave). Single leaf-points if found in caves (Turold, Rytířská Caves) or in exposed positions below rock walls (Horní Věstonice), were traditionally attributed to the Szeletian; however, with the new evidence of a later wave of leaf-point production during the Late Gravettian and the Epiaurignacian (Chapter 6), these sites may also belong to a later stage of cave occupation, around the last glacial maximum.

From a quantitative viewpoint, well-documented Late Middle Paleolithic sites are generally rare throughout Moravia, so that the dramatic increase in the number of sites and artifacts in the EUP suggests a rapid demographic growth between 45,000 and 30,000 B.P. It seems that the Upper Paleolithic hunters generally appreciated the geographic advantages that a geomorphological corridor such as Moravia offered. However, there were slight differences in the behavior of the various EUP cultures in the Moravian landscape: the Bohunican sites are not numerous, but in some areas around lithic outcrops, they become densely clustered and contain large industrial assemblages (several tens of thousands of artifacts at a site; Svoboda, 1983). In the Szeletian, certain parts of Moravia, western Slovakia, Silesia, and Hungary were covered by dense settlement networks that include sparse occupation traces in nearby caves. In Moravia, an almost continuous chain of Szeletian sites follows the exposed eastern margins of the Bohemian Massif, from the Krumlov area in the southwest to the Prostějov area in the northeast. Furthermore, the Szeletian penetrated into the Bohemian Massif deeper than any other Upper Paleolithic culture (the Boskovice Furrow) and intensively exploited the lithic sources there (Figures 5.1, 5.15). A complex settlement pattern with a central site on a marked elevation, surrounded by a cluster or related minisites, is quite typical of both the Bohunician and the Szeletian. The distribution of the Aurignacian is the widest and the densest, especially in the Moravian–Lower Austrian territory, and in eastern Slovakia; there are few Aurignacian sites in Bohemia as well. In Moravia, the distribution shows a structured pattern of spatially delimited and dense regional clusters (Figure 5.2).

The literature traditionally stresses the appearance of structures in the form of dumps, hearths, pits, and huts from the beginning of the Upper Paleolithic onward. Excavations of living floors at the Bohunician and Szeletian sites of Stránská skála and

Vedrovice (Figures 5.8–5.10) yielded settlement units formed by hearths and artifact concentrations, but no traces of dwelling structures (Svoboda 1987d, 1991e; Valoch, 1993b). More data on hearths, partly damaged by earth movements, are available from the Aurignacian living floors (Figure 5.11; Stránská skála IIa, IIIa, Milovice), and especially from Stratzing in Lower Austria (Neugebauer-Maresch, 1993), where they are found undisturbed and provided with well-preserved stone alignments. In association with the hearths with artifact accumulations, and with areas of larger thickness of the cultural layer, Stratzing provides small pits, probably boiling pits, as we know them from later Gravettian sites. Stratzing actually offers the optimal conditions for solving the question of Aurignacian living-site organization and features within the Lower Austrian–Moravian area.

The Lithic Exploitation Areas

The changes observed during the Early Upper Paleolithic are twofold: first, a significant increase in the intensity and effectiveness of local raw-material exploitation, especially of the various Moravian cherts, and second, the introduction of systematic long-distance lithic importations (see Figure 90).

In 1983, the places of concentration of stone industries at the raw material outcrops, mostly of specialized workshop character (primary workshops), were defined as lithic exploitation areas (Figures 5.12–5.15; Svoboda, 1983). They were defined as regions either in an area several kilometers from localized raw-material

Figure 5.8. Vedrovice V: A concentration of the Szeletian industry during excavation by K. Valoch.

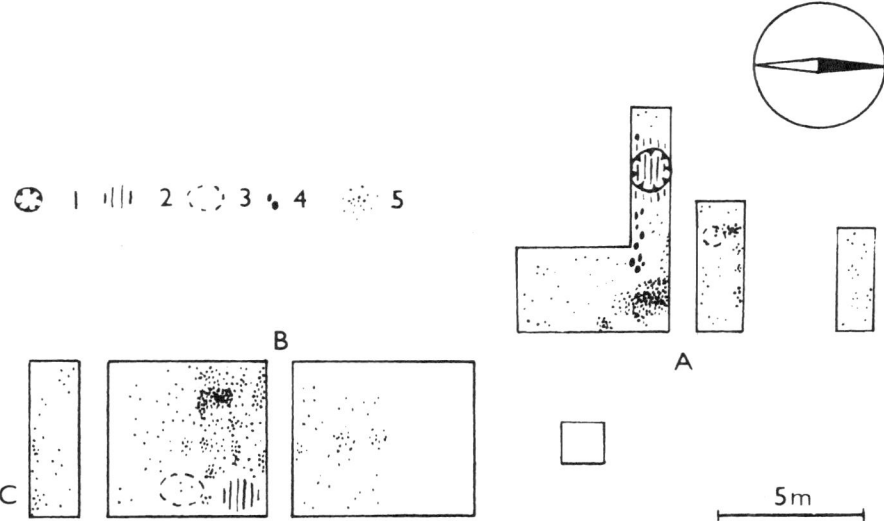

Figure 5.9. Stránská skála III: General plan of the Bohunician living floor, units A, B, C; 1—depression; 2—charcoal concentration; 3—concentration of imported lithic material; 4—ocher; 5—lithic artifacts.

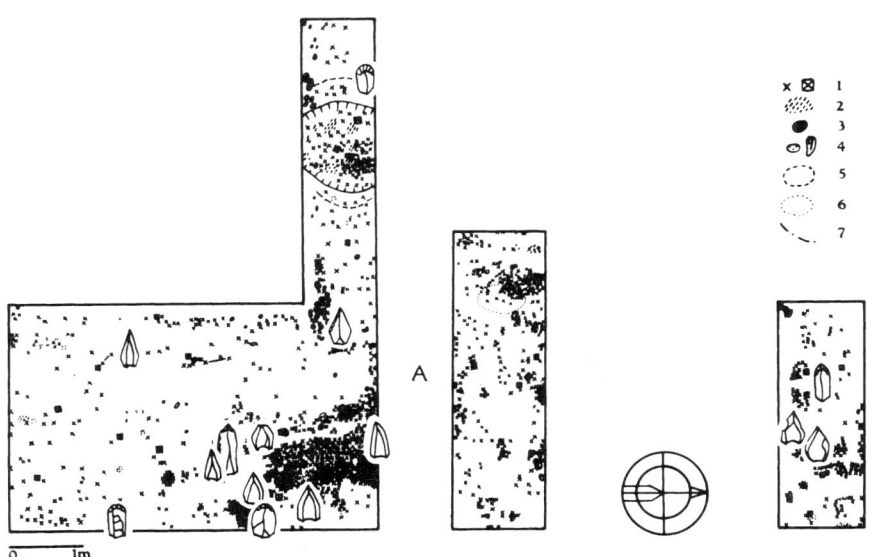

Figure 5.10. Stránská skála III: Detailed plan of the Bohunician unit A. 1—lithic artifacts; 2—charcoal; 3—ocher; 4—bones; 5–cumulation of charcoal; 6—cumulation of cherts of the Krumlovský les type; 7—unit boundaries.

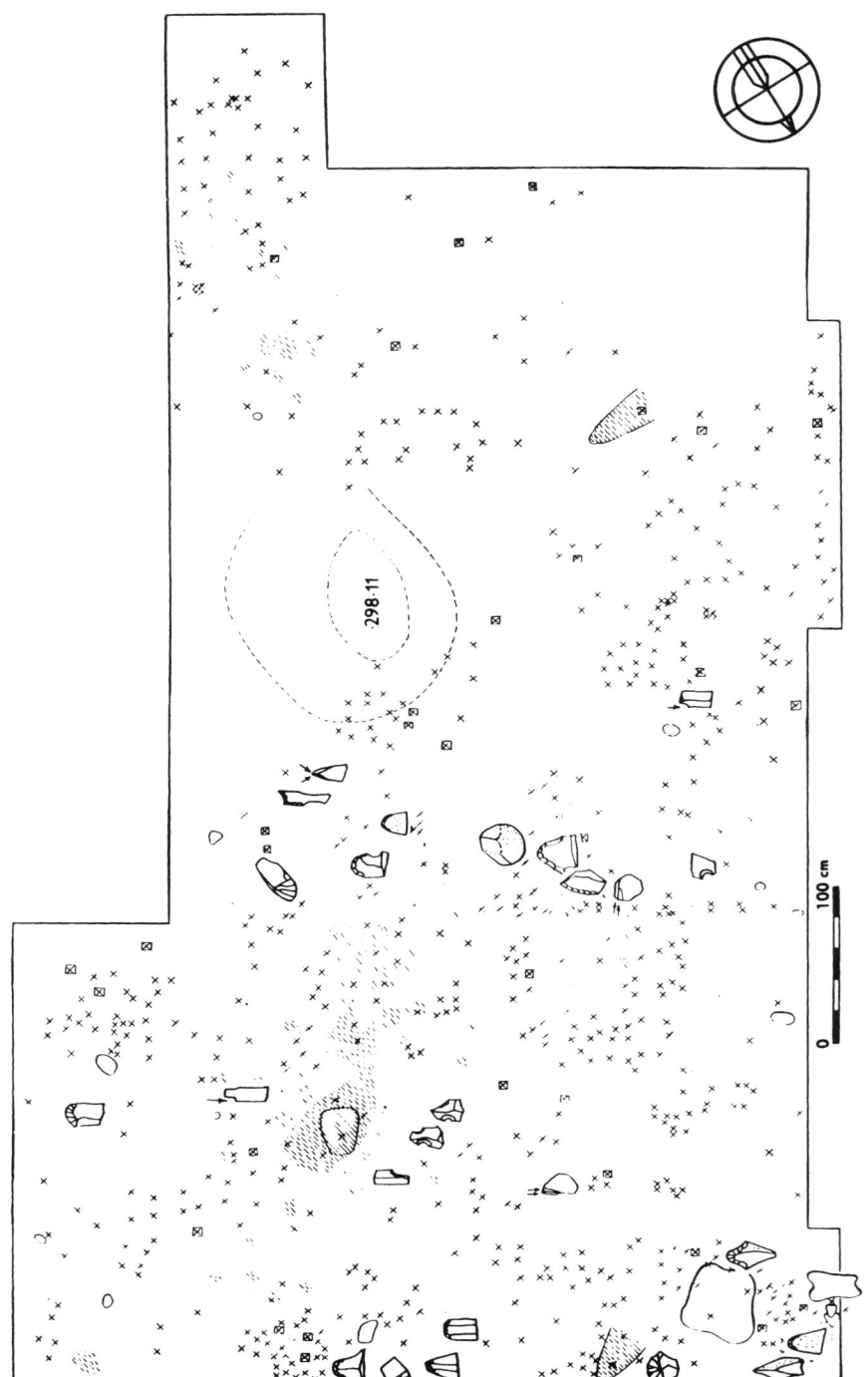

Figure 5.11. Stránská skála IIIa: Plan of the Aurignacian living floor. For key, see Figure 5.10.

Figure 5.12. Stránská skála exploitation area: Map of sites showing the location of outcrops (1—Jurassic cherts; 2—river gravels) and representations of the various lithic materials in lithic industries (3—Jurassic cherts; 4—radiolarite; 5—Cretaceous cherts, 6—Krumlovský les cherts; 7—others). A—Stránská skála IIIa, B—Stránská skála III; C—Podstránská; D—Líšeň; F—Maloměřice, Borky; G—Maloměřice, Občiny; H—Bohunice; I—Tvarožná.

outcrops or in places with a concentration of nonlocalized raw materials, where numerous industries were made mostly of local rocks; some of these industries have a more pronounced workshop character (number of raw material pieces, precores, cores, debris, and nonretouched flakes of larger dimension). The reason that the technologies used at the various outcrops are not exactly the same seems to be "social-geographic" patterning rather the qualities of the materials. The exploitation areas of Stránská skála (cherts) and Ondratice (quartzites) were settled by the Bohunicians, and the Levalloisian-leptolithic technology was applied there; at roughly the same time, the Krumlovský les and Bořitov exploitation areas (both with chert outcrops) document a Szeletian occupation and the use of specific Szeletian techniques, especially for leaf-point production.

A look into the possible spatial differences in lithic procurement was realized with materials from the Ondratice and Stránská skála exploitation areas (Figures 5.12 and 5.13; Svoboda, 1980, 1987d). A settlement complex at Líšeň, about 2 km from the Stránská skála outcrop, was compared, from the point of view of production dynamics, with the primary workshop directly at the source: site Stránská Skála (SS) III. It appeared that the first products of core preparation (prepared raw-material pieces, cortical flakes) and also the last ones (core residuals) were more frequent at Stránská skála than at Líšeň. Furthermore, retouches were rarely observed on the blanks produced at SS III, since retouched tools here were made of imported materials. Another site, SS IIIa (Figure 5.16), was later analyzed by the same method. Surprisingly, this site, even though located near site III, yielded a smaller percentage of primary products and a higher percentage of residuals and last-series flakes. Unlike at

Figure 5.13. Map of the Ondratice exploitation area. A—EUP sites; B—cumulations of quartzite blocs.

SS III, blanks of local material were transformed directly into retouched tools. In general, the differences in production dynamics at sites within a single lithic exploitation area are minor. Logically, a radical difference is observed at later sites, such as the Gravettian sites, based solely on the long-distance import of materials.

Further evidence is supplied by studies of lithic distribution areas in wider vicinities of the outcrops. The Stránská skála chert, as an optimal raw material for study (it emerges from well-localized outcrops), clearly shows a linear distribution along the margins of the Bohemian Massif related to the Bohunician technological influence (Oliva, 1981a; Svoboda, 1983, 1987d). The distribution of the other Moravian materials is much broader, and the interpretation is more difficult, because of the more dispersed occurrence of these outcrops and their redeposit by natural, especially fluviatile, processes.

The Aurignacian already demonstrates a highly differentiated and variable pat-

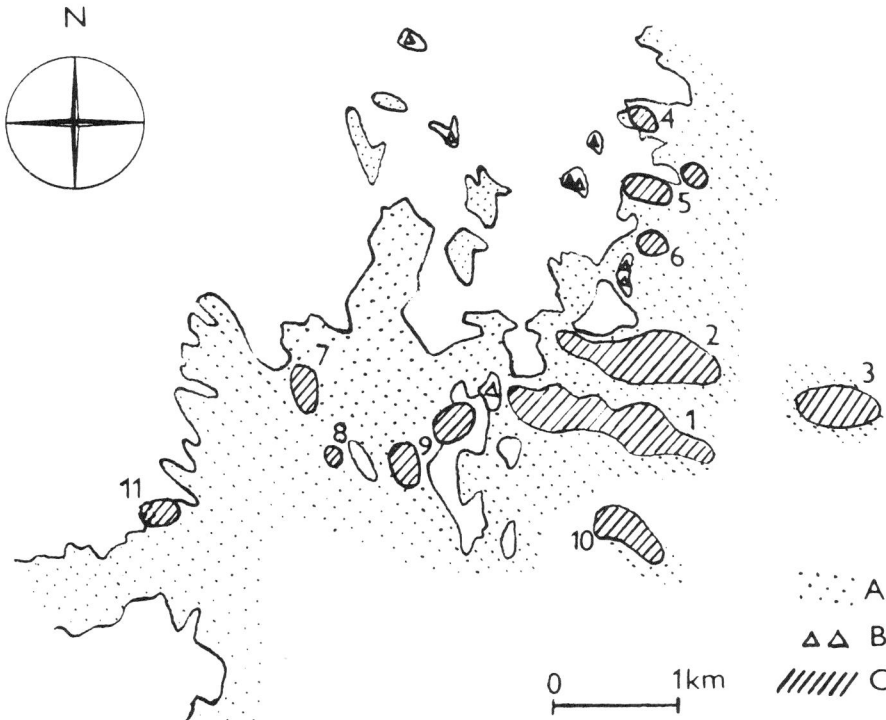

Figure 5.14. Map of the Krumlovský les exploitation area. A—extension of the Upper Tertiary deposits with chert pebbles; B—silicified breccias; C—EUP sites (1–3—Jezeřany I–III; 4–6—Maršovice I–III; 7–11—Vedrovice I–V).

tern of both raw and material exploitation and imports. Some lithic exploitation areas of Moravia (Stránská skála, Krumlovský les: Svoboda, 1987d; Valoch, 1985a) were still settled, and the raw material continued to be worked locally, but the Stránská skála cherts were more randomly exported outside the area. Some Aurignacian sites, typologically "evolved" and probably more recent, show an increasing dependence on exotic lithic materials, such as radiolarite at Tvarožná (Valoch, 1976b; Blades, 1993), rock crystal at Nová Dědina (Klíma, 1977a), and especially flint of northern Moravian and southern Polish origin. This tendency should not be surprising, given the presumed dating of these sites: they may be contemporary with the Gravettian, a culture almost totally dependent on lithic imports. Clearly, there is a social background behind these trends.

A usual assumption here is that evidence of long-distance transport reflects the existence of open networks of social interactions (Gamble, 1986; Mellars, 1989). If exotic rocks appear at a site in limited quantities, one might infer that gift giving or

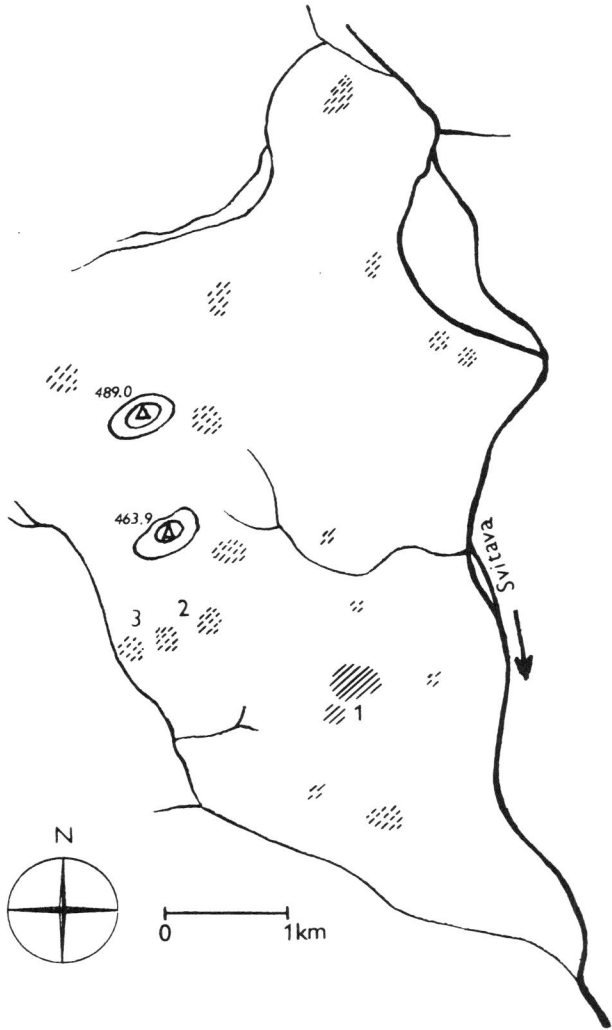

Figure 5.15. Map of the Bořitov exploitation area. The subsoil is formed by Permian and Cretaceous deposits with cherts. EUP sites: 1—Bořitov-Horky; 2—Bořitov-Písky; 3—Bořitov I.

some other kind of exchange network among different groups was involved. Similar conclusions have been suggested on the basis of nonutilitarian lithics and marine shells from extreme distances in Western and Central Europe.

Because of the amount of imported material that forms a major part of the production base at some Aurignacian sites, and especially in the Gravettian, greater group mobility seems more probable than extended exchange (Svoboda, 1994b:72).

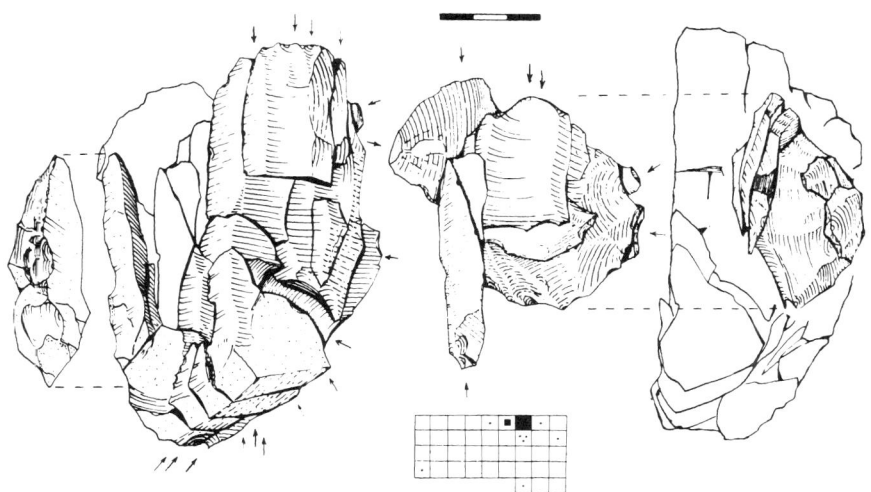

Figure 5.16. Refitting from Stránská skála IIIa documents the Bohunician technology as a conceptual fusion of Upper Paleolithic and Levalloisian principles..

Optimally, such mobility should be studied in relation to the complex of resource exploitation activities, namely, to game migrations and hunting strategies.

Subsistence

Because obtaining nourishment is one of the most important aspects of adaptation, the investigation of changes in subsistence behavior—namely, the beginning of hunting specialization—should enlighten us on the beginning of the Upper Paleolithic. Unfortunately, because of unfavorable conditions for bone preservation in the EUP open-air loess sites in Moravia, it is difficult to reconstruct the composition of the hunted fauna and the diet during this period. In the sites of southern Germany, Hahn (1987) notes the dominance of reindeer, horse, and, less frequently, mammoth and rhinoceros, but there are no signs of heavy reliance on a single species. Where bones have been preserved in Moravian living sites (Stránská skála, Bohunice, Milovice), they are single specimens of horse and mammoth.

Changes in hunting strategies may be inferred indirectly from the facts that caves no longer served as the hunters' home bases (Chapter 4), and that the settlement network moved to strategic positions controlling the lowlands and aimed at eliminating haphazard factors by operating in larger territories.

Sporadically, the hunters in Moravia penetrated the caves occupied by bears, but to what degree their aim was to hunt these animals in particular is open to discussion (Wankel, 1892; Allsworth-Jones, 1986). Gargett (1994) recently studied the bone accumulation at Pod hradem Cave, where 60%–80% of the bone assemblage is of cave bears. He concluded that the carcasses of animals that had died during hibernation were scavenged by carnivores, predominantly wolves, and that the modified bones have not been found in an articulated state. He suggests that more effort should be made to understand processes—both natural and artificial—that are beyond the observed patternings.

Symbols, Rituals, and Art

As the above discussion suggests, the role of social factors during the Middle and Upper Paleolithic transition is most clearly visible in the relatively rapid spread of various art forms (Hahn, 1986) and items of personal decoration (White, 1993), first in certain parts of Europe, and later over larger areas of Eurasia. We may generally suppose that the population increase, population movements, and technological and social changes at the beginning of the Upper Paleolithic were basically related to the need for new means of communication and, consequently, to the origin of art.

However, evidence of artistic creativity during the transitional period (Szeletian and Bohunician) is still scarce and seems no more meaningful than in the Middle Paleolithic. At the Bohunician site of Stránská skála III, several kilograms of imported yellow and red ocher pieces were found (Svoboda, 1987d). The role of coloring material at a profane place like a workshop located at the lithic extraction site is unknown, but ethnographic analogies suggest that both utilitarian and nonutilitarian activities were performed at workshop sites.

It was not before the Aurignacian that the earliest realistic art—plastic ivory carvings of animals, humans and animal-human beings provided with cutmarks and symbolical patterns—flourished in the cave sites of southern Germany (Vogelherd, Geissenklösterle, Hohlenstein: Marshack, 1972; Hahn, 1986). In 1988, a human figure cut of amphibolitic schist was also found at Stratzing, Austria, at the southern margin of a rich accumulation of artifacts and features (Neugebauer-Maresch, 1988). Fine pebbles, one of them with a linear engraving, come from Grossweikersdorf, Austria (Brandtner, personal communication, 1992).

Despite the high density of sites in Moravia, no Aurignacian art is recorded from this territory, possibly because of the unfavorable conditions for organic material preservation at the open-air sites. An evidence of Aurignacian personal ornamentation, however, comes from the Mladeč Caves (Figures 5.17 and 5.18; Appendix A),

Figure 5.17. Mladeč I: A point of the Mladeč type. Photo by the Natural History Museum, Vienna.

Figure 5.18. Mladeč I: Pierced pendants of animal teeth. Photo by the Natural History Museum, Vienna.

where human skeletal remains were found together with fauna, bone weapons and implements, and about 20 perforated teeth of beaver, reindeer, wolf, horse, and bear (Szombathy, 1925; White, 1993). The finds lay in a large dome (site Mladeč I), at the foot of a debris cone accumulated under a chimney. The movement of sediments within the cave, therefore, affected the original positions, and recent interpretations are biased by the long time interval since the discovery. Nevertheless, the association provides interesting evidence of the emergence of "self"-definition and social display. There was probably an analogical situation in the partly destroyed cave Mladeč II (Knies, 1905), and in the Koněprusy Caves, Bohemia: again, fossil human remains lay in a debris cone under a chimney, together with a few scattered lithics and a fossil shell.

From the time of its discovery, the situation at Mladeč has evoked discussion. Bayer (1925) interpreted the site as a settlement and a burial site accessible by an entrance. J. Szombathy (1925) added the possibility that anthropophagy was practiced at the site. According to Smyčka (1922), the bodies had been thrown into the cave through the chimneys. In 1937, Skutil (1938c:32) found a few archaeological artifacts at the present entrance of the cave; these suggest that the cave may have been accessible in the same way that it is today. Oliva (1989b) supported this interpretation by announcing that there are parietal wall paintings of signs and lines, Paleolithic in his view, inside the cave. The complex situation inside the dome, however, does not correspond to a settlement nor to a frequented site (Appendix A). The almost total absence of reliable traces of activities, the lack of lithic implements, and especially the pattern of redeposition under the chimney (as far as we are able to reconstruct it), supported by analogical situations in two other caves of the same period, would favor instead the original view of Smyčka. It is even possible that throwing dead bodies into caves through the chimneys was practiced repeatedly and had a ritual meaning in that particular area and period.

Chapter **6**

Culmination and Decline of the Upper Paleolithic
The Gravettians and Epigravettians

The most complex record of a successful Upper Paleolithic adaptation is offered by evidence from the Gravettian sites. In fact, the Middle to Upper Paleolithic transitional process did not end before the Gravettian (Svoboda, 1993b).

The availability of rich evidence covering a wide range of behaviors is due to a fortunate coincidence of activities (such as settlement aggregation, more specialized resource exploitation, and a diversity of ritual and artistic behavior) and favorable depositional circumstances for the preservation of their remains (large sites covered by thick loess deposits). From a developmental perspective, the later Gravettian is important to our understanding of change in adaptations before and around the last glacial maximum (Jochim, 1987; Soffer, 1987; Soffer and Gamble, 1990).

Although Gravettian sites such as Předmostí and Jaroslavice were among the first recorded in Moravia, the description of this culture began relatively late and is still in the process of modification. First identified as being from the "mammoth age" (Wankel, 1884), these sites were later considered Upper Aurignacian (Absolon, 1938a,b). Several authors observed more-or-less important typological and stylistic differences from the typical Aurignacian (Bayer, 1925; Knies, 1925) and even suggested local names (Aggsbachian). The term *Gravettian* however, as suggested by Garrod (Prošek and Ložek, 1954) and sometimes further defined by phrases such as "eastern Central European" and "Lower Austrian-Moravian-Slovakian" (Felgenhauer, 1951), was not applied until after World War II. Subsequently, Klíma (1959e) and Delporte (1959) used the term *Pavlovian*.

Chronological subdivisions of the Gravettian (Pavlovian) have been suggested by Klíma (1961c), Valoch (1961c), Kozlowski (1986), and Otte (1981, 1991). Bárta (1987) separated an earlier and a later Gravettian stage in Slovakia, while Kozlowski and Sobczyk (1987) named the earlier stage Pavlovian and the later Kostenkian. Soffer

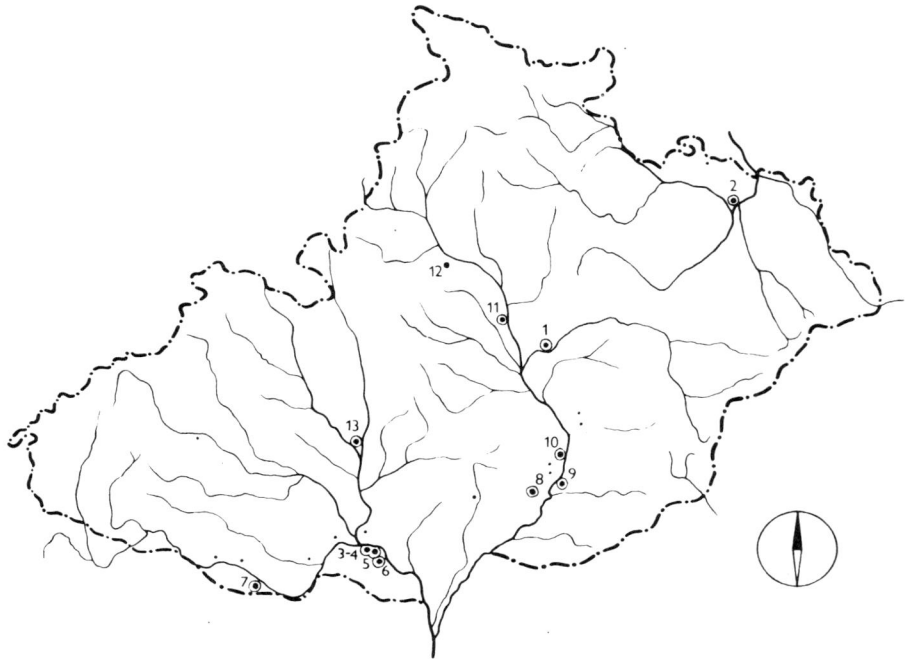

Figure 6.1. Map of the important Gravettian sites. Circle: Excavated site; point: Surface site. 1—Předmostí; 2—Petřkovice; 3-4—Dolní Věstonice I–II; 5—Pavlov; 6—Milovice; 7—Jaroslavice; 8—Boršice; 9–Jarošov; 10–Spytihněv; 11—Blatec; 12—Mladeč (Plavatisko); 13–Brno (burials II–III).

(1993) wrote about a Willendorf-Pavlov-Kostenki-Avdeevo unity but emphasized its inner diversification. Svoboda et al. (1994) and Svoboda (1996) repeated the succession of the Pavlovian and the Kostenkian stages of the Gravettian, followed, after 20,000 B.P., by the Epigravettian.

Beginning around 30,000 B.P., the Gravettian in the middle Danube area represents one of its earliest occurrences in Europe, and most archaeologists agree that it is of local origin (an eastern origin was recently suggested by Otte). Typologically oriented archaeologists therefore searched for a predecessor and found it mostly in the Szeletian of Moravia (Valoch, 1981a) or in the upper layer of the Szeleta Cave (Svoboda and Simán, 1989). This view, however, cannot be supported by physical anthropology, even though we have relatively large samples of the Gravettian population: there are no fossils of Szeletian predecessors (according to some authors, Szeletians may have been late Neanderthals), and the Aurignacian sample from Mladeč is polytypic. In our present state of knowledge, especially with our lack of data on the late Szeletian, it seems more appropriate to see the Gravettian as a product of complex interactions in an area of several competing groups.

The comparatively large number of data from well-preserved settlements has evoked discussion of topics that could hardly be mentioned with the limited evidence from earlier sites, and that are held on a truly international level. These concern the complex process of adaptation, hunting, lithic raw-material imports, the organization of the settlements, seasonality, rituals, and art.

In analyzing the settlements, Absolon (1938a,b, 1945b) contributed to the knowledge of their spatial organization by inventing a systematic unearthing of parallel longitudinal zones. Klíma (e.g., 1963b,f) developed this method by excavating in squares and recognizing hearths and outlining features, mostly interpreted as dwellings. Whereas Klíma (1984a) has reconstructed the various dwellings as being more-or-less contemporary, forming a sort of a village, the actual research aims at a more precise understanding of their chronological relationships.

A very old (and still unresolved) problem in understanding Gravettian hunting concerns the nature and origin of the mammoth bone accumulations adjacent to settlements: whether they are due to human activity (Wankel, 1884; Absolon, 1945b; Klíma, 1969a) or to natural deaths (Steenstrup, 1890; Wankel, 1890; Soffer, 1993; Mithen, 1993).

In studies of art, the approaches used in Central Europe seem to have been less variable than in Western Europe (cf. Conkey, 1987). Archaeological thinking has been influenced by hunting-magic theories more profoundly than by all later structuralist and analytical models. Therefore, elements suggesting symbolic wounding and weapons have been continuously searched for in the art, such as the deep incision made by a sharpened stick in the ceramic lion head from Dolní Věstonice (Absolon, 1945b:17). More recently, the understanding of the rituals associated with artistic creations has been enriched by technologically oriented studies on an international level (Vandiver et al., 1990; Soffer et al., 1993; Soffer and Vandiver, 1994).

STRATIGRAPHIC BACKGROUND

Stratigraphically (Table 6.1), the period we are concerned with here is correlated principally with the upper Stránská skála soil of the interpleniglacial (including Middle Aurignacian and Early Gravettian, with C-14 datings between 32,500 and 29,000 B.P.; see Chapter 5; Haesaerts, 1990; Svoboda, 1991e, 1993a) and the deposit of the last loess cover (Upper Aurignacian and Gravettian), up to the last glacial maximum (20,000–18,000 B.P.: Soffer and Gamble, 1990). The overlying loess cover was studied in detail by Klíma (1958a, 1969a; Klíma et al., 1962) at Dolní Věstonice and by P. Haesaerts (1990) at Willendorf and Grubgraben. Both authors observed several pseudogley horizons, eolian sand, and solifluction layers within the loess. Further excavations at Dolní Věstonice II and Milovice repeatedly revealed further pseudogley horizons (Smolíková, 1991), obviously representing periods of increased humidity rather than increased temperature.

Whereas the most complete chronological sequences are recorded from multi-layer sites such as Willendorf (Haesaerts, 1990) or Molodova V, at the large Moravian sites a single cultural horizon evolved during longer periods of interrupted or limited

Table 6.1. Comparative Chronological Table of the Gravettian

B.P.	Willendorf, site II	D. Věstonice, site I	D. Věstonice, sites II and III	Pavlov I, a,b	Předmostí, sites I and II	Milovice	Petřkovice	Spadzista, site C2	Molodova, site V
20,000									
21,000					X		20,790		
22,000	layer 9				X	22,100			
23,000									layer 7: 23,000
24,000			Site III: 24,560				23,370	layer III: 24,040	23,700
		Middle and			Site II:			24,380	
25,000	Layer 8: 25,800	upper parts: 25,820 25,950	1. unit: 25,570–25,740 Unit LP: 26,390	25,020-b 25,530-b	25,040 Site I:	25,220			
26,000			Triple Burial: 26,640 Majority of units: 26,900–27,100	26,170-a 26,620-b 26,650-b 26,730-b	26,320 26,870				
27,000	Layer 7	Lower part: 27,250	Units A–C: 27,660					Layer IV	
28,000	Layer 6		Lower part: 28,300						Layer 9: 28,100
29,000	Layer 5: 30,500	Lower part: 29,300	Lower part: 29,000						Layer 9: 29,650

Note X = undated occupation.

loess deposits. The matter originates from anthropogenic activities, and as shown by Smolíková, the matrix also includes soil particles. Horizontal movements (solifluction) and other deformations of the layer are visible, but archaeological features such as hearths, pits, or human skeletons are little or not affected by these deformations as much as would be supposed. Stronger deformations along vertical fissures took place immediately at the end of the occupation of Dolní Věstonice (DV) I and Petřkovice, before the deposit of the last loess cover.

The chronological relationships of the various settlement units at the large Moravian sites (Klíma, 1963b,f, 1994a; Svoboda, 1991b, 1994a) have been studied on the basis of stratigraphic observations such as the overlapping of slope-slipped loessic blocks (DV I), the overlapping of settlement units (unit 1 and 2 at DV II), the thickness of the underlying loess separating the cultural layer from the 30,000-year-old soil below (DV I and II), and radiocarbon dating. The C-14 samples, all of charcoal, were measured in several laboratories, but the Groningen data usually present higher values, smaller deviations, and a more meaningful developmental pattern. Therefore, in order to make comparisons, we have based our chronological framework on the Groningen data (Tables 6.1 and 6.2). Then we have correlated the C-14 data with typological evidence from the spatial analysis of some sites, with changes in the lithic raw-material selection, and with the environmental data.

On the basis of the new datings and comparisons, it seems that DV I and II were repeatedly settled during relatively long intervals between 29,000 and 25,000 B.P., DV III around 24,500 B.P., Pavlov I during the surprisingly short time span between 27,000 and 25,000, Předmostí between 27,000 and 25,000 (and once more around 20,000 B.P.), Milovice between 25,000 and 22,000, and Petřkovice between 23,500 and 21,000 B.P.. Finer, within-site chronological relationships have been searched for among the individual settlement units on the basis of spatial relationships, typology, and refittings.

As a result, it is suggested that the Gravettian be separated in two major stages, both prior to the upper pleniglacial maximum: the Pavlovian and the Willendorfian-Kostenkian. Eventually, the Pavlovian may be subdivided in two substages.

The Epigravettian sites (Table 6.4; Kozlowski 1986) are located in the uppermost parts of the last loess, after the upper pleniglacial maximum, and are dated to 18,000 B.P. (Stránská skála IV) and 14,500 B.P. (Brno-Vídeňská Koněvova and Velké Pavlovice: Svoboda et al., 1994:Table 16; Valoch, 1980b).

ENVIRONMENT

The data on climate and vegetational cover by the end of the Würmian interpleniglacial suggest relatively favorable conditions: the existence of large mammal herds, as documented in the paleontological record of both archaeological and natural contexts. According to R. Musil (1994), the animal composition (mammoths, reindeer, foxes, wolves, and hares) fits well into such landscape reconstructions. Even if pedogenetical processes ended right in the initial stages of soil development, the

Table 6.2. Gravettian Datings (Mostly of Charcoal) from Lower Austria and Moravia (Table Based Only on Groningen Datings)

GrN 11193	Willendorf II, layer 5	30,500 + 900–800 B.P.
GrN 17803	Willendorf II, layer 6	27,600 ± 480 B.P.
GrN 17804	Willendorf II, layer 7	28,560 ± 420 B.P.
GrN 11191	Willendorf II, layer 8	25,800 ± 800 B.P.
GrN 17801	Willendorf II, layer 8	25,230 ± 320 B.P.
GrN 17802	Willendorf II, layer 8	25,660 ± 350 B.P.
GrN 3011	Krems, Wachtberg	27,400 ± 300 B.P.
GrN 2513	Aggsbach	26,800 ± 200 B.P.
GrN 1354	Aggsbach	25,760 ± 170 B.P.
GrN 11189	Dolní Věstonice I, lower part	31,700 ± 1000 B.P.
GrN 18187	Dolní Věstonice I, lower part	29,300 + 750–690 B.P.
GrN 18188	Dolní Věstonice I, lower part	27,250 + 590–550 B.P.
GrN 1286	Dolní Věstonice I, middle part	25,820 ± 170 B.P.
GrN 18189	Dolní Věstonice I, upper part	25,950 + 630–580 B.P.
GrN 2092	Dolní Věstonice II, brickyard	28,300 ± 300 B.P.
GrN 2598	Dolní Věstonice II, brickyard	29,000 ± 200 B.P.
GrN 13962	Dolní Věstonice II, units A–C	27,660 ± 80 B.P.
GrN 14831	Dolní Věstonice II, triple burial	26,640 ± 110 B.P.
GrN 15276	Dolní Věstonice II, burial DV XVI	25,570 ± 280 B.P.
GrN 15277	Dolní Věstonice II, unit 1	25,740 ± 210 B.P.
GrN 15279	Dolní Věstonice II, unit 2	26,920 ± 250 B.P.
GrN 15278	Dolní Věstonice II, unit 3	27,070 ± 300 B.P.
GrN 21122	Dolní Věstonice II, unit 4	26,970±200 B.P.
GrN 15324	Dolní Věstonice II, southern hearth	27,070 ± 170 B.P.
GrN 15325	Dolní Věstonice II, eastern hearth	26,970 ± 160 B.P.
GrN 15327	Dolní Věstonice II, western hearth	27,080 ± 170 B.P.
GrN 21123	Dolní Věstonice II, unit LP/1-4	26,390 ± 190 B.P.
GrN 14830	Dolní Věstonice II, mammoth deposit	26,100 ± 200 B.P.
GrN 20392	Dolní Věstonice III	24,560 + 660–610 B.P.
GrA 192	Pavlov I, 1953 area (b)	25,530 ± 110 B.P.
GrN 19539	Pavlov I, 1953 area (b)	26,650 ± 230 B.P.
GrN 1272	Pavlov I, 1956 area (b)	26,620 ± 230 B.P.
GrN 1325	Pavlov I, 1956 area (b)	25,020 ± 150 B.P.
GrN 4812	Pavlov I, 1956 area (b)	26,730 ± 250 B.P.
GrN 20391	Pavlov I, 1957 area (a)	26,170 ± 450 B.P.
GrN 6801	Předmostí I, cemetery	26,870 ± 250 B.P.
GrN 6852	Předmostí I, cemetery	26,320 ± 240 B.P.
GrN 19540	Petřkovice, 1953	20,790 ± 270 B.P.
GrA 891	Petřkovice, 1994	23,370 ± 160 B.P.
GrN 14824	Milovice, feature G	25,220 ± 280 B.P.
GrN 14825	Milovice, mammoth deposit D	22,100 ± 1100 B.P.

Table 6.3. Late Aurignacian Datings (Bone, Antler) from Lower Austria

GrN 6660	Langmannersdorf	20,260 ± 200 B.P.
GrN 6659	Langmannersdorf	20,580 ± 170 B.P.
VRI 676	Horn, Raabserstrasse	23,210 ± 510 B.P.
VRI 1272	Alberndorf	20,500 ± 1400 B.P.
VRI 1536	Alberndorf	25,350 ± 450 B.P.

vegetation suggests a milder environment compared to that of preceding periods. Pollen and charcoal analyses from the Gravettian cultural layers at the south Moravian sites, and from contemporary peat sediments in the nearby core at Bulhary, show that the landscape was partly covered by wooded areas (usually more than 50%), with conifers (*Pinus cembra* and *Pinus sylvestris*) dominating, as well as numerous grains of *Picea, Juniperus, Betula*, and *Larix*. Decidous taxa were also present, including a few more pretendous species (oak, beach, and yew), probably restricted to favorable locations. Open landscapes were covered predominantly by *Poaceae, Cyperaceae, Artemisia*, and *Centaurea*. Finally, these spectra also showed that the quantity of hygrophilic plants and spores in the spectra was profoundly affected by the immediate environments surrounding the sampled localities (Rybníčková and Rybníček, 1991; Svobodová, 1991a,b; Opravil, 1994; Mason et al., 1994).

Studies of the mollusks from Dolní Věstonice, in contrast, suggest colder environmental conditions than the plants (cold subarctic tundra: Kovanda, 1991). The reason may be climatic instability during the longer time span of the deposit of the cultural layer (see rthe C-14 datings) or the variability of the altitudinal zones in the Pavlovské Hills area (Svoboda, 1995b).

In the faunal evidence of the later Gravettian period, Musil (1994) observed an increase in the number of deer, elk, reindeer, and bovids. It appears that such a fauna requires a slightly different landscape. Even if the paleobotanical evidence for this period is still scarce, the situation at Předmostí (samples 6 and 7: Svobodová, in Svoboda et al., 1994) suggests a decrease in arboreal pollen (from 31% to 16%) and an increase in heliophilous plants.

Table 6.4. Epigravettian Datings (Bone) from Lower Austria and Moravia

AA-1746	Grubgraben AL 4	18,960 ± 290 B.P.
Lv-1680	Grubgraben AL 4	18,400 ± 330 B.P.
Lv-1660	Grubgraben AL 3–4	18,170 ± 300 B.P.
GrN-13945	Stránská skála IV	18,220 ± 120 B.P.
GrN-14351	Stránská skála IV	17,740 ± 90 B.P.
GrN-9350	Brno-Vídeňská (Koněvova)	14,450 ± 90 B.P.
GrN-16139	Velké Pavlovice	14,460 ± 230 B.P.

During the Epigravettian, we observe the disappearance of large mammoth-bone deposits, and hunting becomes oriented to reindeer (Grubgraben) and horse (Grubgraben, Stránská skála IV). A pollen analysis from Stránská skála IV, a site open to horse hunting, documents the presence of *Tilia, Betula, Pinus, Salix, Corylus,* and *Alnus,* as well as a large number of herbs and other plants of open landscapes.

TECHNO/TYPOLOGICAL INTERACTIONS THROUGH TIME

At Willendorf II, a continuous loess deposit, dating to 30,000–20,000 B.P., enabled excavators to separate five stratigraphic layers (5–9), stylistically assigned to the Gravettian (Felgenhauer, 1959). Thus, all efforts in Gravettian chronology should combine the vertical stratigraphy at Willendorf with the spatial analysis at the Moravian sites (Table 6.5; Otte, 1981, 1991; Svoboda, 1994b, 1996). The numbers of endscrapers, burins, and backed implements reach their maximum in the lower and upper parts of the sequence (layers 5 and 9). There is an increase of retouched blades in the middle part of the sequence, reaching its maximum in layer 8; a very marked increase of pointed blades, with a maximum in layer 7; and a smaller increase of sidescrapers in both these layers. Some of the retouch style is elaborate, including artifacts with a steep retouch (see Felgenhauer, 1959:Figures 33 and 35). The typologically significant shouldered points of the Kostenki type do not appear before layer 9, and an even larger number of them was collected in the nearby Willendorf I site. On the basis of the data of Zirkl (in Felgenhauer, 1959) and, later, Svoboda's own analysis, it should be added that a parallel change occurs in the raw materials, with flint dominating at the base and top of the sequence (layers 5 and 9) and radiolarite in the middle (layers 6–8). With respect to both typology and raw materials, we suggest a separation of the Willendorf sequence into three chronological units: layers 5, 6–8, and 9.

In further typological comparisons of the Gravettian (Table 6.6) and the Epigravettian, certain techniques and types show cross-cultural parallels to other cultures and cultural complexes:

Table 6.5. Development of Significant Typological Indices in the Stratigraphy of Willendorf (in %)

Layer	5	6	7	8	9
Endscrapers	17.8	11.8	6.3	9.4	9.9
Burins	21.5	19.7	6.3	8.2	20.5
Backed implements	8.9	6.6	4.4	6.9	23.7
Other microliths	14.9	—	—	1.7	0.2
Retouched blades	10.4	25.0	21.5	24.5	15.5
Pointed blades	5.9	3.9	33.5	24.5	7.9
Sidescrapers	—	—	1.9	2.1	0.6

CULMINATION AND DECLINE

Table 6.6. Change of Typological Indices, Pavlov I and Dolní Věstonice II

Unit	Pavlov 1952		Pavlov 1953		Pavlov 1957		DV II/1		DV II/2+3	
	n	%	n	%	n	%	n	%	n	%
Endscrapers	48	8.1	137	9.2	159	7.6	3	4.5	8	8.2
Burins	143	24.1	501	33.5	449	21.5	14	21.2	33	33.7
Backed implements	235	39.9	327	21.9	234	11.3	39	59.1	28	28.6
Other microliths	66	11.1	208	13.9	352	16.9	5	7.6	7	7.1
Retouched blades	13	2.2	69	4.6	319	15.2	—	—	3	3.1
Pointed blades	4	0.7	26	1.7	49	2.4	—	—	1	1.0
Sidescrapers	4	0.7	10	0.7	20	1.0	—	—	—	—
Total tools	593		1494		2084		66		98	

1. The Aurignacioid elements: A few thick and rather atypical endscrapers are present in the Early Pavlovian stage (Dolní Věstonice I, II), but typical Aurignacian endscrapers and burins reappear in the Epigravettian (Grubgraben, Stránská skála IV).
2. Elaborate marginal retouching of blades and pointed blades limited to certain assemblages (Willendorf II, layers 7–8; Předmostí; Dolní Věstonice II-unit LP; Petřkovice) throughout the Gravettian development.
3. Microliths (crescents and derived forms are typical of Pavlov I, while backed microdenticulates are typical of DV I and II).
4. Derived Jerzmanowician elements. Blade points with ventroterminal retouches were frequent during the Late Middle Paleolithic and the Early Upper Paleolithic (see the so-called Jerzmanowician, Chapter 5), but a derived, less richly retouched form was subsequently recorded from the Pavlovian (Willendorf, Pavlov, Předmostí) and from Kostenki 8-I.
5. Bifacial leaf-points developed from the Middle Paleolithic to the Early Upper Paleolithic of the area (Szeletian). New analyses of the Pavlovian typology show that, contrary to earlier views, leaf-points were almost absent during this stage and reappeared as late as the Upper Gravettian (Petřkovice, Figure 6.3, number 17; Trenčianské Bohuslavice) and the Late Aurignacian, that is, in a time slightly preceding the Solutrean of Western Europe.
6. The Kostenkian elements. Shouldered points of the Kostenki type (Figure 6.3, number 1) are the leading fossil uniting the Upper Gravettian of Central and Eastern Europe (Kostenki I-1: 24,000–19,000 B.P.).
7. Microblade technique. Some wedge-shaped microblade cores, resembling the ones existing in Northern Asia around 20,000 B.P., were recently recorded in the Epigravettian and the Late Aurignacian.

Occurrences of these techniques and types may reflect the continuity of a tradition (Jerzmanowician types in the Pavlovian, Aurignacian types in the Epigravettian), a direct interaction (migration or acculturation—Kostenkian types in the Upper

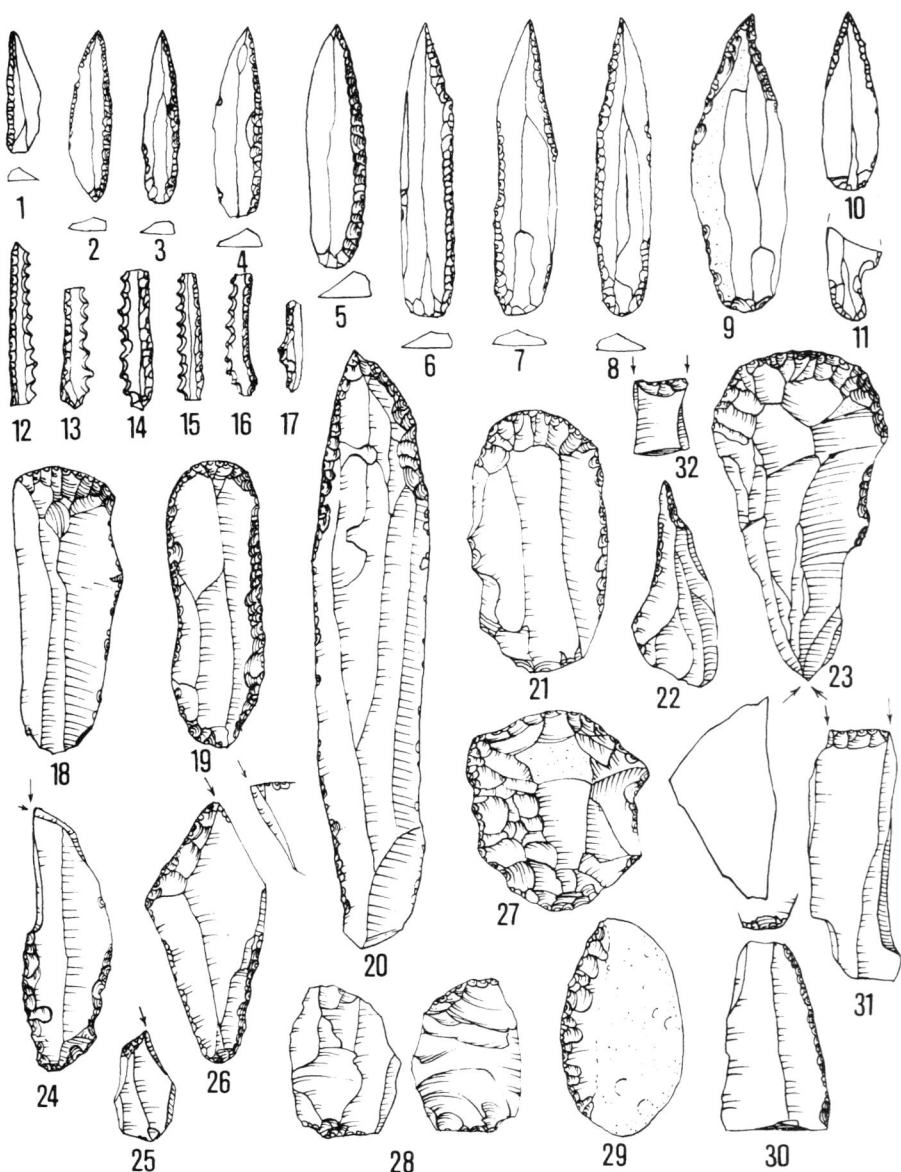

Figure 6.2. Gravettian lithic industry (Pavlovian stage, 27,000–25,000 B.P.): Dolní Věstonice I.

Gravettian: Sofer, 1987), or common Paneuropean or Eurasian tendencies in technological and stylistic concepts (bifacial leaf-points in the Upper Gravettian and microblade technique in the Epigravettian; Svoboda, 1996).

The Early Pavlovian (30,000–27,000 B.P.)

The earliest Gravettian in the middle Danube territory is documented at Willendorf II (layer 5), Dolní Věstonice I (the lower part of the site) and II (the lower part of the site and certain locations in the upper part). The industries are dominated by burins, backed implements, and endscrapers. Burins are about twice as numerous as endscrapers, and the number of geometric microliths is usually lower. Rarely, some of the endscrapers have high, Aurignacian-like shapes.

The industries are predominantly of flint, and radiolarite and local lithic materials (i.e., Moravian cherts in the lower parts of sites Dolní Věstonice I and II) occur in low percentages.

The Evolved Pavlovian (27,000–25,000 B.P.)

This chronological stage was observed in layers 6–8 at Willendorf II, at Dolní Věstonice I (the middle and upper parts of the site), Dolní Věstonice II (the majority of the site surface), Pavlov I (all materials analyzed so far), and Předmostí (the larger part of the industry). The rich bone industry documents the unity of this stage (Klíma, 1994b), while in the art, we observe certain differences between the Dolní Věstonice–Pavlov style and the Předmostí style (Svoboda, 1995a). This latter view seems to be supported by the lithic typology, where one may observe separation into two facies: the first one, represented by Willendorf II, Předmostí, Pavlov I (1957 area), and Dolní Věstonice II (unit LP/1-4), is characterized by elaborate marginal, steep, or scalariform retouches on blades and flakes, by retouched pointed blades, and by some typical sidescrapers. The second facies, found at Dolní Věstonice I, in two chronological substages at Dolní Věstonice II (around 27,000 and 25,500 B.P.), and most characteristically at Pavlov I (1952–1953 area), can be differentiated by a rarity or absence of marginal retouch, and by an abundance of microliths such as crescents, trapezoids, and triangles at Pavlov, and by microdenticulates at Dolní Věstonice (Figure 6.2). The points with ventroterminal retouches, derived from the Jerzmanowice type, are present in both facies, while the bifacial leaf-points seem absent during this stage.

Imported raw materials, especially flint, substituted totally the local ones. In certain assemblages (a-area at Pavlov I, Willendorf II), we observe a marked increase of radiolarite.

The Willendorfian-Kostenkian (24,000–20,000 B.P.)

This Upper Gravettian state is represented by the sites of Willendorf I and II (layer 9), Předmostí (a hypothetical recent stage), and Petřkovice (Figure 6.3). Outside the Austrian-Moravian-Silesian territory, the sites of western Slovakia (Mora-

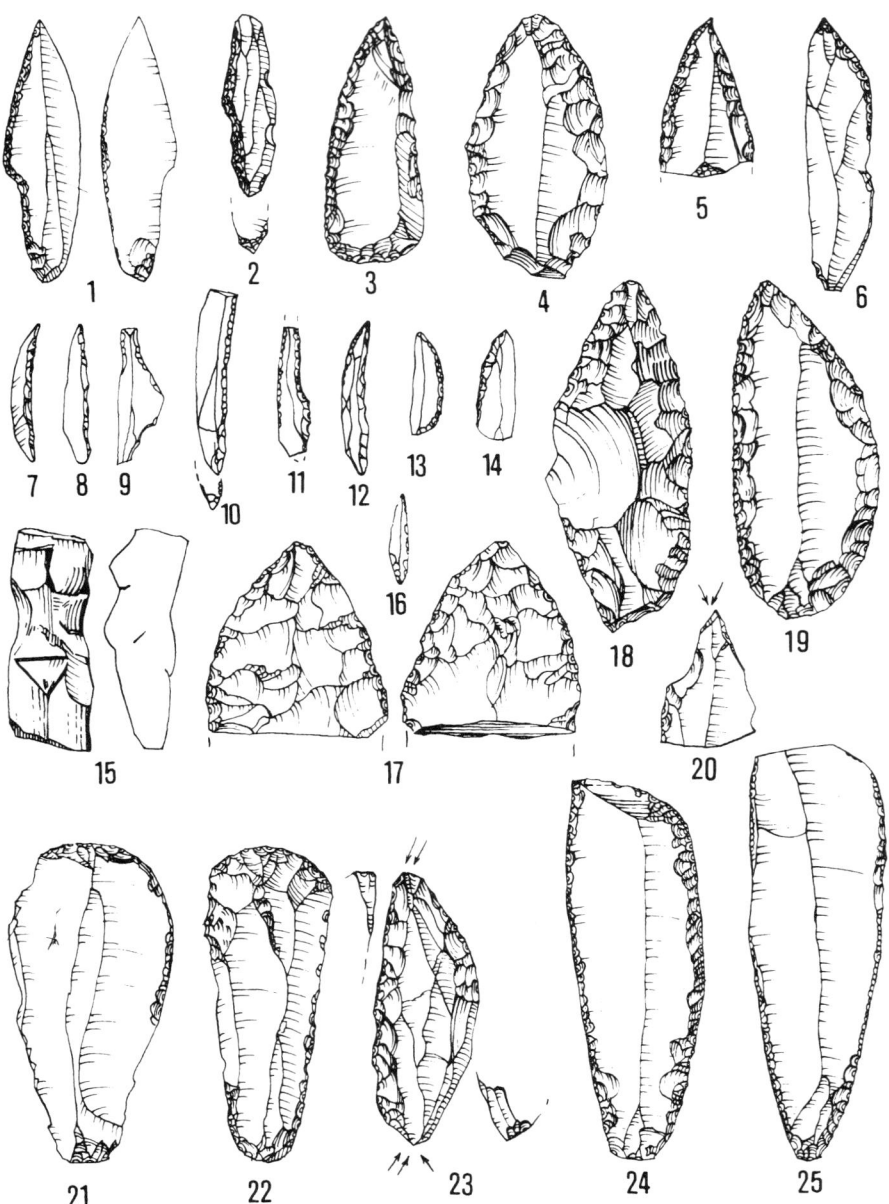

Figure 6.3. Gravettian lithic industry (Willendorfian-Kostenkian stage, 23,000–21,000 B.P.): Petřkovice.

vany, Nitra-Čermáň, Trenčianské Bohuslavice) should be added, as well as Spadzista in Poland and Molodova, layer 7, in Ukraine. The most important typological feature uniting all these assemblages is the appearance of shouldered points of the Kostenki type, showing a link to Eastern Europe typical of the period. Therefore, J. K. Kozlowski and K. Sobczyk (1987) called this stage Kostenkian.

Some sites also have bifacial leaf-points (Trenčianské Bohuslavice: Bárta, 1988; Předmostí, Petřkovice). In the period slightly preceding the development of the Solutrean in Western Europe, these implements should no longer be considered a Sezletian reminiscence, but an expression of a new wave of leaf-point production. The marginal, sometimes steep, retouches on the artifacts and the decrease in the number of microliths recall the former Předmostí style rather than Dolní Věstonice.

Some of the sites yielded single female figurines (Willendorf, Moravany, Petřkovice), and therefore, this stage has also been named the *horizon with single Venuses* (Svoboda, 1995a). The shapes of the first two mentioned figurines have striking analogies in Eastern Europe (Kostenki 1-I, Avedeevo), suggesting a close relationship between the two distant regions (cf. Gamble, 1986).

The Late Aurignacian (Epiaurignacian)

Stratigraphic evidence from Moravian sites (Stránská skála IIa: Svoboda, 1991e), certain C-14 datings from Lower Austria (Table 6.3), and typological chronologies based on surface assemblages (Oliva, 1987a) suggest that the Aurignacian survived until 20,000 B.P. (Chapter 5).

According to current scenarios, the Late Aurignacian and Gravettian populations would have lived side by side, but would have occupied different territories (Chapter 8); this implies that their behavior was also different.

The Epigravettian (after 20,000 B.P.)

The ongoing excavations of a living site at Grubgraben, Lower Austria (Brandtner, 1990; Montet-White, ed., 1990), a horse-killing site at Stránská skála IV (Svoboda, 1991e), and a relatively dense network of related surface sites in Moravia (Svoboda et al., 1994:155–161) suggest a more important Epigravettian occupation than has previously been supposed (Soffer and Gamble, 1990). However, the term *Epigravettian* covers typologically variable assemblages, and the meaning is still more chronological than cultural: possible continuities point not only to the Gravettian, as suggested by the name, but also to the Late Aurignacian.

The raw material base is rather versatile, with a more important share of local cherts compared to the Gravettian, but also with some imports from rather distant areas (obsidian) or from places difficult to access (rock crystal). In typology (Figure 6.4), the proportions of small burins to endscrapers changes radically from site to site (or, as shown by the Grubgraben sequence, within the same site: Montet-White, 1990). Another typical feature is the Aurignacioid character of some of the burins and endscrapers (Stránská skála IV, Brno-Jundrov, Zelená Hora, Otaslavice, Ostrožská

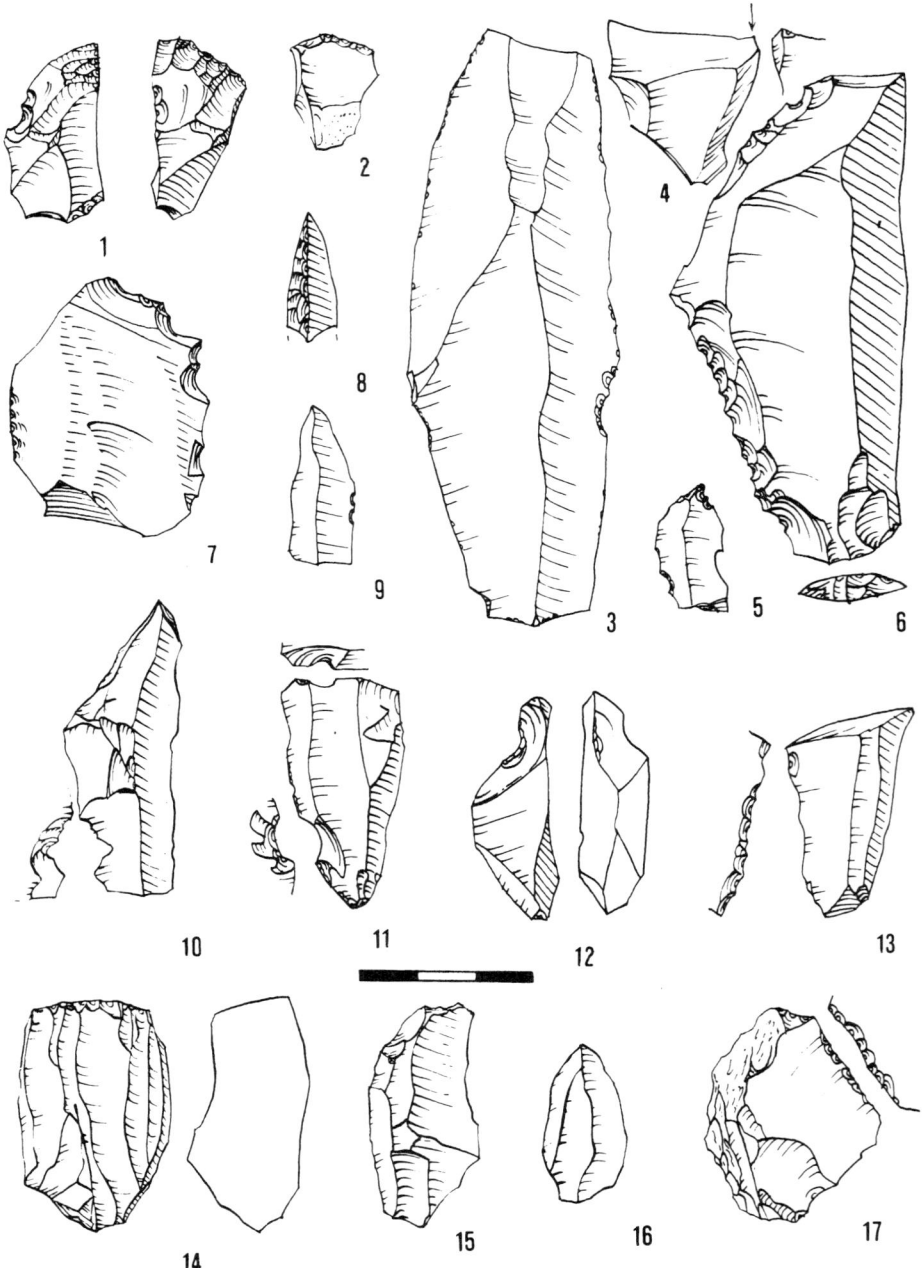

Figure 6.4. Epigravettian lithic industry (around 18,000 B.P.): Stránská skála IV.

Nová Ves) and Middle Paleolithic character of some sidescrapers (Grubgraben). Microblades are common, and backed bladelets appear in most of the assemblages (Brno-Vídeňská Koněvova, Zelená Hora, Otaslavice, Ostrožská Nová Ves, Hranice, Záblatí), but microlithic triangles are limited to the site of Hranice. Typical La Gravette points are absent, which seems paradoxical if we label this period *Epigravettian*.

A new technological feature, possibly related to the use of a pressure technique, is the wedge-shaped microblade cores (Svoboda, 1995c). Such cores, still little known in Moravia, appear in the context of either the Late Aurignacian (Dobrochov, Nová Dědina, Karolín II) or the Epigravettian (Opava, Pístovice II, Stránská skála IV). The appearance of this technology is calculated to date before and around 20,000 B.P. in Northern Asia.

The excavations at Grubgraben (Brandtner, 1990; Montet-White, 1990) added some data on the bone and antler industry, absent in Moravian sites. A *baton de commandement*, the earliest in the region, and the very fine needles are comparable to later Magdalenian specimens, while the remaining antler artifacts suggest instead Gravettian traditions.

THE GRAVETTIAN ADAPTATIONS

The relatively complex evidence from the Gravettian sites enables us to approach not only activities and technologies in relationship to environment, as in the Early Upper Paleolithic (EUP), but also, more directly, the presumed social, symbolic, and ritual frameworks that lay beyond these adaptations. Another aspect now involved, even if only on the level of relative comparisons (using general terms such as *longer* and *shorter*), is the time, that is, the duration of occupations and seasonality. Role of planning, as emphasized by Binford (1989), may now be followed in attitudes toward landscape, resources, storage, and rituals (Soffer, 1989; Soffer et al., 1993), and also toward competing cultural systems operating within the same territory (Late Aurignacian; Svoboda et al., 1994).

Various authors have suggested that the Gravettian sites in Moravia have world or European primacy in introducing new adaptive patterns and technologies: ceramics (Absolon, 1938a; Klíma, 1963b; Vandiver et al., 1990), the possible use of coal for heating (Klíma, 1953b), textiles or basketery (Soffer, personal communication, 1995), possibly the earliest evidence of plant food consumption (Mason et al., 1994), and possibly tendencies toward wolf domestication (Benecke, 1995). Naturally some of these surprising possibilities require further testing. As a complex system, however, the Gravettian model of adaptation seems to be one of the most efficient ones in human pre-Neolithic history.

Settlement Pattern: Regional Viewpoint

The Gravettian strategy in selecting a microregion or a site differs from that of the EUP (Svoboda, 1995b); therefore, the Aurignacian–Gravettian superpositions at the same site are exceptions (Willendorf II, Milovice). The Gravettian (Pavlovian) is usually found in extended sites under loess deposits near river valleys, at 200–300 m a.s.l. (Figure 6.1). These sites are less numerous than in the EUP and are arranged axially, along the main route connecting the Danube valley and the Northern European Plain (Willendorf, Dolní Věstonice and Pavlov, Předmostí, Spadzista [Kozlowski, 1974]). Further to the west, a similar east–west communication axis along the Danube connected Bavaria with the upper Rhine region.

The quantification of the Gravettian (Pavlovian) sites, however, is more difficult than in the other cultures (Chapter 8; Appendix B) because the large sites like Dolní Věstonice are, in fact, clusters of individual minisites, while the numerous small sites of the Znojmo, Uherské Hradiště, and other regions may be classified Gravettian only with respect to geography, context, or patination, rather than typologically.

By the end of the Gravettian, a horizon of several sites with artifactual elements reminiscent of Eastern Europe, here called the Willendorfian or Kostenkian, emerges in strategic places along the same passage (Willendorf, Předmostí, Petřkovice, Spadzista). Especially the shouldered points, dispersed quickly over a large part of the continent, suggest increased mobility, probably as an adaptive response to the climatic change of the last glacial maximum (Soffer, 1987, 1993).

With the exception of the large settlement at Grubgraben, the Epigravettian occupation seems to have been peripheral and episodic. The sites, more dispersed in time and space (Figure 7.1), and more dependent on a variety of lithic sources, were also more variable in site location. More sheltered locations were usually searched for near the mouths of smaller valleys (Brno-Stránská skála IV, Vídeňská and Jundrov, Pístovice, Zelená Hora, Otaslavice), but exposed elevations (Hranice) or open valleys of larger rivers (Ostrožská Nová Ves) were not avoided.

Settlement Pattern: One-Site Focus

Analysis focused on the one-site level shows that the large Moravian sites (Appendix A) are composed of various "settlement units," each with a central hearth or hearths, and with pits on the surrounding floors, some of them located in shallow depressions and sometimes with larger stone or bone alignments along the external margins (Figures 9.2 and 9.7). Because of the present state of research, we refuse the a priori assumption that these units were contemporary and composed a sort of a "village" (e.g., Absolon, 1945b; Klíma, 1963b). Instead, their relationships (chronological, seasonal, and functional) should be the result of ongoing and future analysis. It seems today that large surfaces of the sites really fall into relatively short time spans (Dolní Věstonice II, Pavlov I), but the individual settlement units may have dated to different occupation stages within these time spans.

A second point concerns a more detailed analysis of various zones within one particular settlement unit. In this case, differences are interpreted from the point of view of behavior rather than of chronology. In the following, we describe several case studies of this kind.

Any spatial analysis of southern Moravian sites is limited by the primary data about the location of the objects. At Dolní Věstonice I and II and at Pavlov I, the position of artifacts has been documented mostly by square meters only. Even if we have not been able to realize an analysis in the sense of Stapert, some of the results achieved with this kind of evidence are encouraging (Svoboda, Škrdla, and Jarošová, 1993). Beginning in 1990, the position of each piece is being recorded two- or three-dimensionally and computerized (Dolní Věstonice I and III, Předmostí, Petřkovice).

At Dolní Věstonice I, in the uppermost part of the site, Klíma (1952a, 1963b) recognized settlement unit 2 as a structure clearly outlined by stone enclosure and with a central hearth, ceramic fragments, ocher, and a medium artifact density inside (Figure 6.5). However, areas of a higher artifact density, with shells and several small pits, but no hearts, occur about 3–4 m to the southeast. This situation suggests the existence of an adjacent activity area outside the dwelling.

At Dolní Věstonice II, several settlement units were distinguished, each with a central hearth and a system of features, mainly pits, but without visible outlines (Klíma, 1995; Svoboda, 1991b). The patterns of artifact distribution around these units show relatively regular clusters that either overlap with the visible terrain features or, more frequently, lie asymmetrically, slightly downslope from the central hearths (Figures 6.6–6.9).

A more detailed case study was presented for unit 4 at the same site, located downslope from Klíma's western hearths (Svoboda et al., 1993). In this area, the position of the hearths in relation to the central artifact concentration is clearly peripheral. One of these hearths, instead, was surrounded by Tertiary shells and ocher.

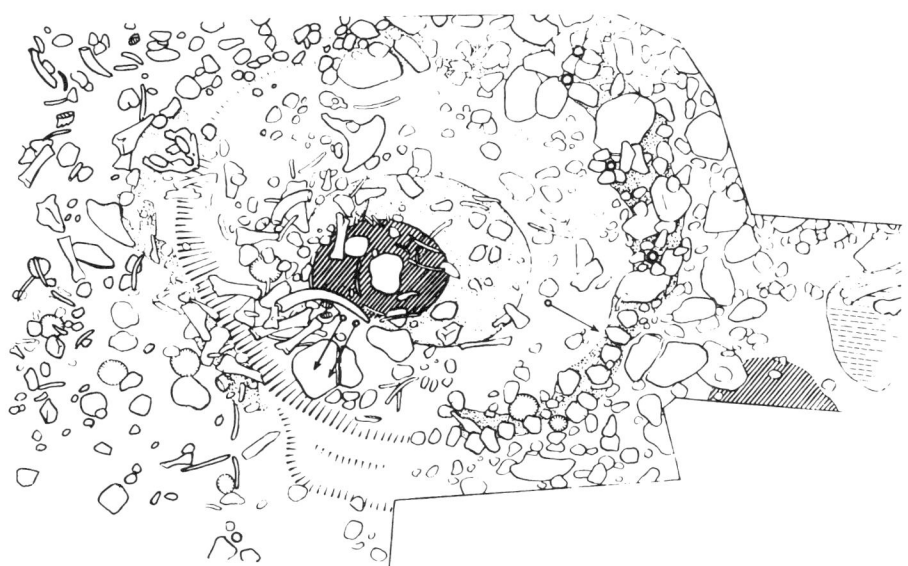

Figure 6.5. Dolní Věstonice I: Plan of settlement unit 2 (after B. Klíma).

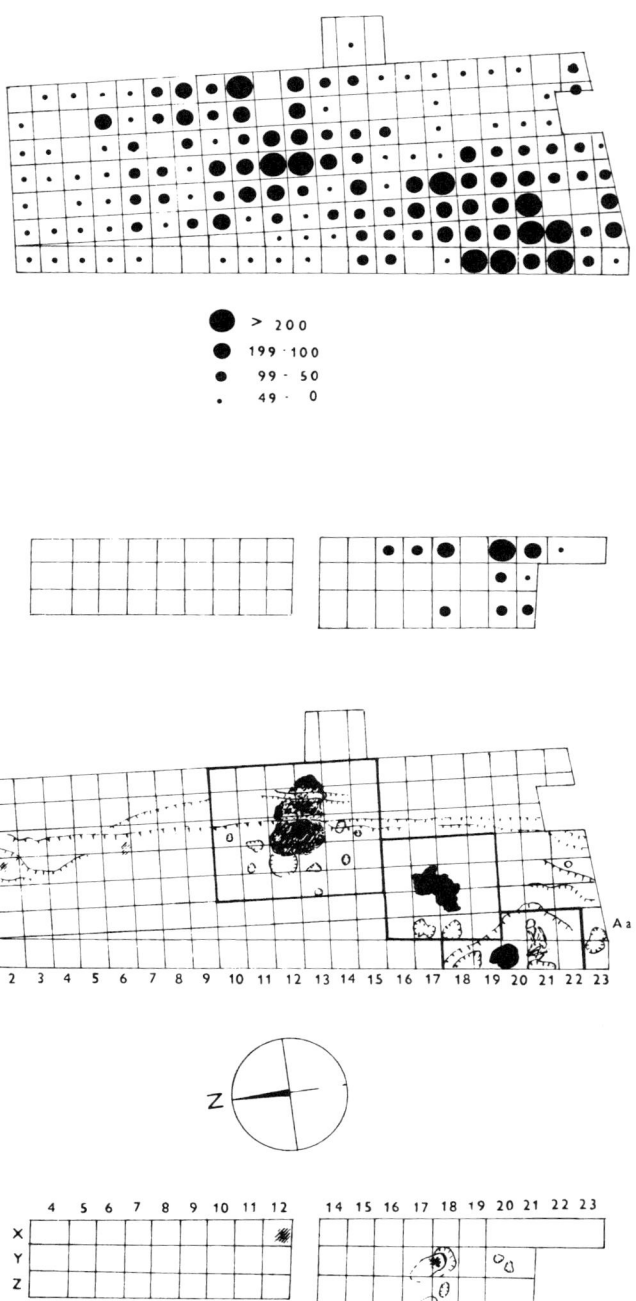

Figure 6.6. Dolní Věstonice II: Settlement units 1–3: Density of lithics in the excavated area.

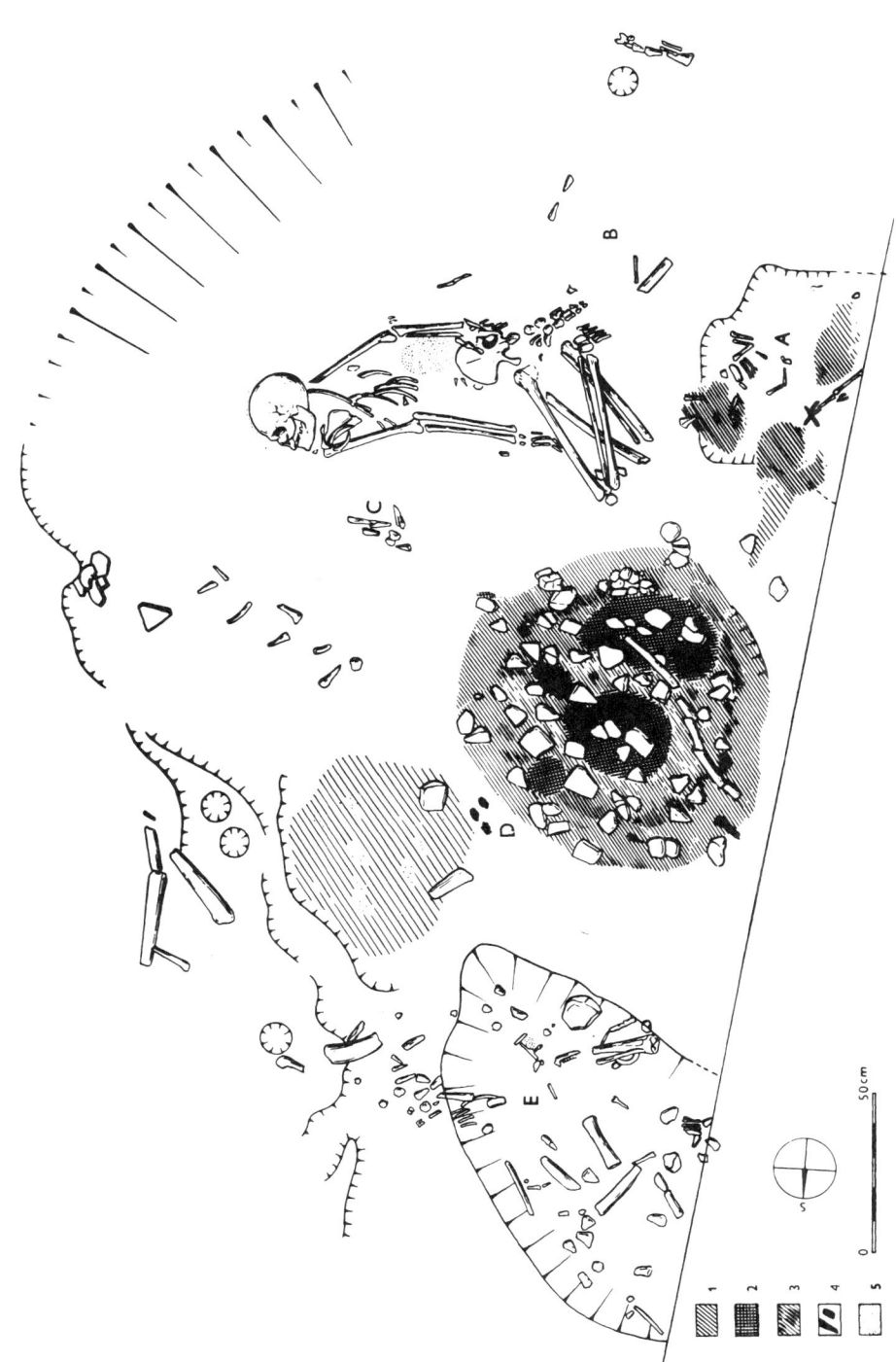

Figure 6.7. Dolní Věstonice II: Plan of unit 1 including the male burial DV XVI. 1—charcoal deposit; 2—red-burnt loess; 3—charcoal concentration; 4—wood; 5—ocher.

Figure 6.8. Dolní Věstonice II: Settlement unit 3 (hearth encircled by pits).

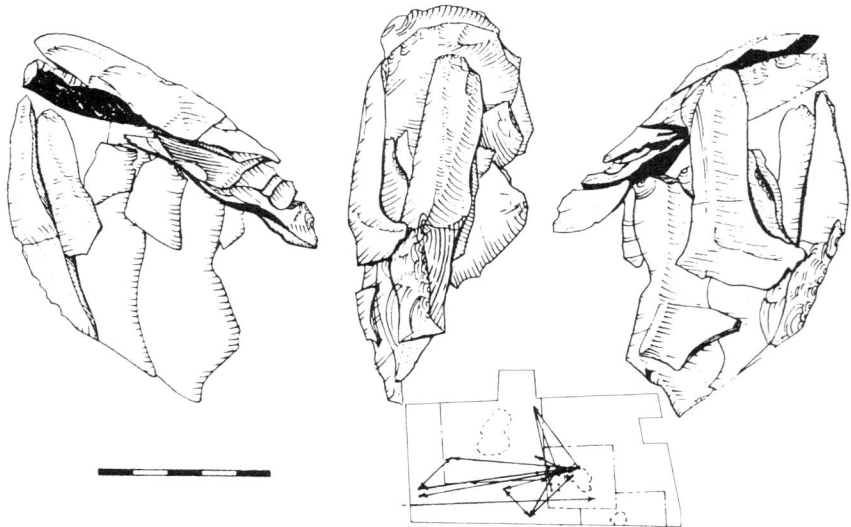

Figure 6.9. A refitted core from the same areas as Figure 6.6.

Microliths dominate in the center; approaching the periphery, we observed an increase in burins, in radiolarite, and in all kinds of larger bones and stones (the centrifugal effect).

At Pavlov I, a more detailed analysis is actually available for the 1952–1953 excavation area. The analysis takes as its starting point the central feature outlined by B. Klíma during the excavation (Svoboda, 1994a), but the outlines were only partly limited by larger objects or by a depression along the northern margin. The shape of the feature—two adjacent circles—suggests that it may have been composed of two circular features, each 4–5 m in diameter. The artifact distribution accords with the shape of the feature and respects its northern outline but continues to reach maximal densities in the western vicinity. The faunal distribution does not respect the feature at all: almost all species are concentrated to the west of it, and some of them to the south. The western vicinity of the feature, therefore, is an area of special importance. It includes several hearths and regular kettle-shaped depressions, most probably boiling pits; Tomášková (1994) observed a semicircular pattern of artifact concentrations around some of the hearths. This area also covers the maximal densities of endscrapers and burins, as well as maximal densities of wolf, hare, and reindeer remains. If we accept the central feature as a dwelling structure, the western zone would represent an adjacent activity area, the two most probably connected by an entrance.

Generally, we find two types of patterning at our sites: (1) structures with an adjacent activity area outside (Dolní Věstonice I, Pavlov I) have a number of analogies in Eastern Europe, namely, the solid mammoth-bone dwellings; (2) the structures with artifact clusters that overlap the structures asymmetrically (Dolní Věstonice II) recall instead the light, tentlike structures from Western Europe. Therefore, these comparisons may contribute to the classification of dwelling structures and to insight into the spatial organization of the activities performed there.

The most important Epigravettian evidence comes from Grubgraben, where F. Brandtner and B. Klíma have recently reconstructed a yurt-type dwelling, outlined by a circle of antler pegs presumed to have stabilized the skin coverage.

Duration of Occupation

In the current literature, there is only one rough estimation of the terms *short* and *long* duration of occupation: R. Musil (1994), basing his estimate on the amount of hunted game at Pavlov I (the 1952–1953 area), estimates the length of occupation of this part of the site at one or two years, or at one year with two winters. Our further comparisons are of only a relative value.

All sites at the foot of the Pavlovské Hills were supplied with the same raw materials, possibly in a regular, seasonal rhythm. The economy of lithic production, however, was not exactly the same. The pronounced microlithic character of a large part of the Pavlov I industry studied thus far, together with the higher proportion of retouched tools (Svoboda, 1994a,b) and worn artifacts (Tomášková, 1994), suggests a higher intensity of material use than at Dolní Věstonice II. Refittings of the radiolarite in Pavlov (the 1953 area; Škrdla, 1994) show that, in contrast to the 1957 area of the same site and to DV II, the artifacts rarely fit together; this observation suggests that the time period of the input and output of material into and from the area was long enough to interrupt the relationships among the artifacts as they emerged from lithic production. The dwellings, as they were reconstructed at Pavlov I and DV I, are more frequently semisubterranean and are sometimes outlined by marginal enclosures of stones and bones (types "A–C," Figures 6.5, 6.10), while those at DV II are rather light surface structures of the tent type (type "D," Figure 6.8; Svoboda, 1991b). Pavlov I is the only site in Moravia where a storage pit comparable to the ones known in Eastern Europe has been found (Klíma, 1977b; cf. Soffer, 1989). Furthermore, Pavlov I and DV I have thick ashy deposits, sometimes separated into several microhorizons, with concentrations of fired clay and decorative objects around them (e.g., Klíma, 1981b); Pavlov I and DV II lack representational art, the production of fired clay was limited, and the ash deposits are smaller and thinner. It seems reasonable, therefore, to conclude that the differences between sites like Pavlov I and DV I, on the one hand, and Pavlov II and DV II, on the other, may be related to a relatively longer duration of occupations.

Seasonality

Data on seasonality are still extremely limited, and the question calls for more systematic study in the future. R. Musil (1994) at Pavlov I (the 1952–1953 area), on the

Figure 6.10. Milovice, a mammoth-bone dwelling, during excavation by M. Oliva.

basis of the quantity of animals hunted for furs (wolves and foxes), suggests a winter occupation. Tomášková (1994) seems to support this view by observing traces of work with frozen and dry materials near some of the hearths.

Dolní Věstonice II, a site calculated to have had a shorter occupation, also has a good proportion of foxes. Furthermore, we have the evidence from tree rings by Opravil (1994) suggesting a winter occupation. Thus, the sites of the area, in our present state of knowledge, show differences in duration of occupation but not in seasonality. Certainly, this evidence does not mean that the sites were not occupied in other seasons as well.

For the Epigravettian, faunal studies of Stránská skála IV, prepared by D. West (1996) may reveal certain evidence on seasonality as well. The presence of dermestid (coleoptera) pupation chambers on one of the bones suggest that the killing episode evidenced at this site took place in summer.

Lithic Raw-Material Imports

The message presumably reflected in changing behavioral patterns toward the various siliceous materials throughout the Upper Paleolithic becomes especially important in the Gravettian. Therefore, geochemical analyses are being undertaken (Přichystal, 1994a) to locate the network of lithic imports as precisely as possible. A combined geological-archaeological project is in preparation.

The increase of high-quality lithic imports observed from the beginning of the Upper Paleolithic reached its maximum during this period (Figure 8.2). Only some assemblages of the Early Pavlovian retain higher proportion of local materials (Cretaceous chert at unit A, Dolní Věstonice II, and Krumlovian chert at unit B of the same site). During the Evolved Pavlovian, about 50%–90% of the recorded silicites originated from the flint outcrops in the Silesian glacial sediments, or in the Krakow–Czestochowa Jurassic of South Poland, and 10%–50% from the radiolarite outcrops, either on the Slovakian–Moravian boundary or in the Austrian Danube valley. Further, even more distant sources cannot be excluded (Přichystal, 1994a). It would be absurd to invoke exchange to explain this almost total dominance of exotic silicites, clearly for utilitarian use, particularly when this use was not extended to its fullest potential (Blades, 1993; Svoboda, 1994b). We argue that these imports are related to increased group mobility along the southwest–northeast route. This is even more probable given the possibility of easy movement provided by the regional topography, which also permitted animal migration.

Lithic exploration in the vicinities of the Gravettian sites has been directed mostly to the nonsiliceous material used for coarser tools and other components of heavy-duty industry. Still other operational ranges are indicated by imported shells from Neogene deposits of the Vienna Basin, and of ocher from the Ždánice flysch and from the Bohemian Massif.

Later in the Epigravettian, as the selection of the silicite sources became more variable, we may presume either a combination of group mobility with intergroup exchange, or the random movements of a group over eastern Central Europe.

Subsistence Strategies

The earliest finds of huge mammoth-bone concentrations were generally classified as being from the "mammoth age" and were interpreted as being the remains of hunting (Wankel, 1884). However, the authority of a visiting Danish scholar, J. Steenstrup (1890), finally convinced Wankel that humans were not contemporaneous with mammoths, as could be so easily deduced from the context. In his later work, Wankel (1890) accepted the view of Steenstrup that, in fact, later hunters of the Reindeer Age had come to the site to explore the bones from the earlier natural mammoth extinction.

Further excavations of Gravettian sites enlarged the available evidence substantially, and the "mammoth hunters" model was no longer questioned (Absolon, 1938b; Musil, 1955, 1959a,b, 1968; Klíma, 1963b, 1983a, 1990b). At Předmostí, evaluations of the early reports suggest that mammoth bones were either concentrated or scattered throughout the cultural layer in quantities, while at the southern Moravian sites, huge deposits of mammoth bones lay sorted, apart from the settlements, mostly in depressions, and sometimes in water, but the stratigraphy and dating confirm their contemporaneity with the settlements (Figure 6.11; Dolní Věstonice I: Klíma, 1969a; Dolní Věstonice II: Svoboda, 1991a; Milovice: Oliva, 1989a); in the last mentioned case, the mammoth bone deposit was even larger than the adjacent settlement. Individual mammoth bones found inside the southern Moravian sites mostly show traces of artificial modifications, and some of them were used in constructions.

Figure 6.11. Dolní Věstonice I: Mammoth bone deposit excavations by B. Klíma.

CULMINATION AND DECLINE

Most recently, the question has been reopened whether the mammoth bones accumulated through human hunting activities (Musil, 1994), or whether they represent natural mammoth cemeteries, exploited by humans for organic materials for tools and carvings or, as in Russia and Ukraine, as building material and fuel (Soffer, 1993; Mithen, 1993).

From the broader viewpoint of settlement geography (Figure 6.1), the Gravettian settlement seems to have followed the osteological finds of large mammals along the rivers (e.g., Hrubý, 1951; Skutil and Stehlík, 1932b), whereas it avoided the other possible, but dry, passages (the Vyškov Gate: Svoboda, 1994c). Analyses of lithic imports perfectly confirm the existence of such a passage. We may therefore conclude that there was a sort of direct relationship between the mammoth herds' movements and the operations of the hunters, but we cannot separate planned hunting from random collecting or carcass scavenging (Mithen, 1993). Some evidence of hunting may be derived from the settlement topography, which offers strategic places with good control over river valleys (Dolní Věstonice, Pavlov, Předmostí, Petřkovice), as well as a number of blind valleys, gorges, and other "natural traps" along the slopes (Dolní Věstonice, Milovice). Unfortunately, modern archaeozoological analyses of the Gravettian bone material that would support these viewpoints are not available from Moravia. Concerning the end of this mammoth-remains deposit, the archaeological record demonstrates that it ended with the Gravettian, around 20,000 B.P.. Here, both climate deterioration, implying vegetational change and a deterioration in carrying capacities, and systematic human predation should be evaluated as possible causal factors.

Another surprising pattern inside the Gravettian settlements is the frequent occurrence of carnivore bones (fox and wolf), some of them showing cutmarks (Musil, 1994): apart from the use for furs, it is difficult to imagine other possible uses. According to Benecke (1995) some of the wolves from Předmostí suggest a trend toward domestication.

Among the animals undoubtedly hunted for consumption, reindeer and hare dominate, while the decrease in the importance of the horse compared to earlier and later periods is, after Musil, due to a change in hunting techniques. In Russia, Soffer (1985, 1989) emphasized the role of the in-ground storage of herbivore meat in pits dug into permafrost. In Moravia, which was more influenced by periglacial climates, comparable evidence is extremely scarce, and the digging of pits was generally a very rare practice (Pavlov I: Klíma, 1977b); other pits at DV II (feature E in unit 1 at the western slope: Svoboda, 1991b) seem to be rather shallow for this purpose. However, as shown by Binford (1993), the absence of pits in no way means the absence of long-term storage.

After the last glacial maximum, the Epigravettian site of Stránská skála IV gives evidence of specialization in horse hunting (Figure 6.12; Appendix A; Svoboda, 1991e), and the geomorphology of the site, located under a rock cliff, seems to make it a favorable location for this purpose. An archaeozoological analysis of the horse bones in comparison with standard Epigravettian settlements (Grubgraben and Sagvar) has actually been prepared by D. West (1996).

It should be added that interpretations of the importance of meat in the Upper

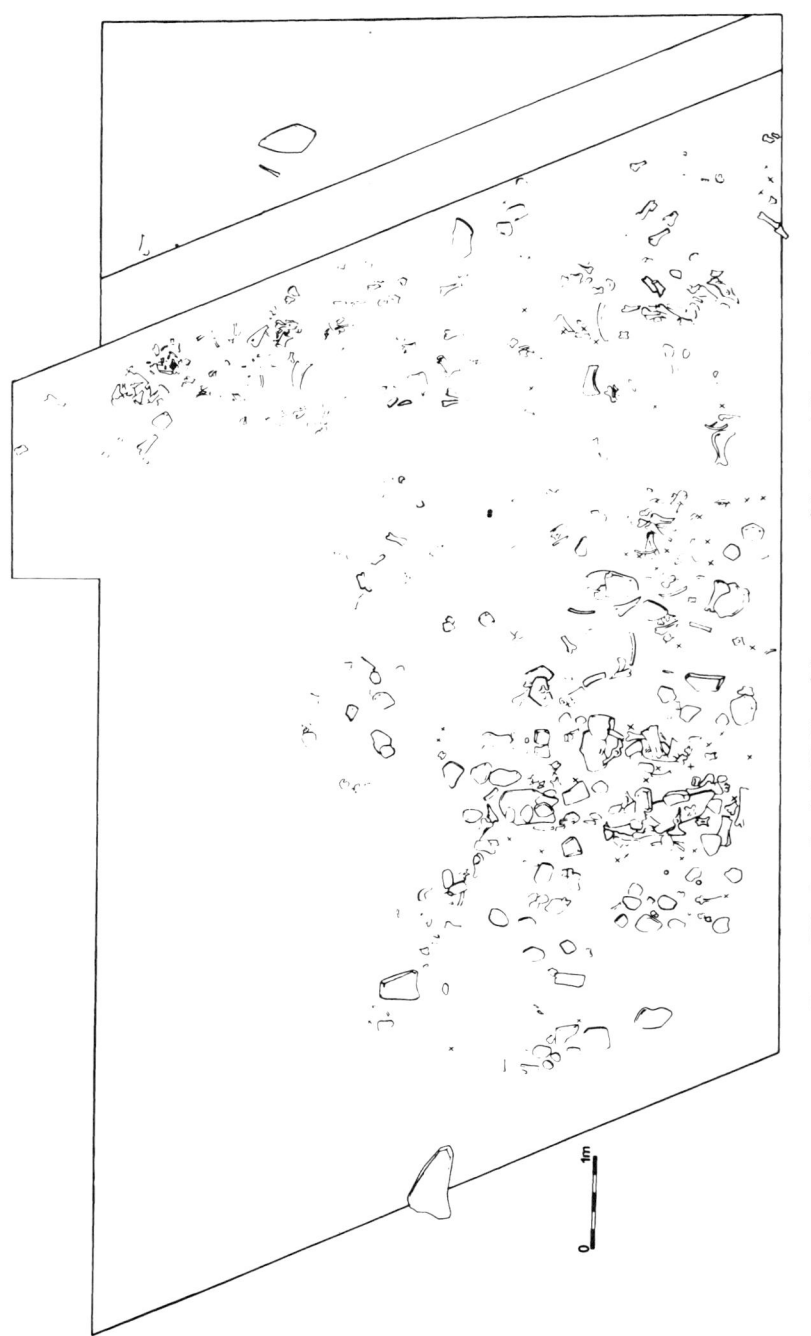

Figure 6.12. Stránská skála IV: Plan of the western part of the horse-killing site.

CULMINATION AND DECLINE

Paleolithic diet recently has undergone certain criticisms, as the discoveries from Dolní Věstonice II suggest, according to Mason et al. (1994), that plant foods may have been consumed. These discoveries are of fragments of charred plant tissue or amalgamations of plant fragments with mineral matter. At Late Paleolithic sites in the Near East, similar finds have been interpreted as being the charred feces of infants fed on finely-ground plant food. On the other hand, Soffer (1985) argues that very few staple plants were available in periglacial regions, and that residues on the grinding stones found at the sites (including DV I and II) suggest their use for grinding pigment and bones rather than plants.

In general, and compared with the other Upper Paleolithic cultures in Moravia, the Gravettian model of resource exploitation shows the highest complexity, and long-distance raw-material transport, combined with systematic mammoth exploitation (hunting or scavenging), and seems to have been the most labor-intensive.

Art

During the Gravettian, a real center of artistic creativity was established in Moravia. In this region, art may now be followed in a widespread variety of forms, including the decoration of tools and weapons, personal decoration, and representative art. This phenomenon of art history should probably be understood to be a result of the complex development and interaction among the former EUP cultures, of communication and competition, and also of the need for a symbolic manifestation of the self-awareness of individuals and groups. A more detailed look at Moravian art (Figure 6.13) shows slight stylistic differences between the two largest centers in the south (Dolní Věstonice and Pavlov) and the north (Předmostí; Svoboda, 1995a).

In decoration, the Dolní Věstonice–Pavlov style is characterized by geometric ornament composed of rows of incisions, sometimes arranged in a herringbone pattern (Klíma, 1981b: Figures 39 and 40) and other complex patterns (Absolon, 1938b: Figure 30). In 1957, Absolon speculated about the arithmetical capacities of

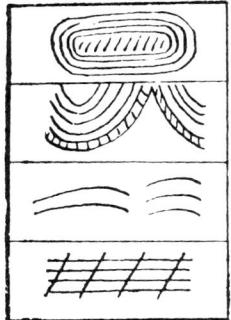 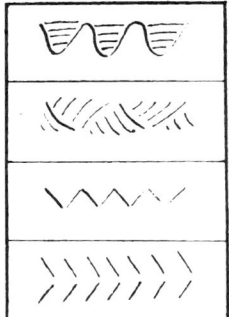 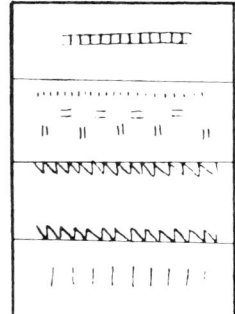

Figure 6.13. Comparative table of Gravettian decorative patterns.

Upper Paleolithic hunters, just on the basis of these incisions, an issue later followed, refined, and developed by Marshack (1972). Another typical features is ceramics, the earliest of its kind in the world: figurines of burnt clay, sometimes broken, deformed, or incised, probably in a ritual context (Soffer et al., 1993). The famous Black Venus of Dolní Věstonice I (Figure 6.14, Absolon, 1938a) is a ceramic object as well, but it differs from the others in its larger size, sophisticated shape, and a relatively good state of preservation (a fracture at the base seems to have occurred after firing): this may suggest a more important role, and possibly a more durable use than as the object of a ritual. Furthermore, the Black Venus probably served as a "prototype," and its classical

Figure 6.14. The Věstonice Black Venus.

shape was imitated in other female torsos from the same site, both modeled in clay and carved in ivory.

Ivory was the material in which the representation of the human body at Dolní Věstonice reached maximal simplicity in a most sophisticated way. Such objects were clearly intended for a longer use that the ceramics, and some of them were pierced as pendants. A typical abstraction, exaggerating the sexual organs, is traditionally seen as female breasts: this motif appears shaped in a figure or in whole series of pendants. In the view of Kehoe (1991), however, the breasts change to testicles and the stylized body to a penis. We only comment that seeing a dual or bisexual sense in an object is not uncommon in primeval thinking. Apart from abstract concepts of humans, there is a realistic, but still stylized, female face of ivory, provided with eyes, eyelids, eyeballs, nose, and coiffure (Figure 6.15).

The art of Pavlov I (Appendix A) is known from specialized studies concerning the lioness carving (Klíma, 1964a), the engraving of a "map" (Klíma, 1988), and plastic art (Klíma, 1989). The decorative objects of ivory are site-specific: a series of extremely finely carved rings, other rings with decorations, and fine, richly decorated fragments of bands, which, if complete, may be interpreted as headbands (Figure 6.16). The style of the decoration differs in the curvature of the lines, usually very slight, but sometimes forming arches. These curves are parallel and combined into various geometric patterns, covering the surface of the bands. The complex pattern interpreted as a map (Figure 6.17; Klíma, 1988), engraved in mammoth tusk, is made in this same "curved-line style" but is more complicated. Klíma's argument about its specific (symbolic) meaning, perhaps in the spatial sense, seems to be supported by Eastern European parallels (Kirillevskaya).

The excavations at Pavlov I also enriched the collection of ceramics by adding further figurines of animals and humans (males and females; Figure 6.18). Two features should be stressed in this context: first, the human heads are stylized into a biconical shape, in both clay (two cases) and ivory (one case). Second, some of the figures have belts, showing either a simple geometric decoration, similar to that on the ivory bands, or, as suggested by Marshack (1991:22), a twined cord (Figure 6.18, below). Figural carving in ivory is documented by a female figure and two *countours découpés* of ivory plates (Figures 6.19 and 6.20): a static mammoth figure and lion in motion. Perforated disks of unknown (symbolic?) meaning were carved of siltstone plaques; these objects occur repeatedly in the Moravian Gravettian.

The Předmostí style of bone decoration is more geometric than the Dolní Věstonice–Pavlov style, and it is based on series of short, straight incisions, sometimes arranged in herringbone patterns and hatched triangles (Absolon and Klíma, 1977). Arches and their combinations are present, but the slight curvatures typical of Pavlov are absent. Geometric patterns cover surfaces of bone tools, pendants, and bones with no evident practical functions (ribs, shoulder bones: Valoch, 1975a). Breuil (1925:Figure 19) even mentions traces of painting on a mammoth bone, but unfortunately, the object is not available today. The geometric stylization of a female figure (Kříž, 1896), engraved in a mammoth tusk, is rooted in the particular style and vision typical of the

Figure 6.15. Female head from Dolní Věstonice.

site (Figure 6.21). Some of the ivory pendants have a shaped head for fixation, and the same kind of a head is observed on several mammoth phalanges (Maška, 1913; Valoch, 1969a): these may have served as weights, but some of them strongly recall the shape of a seated pregnant female. Realistic figures are rare. The single carving of a mammoth discovered by Kříž and recognized as such by Maška (1912) is relatively large and monumental in style (Figure 6.22). Evidence of ceramic production is very limited. Finally, further perforated disks of Tertiary siltstone, 18–19 cm in diameter (Valoch, 1960a), are comparable to the ones from Pavlov I.

In the Upper Gravettian, three sites in the neighborhood of Moravia became famous for single female figurines. The well-known female statue from Willendorf II,

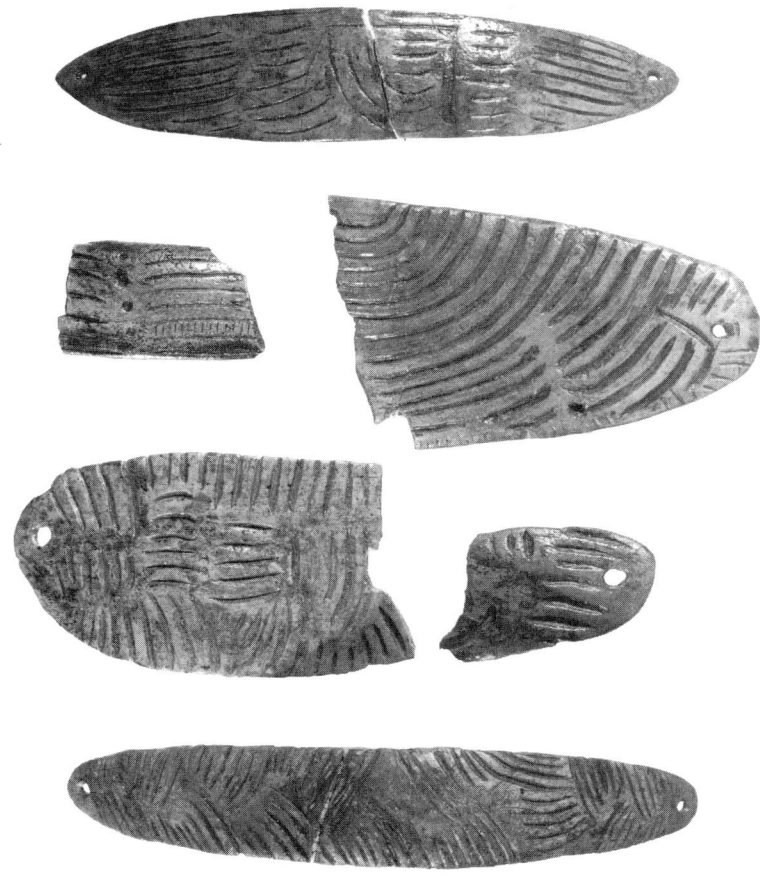

Figure 6.16. Pavlov I: Decorated headbands of ivory.

layer 9 (e.g., Marshack, 1991), made of limestone, reminds one of some figures of the Gagarino site. The female figure from Moravany, Slovakia (Bárta, 1980), carved of ivory, recalls the Kostenki style of female figurines. Finally, the site of Petřkovice, Silesia, yielded a slim female torso, carved of hematite in a rather original style (Figure 6.23; Klíma, 1955b).

The Epigravettian evidence from eastern Central Europe suggests a rapid decrease in all artistic activities. In our region, we may recall the *baton de commandement*, decorated with a zigzag line pattern, a few pierced fragments of ivory rondels, pierced animal teeth, and a whistle, all from Grubgraben. Stránská skála IV has only a possible,

Figure 6.17. Pavlov I: Decorated mammoth tusk interpreted by Klíma as a map.

more simple whistle made of a reindeer phalange. All in all, the paucity of these remains offers a striking contrast to the richness of earlier Gravettian art.

Rituals

All efforts to interpret rituals are widely influenced by ethnographic evidence. Such evidence usually involves spirits and can therefore hardly be supported by the material from excavation (Noble and Davidson, 1993). In the following, we concentrate on the context and subjects of the excavated objects in order to discern social actions.

Central Europe lacks solid evidence of parietal art and the related deep-cave rituals. The diversity of mobile art techniques and forms, however, is not less complex than in Western Europe. We assume, first, that ritual behavior existed, and second, that it took place at open-air sites or in caves opened to daylight by other means than decorating the walls. Almost all artistic evidence presumably related to rituals, as well as a large number of the human burials, was discovered in the context of settled areas. The bulk comes from large sites with intensive reoccupation: the hearths where ceramic figurines were produced and destroyed (Figure 6.5; Dolní Věstonice I, Pavlov I) or areas plastered by red ocher and surrounded by hearths (Petřkovice), with a direct association to a female figurine cut of the same hematite material (cf. Figures 6.23 and 9.9). The Moravian evidence, therefore, supports the view of Conkey (1987) by stressing the social functions of art and rituals, performed in living places and in places of aggregation.

Time has been measured and recorded in Upper Paleolithic Moravia (Absolon, 1957; Marshack, 1991; Emmerling, Geer, and Klíma, 1993). With respect to the context, art objects may be separated into items of short-term and long-term use (Svoboda, 1976, 1986). Carving sculptures of animals and humans, and items of personal adornment is time-consuming, and these products served their purpose for a longer period. Larger sculptures were certainly stationary, while the smaller, pierced

CULMINATION AND DECLINE 163

Figure 6.18. Pavlov I: Ceramic figural plastics.

ones contributed to personal adornment as pendants or were carried in a pouch. A. Marshack (1972) confirmed this by observing the wear polish on surface of some of the carvings. Some objects contribute to the concept of "self-awareness" of an individual within the society (Marshack, 1992:183). It is surprising that we do not find such carvings with the ritually buried human skeletons, among the items of personal

Figure 6.19. Pavlov I: Ivory carving of a mammoth.

Figure 6.20. Pavlov I: Ivory carving of a lion.

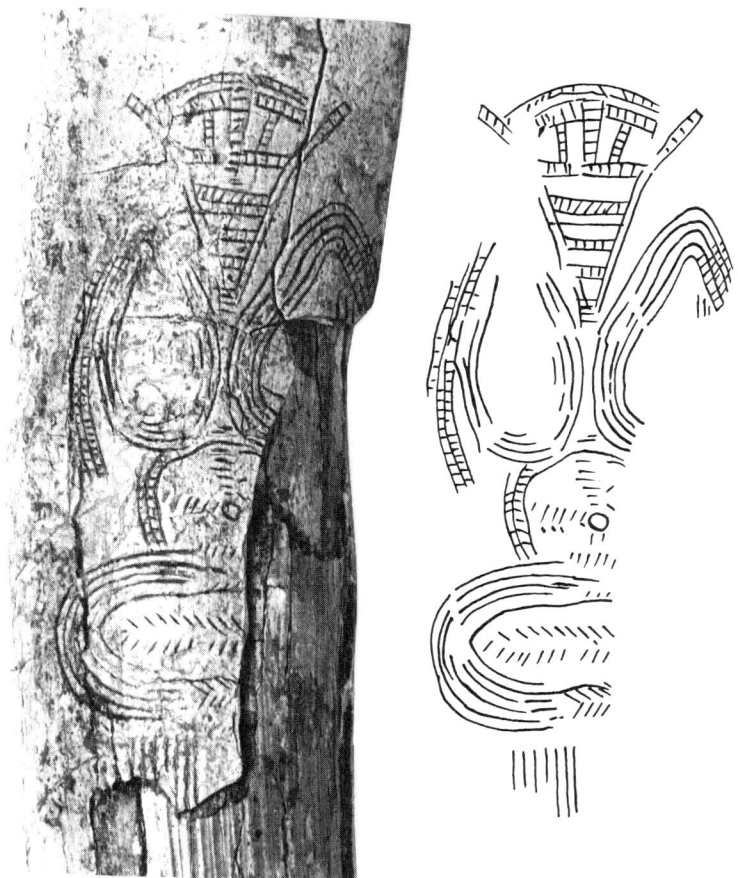

Figure 6.21. Předmostí: Female engraving on a tusk.

adornment. The only statue found in a burial, the ivory carving of Brno II (Makowsky, 1892), is too large to have been carried around.

Long-term use is conjectured for decorated bone, antler, and ivory tools and weapons as well. An image decorates the object once forever. Besides its aesthetic meaning, the image may have supplied some kind of supernatural power to the implement, strengthening its functions. In all these categories, the aim was an object per se and its magical powers.

The short-term art is observed first in the Gravettian ceramics, and later in the Magdalenian engraved plaques (Chapter 7). In both cases, the importance seems to lie not in the object, but in the moment of its creation and destruction. An experienced artist may produce such objects relatively quickly. The pattern of subsequent destruc-

Figure 6.22. Předmostí: Carved mammoth statue.

tion is sometimes demonstrated by breakage, deformations (ceramics), and reutilizations (stone plaques). This kind of art clearly represents only the nonperishable remains of a more complex ritual creation.

Baked clay figurines represent one of the most typical phenomena of Gravettian (Pavlovian) sites in Moravia. These figures, sometimes broken, deformed, or incised, are found clustered together with a number of unshaped clay pellets around the hearths where they were obviously made (Figure 6.18). Large collections were found at Dolní Věstonice I (Absolon, 1938a,b, 1945b; Klíma, 1979b, 1981b) and Pavlov I (Klíma, 1989), while smaller samples originate from Pavlov II, Dolní Věstonice II, and Předmostí. Absolon and B. Klíma suggested that the ceramic objects served in some kind of ritual, located in "places of mystical hunting cults" (Absolon, 1945b:17).

The results achieved recently in the physicochemical studies of P. Vandiver et al. (1990) have shown how these rituals may have functioned. The raw material was local loess, generally fired to temperatures between 500–800°C. These temperatures correspond to the results of analyses from some of the hearths. Certain deformations observed in the shape of the figurines are due to thermal shock. Such effects of rapid temperature change appear repeatedly, showing that this approach was not accidental

CULMINATION AND DECLINE 167

Figure 6.23. Female figure from Petřkovice.

but intentional. Some pellets also show imprints (possible evidence of weaving or basketery; Soffer, personal communication, 1995), and these may be utilitarian.

Another question is how far such presumed ritual accords with the hunting-magic scenario, so widely referred to in Central European prehistoric research. If this relatively simple model is true, we would expect certain parallels in the quantity of hunted animals, as preserved in bones, and the ones depicted in art. Instead, strong disproportions are systematically observed in the record, reaching from Cantabrian cave art to Central Europe, and several hypotheses have been raised to explain it. Klíma (1979b, 1981b:Figure 24) observed such a disproportion at Dolní Věstonice I: in faunal remains, we have, in the first place, the huge accumulations of mammoth bones along the sites. Whatever disagreement there may be in interpreting them, this animal was of primary importance to the human economy, together with hares and reindeer, but among the ceramics at the same site, the species most frequently represented are bear, lion, and other carnivores. Furthermore, there are figurines of females, males,

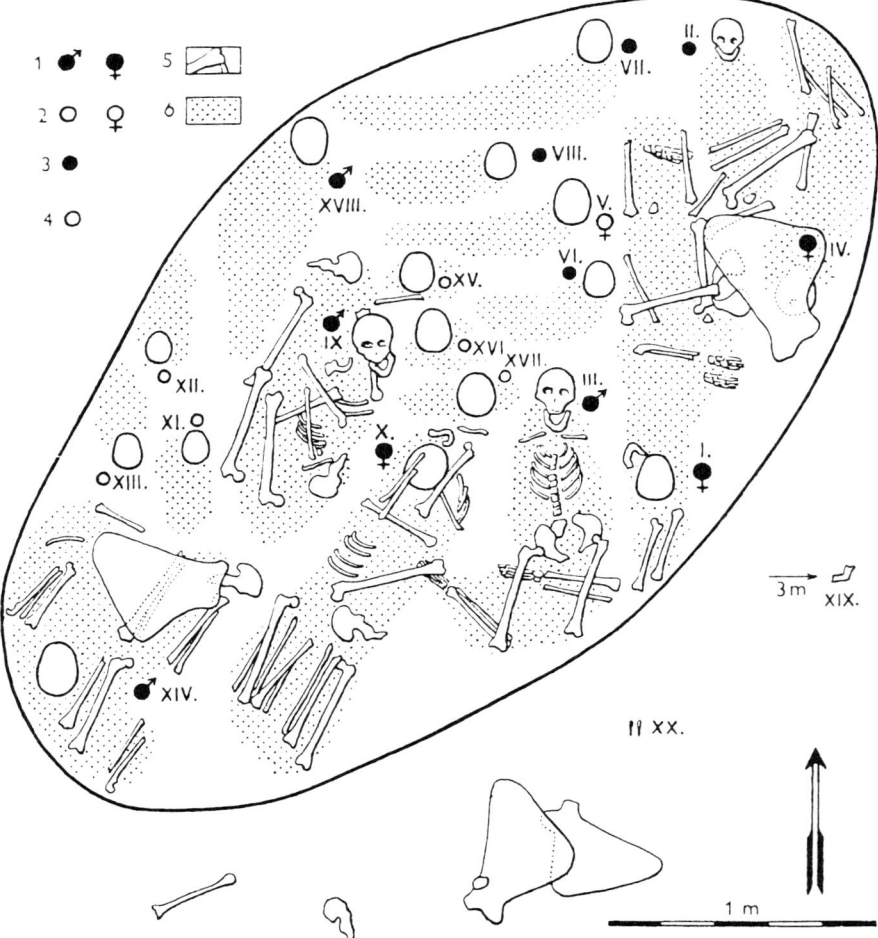

Figure 6.24. Reconstruction of the Předmostí burial (after B. Klíma, using the original documentation by K. J. Maška). 1—adult individual; 2—young individual; 3—child; 4—baby; 5—bones; 6—probable position of the postcranial part of the body.

and hybrids in the same contexts. Mammoth is much more important in the ceramic sample from Pavlov I, but this site lacks the typical mammoth-bone accumulation.

It may therefore be concluded that, during ceramic production, as in the ivory carvings, the important or imposing animals (the largest herbivores, such as mammoth, rhinoceros, and horse, together with dangerous carnivores) were among the preferred subjects.

CULMINATION AND DECLINE 169

Figure 6.25. Dolní Věstonice II: The triple burial (DV XIII–XV).

Burials

Moravia has yielded the largest sample of burials known in Europe from the period between 30,000 and 25,000 B.P. This material is precious for studies not only of anatomy (Chapter 3), but also of ritual practices with the deceased. Hypotheses on burial rituals are being derived from contextual interpretations of the original terrain situations (Klíma, 1990b, 1991), and from examinations of injuries to bone (Vlček, 1993b). For example, Vlček examined the healed wounds repeatedly found on frontal and temporal parts of the skull and suggested ritual fighting, possibly in the context of initiation.

The position of the deceased, flexed or on the right side (Figure 6.7), seems to have been quite common (cf. the female burial from Dolní Věstonice I and the male burials in site II, to mention only the well-documented cases) and one evidently used without regard to the sex of the deceased. Furthermore, there are burials of several individuals, such as at Předmostí (over 20 individuals; Figure 6.24; Appendix A), unfortunately unprecisely documented (Maška's diaries; Klíma, 1991:74), and the triple burial recently found at Dolní Věstonice II (Figure 6.25; Klíma, 1987b). The child's burial at Dolní Věstonice I is extraordinary because of the partial burning of the skeletal remains (Absolon, 1945b). Mammoth scapulae and stones, used to cover some of the burials (DV I, Pavlov, Brno II, Předmostí) were probably replaced by wooden constructions at Dolní Věstonice II (Svoboda, 1991b).

Some regular burials at Pavlov I and Dolní Věstonice I and II seem to have been accompanied by fragments of the skulls of other, perhaps accompanying individuals (Klíma, 1990c), but little evidence is available in the form of associated objects or funerary gifts. The problem is that the bodies are covered by cultural layers with current archaeological content (artifacts, Tertiary shells, and bones), and it is difficult to prove the association of a particular object with the skeleton. We are sure only in the case of a few pierced ivory pendants and pierced carnivore canines, found directly with the bodies (Dolní Věstonice I and II). The skull and sometimes the pelvis may be covered by red ocher—like some female figurines from the Upper Paleolithic of Europe.

A notable exception is the male burial numbered Brno II, rescued by Makowsky in 1891 (Makowsky, 1892; Appendix A). There is no evidence of a settlement at the finding spot, which seems to have been limited in space; thus, the association of the objects, some of them quite spectacular, and the buried body is more than probable. There was a male sculpture in ivory; about 600 Tertiary shells; small ivory and stone circles, some of them with a simple decoration; and two large, perforated disks of siltstone of the kind we noted at Předmostí and Pavlov. The decoration of some of the small disks, even if very simple, clearly represents female symbols; in the context of a male body and a male statue, such an association may be meaningful. In general, this well-equipped burial proves the high degree of variability we face in funerary rituals, which may reflect a variability in the social position of certain individuals.

Chapter 7

Western Invasion
The Magdalenians and Epimagdalenians

Until about 15,000 B.P., the Gravettian and Epigravettian development of eastern Central Europe was, in its broad outlines, comparable to what was happening on the Eastern European plains. The majority of researchers now agree that, after the date, these trends were radically interrupted by a Magdalenian cultural inflow from the west. Therefore, this chapter points out the possibility of comparing adaptations of two continentwide cultural units within the same geographic setting, but under environmental conditions gradually changing toward the late glacial and postglacial. One of the major characteristics of this development was the shift of occupation from the open landscape and back to the karst regions. Therefore, speleoarchaeology becomes a key discipline in understanding the late glacial adaptations in this part of Europe.

Cave studies played an important role during the formation and establishment of stratigraphic and developmental schemes concerning the Moravian Paleolithic, but today, with new methods of study, we mostly find ourselves in empty cavities or on redeposited sediments. As early as the last century, researchers recognized that caves in Moravia had been settled mainly during the cave-bear period and the reindeer period (Wankel, 1884), the first of which could be compared to the classical French sites *Le Moustier* and the second to *La Madeleine* (Maška, 1886): unlike in the neighboring areas of southern Germany, Poland and Slovakia, an important hiatus in cave occupation separated the two (the mammoth period, or Aurignacian and Gravettian, during which open-air sites were preferred).

Over many years of research, several efforts were made in the literature to demonstrate a local, Gravettian origin of the Magdalenian, but the arguments were restricted to assuming lineages between single artifact types. A later synthesis of the complex archaeological evidence (Valoch, 1960c), and especially the comparative studies of the art (Svoboda, 1976), are convincing enough to prove an external, western influence.

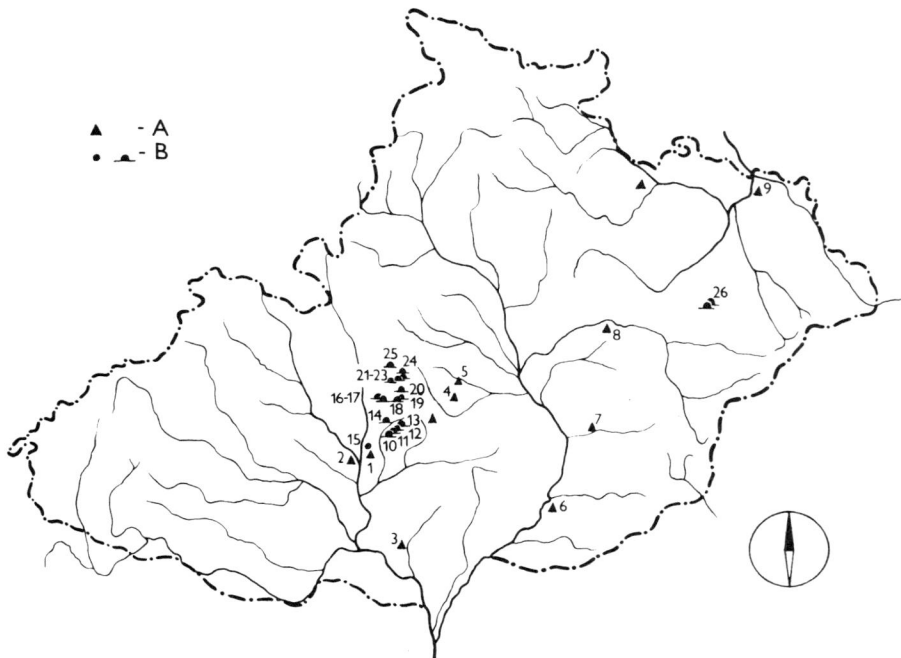

Figure 7.1. Map of the Epigravettian (A) and Magdalenian (B) sites. 1—Brno-east (Stránská skála IV); 2—Brno-west (Vídeňská and Kamenná Streets, Jundrov); 3—Velké Pavlovice; 4—Zelená Hora; 5—Otaslavice; 6—Ostrožská Nová Ves; 7—Zlín, Louky; 8—Hranice; 9—Záblati; 10—Pekárna; 11–Hadí Cave; 12—Křížova Cave; 13—Adlerova Cave; 14—Švédův stůl; 15—Maloměřice; 16—Býčí skála; 17—Barová Cave; 18—Nová Drátenická Cave; 19–Žitného Cave; 20—Kolíbky; 21—Rytířská Cave; 22—Veruněina Cave; 23—Srnčí Cave; 24—Balcarova Cave; 25—Kůlna; 26—Šipka and Čertova díra.

Further problems concerned the inner chronology (and relative relationships) of the Magdalenian. The stratigraphy of Pekárna Cave was not used for this purpose, because Absolon and Czižek (1926–1932) noted no basic differences between the two layers (g and h) attributed by them to the Magdalenian, and the lower, earlier Magdalenian layer (i) was then believed to belong to the Upper Aurignacian. Later attempts at dating were based on the concept of a gradual disappearance of glacial fauna (Musil, 1958), or on the change in sedimentation related to the end of loess deposit (Valoch, 1960c). These authors and their concepts, however, were quite limited by the quality of the evidence from earlier excavations.

Between 1961 and 1976, Valoch (1988) organized a large excavation in Kůlna Cave. After that, it seemed that the Paleolithic evidence from the karst had been exhausted. To check this, a survey throughout the territory of the karst was undertaken between 1981 and 1987, aimed at reconsidering the caves already excavated and at revealing information about new caves. Trenches were laid in a total of 20 caves, but only 5 of them yielded traces of Paleolithic settlement (Seitl et al., 1986; Svoboda, 1991c; Svoboda, Ložek, Přichystal, Svobodová, and Toul, 1996). The importance of this interdisciplinary project lies in the new data on the chronology and the ecology of the late glacial rather than in Magdalenian archaeology.

It may therefore be concluded that the majority of the Magdalenian sites in Moravia have already been excavated, and thus, this important period actually receives too little attention. However, an urgent task of future studies lies in reconstructing the adaptive and behavioral processes that lie behind the rich evidence now in hand, and in placing it in a seasonal framework. Special attention should be paid to the hitherto underestimated faunal studies. Naturally, any studies of this kind will be very limited by the lack of solid contextual data from the early excavations.

STRATIGRAPHY AND ENVIRONMENT

In the Moravian caves (Table 7.1), the Magdalenian industries appear both in the upper part of the last glacial loess or superposed over it. Therefore, the possibility of using this material for chronological purposes was discussed several times in the earlier literature (Musil, 1958; Valoch, 1960c). In the neighboring countries (southern Poland, western Germany), the last loess is usually dated to the pre-Alleröd (Dryas II) or the latest Alleröd periods (Ginter et al., 1987).

Paleontology supplies another possibility of drawing a chronological division

Table 7.1. Stratigraphic Comparison of Late Glacial Sites

	Barová Cave	Nová Drátenická	Pekárna Cave	Kůlna Cave
Alleröd	Layer 10: Epimagdalenian			Layer 3: Epimagdalenian 10,070 B.P. Layer 4: Epimagdalenian 11,470 B.P.
Dryas II	Layer 11: Magdalenian	11,670 B.P.		Layers 5 and 6: Magdalenian 11,590 B.P.?
Bölling	Layer 12: Magdalenian		Layers g and h: Magdalenian 12,500 B.P. 12,670 B.P. 12,940 B.P.	
Dryas I	(Erosion) Layer 14	Magdalenian 13,870 B.P. 12,900 B.P.	Layer i: Magdalenian	?

in the Magdalenian. Musil (1958) based his hypotheses mainly on the presence or absence of glacial animals (mammoth, rhinoceros, cave bear, cave hyena). He recorded all of these species in the Balcarova Cave, and the last mammoth specimens were noted at Kůlna and Pekárna (layer h). More recently, we have also found mammoth and rhinoceros in the Barová Cave (in the last loess layer, 11).

With the introduction of C-14 chronology (Table 7.2), we may state that the earliest Magdalenian dates in eastern Central Europe, around 15,000 B.P., are from the Maszycka Cave, southern Poland (Ginter et al., 1987). The earliest data from Moravia, about 14,000–13,000 B.P., are from the Nová Drátenická Cave in the central part of the Moravian karst (Klíma, 1949; Valoch, 1993a), from a clay layer relatively deep in the loess and debris deposits.

In the Pekárna Cave (Absolon and Czižek, 1926–1932; Klíma, 1974a; Svoboda, 1991c; Appendix A), the Magdalenian is still found in the uppermost part of the loess (layer i) and in two or three overlying humus and clayey horizons (layers g and h). These sections, most completely developed in the entrance area (Svoboda, 1991c), vary with increasing distances both into the cave and out from it, and a separation of the cultural horizons in these areas on the basis of the preserved documentation of R. Czižek is difficult. The basal loess (layer i) includes mollusks and microfauna corresponding to the open landscapes of the late glacial. The complex in layers g and h, now dated by C-14 to the Bölling (13,000–12,000 B.P.), corresponds to an increase in temperature and moisture, however, not showing remarkable changes in the structure of faunal assemblages. The layers above the Magdalenian (layer f) include microfauna characteristic of the earlier Dryas, while the mollusks already reflect the Holocene climatic optimum.

From Kůlna, layer 6 (Valoch, 1988; Appendix A), there are surprisingly late Magdalenian dates, around 11,500 B.P., attributed to a fireplace found in the brownish yellow loess inside the cave. This late loess is covered by two clayey layers (4 and 3)

Table 7.2. C-14 Datings, Magdalenian and Epimagdalenian

	Maszycka Cave, Poland	15,490 ± 390 B.P.
	Maszycka Cave, Poland	14,520 ± 240 B.P.
OxA 1953	Nová Drátenická Cave	13,870 ± 140 B.P.
OxA 1954	Nová Drátenická Cave	12,900 ± 140 B.P.
OxA 1952	Nová Drátenická Cave	11,670 ± 150 B.P.
Ly 2553	Pekárna, layers g and h (1925–1930)	12,940 ± 250 B.P.
GrN 14828	Pekárna, layers g and h (1986)	12,670 ± 80 B.P.
OxA 5972	Pekárna, layers g and h (1986)	12,500 ± 110 B.P.
OxA 5973	Kolíbky (1982)	12,680 ± 110 B.P.
Ly 1108	Hostim, Bohemia	12,420 ± 470 B.P.
GrN 5097	Kůlna, layer 6, cave interior	11,590 ± 80 B.P.
GrN 11053	Kůlna, layer 6, entrance	11,450 ± 90 B.P.
GrN 6102	Kůlna, layer 4	11,470 ± 105 B.P.
GrN 6120	Kůlna, layer 3	10,070 ± 85 B.P.

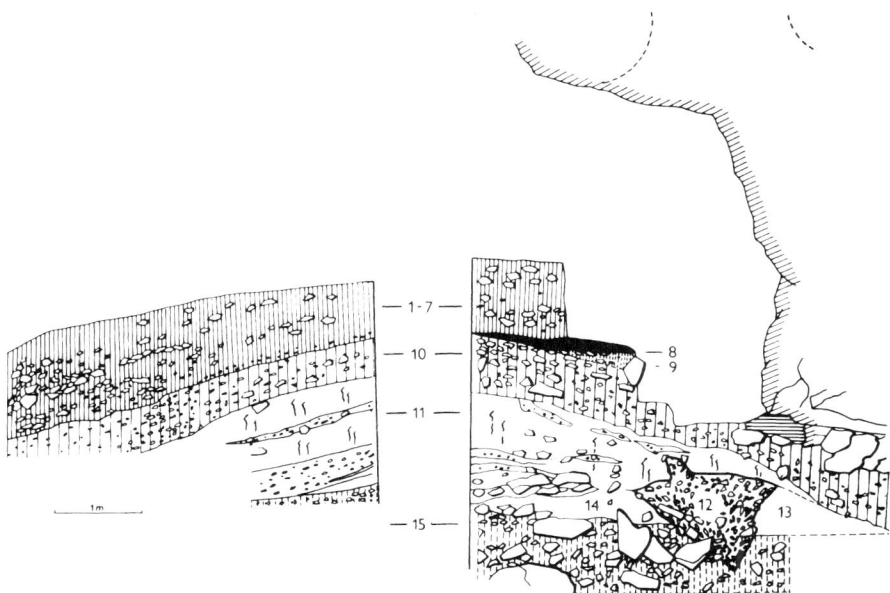

Figure 7.2. Stratigraphic section at the entrance of Barová Cave. 1–7—dark humic loams with limestone scree (Holocene); 8—Neolithic hearth; 9—light loam with scree; 10—coarse limestone scree with light loesslike matrix (Alleröd to early Holocene); 11—loess; 12–infill of a wedge-shaped crevasse; 13—redeposited loess; 14–light brown loess; 15–coarse limestone scree with brownish red loamy matrix.

of the Epimagdalenian, corresponding to the Alleröd and dated to 11,470 B.P. and 10,070 B.P. (Smolíková, 1988).

Finally, Barová Cave (Figure 7.2; Seitl et al., 1986; Svobodová and Svoboda, 1988; Svobodová, 1992) has the most complete stratigraphic and especially biostratigraphic evidence (microfauna, mollusks, pollen), but C-14 dating is unfortunately not available, and the archaeological context is scarce. The base of this sequence (layer 15) consists of rock debris filled with brown-reddish clays. Pollen spectra from this layer indicate that the arboreal vegetation (*Pinus*, *Betula*, *Salix*, and *Corylux*) did not exceed 14% and that grains of *Asteraceae* predominated among the nonarboreal pollen. This combination of pollens suggests the presence of a rather open landscape that was glacial in character. An important climatic amelioration is observed in the overlying loess sediment (layer 14). Here, arboreal pollen increases to 46.3% and includes *Pinus*, *Picea*, *Betula*, *Juniperus*, *Corylus*, and *Salix*. Nonarboreal taxa include *Poaceae*, *Asteraceae*, and *Cyperaceae*. Layer 13, which included a poor lithic assemblage, represents a period of erosion and resedimentation, after which an erosive depression was formed and subsequently filled by debris and loess (layer 12).

The percentages of arboreal pollen are low at the base of this depression (19.5%–24.6%), increase toward the middle (56.3%), and decrease toward the top of the filling (16.5%). The arboreal pollen at the top of the depression includes *Pinus, Betula, Alnus,* and *Ephedra distachia, Juniperus,* and *Salix.* The microfauna recovered from this sequence contain both steppe and woodland species (*Arvicola terrestris, Dicrostonyx torquatus, Lemmus lemmus, Microtus agrestis,* etc.). The lithics of layer 12 date to the Magdalenian, while the extension of woodland at this early Magdalenian time would suggests a Bölling age. The loess sediments (layer 11) covering the erosive depression represent the last dated loess in Moravia. The percentages of arboreal pollen (especially of pine and birch) in this layer fluctuate from 29.5% to 43.7%. Late glacial species are represented by *Selaginella* and *Helianthemum.* The pleniglacial mollusks present in the middle part of this layer are replaced by the late glacial species toward the top of the layer. The remains of large fauna include the last rhinoceros and mammoth dated in Moravian loess, accompanied by bovids. The cultural inventories consist of some Magdalenian lithics documenting working of the local cherts.

The last glacial layer (10) is no longer constituted of loess, but of earth with much limestone debris. The pollen analysis demonstrates an extension of woodland, however, with a different composition, dominated by birch and hazel; at the top of the layers, all arboreal elements rapidly decrease in number. After the mollusks, this layer dates to the late glacial–early Holocene boundary, while a boreal assemblage is documented higher in the overlying layer. Culturally, this layer is attributed to the Epimagdalenian, with an increased number of raw material imports (flint, rock crystal) and two backed microblades. The observed woodland extension in this cultural context suggests an Alleröd age.

More precise evidence of late glacial vegetational development, however, with no archaeological associations, is evidenced by pollen analyses from several peat bog sections of the southern Moravian lowlands. The most important section is at the former Vracov Lake (Rybníčková and Rybníček, 1972; Svobodová, 1991c). It documents part of the cool and dry early Dryas (I) at the base, with steppic vegetation and shrublike patches of *Ephedra, Pinus,* and *Juniperus.* The following warmer and moister Bölling is characterized by patches of pine and birch woodland.

CULTURAL PATTERNS

The Magdalenian

The lithic typology of the large Magdalenian sites (Table 7.3; Figure 7.3), as represented at Pekárna (layers g and h), is composed primarily of four groups: endscrapers, burins, borers, and backed implements. The backed implements are mainly simple backed blades and, rarely, points and truncated blades. Compared to those of the Gravettian, the backed microliths become more rare. It seems certain that the variability in frame of this structure reflects the lack of comparability in the number of tools in the assemblages (which may vary from hundreds to several classified types) rather than chronological or facial differences. Therefore, it is difficult to develop evolutionary schemes of the Magdalenian industries in Moravia (Valoch, 1960c) and to compare them within the chronological and stratigraphic frameworks.

Table 7.3. Magdalenian, Comparative Typology

	Pekárna, platform	Hadí Cave	Křížova Cave	Ochozská Cave	Žitného Cave	Býčí skála	Balcarova Cave	Maloměřice Borky 1	Kůlna, layer 5	Kůlna, layer 6
Endscrapers	19.5	13.7	9.8	10.5	12.3	18.6	17.1	7.5	14.7	12.0
Burins	12.1	13.7	8.2	19.3	13.2	9.5	6.8	35.3	14.7	12.0
Borers	11.4	17.9	16.4	9.5	10.8	18.6	8.6	15.9	8.0	11.2
Backed blades	28.8	6.3	31.2	33.0	44.1	14.9	51.3	21.0	29.3	23.2
Sidescrapers	0.4	1.9	0	0.7	0.6	1.6	0	1.2	6.6	8.8
Combinations	2.3	10.5	0	0.4	0	1.2	X	4.6	2.7	1.6
Others	25.5	36.0	34.4	26.6	19.0	35.6	X	14.5	24.0	31.2
Total tools	735	95	61	285	538	242	117	603	75	125

Note: X = present but not calculated.

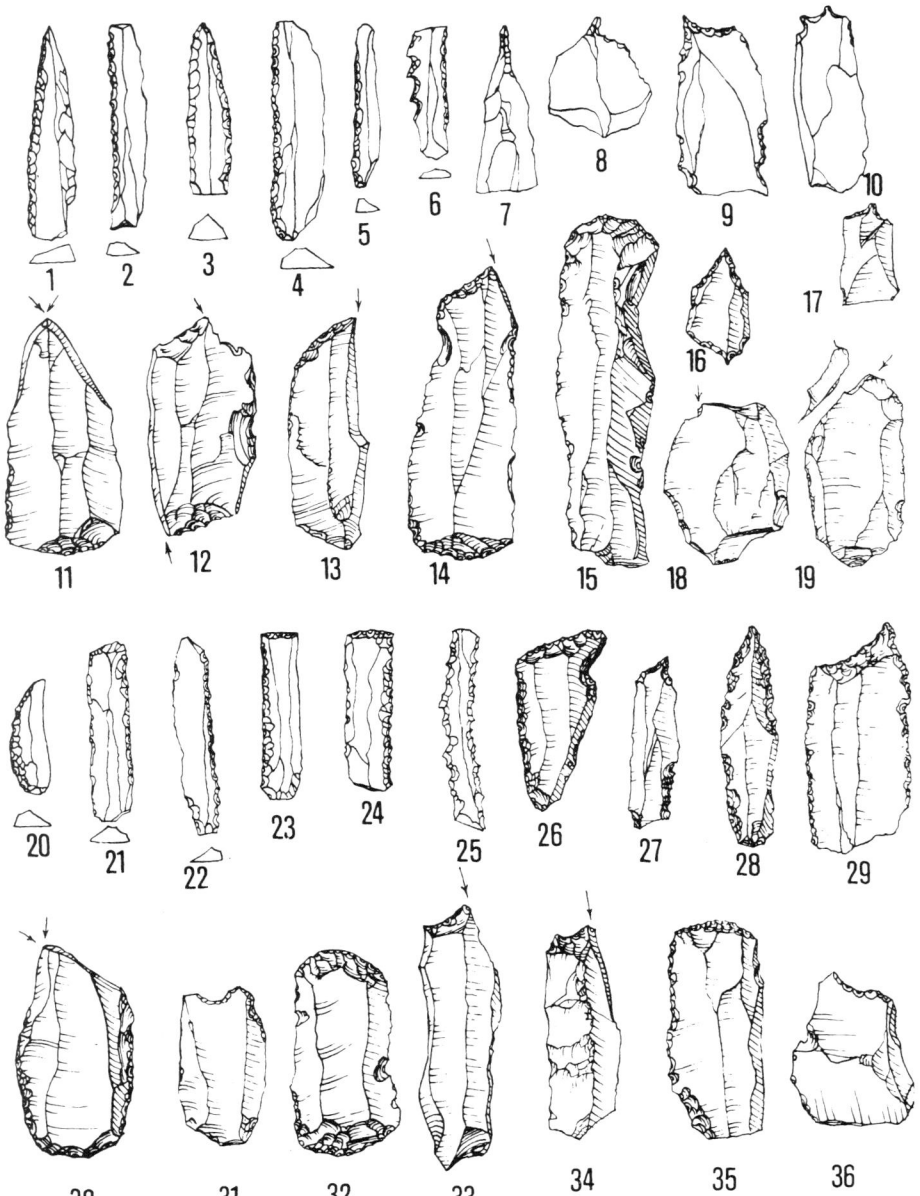

Figure 7.3. Magdalenian lithic industry (around 12,500–13,000 B.P.): Pekárna Cave. 1–19—layers g and h; 20–36—layer i.

New bone and antler tools and weapons, such as spears with single or double beveled bases, accompanied by rare *navettes*, barbed points (harpoons), *batons de commandement*, and sewing needles, appear in the Magdalenian and, again, especially in Pekárna (the longest needle, however, was found in the Žitného Cave; Appendix A). For some authors, the fact that certain distinctive tools—*batons de commandement* and needles—were previously known in the Epigravettian of Grubgraben or in the Gravettian of Russia, serves as the major argument for assuming Magdalenian origins in the Gravettian and Epigravettian traditions of Central Europe.

The Epimagdalenian

In certain cave sites, the small assemblages of the Epimagdalenian represent a stratigraphic continuation of the Magdalenian development. In lithic typology (Figure 7.4), they are primarily characterized by the appearance of short endscrapers and burins (Kůlna Cave), and of backed microblades (Kůlna and Barová Caves: Seitl et al., 1986; Valoch, 1988).

The Tišnovian

Industries of the Tišnovian group are chronologically comparable to the Epigravettian, but they occupy larger, open landscapes, including regions previously scarcely colonized or else deserted. Typologically (Figure 7.4), they differ mainly in the presence of microlithic backed points (Kos, 1971; Svoboda et al., 1994).

THE LATE GLACIAL ADAPTATIONS

As an invasive culture, the Magdalenian documents new preferences in site location and in adaptation to the faunal resources of the late glacial, but it shows a continuity in the use of the old communication routes throughout Central Europe. Ideology, as reflected in symbolic behavior and art, had clearly been introduced from the west, but more detailed comparisons will show how far its original formal and symbolic content had been modified in the newly settled territories.

Settlement Pattern

Magdalenian settlement in Moravia lay at the easternmost boundary of the Magdalenian in Europe, in a peripheral location broadly comparable to that of the Acheulean (Chapter 4).

The preference for karstic areas (Figure 7.1) in the Magdalenian of Moravia is also observed along the eastern boundaries of this culture: in southern Poland (Maszycka Cave), Lower Austria (Gudenus Cave), and further to the west along the upper Danube (Klausen Caves, Kleine Ofnet, Kaufertsberg, Vogelherd, Felsställe, Geissenklösterle, Brillenhöhle, and Petersfels) and as far as Switzerland (Schweizersbild and

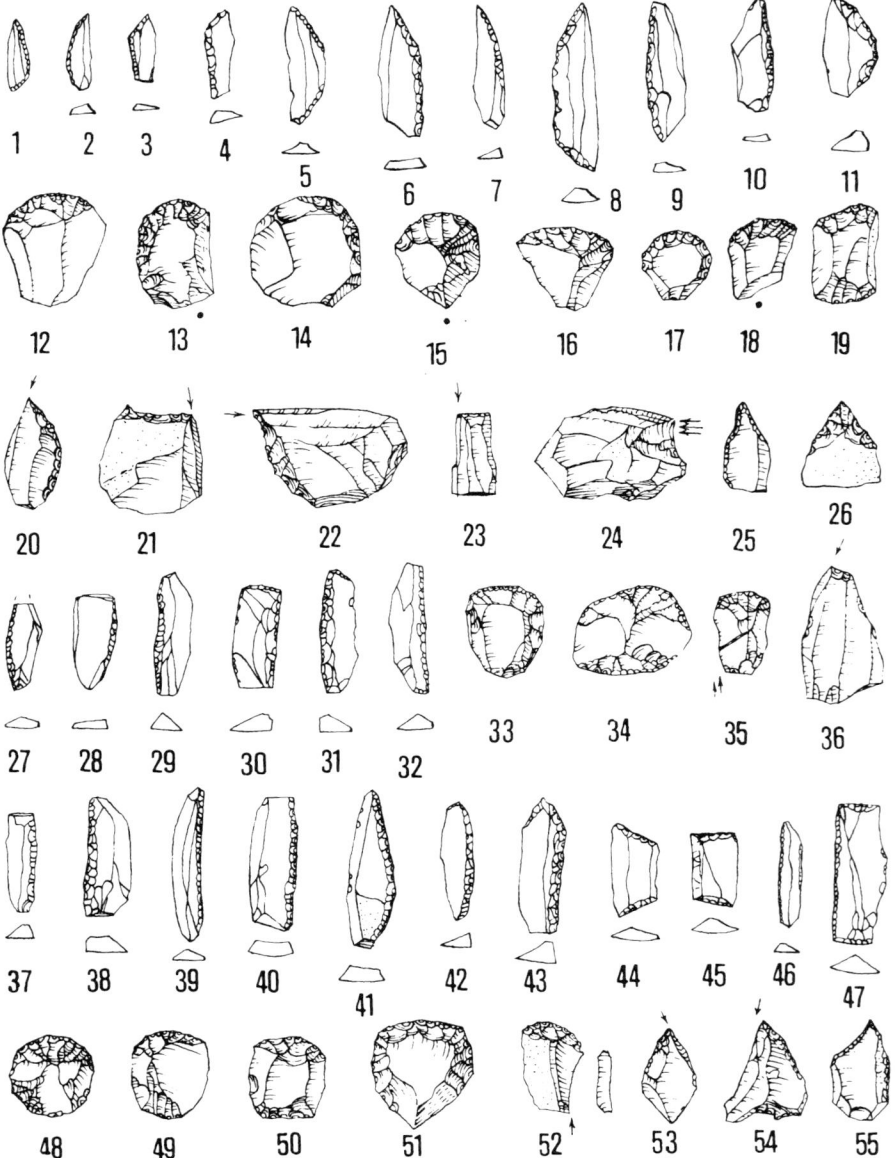

Figure 7.4. Tišnovian (1–26) and Epimagdalenian (27–55) lithic industries: Tišnov and Kůlna, layer 4.

Kesslerloch). On the other hand, large open-air sites are known from the Rhineland (Gönnersdorf and Andernach), central Germany (Oelknitz and Nebra), and Bohemia (Hostim); what is probably the easternmost one is located in central Poland (Klementowice). This second group of sites also provides evidence of a different hunting specialization and slightly different symbolic behavior (traces of rituals in the open air and a preference for the use of slate plaques for art). Given the existence of these two large Magdalenian areas in Central Europe, let us say the "southern" and the "northern," Moravia would clearly fall into the first area.

In the Moravian karst, a longitudinal area about 25 km in length, the location of the caves follows the geographic and hydrological separation of this area into southern, central, and northern parts. Each of these parts has a large central site: Pekárna in the south, Býči skála in the center, and Kůlna in the north. These are surrounded by clusters of smaller sites, again mostly caves, but sometimes, and especially in the south, strategically located open-air sites controlling the adjacent lowlands. From south to north, as the karst reaches further into the highlands, the valleys become deeper, and the absolute altitudes higher (altitudes range from 300 to 400 m in the southern and central karst, and from 400 to 500 m in the north), and settlement is more and more scarce. Whereas almost every accessible cave or shelter provides a trace of the Magdalenians in the south, large and suitable caves were never settled in the north (Valoch, 1960c; Svoboda, Seitl, and Štrof, 1983).

A substantial part of the archaeological and paleontological record of the Moravian Magdalenian, and almost all the art objects, originates in the Pekárna Cave (Figure 7.5; Appendix A; Absolon and Czižek, 1926–1932). The role of this cave in the Magdalenian settlement system may now be evaluated in the context of the adjacent sites, especially the platform in front of it (Klíma, 1974a; Svoboda, 1991c), smaller caves in the vicinity (Hadí, Adlerova, Křížova, Švédův stůl, Kůlnička), and the settlement along the brook below Pekárna in front of Ochozská Cave, where Klíma (1970a, 1984a) observed a longitudinal depression and interpreted it as a dwelling. Within the broader vicinity, there is the largest Magdalenian open-air site at Maloměřice-Borky I in the Brno basin (Valoch, 1963), as well as several strategic locations at the outskirts of the Bohemian Massif around Mokrá (Škrdla, personal communication, 1995).

The interpretations of occupation in Pekárna alone, supplying the largest concentration of artifacts but little evidence of features, faces several problems, even if the largest excavation by Absolon and Czižek has been relatively well documented for that time. Given the character of the sediments, as well as the early time of their excavation, following the habitation structures in the 60-m-long cave is quite difficult. On the basis of Czižek's diaries, Svoboda (1991c) reconstructed a continuous line of hearths about 2–3 m deep from the entrance, as well as a second line about 33–36 m from the entrance. In the center of this delimited area lies a group of four larger limestone blocks surrounded by a flake accumulation. However symmetrical such a structure may seem to be (Figure 7.6), it is difficult to prove the contemporaneity of the various hearths. In the lower Magdalenian horizon (layer i) are documented traces of workshop activities using local cherts.

Figure 7.5. View of Pekárna Cave.

Another of the central caves, Býčí skála (Absolon, 1945a; Appendix A), differs from all the other sites because of its location of the settled area far from the entrance and daylight. Art is preserved, but only in the form of engraved pebbles (Figure 7.13, number 2). Similarly to Pekárna, the lower horizon most probably documents a workshop specialized in the local cherts (Valoch, 1966b; Sobczyk, 1984).

Kůlna, the central site in the north of the Moravian karst (Valoch, 1988), is the largest of all the caves, but the occupation was less intensive, and the representative art is absent.

Among the smaller sites, the newly reexcavated site of Kolíbky (Figure 7.7; Knies, 1905; Svoboda et al., 1996) deserves attention not only because of the evidence of local-raw-material working (cherts and ocher), but especially because of the exceptional discovery of a series of graywacke slabs with circular depressions, possibly lamps (Figure 7.8; Appendix A). According to the original observation by Knies (1905), the slabs should have formed "a row" (if Knies did not mean "a row" in a numerical sense). The presence of charcoal and burnt loess observed by him around these objects suggests a function related to heating. To interpret a container as a lamp, de Beaune (1987) strongly requires appropriate traces of its use as a lamp. With the negative results of chemical analyses (Toul, in Svoboda et al., 1996), we base our comparison with the French lamps on a probability derived from Knies's observations and on the morphology and small volume of the depression (not useful as containers).

During and after the Alleröd, the Late Paleolithic sites became more dispersed and generally smaller, and most of them are known from surface surveys only. Possible settlement features were recorded only from Tišnov (Kos, 1971); however, the terrain

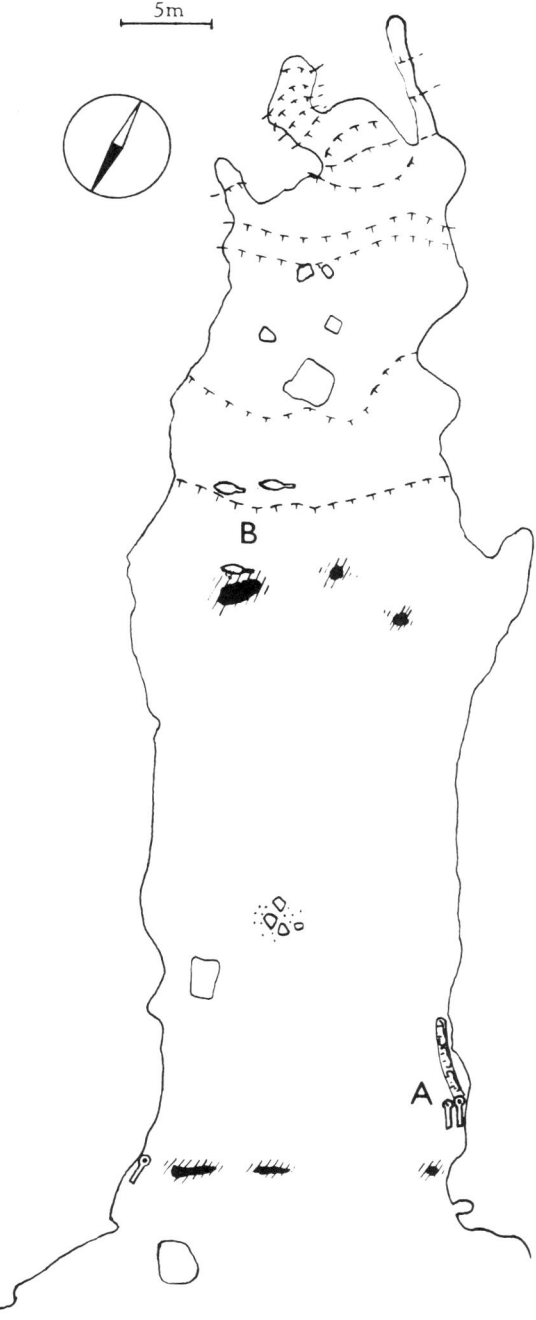

Figure 7.6. Plan of Pekárna Cave: Position of the large hearths and concentration of bone objects. A—ribs with drawings of bisons, *batons de commandement*; b—decorated *spatulae*. Reconstruction using the data of R. Czižek.

Figure 7.7. View of the Kolíbky site.

Figure 7.8. Kolíbky, one of the graywacke plaques with depressions, possibly a lamp.

situation at this site was not quite clear. Some caves were repeatedly settled by the Epimagdalenians (Kůlna, Barová Cave), but the general trend of Tišnovian settlement was to expand into newly opened territories of the Bohemian–Moravian Highland (Diviš and Grepl, 1984; Oliva, 1986), to the Bučovice region (Mazálek, 1960; Valoch, 1966c), or, within the traditionally settled regions, to higher and more exposed positions (Pavlovské Hills and Kobylanka; Ložek, 1985; Ložek, Tyráček, and Fejfar, 1959).

Duration of Occupation

As in analyses of the Gravettian settlement pattern, the size of the sites, the volume of the layers, and the hearths still remain major criteria in distinguishing between "long" and "short" occupation periods. Naturally, this kind of analysis, especially in caves, cannot separate a continuous occupation from an accumulation of short, repeated visits to a favored shelter.

In Germany, the size of the Magdalenian sites and their relationship to the complex archaeological evidence have been analyzed by Weniger (1989). These include large sites with more than 100 cores, several hundred retouched tools, rich faunal assemblages, examples of portable art, and habitation structures. Furthermore, there are medium, small, and extremely small sites. According to Weniger, the small sites were usually short-term field camps occupied mainly in spring and summer: bone and antler tools are rare, habitation structures are not evident, and the presence of fire is often evidenced by burned artifacts only.

In Moravia, Pekárna Cave represents, in its volume and extension of archaeological layers, the most splendid example of a large, and/or repeatedly occupied, site. Among the other more important sites are Býčí skála and Kůlna.

Numerous small (episodic) sites are recorded in the Moravian karst (Appendix B), and Barová Cave offers an example well documented by modern excavations (Seitl et al., 1986). Weniger has also noted that the small sites are more varied functionally than the large ones and gives several examples of special activities performed at such sites in Germany. Similarly, in Moravia, the various activities are more readable at small sites (local-raw-material working at Barová, the systematic import of rock crystal at Žitného, and the concentration of ocher and the possible lamps at Kolíbky; cf. Appendix A).

Seasonality

From a European-wide perspective, seasonality in Moravia has so far been addressed by Sturdy (1975), who suggested long-distance seasonal migrations of the reindeer between the Central European Highlands and the Northern European Plain. It is important, however, to base general models on detailed osteological analyses of the individual sites. As in the Gravettian, the evidence of the presumed seasonal rhythms is limited, and hibernation is more clearly documented in the large sites than the presumed summer camps in the small sites. A winter occupation at Býčí skála may be deduced from its unusual location deep in the cave: the interior climatic condition of the cave, a subterranean brook deeper in the cave, and the local source of the cherts would have made it an optimal hibernation site. From Pekárna, Berke (1989) analyzed a series of 12 mandibles of young reindeer between 6–9 months old corresponding to occupation from November to February. Naturally, this observation does not exclude occupation during other seasons of the year.

An earlier study of reindeer antlers from Moravia suggests that the animals may have stayed in the karst during the whole year (Musil, 1958:18). It would be especially promising to analyze materials from the small and exposed cave sites of the Moravian karst to see whether the differences in site size and location are related to seasonality.

Variability in Raw Material Acquisition

At first glance, the Magdalenian pattern of lithic raw-material procurement does not differ from the Gravettian one (Figure 8.2). The production of the Magdalenian industries still depended largely on imported raw materials, and most of the flint material continued to come from the northeast (Poland: Sobczyk, 1984); the closest occurrences of related glacial sediments are found in the Moravian Gate, about 90 km northeast of the Moravian karst.

In contrast to our lack of evidence on the Gravettian, we now have good evidence of primary workshops at the flint outcrops along edges of the Northern European Plain from Poland (Brzoskwinia and Wolowice) to Germany (Groitzsch), and analyses of the primary procurement imply a better understanding of technology (Ginter, 1974; Sobczyk, 1993). Subsequently, flint importation to the Moravian karst may be illustrated, for example, by the unusually large and carefully prepared precore of flint from Adlerova Cave (Svoboda, 1987c). If the raw material imports reflect regular (seasonal) population movements that connected the Moravian territory with lithic exploitation areas in the north and northeast, Sturdy's (1975) hypothesis about long-distance reindeer and hunter migrations would be supported.

Sobczyk (1984) analyzed the Magdalenian sites of Central Europe from the viewpoint of lithic raw-material processing and its dynamics. Special attention has been paid to the percentage of core preforms within the core assemblages, which, logically, reaches maximal values at the primary rock-extraction sites in Poland and Germany (Wolowice, 75%; Brzoskwinia, 25%–30%; Groitzsch, 43%). In the Moravian karst, an area more dependent on imported materials, this percentage is usually low (Pekárna, 4%), and it reaches a higher value in the large cave workshop at local chert sources in Býčí skála (27%).

The radiolarites of eastern or southern origin are present in a lower percentage, as in most of the Gravettian sites. The presence of quartzites of the Bečov type at Maloměřice-Borky is an exception (primary outcrops of this material are localized in northwestern Bohemia; however, a similar material is surprisingly frequent at Austrian sites, where its occurrence suggests another outcrop). Weniger (1987, 1989) recorded that, further to the west, the Gravettian east–west communication axis, which ran along the Danube and connected Bavaria with the upper Rhine, continued to be frequented. This importation network suggests that, even if we suppose a change in population, the old communication routes retained their function.

Another difference in comparison to the Gravettian is relatively good evidence of local chert exploitation in Moravia (Přichystal, 1994b; Svoboda et al., 1996); however, from the variety of local materials used in the Early Upper Paleolithic, only the types available in the vicinity of the Moravian karst were used more frequently: the Cretacous cherts rich in sponge spicules of the Boskovice Furrow (10–15 km from the karst), various cherts of the Rudice formation (the Olomučany type and the Býčí skála type, located directly in the karst), and the Drahany quartzites, which were scattered over the adjacent highlands. Evidence of local processing is supplied by the lower layers of the Pekárna and Býčí skála Caves, by Kolíbky Cave, and by a number of smaller caves. The Moravian karst and its immediate vicinity yielded other lithic sources as well: ocher (the Rudice formation), Lower Carboniferous graywackes, shales, and Lower Devonian sandstones, used for the decorated pebble hammers, for plaques, and for the possible lamps.

Subsistence Strategies

Unfortunately, most of the late glacial paleontological materials come from early excavations in caves, so that we lack exact stratigraphic and contextual data. According to the last summary presented by Musil in 1958, the most important game was hare, followed by reindeer, horse, and birds; after 1958, Musil concentrated more on material from central German sites (Kniegrotte and Oelknitz) than on Moravia.

A review of the preferences in hunting game throughout Central Europe suggests a dominance of reindeer over horse in the "southern" group of sites (ranging from southern Germany to Switzerland) and horse over reindeer in the "northern" group (Middle Rhine valley, Central Germany, Bohemia). Naturally, such a division is simplistic and does not take into account various exceptions. However, the Germany data generally confirm this division (Weniger, 1989), and further parallels appear in the artifactual context. In Moravia, the ratios of reindeer and horse are very variable in the individual sites, and Valoch (1980b:385) once suggested that a preference for one or the other of these two animals was influenced by factors other than ecology (symbolism?).

The restoration of a settlement network in caves may, at the first sight, recall the situation during the Middle Paleolithic rather than the pattern of Upper Paleolithic hunting strategies (Chapter 5). Nevertheless, differences should be searched for in the more complex system of relationships between the individual sites (cf. Musil, 1974; Sturdy, 1975; Berke, 1989; Weniger, 1989), with possible implications about more complex social organization.

The data now in hand about the settlement geography in karstic regions are more complex compared to the still limited faunal database. The Magdalenian settlement pattern suggests a more efficient type of hunting using both the large home bases and smaller hunting posts at strategic places. Since the valley location of the largest caves seems not to have been favorable for hunting, Pekárna is surrounded by a system of smaller, more exposed hunting sites controlling the adjacent lowlands (the Brno Basin and Mokrá). A large part of the bones and meat was clearly transported from considerable distances. Berke (1989) analyzed the horse bones from Pekárna (layers g and h) in detail: the long-bone splinters and the vertebrae are very few compared to the mass of phalanges (including the third phalanges), teeth, and mandibles. The butchering marks are similar to those from Petersfels in southern Germany and occur at the same places (the pattern of breaking the pelvis or extracting the tongue from the mandibles). Berke therefore argues that parts of the bodies were selected and transported to the cave. It seems that, in the Magdalenian, the unfavorable location of the home-bases for hunting may have been reduced by more efficient group organization and planning; therefore, the presumed difference from the Middle Paleolithic should be searched for in human behavior.

Symbols, Rituals, and Art

As suggested by Jochim (1983), the splendid Magdalenian paintings are found only in the West of Europe because the Franco-Cantabrian regions were a climatic refuge during and after the last glacial maximum and there was a resultant need for symbolic negotiations. After the present scenarios, the late glacial amelioration enabled Magdalenian expansion to Central Europe. Therefore, this chapter is based on a comparison of the art of the two regions: their form and, as far as possible, their interpretation.

In its technique and styles, the Magdalenian art of Central Europe demonstrates a unity with the Franco-Cantabrian zone even more convincingly than the other archaeological material, such as the lithics. The differences lie especially in the lack of parietal art and the paucity of plastic animal carvings. Central European plastic art has region-specific forms, such as abstract female statues (the buttocks style), especially from Germany (Bosinski, 1982a), with a single occurrence in Moravia (the ivory statue from Pekárna: Absolon and Czižek, 1926–1932), and with parallels outside the Magdaleniam territory, further to the east (Mezin). This characteristic shape not only was shaped of organic materials (antler and ivory), but was also searched for in natural pebbles (sometimes engraved), which were found in the Moravian sites (Figure 7.13: numbers 1 and 2 from Pekárna and Býčí skála). In France, the buttocks-style abstraction is evidenced as well, but in rock engravings rather than in a plastic form.

From Absolon's excavation in the Rytířská Cave in the northern Moravian karst, K. Valoch (1965e) published a quite different vision of the female, exaggerating the breasts; as one of the possible arguments for local affiliation during the Magdalenian, this piece recalls the former Gravettian abstractions from Dolní Věstonice (Chapter 5).

The forms of decorative patterns on bone and antler tools and weapons, as well as on stone pebbles, were analyzed by Svoboda (1976, 1986). It appears that, throughout Central Europe, they may be separated to two groups: one arising from simple geometric patterns, called *static* (Figure 7.9), and the other combining arches, welled lines, and lentil-like patterns, called *dynamic* (Figure 7.10). The latter of the two identifies Magdalenian style while the first one is recorded elsewhere. However, the

WESTERN INVASION

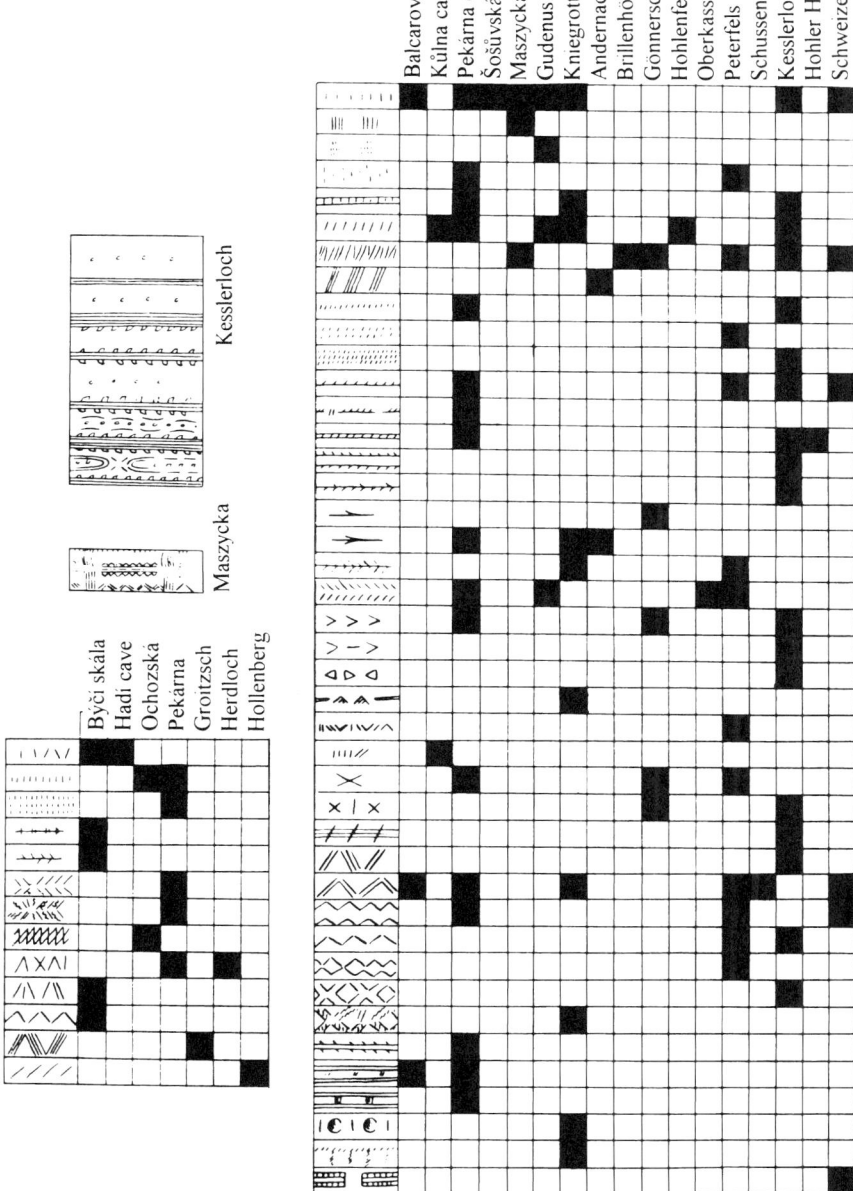

Figure 7.9. Table of Magdalenian decorative patterns in Central European sites: The geometric group. Large table and additions—bone; small table—stone.

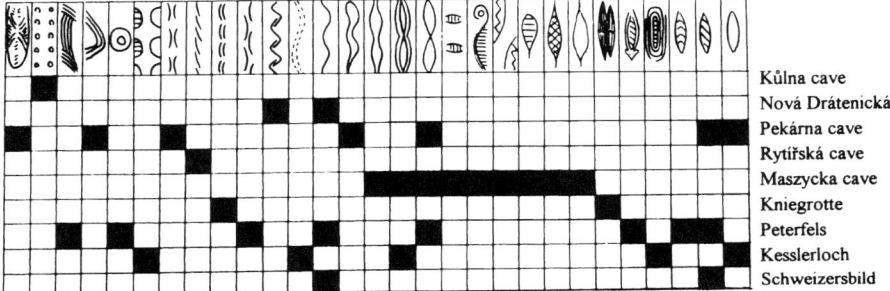

Figure 7.10. Table of Magdalenian decorative patterns in Central European sites: The dynamic group. Large table and additions—bone; small table—stone.

both groups appear in the same assemblages, and this decoration has no relationship to the subdivision of Magdalenian into the "northern" and "southern" groups, except the observation that the majority of the decorated items originates from the south.

A more restricted regional occurrence is the engraved slate plaques, recovered from numerous Magdalenian sites throughout Central Europe (Schweizersbild, Kesslerloch, Hohlenstein, Mittlere Klause, and Petersfels), but typically from the "northern" group of sites (Gönnersdorf, Andernach, Oelknitz, Saaleck, Hostim, Děravá Cave, and Ražice; Klíma, 1985a). The largest assemblage of this sort, from Gönnersdorf, yielded more than 400 female representations, more than 200 zoomorphic engravings (mostly of horse and mammoth), and symbols (Bosinski, 1981; 1982a). In Moravia, plaques of this kind are extremely rare (a sandstone plaque from Pekárna: Klíma, 1974a), and various engravings are made on small schist pebbles instead (Valoch, 1961a).

In the German sites, the context clearly shows an association of the plaques with cultural layers and pits. The plaques, both engraved and unengraved, are concentrated on the floors of three habitation structures, and it seems that this position was secondary. Some of the plaques were broken and reused. Bosinski (1982a) showed experimentally that most of the engravings remained visible for only a short time, until the stone powder disappeared. Then, the plaque could be used again. Therefore, the associations of the various subjects, as accumulated on a plate, have little or no meaning. Furthermore the plaques show a network of lines; apparently accidental and

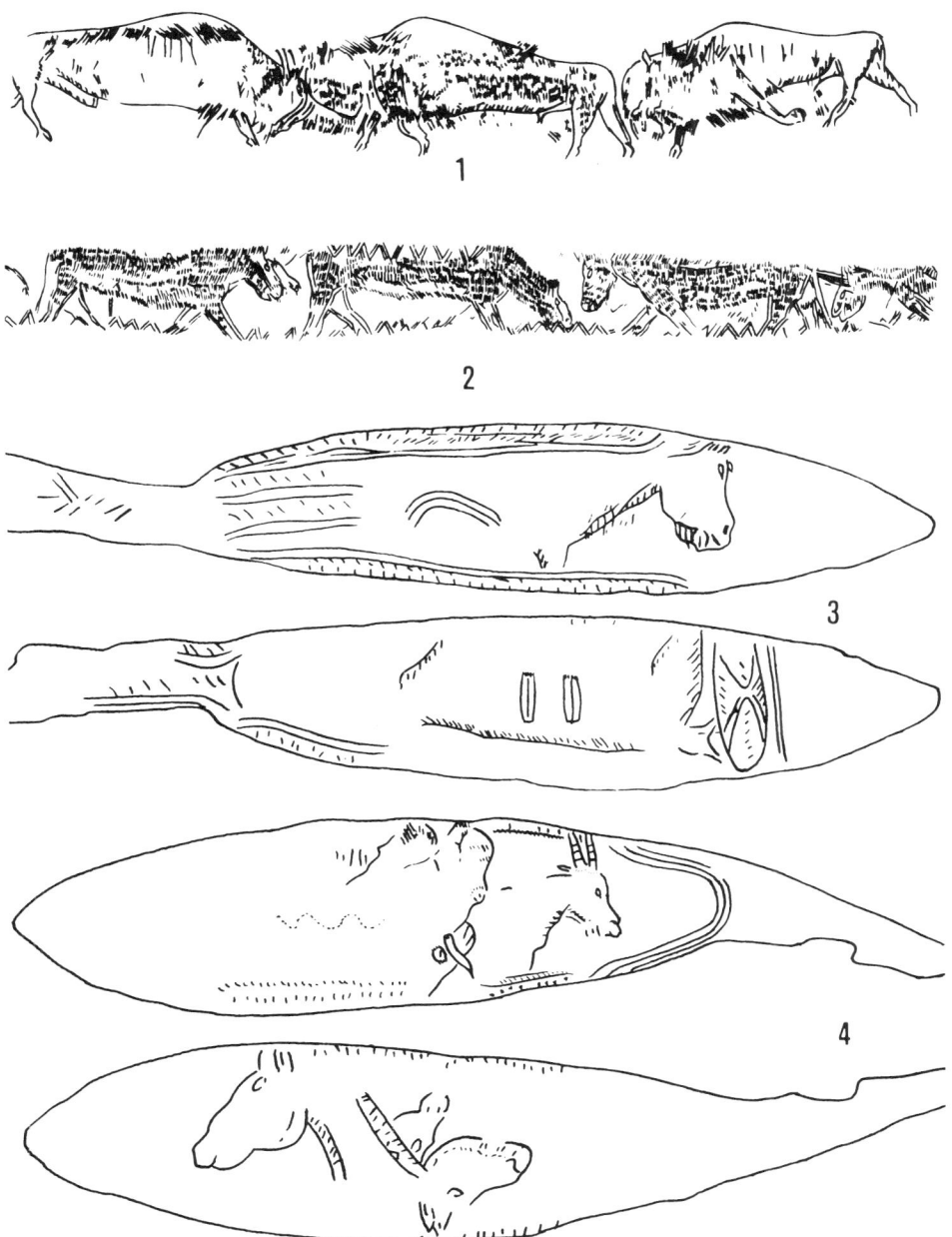

Figure 7.11. Magdalenian art: Pekárna Cave.

complicating the search for figures. These networks may be traces of a ritual performed with the plate (Marshack, 1992: 189). As in case of the Gravettian ceramics, such a ritual would have concerned carnivore and herbivore subjects as well as females. The style of the animals is realistic, even "photographic," but the lines are quick and fluent, drawn by an experienced hand. By contrast, the females are schematized in the Magdalenian buttocks style.

In Moravia (namely, the Pekárna Cave), animal engravings in bone are more typical than engravings in stone (Figure 7.11). The *batons de commandement* of Pekárna are directly comparable to the Western European objects, and two of them are engraved with animal figures (bears and horse's head); closer parallels exist of Petersfels, Schweizersbild, and Kesslerloch (Svoboda, 1976, 1986; Bosinski, 1982a). Some importance may be attached to the spatial distribution of the art objects within Pekárna: two horse ribs decorated with scenes of grazing horses (Klíma, 1965a) (Figure 7.12) and fighting bisons were found at the right side of the entrance area. The *spatulae* engraved with complex zoomorphic and symbolic subjects were concentrated in the deep inner part of the cave, behind the second line of hearths (Figure 7.6). In contrast to the Gravettian sites, the art objects here lie rather at the peripheries than in the presumed geometric center of the cave.

Testing the hunting-magic scenario and all other efforts to understand the content and meaning of this art is complicated by the disproportion in frequency between animal representations in art and the associated faunal remains, as observed earlier in the Gravettian and elsewhere in Europe (Chapter 6). It appears that all the statistics on the depicted species are influenced by the appearance of 61 mammoth engravings at a single site: Gönnersdorf. According to Bosinski, the depiction of animals represented a good personal experience of the artist, but the faunal remains of this animal at Gönnersdorf are as rare as elsewhere. In contrast, a depiction of the hare, so frequently found in the faunal material, was noted in only one questionable case, at Lindenthaler Hyänenhöhle, Central Germany (however, in another orientation, the same curve may represent a mammoth outline). Furthermore, there are bones of animals never found in art (fox and cave hyena) and images which have little or no faunal context (rhinoceros, red deer, and even turtle or seal).

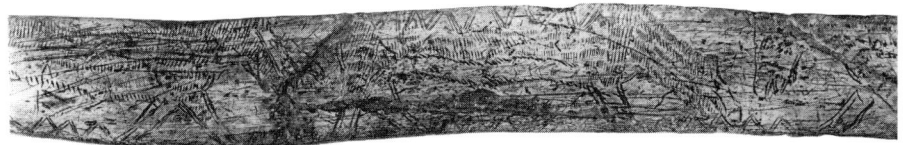

Figure 7.12. Pekárna, detail of the engraving of grazing horses on a horse rib.

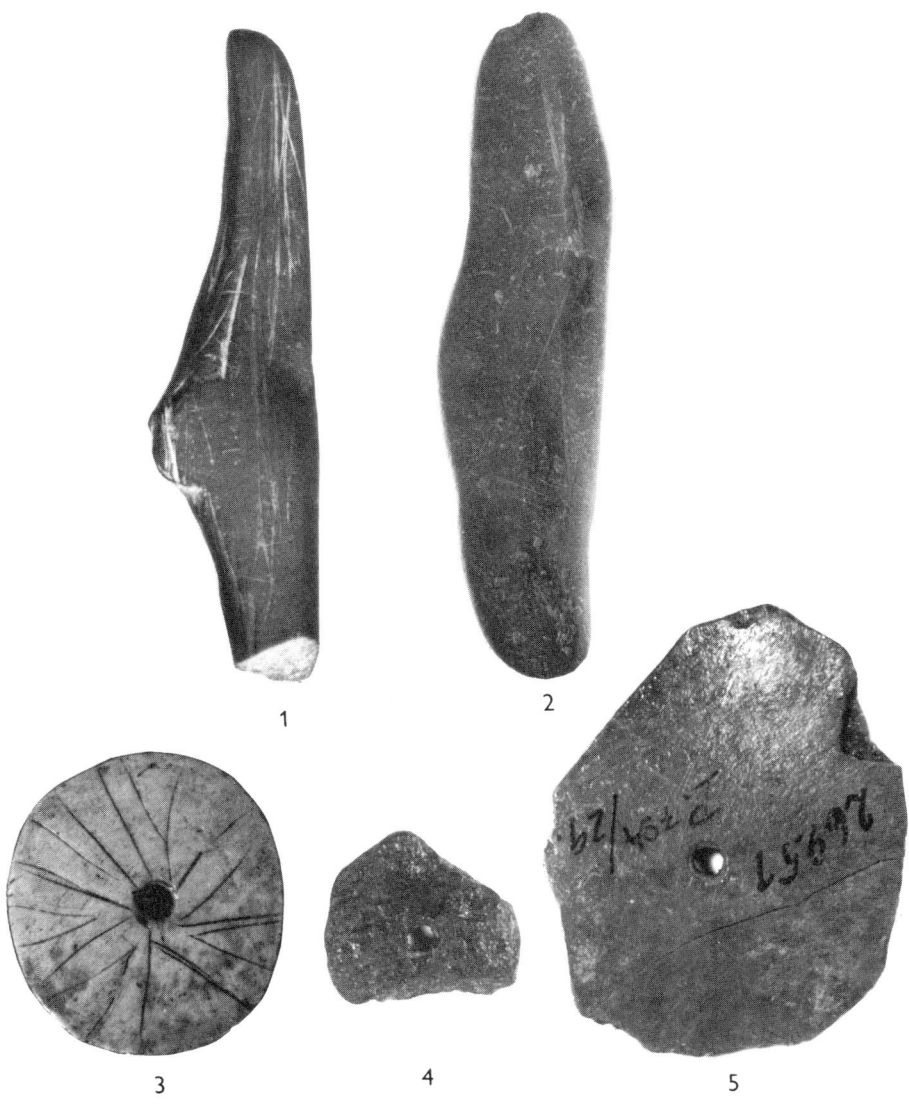

Figure 7.13. Magdalenian pebbles in form of stylized females: 1—Pekárna; 2—Býčí skála. Rondells: 3—Křížova Cave; 4—Ochozská Cave; 5—Pekárna.

The number of animals depicted per species was calculated separately for the "short-term" art (stone plaques) and for objects of longer use, such as carvings in bone and on tools and weapons. It appears that the numerical sequence in the second group (horse, reindeer, bovids, and bear) corresponds to the paleontological evidence better than the numerical stone plates (horse, mammoth, reindeer, and rhinoceros). This finding stresses the ritual character of the stone plaques, tied not so much to economic realities as to the strength and visual importance of the animal (Svoboda, 1976).

Burials

To the east of the Rhine (a region with the noteworthy ritual grave at Oberkassel [Verworn, Bonnett, and Steinmann, 1919]), the evidence about funerary behavior with bodies is very limited. The Early Magdalenian occupation of Maszycka Cave, southern Poland, is related to the discovery of the fragmented skeletal remains of 16 individuals, and it is not impossible that they were ritually killed. Further skeletal fragments have been described from the sediments of three caves in central Germany (Chapter 3). Early excavators reported further human cranial fragments in three Moravian caves (Kůlna, Balcarova, and Michalova) (Knies, 1990, 1901b; Jelínek, 1988). However, given our uncertainties about the stratigraphic context of these early finds, their Magdalenian age remains unproven. If all these repeatedly found cranial fragments date to late glacial sediments, they would only document funerary behavior with human remains that does not differ substantially from that observed in the Middle Paleolithic.

Chapter **8**

Creating Settlement Networks

MACROREGIONAL VIEW: CENTRAL EUROPE

The Paleolithic topography of Central Europe (Figure 1.1) was basically predestined by the upper and middle course of the largest river, the Danube, connecting the west and east of the region. To the north of the Danube, the chains of lower mountains (reaching altitudes around 1000 m above sea level) surrounded the basins of other Central European rivers such as Labe (Elbe) or Saale, grading toward distinct Paleolithic microworlds: the Northern European Plain and the Rhine Valley. To the east and southeast, the Carpathian basin, with a large, scarcely inhabited plain and with concentrated occupation along the margins of the mountaneous ridges (reaching altitudes around 2000 m a.s.l.), follows the course of the Danube further to the microworlds of Balkans. Along these outlines, we may define three subregions within Paleolithic Central Europe: the "southern," or Danube subregion (southern Germany, Austria, and Moravia, with analogies as far as southern Poland); the "northern," or Labe, subregion (Bohemia, central Poland, and central Germany, with parallels to the Rhine valley); and the "southeastern," or Carpathian, subregion (Slovakia and Hungary).

A look at the spatial distribution of Paleolithic cultures shows how important this geographic separation was. First and foremost, there were cultures of western origin that occupied both the southern and the northern subregions but did not (or only scarcely) penetrate further to the southeast: the Acheulean (Bosinski, 1967; Fridrich, 1982) and the Magdalenian (Valoch, 1960c; Svoboda, 1976; Weniger, 1987). In contrast, cultures with southeastern relationships reached as far as Moravia but only episodically penetrated further to the west: the Bohunician (Svoboda, 1987d, 1990a) and Szeletian (Allsworth-Jones, 1986; Oliva, 1991c). Information about the spatial extension of the Epigravettian across Central Europe is still restricted by a limited data base.

There are additional differences between the south and the north. The southern, Danubian region typically shows dense occupations in the Aurignacian (Hahn, 1977) and Gravettian (Otte, 1981), with caves being preferred along the upper Danube (southern Germany) and large open-air sites along the middle Danube (Lower Austria and Moravia). In contrast, the norther region has a larger number of important Lower and Middle Paleolithic (Bosinski, 1967; Fridrich, 1982; Mania 1984) and Late Paleolithic sites. As for the Magdalenian, this culture occupied both regions relatively intensively, but there were slight behavioral differences between the northern and southern groups (Chapter 7).

Moravia clearly belongs to the southern subregion, but during certain periods, it shows influences from the adjacent southeast. An advantage of this region (among others) is that practically all Central European cultures met here, even if some of them left only a sparse record (Lower, Middle, and Late Paleolithic). Even occupation as distant from the Danube as the southern Polish sites around Krakow shows analogies to the southern rather than to the northern subregions, thus underlining the importance of the Moravian Gate as an axis of interregional communications.

MICROREGIONAL FOCUS: MORAVIA

An important aspect of present-day Czech archaeology seems to be its focus on landscapes rather than on the previously well-studied single site.

More than 125 years ago, Paleolithic research in Moravia was initiated in caves (Chapter 1). Between 1867 and 1918, 11 of the 18 sites excavated in Moravia were caves of the Moravian karst. Between 1918 and 1945, 12 sites were excavated, but only 4 of them were caves in this area, including the systematic excavation in Pekárna Cave. Between 1945 and 1989, the number of excavated sites increased to 41, 19 of which were caves of the Moravian Karst. At the same time, Paleolithic research expanded to large sites in loess, such as Předmostí and Dolní Věstonice (Tables 1.1–1.3).

However, the behavior of hunting-gathering groups shows continuity in space, and their archaeological traces are distributed more widely over landscapes than the individual excavations may suggest (Appendix B). The surface research on landscapes in Moravia has a tradition going back to the 1890s, when a regional survey was held by H. Hostínek around Ondratice in the Prostějov region. In the 1930s, K. Absolon supervised systematic surveys in the same area and presented their cartographic documentation (Absolon, 1935c:7), while Skutil (1936) recorded and mapped small surface sites from the whole of Moravia. During the 1960s and 1970s, K. Valoch initiated a large-scale collaboration with several surveyors in various parts of Moravia: J. Ječmínek in the Prostějov region, A. Koutný in the Zdounky region, R. Klíma in the Brno region, and many others (Valoch, 1956, 1961b, 1962b, 1967, 1979b, 1983). This system of exploration brought to light not only a number of new surface sites, but whole ares of Paleolithic occupation hitherto unknown or poorly known: the Boskovice Furrow, surveyed by A. Štrof, and Krumlovský les Highland, surveyed by V. Effenberger (Valoch, 1965d, 1966a, 1971, 1977b, 1978c). In consequence, in some of the Moravian and Silesian administrative districts the regional sites were catalogued (Grepl, 1991; Hrubý, 1951; Jisl, 1971; Klíma, 1986; Mazálek, 1960; Oliva, 1986, 1989c; Podborský and Vildomec, 1972).

During recent years, the methodology of regional surveys has become widely discussed in Czech archaeological theory. Apart from long-term collaboration with local amateur archaeologists, the new trends are dominated by time-limited professional surveys with a predetermined strategy. The methodological value of systematic professional surveys is undoubtedly higher than that of amateur activities. Nevertheless, in an agriculturally cultivated landscape, the work of professional surveyors is more limited by time, changing weather and light, and access to the fields (Svoboda, 1994c).

Since the late 1980s, Paleolithic materials from Moravia have been revised in the regional museums, listed, and—in collaboration with T. Czudek from the Institute of Geography—charted on maps with a scale of 1:200,000 (Appendix B). Solitary finds and dubious sites have been excluded, and the numeration systems used at the site clusters in certain localities (some of them quite complicated because they were labeled by a succession of surveyors) were avoided. Naturally, such a list is still far from complete. Nevertheless, it shows that the majority of the sites are clustered in 20 regions. Czudek remarked that the boundaries of these regions do not correspond to the defined geomorphological units. The site clusters are located in marginal areas between the lowlands and the highlands, expanding up to 500 m above sea level. Therefore, Czudek (1994:14) suggested the following regional names (from south to north): the Pavlov region, the Znojmo–Pouzdřany region, the Klobouky region, the Kyjov region, the Uherské Hradiště region, the Dolní Kounice region, the Mohelno region, the Rosice-Boskovice region, the Brno region, the Vyškov region, the Bučovice region, the Moravian karst, the Zdounky region, the Holešov region, the Prostějov region, the Přerov–Hranice region (the Moravian Gate), the Olomouc region, the Štramberk karst, the Opava region, and the Ostrava region.

Based on the importance of the recorded sites (excavated versus surface sites) and on their density, Czudek (1994) selected eight of these regions as more important than the others (the Pavlov region, the Rosice-Boskovice region, the Brno region, the Moravian karst, the Zdounky region, the Prostějov region, the Přerov–Hranice region, and the Štramberk karst) and described them separately. It is presupposed that altitude (with climatological, vegetational, and other environmental effects), geomorphology (passages and remarkable elevations such as the Pavlovské Hills), riverine networks, game, and raw material resources were responsible for the human selection of a particular area. Models of hunter-gatherer communities suggest that such areas, in fact, may have been structured by various exploitive, social, and ritual activities, but the boundaries are sometimes invisible today—or may never have really existed. What has the optimal chances of being detected today is the exploitation of fauna and lithic outcrops.

The correlation of the spatial distributions of paleontological finds is complicated by the various states of preservation of this material, which have been widely influenced by the sedimentary conditions in a particular areas, whereas the available information has been biased by uneven intensity of regional paleontological surveys. The early maps of the paleontological records of Moravia, as drawn by Skutil and Stehlík (1932b), show areas of mammalian and mammoth distribution along the loess-covered and well-explored western margins of the Bohemian Massif and thus

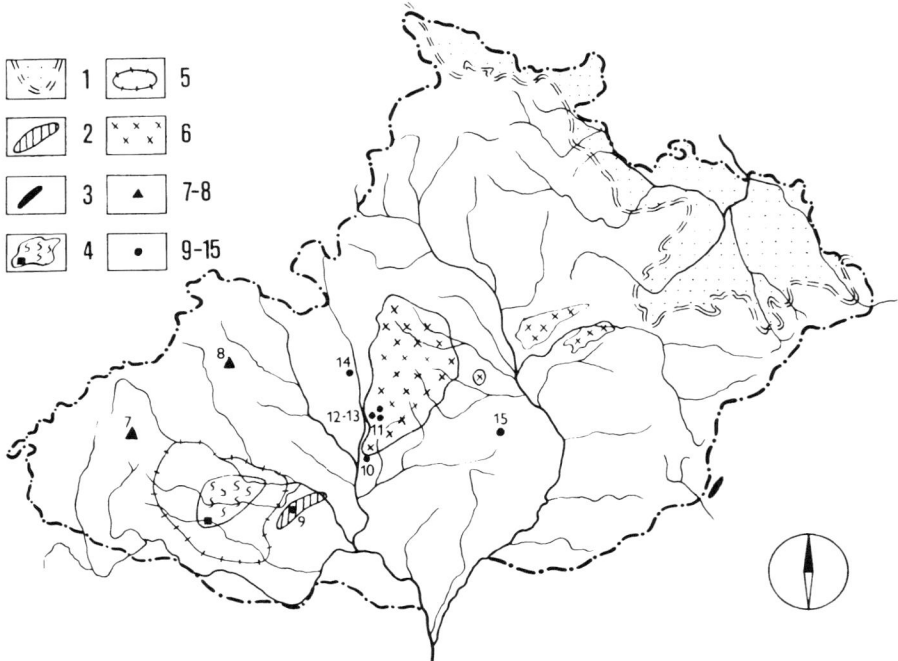

Figure 8.1. Map of the outcrops of lithic raw materials in Moravia (after A. Přichystal). 1—Extent of continental glaciation with erratic silicites and flints; 2—main outcrops of the Krumlovský les cherts; 3—probable area of radiolarite exploitation in the White Carpathians; 4—outcrops of silicified weathered serpentinites ("plasma") around Jevišovice; 5—occurrence of moldavites; 6—approximatice extension of quartzites in the Drahany, Nízký Jeseník, and Maleník Highlands; 7–8—areas of rock crystal exploitation around Kněžíce and Sklené-Rousměrov; 9–15—localized chert outcrops (9—Vedrovice; 10—Stránská skála; 11—Býčí skála; 12–13—Rudice and Olomučany; 14—Bořitov, 15—Troubky-Zdislavice).

reflect the state of research rather than the actual game densities in the Pleistocene. Regional research along Moravian rivers, as in the rich area around Uherské Hradiště (Hrubý, 1951), will therefore complete and largely modify the picture drawn by Skutil and Stehlík.

The geography of the lithic outcrops has received more attention than the osteology (Figures 8.1 and 8.2; Štecl and Malina, 1975; Malina, 1970; Valoch, 1975c, 1987d; Oliva, 1984c; Svoboda, 1987d; Přichystal, 1994b). A new aspect was introduced with the concept of lithic exploitation areas, which shows intensive settlement and raw material use in the areas of outcrops that had favorable conditions for settlement (Ondratice, Stránská skála, Bořitov, and Krumlovský les: Svoboda, 1983: Chapter 5). Another type of behavior was connected with outcrops in highland areas that were less suitable for settlement and hunting: the radiolarite (Kozlowski, Ma-

Figure 8.2. Diagrams showing changes in the exploitation and distribution of lithic raw materials during the Upper Paleolithic.

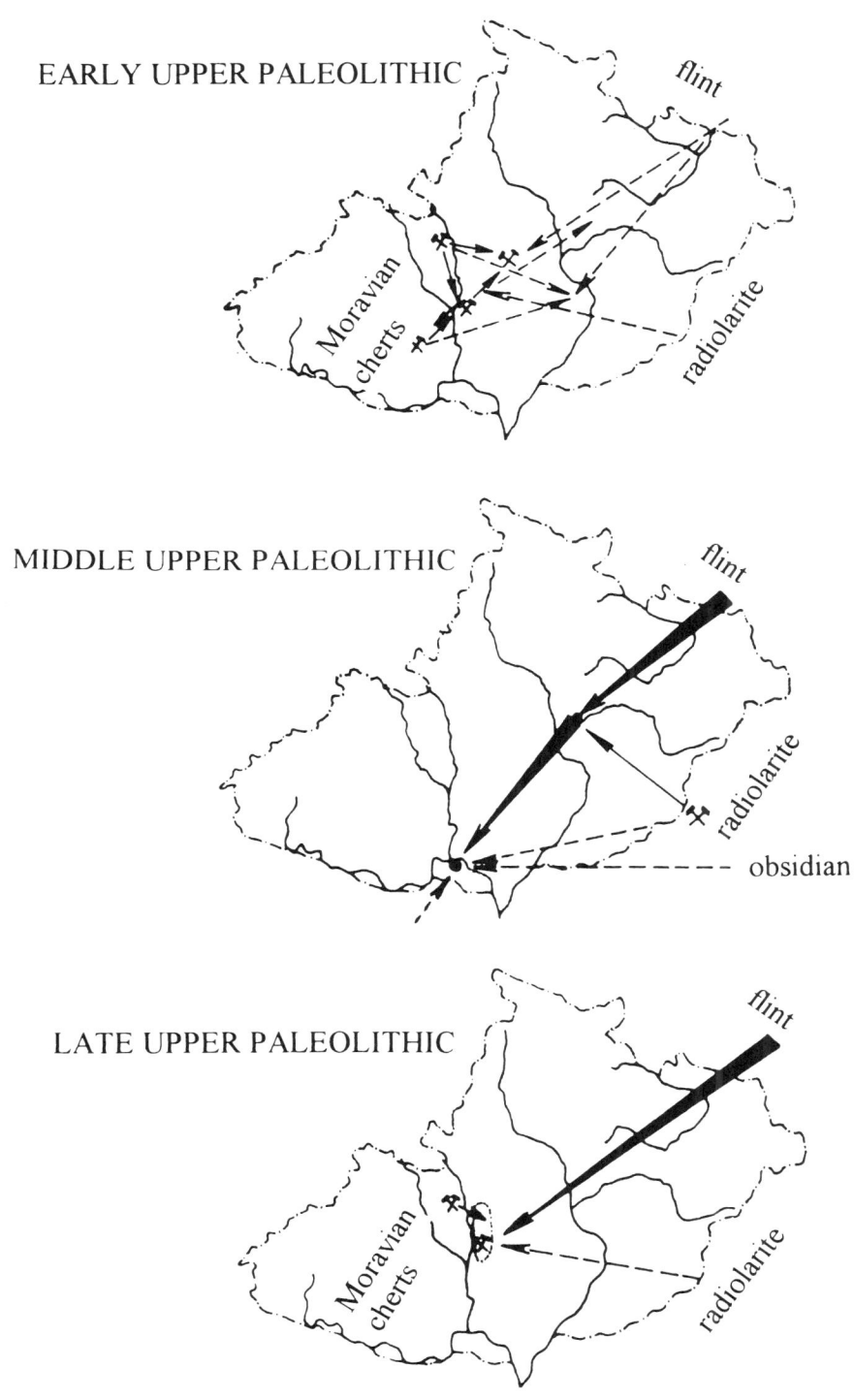

Table 8.1. Characteristics of the Individual Territorial Types

Type	A	B1	B2	C	D
Altitude	300–500 m above sea level	250–400 m above sea level	250–400 m above sea level	200–300 m above sea level	Up to 500 m
Character	Highland/karst	Lowland/highland	Lowland/highland	Valleys	Highland
Lithic	Available	Abundant	Abundant	Mostly absent	Rare
Use	Caves as shelters	Strategic positions	Sheltered valleys	Rivers, passages	Colonization
Cultures	Mousterian	Bohunician			Szeletian
	Micoquian	Szeletian			
	Magdalenian	Aurignacian		Gravettian	
	Epimagdalenian		Epigravettian		Late Paleolithic

necki, Rydlewski, Valde-Nowak, and Wrzak, 1981) or rock crystal (Přichystal, 1989) probably requiring short-term visits.

When the viewpoints of geomorphology and resource availability are combined, the regions of Moravia may be classified into four types (Table 8.1; Figures 8.3 and 8.4).

Territorial Type A

Territorial type A is karst landscapes, located in highlands (the Moravian and Štramberk Karst, 300–500 m above sea level), with minimal contact with the adjacent lowlands areas. The caves supplied relatively dry shelters during the glaciations, but control over the lowland passages from the cave entrances was usually not possible. The surrounding landscapes represent networks of smaller valleys or karstic plains, but no larger riverine networks were associated (only smaller brooks, partly subterranean). The both karstic areas offered limited outcrops of low-quality cherts (the Býči skála cherts, the Olomučany cherts, and cherts from the Štramberk flysch sandstones) and quartzites.

Territorial Type B

Territorial type B covered the marginal areas between highlands and lowlands, 250–400 m above sea level, namely, along the margins of the Bohemian Massif from Znojmo in the south as far north as Silesia in the north (the Dolní Kounice region, the Brno region, the Vyškov region, the Prostějov region, and the Opava region), penetrating along valleys deeper into this Massif (the Mohelno region and the Rosice–Boskovice region), or occupying individual marginal highlands of the Carpathians (the Klobouky region and the Zdounky region). In some cases, individual sites may have descended to 200 m above sea level, especially at the foot of the Krumlovský les Highland. The type B location was preferable for the exploitation of two types of

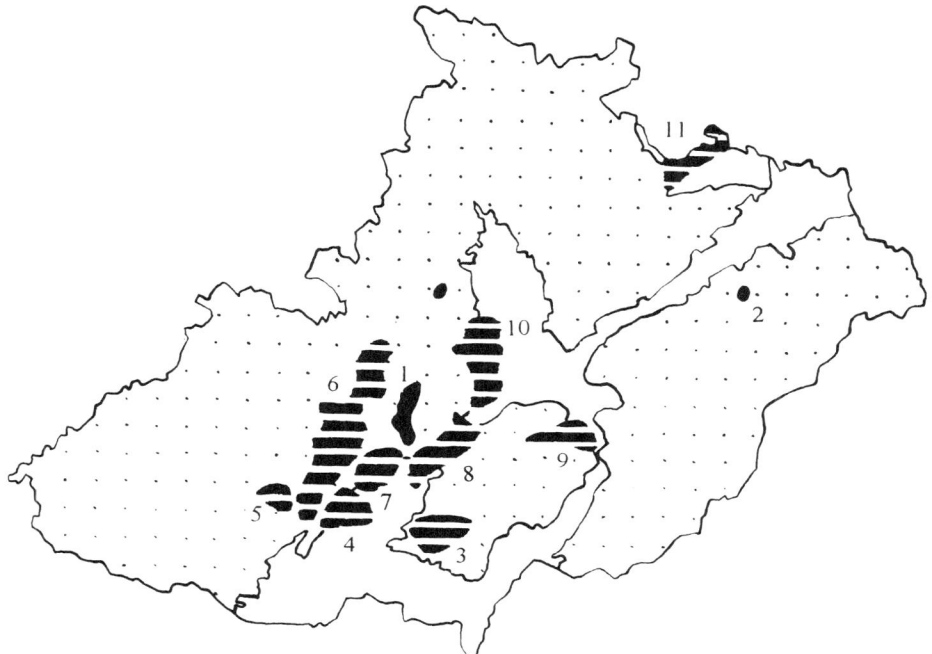

Figure 8.3. Map of the territorial types A (black) and B (horizontally hatched). 1—Moravian karst; 2—Štramberk karst; 3—Klobouky region; 4—Dolní Kounice region; 5—Mohelno region; 6—Rosice–Boskovice region; 7—Brno region; 8—Vyškov region; 9—Zdounky region; 10—Prostějov region; 11—Opava region. The lines indicate the highland (pointed)–lowland (wide) boundaries.

environment (highlands and lowlands with specific vegetational coverage) and offered control over the movements of game in the lowlands. On the other hand, these regions were usually far from larger rivers. Some of them offered sources of good-quality cherts (the Krumlovský les, Stránská skála, and Bořitov exploitation areas: Oliva, 1987c; Svoboda, 1983, 1987d; Valoch, 1993b), quartzites (the Ondratice exploitation area: Absolon, 1935c, 1936; Svoboda, 1980), and glacial flint (the Opava region: Přichystal, 1994b).

Territorial Type C

The valleys of the large Moravian and Silesian rivers—Dyje, Morava, Bečva, and Odra—where interconnected, formed an axial passage through Moravia (the Znojmo–Pouzdřany region, the Pavlov region, the Uherské Hradiště region, the Olomouc region, the Přerov–Hranice region, and the Ostrava region), with only one connecting link more distant from the riverine network (the Kyjov region). The settled locations lay in lower altitudes than the other territorial types (200–300 m above sea level); the reason is the generally lower locations of these valleys. The coincidence of

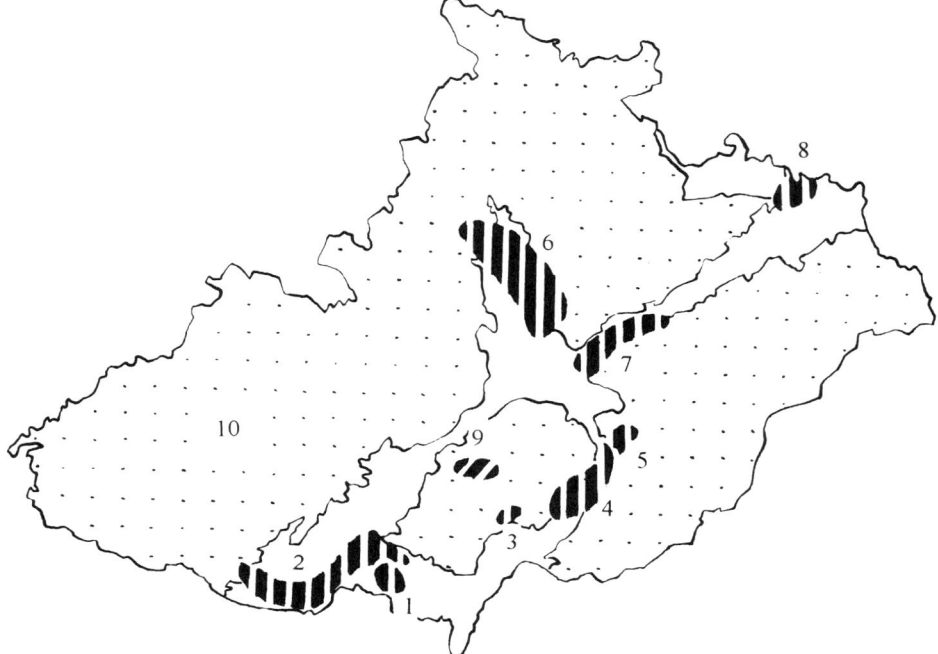

Figure 8.4. Map of the territorial types C (vertically hatched) and D (diagonally hatched). 1—Pavlov region; 2—Znojmo–Pozdřany region; 3—Kyjov region; 4—Uherské Hradiště region; 5—Holešov region; 6—Olomouc region; 7—Přerov–Hranice region; 8—Ostrava region; 9—Bučovice region; 10—Bohemian–Moravian highland.

behavioral patterns (the formation of the largest and most spectacular settlement agglomerations) and favorable conditions for preservation (thick loess deposits in the river valleys) is responsible for the complex archaeological record at our disposal. Numerous finds of Pleistocene mammals are recorded from regions of this type, usually in higher densities than elsewhere (Skutil and Stehlík, 1932b; Hrubý, 1951), and the archaeological sites are located so as to control the movements of game. With the exception of the northernmost part (glacial flints of the Ostrava region), this territory has no local lithic sources. However, the longitudinal passage opened the whole system to the importing of high-quality flints from the north (Přichystal, 1994a; Svoboda, 1994b).

Territorial Type D

The higher parts of the Bohemian–Moravian highland, up to 400–500 m above sea level, and a few other regions functioned as reserves for colonization during periods of climatic amelioration. These areas lay far from larger rivers and important game paths. With the exception of restricted outcrops of rock crystal, they did not offer usable lithic material sources.

Introducing the cultural viewpoint into the analysis (Table 8.2) clearly demonstrates preferences by the various cultures for certain territorial types and raw materials (cf. Figures 4.1, 5.1, 5.2, 6.2, and 7.1). First, the cave sites of both karst regions (territorial type A) were preferentially occupied in the Middle Paleolithic, the Magdalenian, and the Epimagdalenian. They were clearly preferred during the glacials as dry and sheltered locations.

The "out-of-the-cave" movement at the beginning of the Upper Paleolithic may be explained only in terms of human behavior: new hunting strategies involving control over larger landscapes, movement over longer distances, and possibly a change from a radiating mobility pattern centered on a cave to a more circulating pattern. There are several types of territorial selection:

The first are regions of type B with dominating Early Upper Paleolithic (EUP) and/or Epigravettian settlement, forming scattered clusters over the landscape. A

Table 8.2. Numbers of Sites (as Referred to in Appendix B) in the Various Regions and Types

	MP	EUP	Gvt	Egv	Mgd	LtP
Moravian karst	5	6	1?	—	26	2
Štramberk karst	2	—	—	—	2	—
Type A total	7	6	1?	—	28	2
Klobouky region	—	8	—	1	—	—
D. Kounice region	3?	20	—	—	—	—
Mohelno region	—	3	—	—	—	—
Rosice–Boskovice region	5?	24	1	—	—	3
Brno region	6	21	2	5	3	—
Vyškov region	1	13	—	3	—	—
Zdounky region	—	13	—	—	—	—
Prostějov region	1	16	—	4	—	—
Opava region	1	6	—	2	—	1
Type B total	17	124	3	15	3	4
Pavlov region	—	4	8	—	—	1
Znojmo–Poudřany region	—	1	n	—	—	—
U. Hradiště region	—	3	n	3	—	2
Holešov region	—	4	n	—	—	—
Olomouc region	—	6	n	—	—	—
Přerov–Hranice region	1	3	2	1	—	—
Ostrava region	1	1	1	1	—	2
Type C total	2	22	n	5	—	5
Bohemian–Moravian highland	—	6	1	—	—	4
Bučovice region	—	—	—	—	—	7
Type D total		6	1			11

Key: MP = Middle Paleolithic; EUP = Early Upper Paleolithic; Gvt = Gravettian; Egv = Epigravettian; Mgd = Magdalenian; LtP = Late Paleolithic; n = present but not calculated.

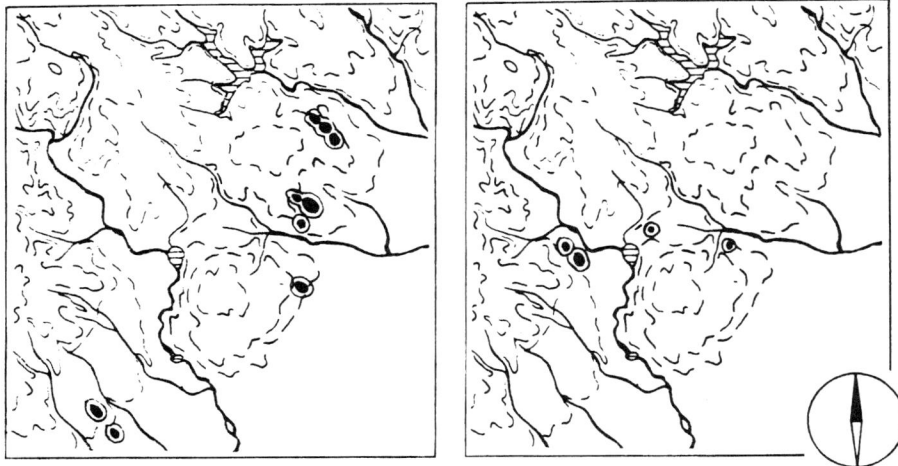

Figure 8.5. Variability in site location within territorial type B, comparing the EUP (type B1, exposed locations; left) and the Epigravettian (type B2, sheltered valleys; right). Case study of the Vyškov Gate area.

more detailed look into the topographies of these regions (Figure 8.5; Svoboda, 1994c) demonstrates that the EUP sites are larger, more numerous, and more exposed (type B1), while the Epigravettian ones are more sheltered (type B2). Deteriorating conditions by the last glacial maximum are a possible cause of this behavioral change.

Second, there are regions with dominating Gravettian settlement, seemingly organized into a longitudinal (axial) communication system (type C). This settlement geography functioned until the last glacial maximum. The divergence in preferential site location between the EUP and the Epigravettian, on the one hand, and the Gravettian, on the other, is remarkable. Chronological studies, showing partial contemporaneity (between the Upper Aurignacian and the Gravettian; Svoboda, 1996), suggest that it was this type of variability in landscape use that enabled the coexistence of various Upper Paleolithic cultures.

Finally, certain cultures demonstrated tendencies toward colonization of the Moravian–Bohemian highland (territorial type D): marginally the Szeletian and, more profoundly, the Late Paelolithic groups such as the Tišnovian. Another example is the Bučovice region, which was probably not attractive enough for earlier, more systematic settlement. In regions which were settled previously (the Pavlov region) the sites move to higher locations (the top of the Pavlovské Hills). The plausible causes seem to be population pressure and the favorable environmental changes by the end of the Pleistocene, which opened the highlands to more permanent settlement.

Appendix A

Catalog of Principal Sites

BALCAROVA CAVE (OSTROV U MACOCHY, FIGURE 7.1, NUMBER 24)

The most important Magdalenian cave site of the Suchý žleb valley (northern part of the Moravian karst), opens onto the valley by an imposing 5.7-m-high entrance, at the altitude of 460 m above sea level. The excavation was carried out rather carefully by Knies (1900, 1901b), who sieved the whole volume of excavated sediments to get a large number of microfaunal remains. Knies observed four accumulations of finds clustered around dark charcoal lenses, interpreted by him to be hearths. Apart from the microfauna, he recorded a large number of birds (about 12,000 bones) and a higher representation of polar fox (Musil, 1958). The composition of the other game, dominated by reindeer and hare and accompanied by cave bear, mammoth, hyena, rhinoceros, horse, aurochs, wolf, and beaver, led to the assumption of a relatively earlier Magdalenian date compared to the dates of the other caves. The lithic industry is composed of the four main groups: endscrapers, burins (and their combinations), various backed blades, and borers (Valoch, 1960c). The exceptional pointed backed blades may, together with some short endscrapers, represent a Late Paleolithic component. The bone industry is represented by awls and fragments of sagaies, some of them decorated (in a zigzag-pattern with short double lines).

At a depth of 0.3 m in the "diluvial clay," next to hearth 2, Knies recorded a fragment of human mandible and, by hearth 3, two human incisors. Later literature threw doubts on the Pleistocene age of these finds; it should be recalled, however, that similar conclusions were made at that time even about Mladeč and Předmostí. The specimen is actually lost, and modern analysis is impossible.

BOHUNICE—ČERVENÝ KOPEC (BRNO, FIGURE 4.1, NUMBER 2; FIGURE 5.1, NUMBER 4)

The Červený kopec (Red Hill) in Brno-Bohunice comprises the most complete sequence of Pleistocene fluvial sediments, loess, and paleosoils (PK I–XII) in Central Europe (Kukla, 1975; Figure 2.3). Isolated traces of human presence (possible artifacts) were found in a paleosoil several cycles earlier than the Matuyama–Brunhes boundary (preliminary mention in Svoboda et al., 1994: Figure 27), in another paleosoil related to the Matuyma–Brunhes boundary (PK X: Valoch, 1977a), and in a Middle Pleistocene paleosoil numbered PK Va (Klíma, 1963a). The main occupation of this important site, however, dates to the time of the final Early Würmian pleniglacial and the beginning interpleniglacial (Figure 9.1). The lithic industry is representative of a specific Levallosian-leptolithic culture, named the *Bohunician*.

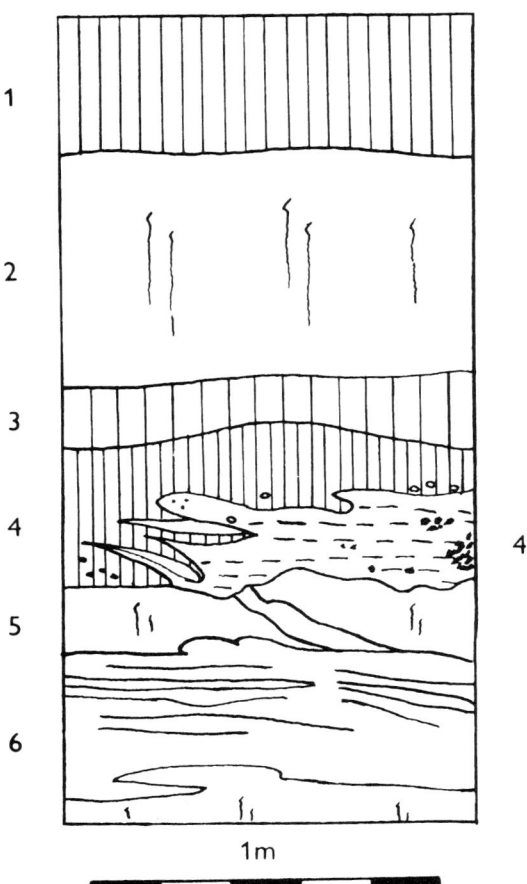

Figure 9.1. Bohunice: Upper part of the section in the Červený kopec brickyard, showing the interpleniglacial soil complex with Bohunician layers (4–4a) and charcoal (black dots); excavations, 1985.

According to K. Valoch (1976a), the industry and the charcoals were located at the base of an interpleniglacial soil complex (layers 3, 4). As the radiocarbon dates (before 40,000 B.P.) are slightly earlier than the supposed date of the first interpleniglacial pedogenesis, this location may be due to the effect of the later pedogenesis on the loessic substrate. Later stratigraphic observations (Svoboda and Svobodová, 1985: Figure 2, Table II) unearthed a horizon of removed loessic earth with charcoals dated as late as 36,000 B.P., also predating the first soil. Pollen analysis indicates a cold tundra, with a dominance of *Salix*.

The industry (Valoch, 1976a, 1982c) is primarily composed of Levalloisian-leptolithic technologies using chert from Stránská skála (about 7 km distant). Some of the bifacial leaf-points and typical sidescrapers are made of hornstones of Krumlovský les chert and Cretaceous chert. These were available from secondary sources (river gravels) in the immediate vicinity of the site (Přichystal, 1987), or by transport from primary sources in the Bořitov and Krumlov exploitation areas. Smaller specialized workshops (Valoch, 1974a) document that even the foreign materials were worked directly at the site. Observations of this kind and the various possibilities of their interpretation have evoked interesting discussions with M. Oliva (1981a, 1984b) on the homogeneity of these assemblages.

The Levalloisian points, simple sidescrapers, notches, and denticulates are the most common types. Simple burins are more frequently found than endscrapers. The endscrapers are flat, often made on wide flakes. Thick Aurignacioid forms of endscrapers are exceptional, as are an atypical Chatelperron-type point and a Quinson-type point.

An early anthropological find, in context to Pleistocene fauna, should be located in the area of Červený kopec Hill (Brno I: Makowsky, 1888, 1890, 1899a,b). It is actually lost, and its Pleistocene age cannot be confirmed.

BORŠICE (FIGURE 6.1, NUMBER 8)

This open-air site in the Moravia River valley (Skutil, 1940b; Hrubý, 1951) was excavated by B. Klíma (1965b), who discovered an ashy cultural layer of the Gravettian age at the base of the last loess cover, with a part of a mammoth bone accumulation. Associated is a rich Aurignacian and Gravettian lithic industry, mostly from the surface. Similar finds continue in the adjacent district of Buchlovice.

BRNO (FIGURE 6.1, NUMBER 13)

Brno II

In 1891, A. Makowsky salvaged the remains of an important human burial during engineering works at Francouzská Street in Brno (Brno II: Makowsky, 1892; Jelínek et al., 1959; Chapter 3). The associated artifacts (a male statue of ivory, decorative objects of ivory and shells, and two pierced siltstone disks with analogies in Pavlov and Předmostí) suggest a Gravettian age, even if the site is located outside the Gravettian territory.

Makowsky (1892:76) described his discovery in the following way:

> At a depth of 4.5 m, a red-colored loess appeared, in which there was a mammoth tusk as thick as a human arm, but so wet and fragile that it fell during separation into innumerable fragments. Below the tusk lay a completely preserved mammoth shoulder bone, and next to it a human skull, on which, unfortunately, one of the workers stepped, pressed it, damaged a part of the mandible, and destroyed a part of it. In the red-colored loess around the skull, there were numerous scattered mollusk shells (*Dentalia*), of which we have collected 600 pieces. Furthermore, we have found rhinoceros ribs up to 1 m long, which fell into pieces during the separation, and, finally, a number of small, partly broken circular objects, and an object of ivory, fragmented into several pieces, which, originally, we considered a part of a tusk, but which later appeared to be a highly interesting idol.

Brno III (Žabovřesky)

In 1927, K. Absolon (1929; Absolon et al., 1933) recorded another human burial from Brno-Žabovřesky (Brno III). He reported that "the female skeleton was deposited in the sand of the lower A-terrace during its sedimentation, covered by ochre and by Miocene silts" (Absolon et al., 1933:19). It is clear today that a modern human burial cannot be contemporary with the mentioned terrace, which is certainly earlier, and that the body must have been deposited in a sort of pit. Cultural relationships to the Gravettian are less clear than in the case of Brno II, and are based only on analogies in the cranial morphology and the ritual (the use of a burial pit and the coverage of ocher).

BÝČÍ SKÁLA CAVE (HABRŮVKA, FIGURE 7.1, NUMBER 16)

The cave of Býčí skála (the Bull Rock) is the largest cave site in the central part of the Moravian karst. It represents a fossil issue cave of the Jedovnický Brook (at 306 m above sea level), which, before reaching Býči skála, flows through an extensive system of caves from Rudice. This cave was the first Paleolithic locality investigated in Moravia. As early as in 1867–1871, J. Wankel (1871a) made his trenches here. In subsequent years, it was studied by A. Makowsky, J. Knies. M. Kříž, F. Čupik, and R. Czižek. The research was concluded in 1936–1938 by K. Absolon. In 1983–1985, J. Svoboda and L. Seitl investigated the Barová Cave, situated about 40 m above the entrance of Býčí skála (346 m above sea level), whose lowest floors belong to the system of the same subterranean brook.

The Paleolithic settlement in Býčí skála is situated in the so-called southern prong of the main cave corridor. The section in this area with two Paleolithic layers, as published by K. Absolon (1945a) and other investigators, called for several interpretations. Whereas the upper position belongs unambiguously to the Magdalenian, the lower one was determined to be Mousterian (Bayer, 1925), Preaurignacian (Absolon, 1945a; Valoch, 1966b), or a workshop facies of the Magdalenian (Sobczyk, 1984). With respect to the overall situation and from the technological point of view, the third interpretation appears to be the most probable (cf. the similar situation at Pekárna), even if an earlier cultural component may be admixed. In the upper Magdalenian layer, the most spectacular finds are numerous schist pebbles and hammerstones with ornamental and sometimes figural engravings (Wankel, 1882, 1884; Valoch, 1961a, 1978a; Svoboda, 1987g). Recently, Oliva (personal communication, 1995) expressed a belief in the existence of an animal drawing, possibly Magdalenian, on the wall of the southern Prong.

In the Barová Cave, at the interface of the late glacial and the Holocene, three periods of forest spreading were documented, the second of which can be archaeologically included in the Bölling (Magdalenian) and the third in the Alleröd (Epimagdalenian: Seitl et al., 1986; Svobodová, 1992). In contrast to the Býčí skála Cave, this site may be interpreted as a space-limited, temporary, but repeatedly occupied hunting post.

DOLNÍ VĚSTONICE (FIGURE 6.1, NUMBERS 3 AND 4)

Site I

Dolní Věstonice (DV) I is an extended and complex settlement accumulation (Figures 9.2 and 9.3; Absolon, 1945b; Klíma, 1963b, 1981b), with evidence of the earliest ceramics thus far known (Vandiver et al., 1990). It has been almost continuously excavated, from 1924 to 1938 by K. Absolon, from 1939 to 1942 by A. Bohmers, in 1945–1946 by K. Žebera, in 1947–1952, 1966 and 1971–1979 by B. Klíma, and in 1990 and 1993 by J. Svoboda. K. Absolon published three monographs (Absolon, 1938a,b, 1945b) concerning his first field seasons: 1924, 1925, and 1926. K. Žebera published another report on his excavations, which is primarily of stratigraphic value (Knor, Ložek, Pelíšek, and Žebera, 1953). Subsequently, B. Klíma published a large monograph summarizing his own fieldwork between 1947 and 1952 (Klíma, 1963b) and the situation in the middle zone of the site (Klíma, 1981b). Finally, B. Klíma published a popular synthesis summarizing the issues covered up to that time (Klíma, 1983a, with further references).

As a whole, the site has yielded ground plans of circular or oval-shaped dwellings (some with stone or mammoth-bone alignments; cf. Figure 6.5); hearths and kilns; faunal remains, including large mammoth-bone deposits (Klíma, 1969a); lithic and bone tools; decorative objects; ceramic figurines (Vandiver et al., 1990) and other art objects; a female burial (DV III); a child burial (DV IV); and several fragmented human fossils (Jelínek, 1953; Klíma, 1990c; Vlček, 1991b). Spatially, the site was separated into lower, middle, upper, and uppermost parts by Klíma, who suggested, on the basis of stratigraphy, that the lower location is the earliest. In order to obtain more C-14 dates for various parts of the site, a series of trenches along the site were excavated in

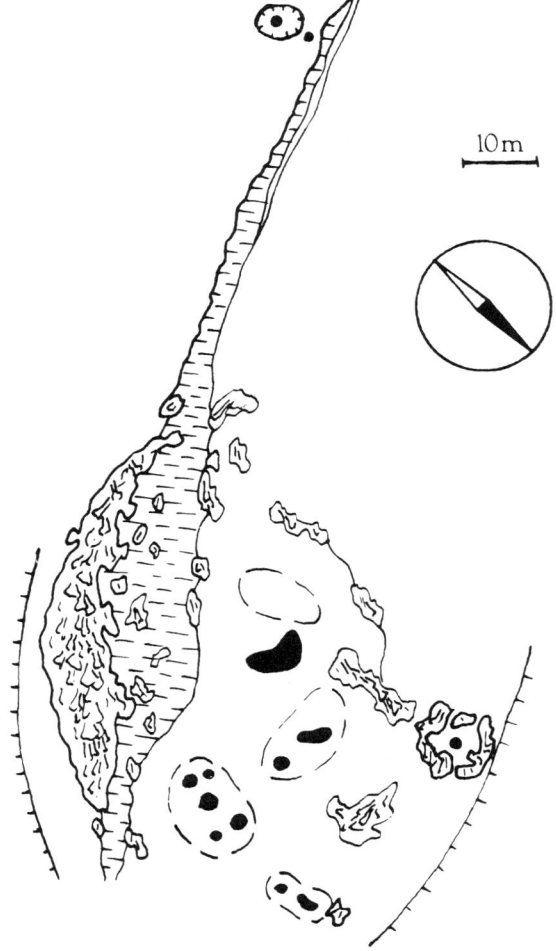

Figure 9.2. Dolní Věstonice I: Plan of the upper part of the site (after B. Klíma).

1990. The Groningen dates confirm the earlier age of the lower location (31,000–27,000 B.P.) compared to the other areas (about 25,000 B.P.; Svoboda, 1993d). Later dates from the Lyon Laboratory seem less coherent within the chronological context.

The major part of the lithic industry is made of imported flints, and a smaller part is made up of radiolarites. A certain proportion of the local Moravian cherts (16%) and quartz appeared only in the lower and uppermost parts of the site. Typologically, the

Figure 9.3. Dolní Věstonice I: Stratigraphic section in the lower part of the site (excavations, 1990) showing (from the top to the base) recent soil, a thick loess deposit with sandy interlayers, the Gravettian layer and soil deposits with a hearth, and redeposited Tertiary subsoil.

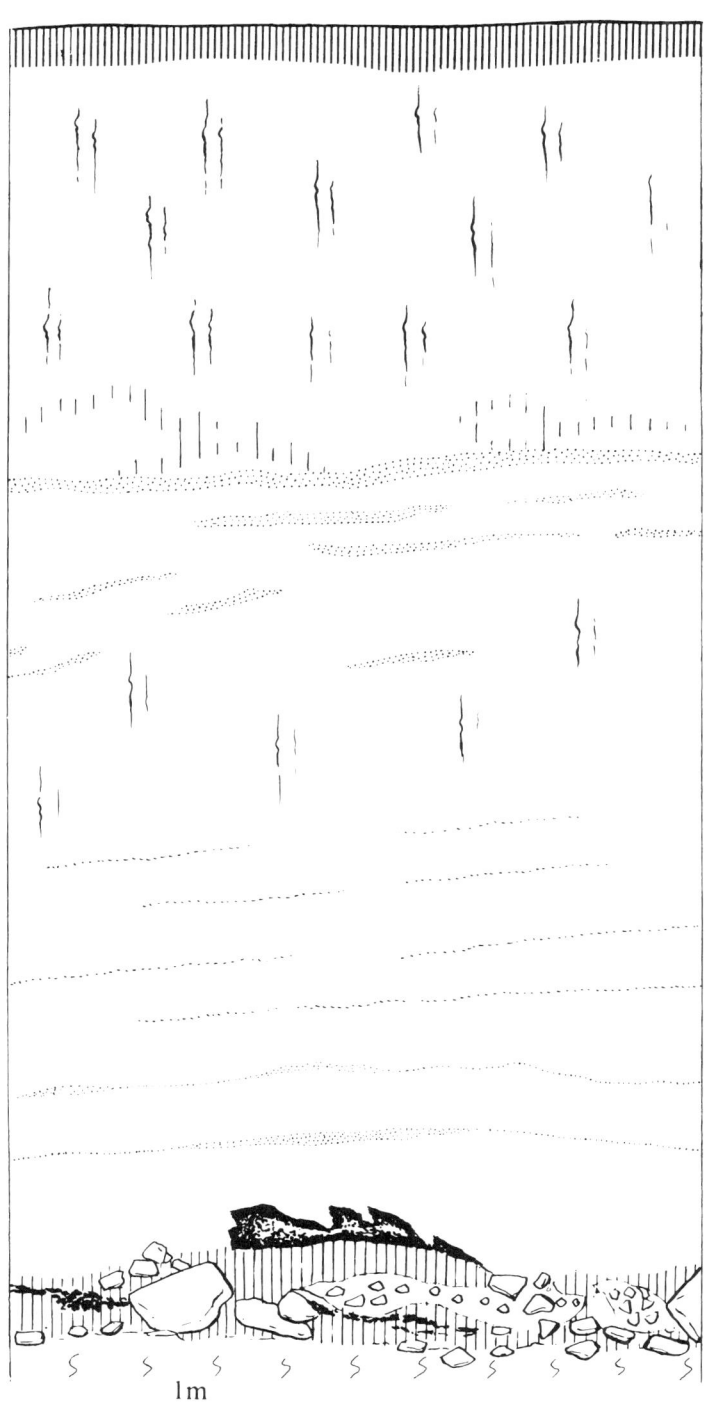

1m

lower location differs in the presence of a few Aurignacioid tool types (2.5%). B. Klíma (1963b, 1969a, 1981b) described in detail the typology of two settlement units in the upper and uppermost locations, of the related mammoth-bone deposit, and of samples originally quantified by Bohmers from the middle location. Generally, burins retain a standard representation of between 30% and 40%. The share of the endscrapers is lower (12%–18%), and Aurignacioid types are absent. Backed microliths are relatively frequent (8%–26%), with numerous microsaws (microdenticulates, 5%–7%) representing the site-specific tool form.

Site II

The site of Dolní Věstonice II forms one of the loess elevations at an altitude of about 240 m, rising above the Dyje River and sloping further to the Pavlovské Hills (Figure 9.4 and 9.5). The loess deposit reaches it maximal thickness at the foot of the elevation, where it was exploited for brick making. The brickyard, at the eastern edge of the village, attracted the attention of researchers at the beginning of the century and became one of the key sections of the Upper Pleistocene in Central Europe (Absolon et al., 1933; Klíma et al., 1962; Demek and Kukla, 1969; Havlíček and Kovanda, 1985; Chapter 2).

In 1985, new and larger industrial exploitation of the loess was initiated above the abandoned brickery. This exploitation unearthed a Paleolithic site almost completely and yielded evidence of its inner structure. The results were published

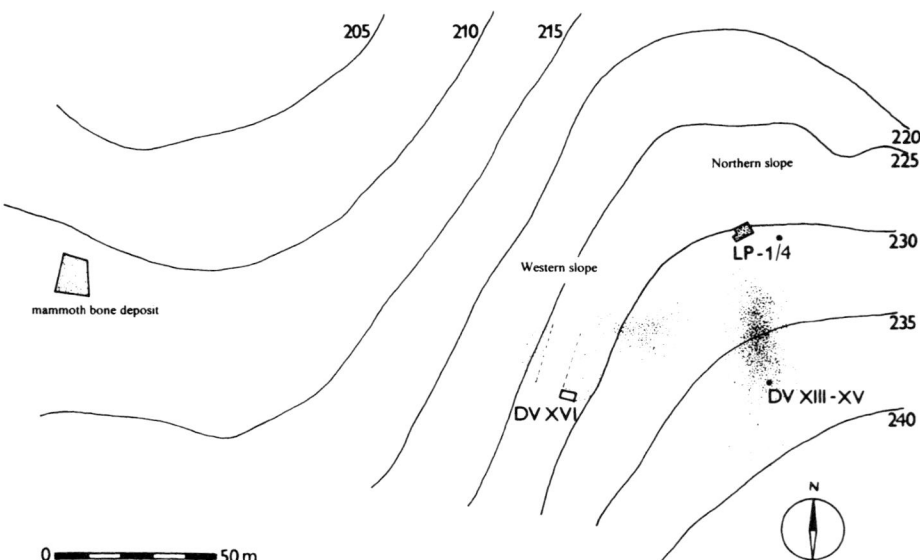

Figure 9.4. Dolní Věstonice II: Plan of the upper part of the site, the western slope, and the mammoth deposit showing the location of human burials DV XIII–XV and DV XVI. Settled areas are dotted.

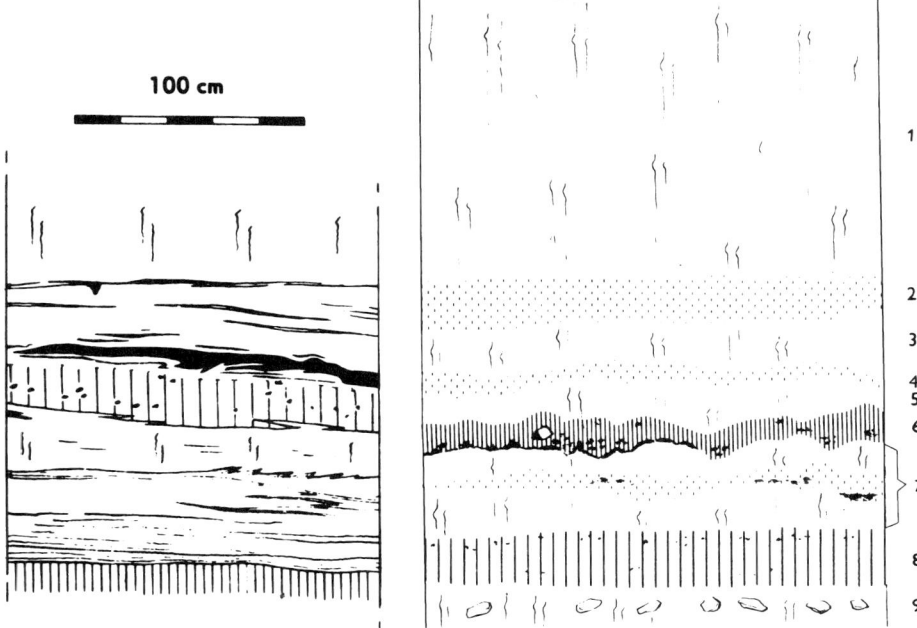

Figure 9.5a,b. Dolní Věstonice II: Detailed stratigraphic sections of the lower part of the site (*left*) and the western slope (*right*); excavations, 1985–1987.

internationally in a series of articles announcing the discovery of human burials (e.g., Klíma, 1987b; Svoboda, 1989a; Svoboda and Vlček, 1991), the possible presence of a wooden industry (Klíma, 1990a), an archaeological analysis of the site and its segments (Svoboda, 1990d, 1991b; Svoboda et al., 1993; Klíma, 1995), and the site's Quaternary geology (Havlíček, 1991). Furthermore, the site may have the earliest evidence of vegetarian consumption (Mason et al., 1994).

The earliest part of the site is the lower location in the northern part (the brickery), dating to 29,000–28,000 B.P. (Klíma et al., 1962). Higher on the northern slope, the industry of unit A (Klíma, 1987d, 1995) has a large share of Moravian (Cretaceous) cherts, radiolarites, and certain archaic features in typology, such as Aurignacian endscrapers and sidescrapers. The nearby unit B has a standard Gravettian industry with burins, pointed blades, and microblades, still made predominantly of Moravian (in this case Krumlovian) cherts, while the industry of unit C is microlithic; all three units were dated at around 27,600 B.P. Unit LP/1-4 (Svoboda, 1990d) lies still higher on the northern slope and is more recent (26,390 B.P.); it already shows the standard raw-material composition of the Gravettian (dominating flint accompanied by radiolarite), and it is characterized typologically by the absence of backed microliths and by a higher proportion of retouched blades and pointed blades.

Most of the complex evidence has been obtained from three settlement agglomerations, all composed of individual settlement units, extending over the top and the western slope of the site (Figure 9.4). The first of the three large settlement agglomerations (A) is oval-shaped and extends north and south. In its southern (upper) part was located the triple burial DV XIII–XV (Figure 6.25; Klíma, 1987b, 1990c, 1995). The second agglomeration (B) is oval-shaped as well, and it gradually declines from east to west. Its lowermost part was subjected to a more detailed case study following changes in the artifact dispersal and composition between the center and the periphery (Svoboda et al., 1993). The third agglomeration (C, western slope, Figures 6.6–6.8) included the single male burial DV XVI (Svoboda, 1989a, 1991b). The C-14 datings (based on Groningen data only), the spatial relationships, and, in certain areas, also the refittings suggest that the majority of the settlement units composing these agglomerations dated from around 27,000 B.P., but the burials are more recent. The triple burial seems to have closed the main occupation stage around 26,600 B.P. A later stage, represented by unit 1 at the western slope, including male burial DV XVI, dates to around 25,500 B.P. The proportionate numbers in lithic typology reflect a typological similarity between certain units of the earlier stage (e.g., units 2 and 3), characterized by the dominance of burins and backed implements. In unit 1, the number and variability of backed implements, mostly microlithic, increase markedly.

The mammoth bone deposit (Svoboda, 1991a) extended into an ancient water-filled basin, about 150 m to the west from the eastern edge of the settlement, at 210 m altitude. Two C-14 data suggest contemporaneity with the main settlement.

Site III

This is a smaller site located between sites I and II. Surface surveys have located scattered Early Upper Paleolithic (EUP) artifacts in the uppermost zone of the site (exceptional in the Dolní Věstonice–Pavlov area) and a Gravettian cultural layer at several places downslope. The excavation in 1993–1994 yielded a central hearth, disturbed by slope movements, and surrounded by a cluster of animal bones, lithic artifacts, charcoal, ocher, and Tertiary shells.

The importance of this site lies especially in its age: the date of 24,560 ± 660–610 B.P. (GrN 20392) suggests that it may be the most recent site within the Dolní Věstonice–Pavlov area. In lithic typology, this observation is supported by the occurrence of an atypical shouldered point, typical of the Upper Gravettian.

JAROŠOV (UHERSKÉ HRADIŠTĚ, FIGURE 6.1, NUMBER 9)

This open-air site is located on the slope of the Černá hora Hill above the Morava River Valley. Earthworks in this area unearthed a layer of mammal bones in loess, probably redeposited along the slope (Procházka, 1983). The fauna is dominated by mammoth, accompanied by rhinoceros and horse. A few lithic tools (blades, a backed blade, a burin) were found associated. The site probably represents the remains of a specialized Gravettian hunting site. Surface surveys in the vicinity have been carried out since 1995.

KOLÍBKY (JEDOVNICE, FIGURE 7.1, NUMBER 20)

This is a small, probably seasonal Magdalenian site, situated apart from the three main settlement clusters of the Moravian karst (465 m above sea level). It was excavated by Knies (1905) and Svoboda et al. (1996). It is dated to 12,680 ± 110 B.P. (OxA 5973). The occupation was located in two small caves (unfortunately, the sediments were destroyed before an archaeological examination) and on a platform in front of them. The appearance of core preforms and hammerstones shows a larger importance of local lithic production than could be deduced from the small size of the site. A few lumps of ocher from nearby deposits suggest further exploitation activities. Finally, the concentration of 26 heavy graywacke slabs with circular depressions, suggesting that they functioned as lamps is even more striking. According to Knies, they were covered by charcoal, and the loess around them was red-burnt. Comparable objects are unknown from other Magdalenian sites in the karst; thus, we can hardly argue that Kolíbky functioned as a specialized workshop and distribution center; rather, we assume that the objects were used on the spot. The observation of Knies (1905) that they were possibly arranged in a row suggests that they may have formed a structure before the cave entrance.

KŮLNA CAVE (SLOUP, FIGURE 4.1, NUMBER 11; FIGURE 7.1, NUMBER 25)

This imposing cave consists of a large, almost horizontal, tunnel-like gallery 92 m long, cut into the left slope of the Sloup semiblind valley (469 m above sea level). It was examined by J. Wankel in 1881, by M. Kříž in 1881–1886, and by J. Knies in 1887–1913. The excavations were continued and completed by K. Valoch in 1961–1976 (Figures 4.6 and 9.6).

According to Valoch (1988), the earliest traces of occupation (a small artifact assemblage from layer 14) fall into the time line of the penultimate (Rissian) glaciation. In the above interglacial layer 11, K. Valoch found a small-dimensional industry (Taubachian). E. Opravil (1988) estimated a dominance of the charcoal of *Abies alba*, accompanied by single charcoals of *Picea excelsa* and *Picea–Larix*. The rather fragmentary osteological material included large numbers of horses, accompanied by rhinoceros (*Dicerorhinus kirchbergensis*).

Following is a sequence of Lower Würmian layers (layers 9b–6a). Layers 8b–7d show a gradual extension of the steppe landscape and of the glacial fauna at the beginning of the last glaciation. In layer 7c, this process was interrupted by a warmer phase, during which there was an extension of the woodlands (Kůlna interstadial, probably equivalent to Brörup). This was followed by layer 7b, formed of a thick and well-bedded deposit. Biostratigraphically, layer 7b is not separated from the overlying layer 7a. Archaeologically, layer 7b is sterile, but there is Micoquian material both in the subsoil (7c) and in the overlying layers (7a and 6a). Layer 7a, in which Neanderthal fossil remains were found, has been dated by C-14, but these datings are minimal and lie at the very limits of this method. The fact that we are not able to date

216   APPENDIX A

Figure 9.6. The Kůlna Cave: Lower part of the section, layers 13b–7a (*left*) and the upper part, layers 7–3 (*right*), in the front part of the cave.

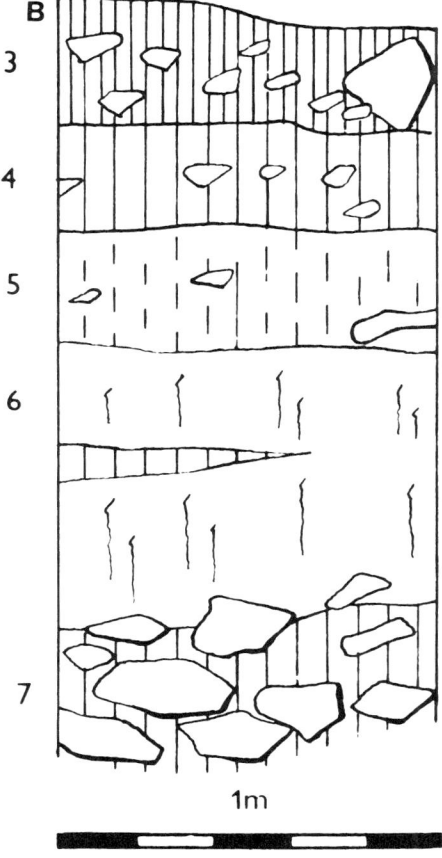

Figure 9.6. (*Continued*)

the end of the Neanderthal occupation more precisely in this most promising case is a serious detriment to our understanding of the Middle to Upper Paleolithic transition in our area. Data on vegetation are available from charcoal only. In layer 7c, Opravil (1988) determined *Abies*, accompanied by single fragments of *Picea*, *Picea–Larix*, and *Pinus*. In layer 7a, there are several fragments of *Fraxinus excelsior* and *Pinus*, accompanied by single pieces of *Acer cf. pseudoplatanus*, *Corylus*, *Picea excelsa*, and *Picea–Larix*. Musil (1988) observed that the horse dominates at the base of the Lower Würmian deposits (layer 9b) and is replaced by reindeer in layer 8a. At the top of the sequence (layers 7d–6a), the most frequently hunted animals become mammoth and reindeer.

Following is a remarkable interruption in the sequence of the Kůlna Cave. Hypothetically, K. Valoch would place here an Upper Gravettian occupation. The

Magdalenian layers, 6 and 5, dating to more than 11,500 years ago, again yielded rich material, especially the lithics; the bone industry is represented mostly by fragments. The paleobotanical analyses were presented by Opravil (1988) and Svobodová (1988, 1992). The pattern of the hunted animals still corresponds to glacial conditions (reindeer, horse, hare, fox, etc.). The excavation of Kříž has yielded a fragment of human mandible, now ascribed by Jelínek (1988; cf. Chapter 3) to the Magdalenian.

These layers are overlain by Epimagdalenian layers 4 and 3, dating back to 11,500–10,000 B.P. The pattern of the hunted animals changes gradually (deer, elk, wild pig, beaver), which corresponds to the spreading of the forest by the end of the glaciation. Layer 3 yielded two human teeth.

MILOVICE (FIGURE 5.2, NUMBER 26; FIGURE 6.1, NUMBER 6)

This site is located in a side valley leading toward the Dyje River. In connection with industrial exploitation of the loess, the salvage excavations were held here by M. Oliva (1988, 1989a) in 1986–1991. There is a small Aurignacian assemblage within the second interpleniglacial soil, dated to 29,200 B.P., and a more extended Upper Gravettian occupation at the base of the overlying loess, dated to 25,000–21,000 B.P. The Gravettian horizon includes mammoth bone deposits in the lower part of the site and a circular feature of mammoth bones (4–5 m in diameter), probably a hut, in the upper part of the site (Figure 6.10). The lithic industry is mainly concentrated in the upper part. It differs slightly from the large Pavlovian sites located 6–8 km to the northwest in its relatively high share of radiolarite, in the remarkable importance of endscrapers related to burins, in the morphology of certain microliths, and in the occurrence of a leaf-point.

THE MLADEČ CAVES (FIGURE 5.2, NUMBER 31; FIGURE 6.1, NUMBER 12)

Site I

The systems of the Mladeč Caves are located in Devonian limestones of Třesín Hill (343 m above sea level) dominating the Upper Moravian Plain. Since the beginning of the 19th century, several early finds of human fossils and artifacts have been reported, but a more systematic survey was initiated by J. Szombathy (1884a,b, 1925) in a dome inside the caves, later named site Mladeč I. A large debris cone emerged here from a chimney in the roof of the dome. The finds obviously lay on the surface and at the foot of the cone, showing a regular dispersal for several meters from the chimney. Today, only the central parts of the cone are still preserved, and they contain Middle Pleistocene fauna. The Upper Pleistocene sediments were almost completely removed (remains of the sediments are visible on the cave walls).

According to the original description and drawing by Szombathy, the cave filling at the foot of the cone may be reconstructed as follows: At a depth of 20–50 cm, he found a major part of a human skull (Mladeč I) and a femur, together with faunal remains. Below lay a travertine layer with charcoal and finely bedded loams with layers of microfaunal remains. Further human fossils (Mladeč II, IIa, and III) and artifacts (pierced animal teeth and a bone point of the Mladeč type) lay in a similar situation in the same vicinity.

Excavations in this dome were continued by J. Knies after 1903. He found more human fossils (skull fragments, etc.), artifacts (bone points of the Mladeč type and awls), and Pleistocene faunal remains. In 1922, the sediments were disturbed by work on accommodations for tourist visits. Smyčka (1922) described some more finds of human and animal bones, strange bone artifacts partly or totally pierced, microfauna, and snails. The following fieldwork was of limited significance to archaeology and anthropology: J. Skutil (1938b) mentioned two lithic artifacts from the entrance of the cave; J. Jelínek (1987) discovered a chopper, possibly of Lower or Middle Paleolithic age; and Horáček and Ložek presented a biostratigraphic study of the Middle Pleistocene filling of the cave. It seems, therefore, that the extension of upper Pleistocene strata that includes the human fossils was restricted and was most probably related to the area below the chimney. Therefore, a reconstruction and documentation of the terrain situation will contribute to the discussion of how the finds were redeposited, including a reconstruction of the possible rituals.

The fauna, composed of aurochs, reindeer, cave bear, wolf, fox (Szombathy), horse, mammoth, rhinoceros, bison, beaver, deer, and elk (Knies), corresponds to the milder climates of the Würmian interpleniglacial, while the typology of the bone points supports the Aurignacian classification.

Site II

From the exterior, the cave system of Mladeč has been damaged by small quarries. In 1904, the workers found and destroyed a small cave in the southern part of Třesín Hill; from the preserved traces, Maška observed that it may have communicated with the surface by a chimney, similarly to site I. The finds were largely damaged. Maška (1905) and Knies (1906) mentioned two human skulls, a child's skull, and a number of postcranial bones, mostly fragmented. Furthermore, the site yielded a Mladeč-type point and another fragment, two lithic artifacts, two pebbles, and glacial faunal remains. From the viewpoint of paleontology and archaeology, the two sites are comparable, but there are slight differences in the skull morphologies.

Apart from the main cave systems, there is a smaller cave called Podkova, with little Upper Paleolithic industry, and a surface Gravettian site on the top of Třesín Hill (Skutil, 1938b; Valoch, 1981a).

NOVÁ DRÁTENICKÁ CAVE (BŘEZINA, FIGURE 7.1, NUMBER 18)

This cave was discovered in 1947 during a speleological survey of the larger Drátenická Cave in the middle part of the Moravian karst (393 m above sea level). Although the orientation toward the north and the whole situation seem unfavorable

220   APPENDIX A

to a settlement, archaeological finds were localized by Klíma (1949, 1951c) in a position called Krápníkový kout. The cultural layer was gray-colored, lying in thick loess. The fauna is dominated by reindeer. New C-14 datings range between 14,000 and 11,500 B.P. (Valoch, 1993a). The lithic industry is characterized by pointed backed blades and truncated blades; both types are rather distinctive in the Magdalenian of Moravia, and therefore, the first type formerly led K. Valoch (1980b) to suggest a Late Gravettian age for the assemblage. However, the Magdalenian character is attested to not only by age, but also by the tree antler sagaies with barbed tips, all decorated by zigzag and sinusoid lines at the base.

PAVLOV (FIGURE 6.1, NUMBER 5)

Site I

Pavlov I was excavated by B. Klíma in 1952–1965 and 1971–1972. The advantage of this site, in contrast to the nearby DV I or Předmostí, is that it was excavated systematically, and by one person. Klíma recognized several dwellings in the excavated area, some of them in depressions with a central hearth or hearths, with pits on the surrounding floors, and sometimes with larger stones or bones along the external margins of the dwellings (Figure 9.7).

The site has world primacy in the earliest ceramics, and also in what is possibly the earliest evidence of weaving or basketry imprints (Soffer, personal communication, 1995). The other evidence has been published in preliminary seasonal reports in journals such as *Archeologické rozhledy* and *Přehled výzkumů*, and in specialized studies

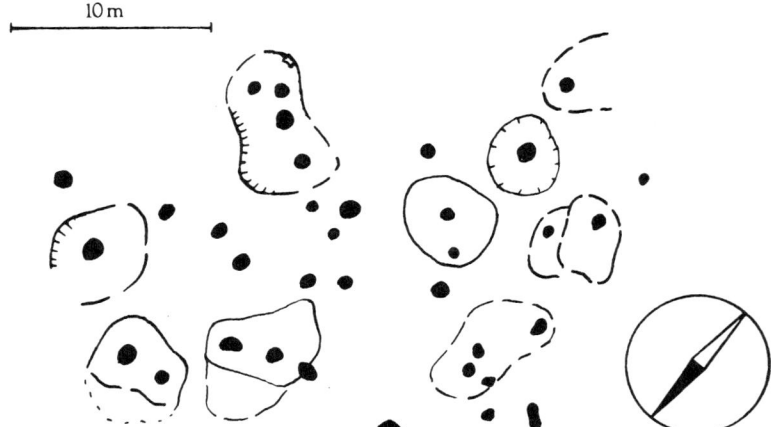

Figure 9.7. Pavlov I: Partial plan of the southern and eastern parts of the site (b) showing the position of the reconstructed settlement units (after B. Klíma).

of the lioness carving (Klíma, 1964a), the engraving of a Paleolithic "map" (Klíma, 1988), the other plastic art (Klíma, 1989), the male burial (Vlček, 1961), the antler tools (Klíma, 1955a, 1987c), the nonsiliceous stone (Klíma 1984b), and the siliceous tools (Svoboda, 1994b). In 1991, the Institute of Archaeology at Dolní Věstonice initiated a long-term project designed to develop a complete description of the site, the various parts of which, including the individual settlement units, are being studied and compared (Svoboda, 1994a; further volumes in preparation).

Spatially, B. Klíma (1963f) suggested that the settled area at Pavlov I may be separated into two parts (a and b), not chronologically contemporaneous. However the six C-14 dates from both parts of the site all fall into a relatively short time span, between 26,700 and 25,000 B.P. In our recent project, two areas were selected of both parts of the site (excavation in 1952–1953 and 1957), and the archaeological material was compared.

By the dominance (double or even a higher proportion) of burins over endscrapers, the samples analyzed thus far correspond to other Gravettian assemblages of the Austrian-Moravian-Silesian territory. The percentage of microlithic backed implements and other microliths in the Pavlov I sample, on the other hand, reaches the highest values so far recorded. Some microliths, fairly standard in size and shape, are rare or absent elsewhere: the crescents, trapezoids, and triangles. Points with ventroterminal retouches, recalling the Jerzmanowice type, are present throughout the assemblage, while shouldered points of the Kostenki type, in their typical form, are absent. A typical stylistic feature of the 1952–1953 sample (area b) is a lack of lateral, steep, or scalariform retouches along the margins of the blades and flakes. The 1957 sample (area a) clearly differs in its higher share of radiolarite, influencing the whole process of raw material selection, economy of use, and typology (the higher share of marginally retouched tools).

Site II

This is a smaller but culturally comparable site with a concentration of artifacts and animal bones around five hearths, axially arranged (Klíma, 1961b, 1976).

Site III

The easternmost site yielded a sample of lithics, charcoal, and mammoth bones during industrial exploitation of the loess (Klíma, 1981a, 1983e). The site is worth further investigation.

PEKÁRNA CAVE (MOKRÁ, FIGURE 4.1, NUMBER 13; FIGURE 5.1, NUMBER 24; FIGURE 7.1, NUMBER 10)

Pekárna (also Kostelík, Díravica) is the central cave site in the southern part of the Moravian karst, 44 m above the Říčka Brook valley and 361 m above sea level (Figures

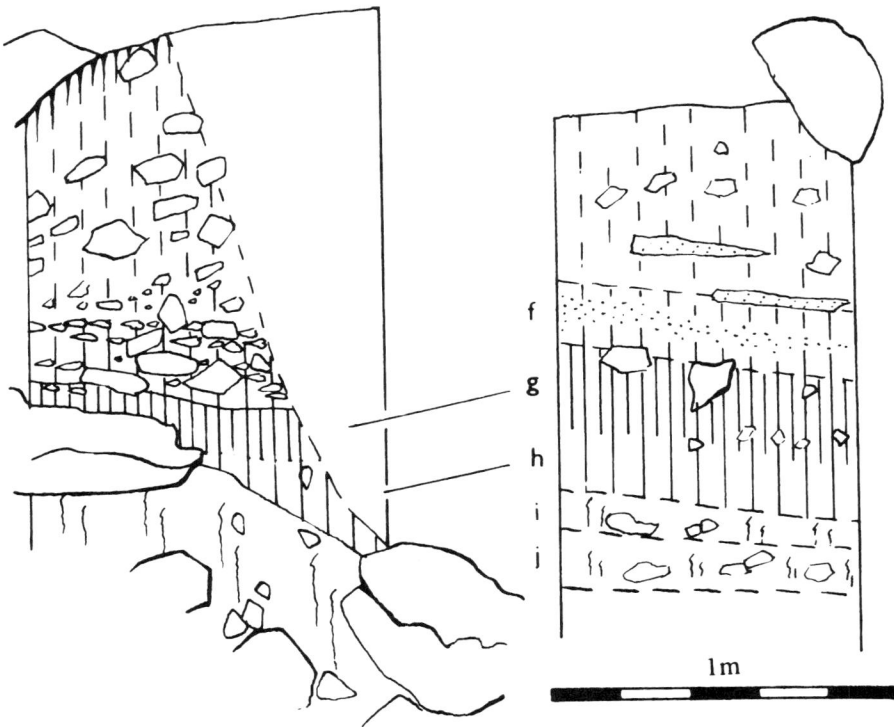

Figure 9.8. Pekárna Cave: Sections in front of the cave from the excavation of 1986–1987 (left) and in the cave entrance (excavations in 1925–1930). Magdalenian occupation is in layers g and h, and partly in i; earlier occupation is also in layer i.

7.5, 7.6, and 9.8). The interior of the cave has been excavated since 1880 by J. Wankel (1881, 1882), J. Szombathy, A. Makowsky, and F. Koudelka; from 1884 to the end of the century by M. Kříž (1891, 1897–1898, 1898), and systematically between 1925 and 1930 by K. Absolon and R. Czižek (Absolon and Czižek, 1927–1932). Excavations of the platform before the entrance were realized by B. Klíma in 1954 and 1961–1965 (Klíma, 1974a), and by J. Svoboda in 1986–1987 (Svoboda, 1991c).

While the major part of the archaeological material recovered belongs to the Magdalenian, the question of pre-Magdalenian occupations was open to discussion. The reason is the changing thickness of the layers in question, their disappearance toward the end of the cave, and, in consequence, the changing stratigraphic situations in various parts of the cave. Even if the excavation reports by R. Czižek were made on a very good standard for that time, it is now difficult to correlate the documentation with the concrete materials stored in the Moravian Museum. Absolon's scheme, suggesting a sequence of pre-Aurignacian, Upper Aurignacian, and Magdalenian occupations, has recently been replaced by a sequence of Micoquian, EUP (Szeletian–Jerzmanowician?), and two or three Magdalenian layers.

The Magdalenian is deposited either in the uppermost part of the late glacial loess (layer i, not dated) or in the overlying humus layers (g and h, with C-14 datings between 12,500 and 13,000 B.P.). The Magdalenian fauna is composed of hare, reindeer, horse, birds, and a polar fox (Musil, 1958). Further environmental studies (microfauna, malaccozoology, palynology) were carried out during the last excavation (Svoboda, 1991c).

The typological differences between the various Magdalenian positions are minor. The main typological groups are endscrapers, burins, borers, and backed implements. Rarely, there appear some backed points and rectangular backed blades. Antler points with a unifacially or bifacially cut base are accompanied by navettes, harpoons, bone awls, and needles.

The Pekárna Cave has yielded the largest assemblage of Magdalenian art objects from our territory: two horse ribs with scenes of grazing horses and fighting bisons, both found in the entrance area (Klíma, 1974a); *spatulae* decorated with symbols and the heads of animals (horses, antelope, and bison), concentrated rather in the distant parts of the cave; *batons de commandement* with engravings of horses and bears; and a highly stylized female figure of ivory (Absolon and Czižek, 1926–1932).

Pekárna is surrounded by a cluster of smaller cave sites (Hadí, Adlerova, Křížova, Švédův stůl, and Kůlnička) and open-air sites (Ochozská Cave platform, Maloměřice-Borky I, and Mokrá; Appendix B).

PETŘKOVICE (FIGURE 6.1, NUMBER 2)

This Upper Gravettian site is located at the northern entrance of the Moravian Gate (in the Czech part of Silesia). Excavations were done by J. Folprecht and K. Absolon in 1926–1929, B. Klíma in 1952–1953, and J. Svoboda and L. Jarošová in 1994–1995. The resulting ground plan (Figure 9.9) comprises a group of hearths, centered on central areas covered by powdered hematite, and a few small pits. Furthermore, the site yielded charcoal, lithics, compact hematite (including a small female statue cut of this raw material: Klíma, 1955b), some ceramic pieces, and coal (possibly used in the hearths). With the exception of mammoth molars, the organic materials were poorly preserved.

Traditionally, this site has been considered rather early in the Gravettian. The charcoal from Klíma's excavations has been newly dated (20,790 ± 270 B.P.), as has charcoal from the new excavations (23,370 ± 160 B.P.). Both data make the site important as a representative of the Upper Gravettian (Willendorfian-Kostenkian) stage, as confirmed typologically by the occurrence of shouldered points and leaf-points.

PŘEDMOSTÍ (PŘEROV, FIGURE 4.1, NUMBER 8; FIGURE 6.1, NUMBER 1)

The Middle and Upper Paleolithic site of Předmostí, one of the richest and most spectacular sites of central Europe, is located at the southern entrance of the Moravian

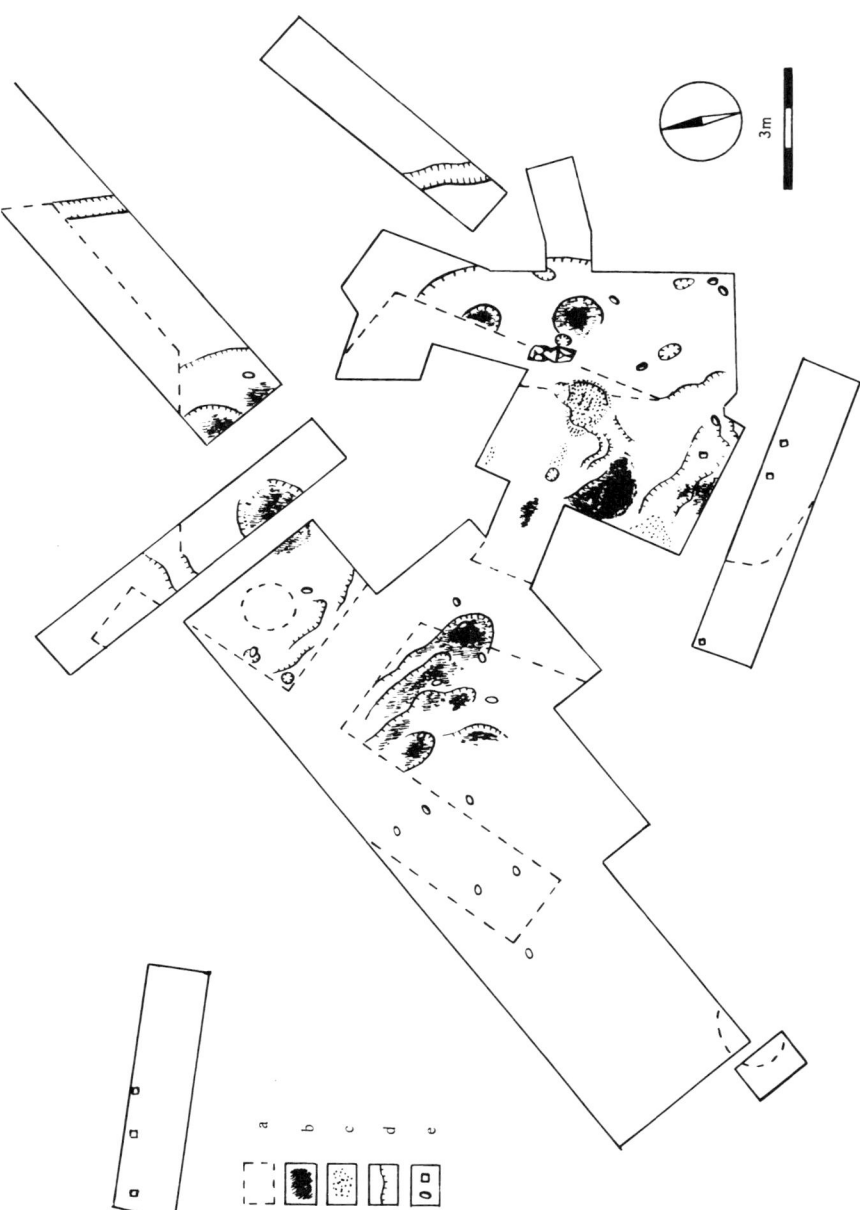

Figure 9.9. Petřkovice: Reconstruction of site 1a, on the basis of excavations in 1952–1953 and 1994–1995. a—earlier trenches; b—charcoal accumulations (hearths); c—areas covered by powdered ocher (hematite); d—depressions; e—mammoth molars, larger stones. The position of the female figurine is indicated.

CATALOG OF PRINCIPAL SITES

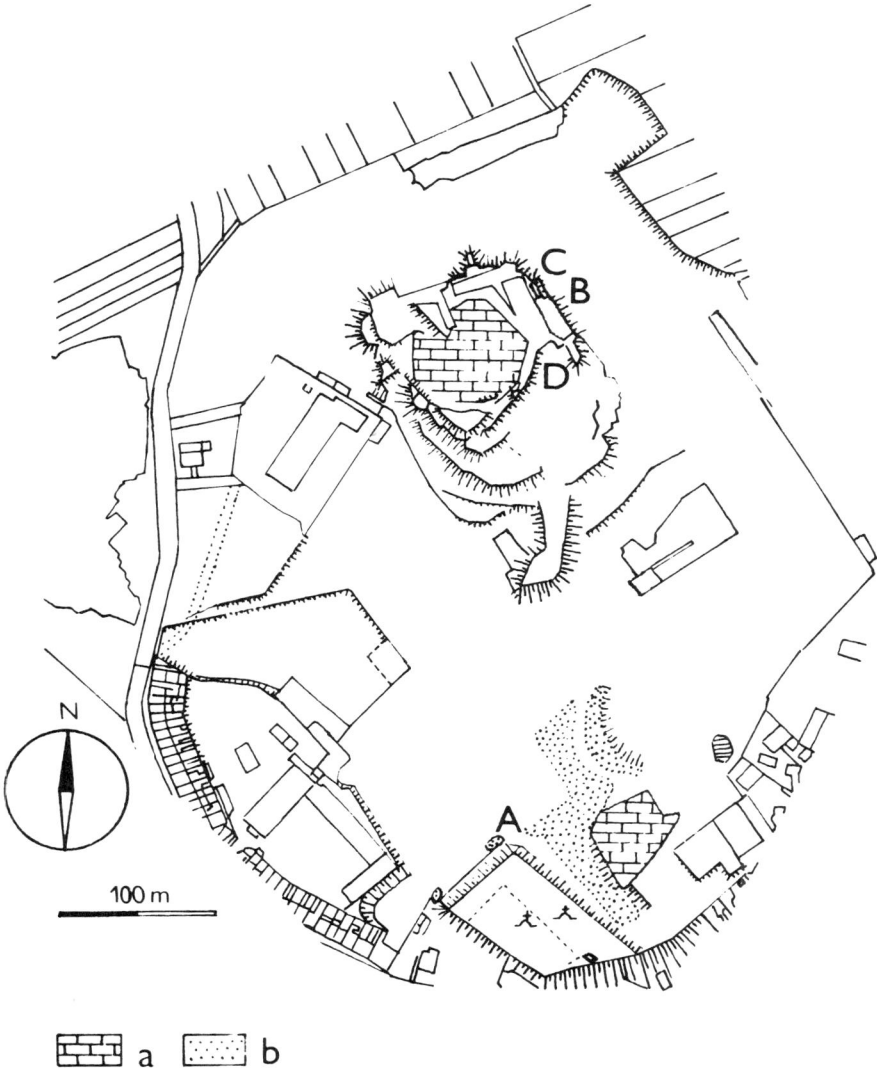

Figure 9.10. Předmostí: Plan of sites I and II. A–D—location of sections (see Figure 9.11): a—limestone; b—upper Paleolithic site.

Gate (Figure 9.10). All the leading personalities in Paleolithic research in Moravia have been engaged to work here: J. Wankel (1880–1882, 1884, 1886), K. J. Maška (1882–1884, 1889–1895), M. Kříž (1895), J. Knies (1923 and later), K. Absolon (1924–1935), H. Schwabedissen (1943), K. Žebera (1952–1954), and B. Klíma (1971–1973, 1975–1976, 1982–1983), but there are several paradoxes in the long history of this site. The method of excavating prehistoric surfaces at open-air loess sites was first applied here, but unfortunately without adequate graphic documentation. In addition, the excavations sometimes took place in the unfavorable atmosphere of the industrial exploitation of limestone and loess and the personal competition of archaeologists. The site has yielded the largest assemblage of early modern human skeletons known thus far, but at the end of the World War II, most of the accumulated material, including the human fossils, was destroyed by fire, and only the illustrations and descriptions are available, in several volumes (Matiegka, 1934, 1938; Absolon and Klíma, 1977).

Originally, two limestone rocks, Skalka in the south and Hradisko in the north, emerged from the Tertiary and Quartenary deposits (Figures 9.10 and 9.11). Both rocks were exploited for limestone, and Skalka soon completely disappeared.

Site I (Skalka)

The first archaeological excavations at Předmostí were concentrated on the promising areas in loess, surrounding the former elevation of Skalka. J. Wankel (1884) explored accumulations of mammoth bones, sometimes selected after sorts (tusks and molars), and accompanied by artifacts; under one mammoth femur, Wankel discovered part of a human mandible. During the excavation of further mammoth-bone clusters, K. J. Maška (1886) explored similar areas until 1894, when he found an extended burnt area encircled by mammoth bones with a group of seven wolf skeletons nearby. Afterward, human bones emerged (Maška, 1894). In August, Maška touched a larger group of human skeletons to the west of Skalka: the largest "grave" from the Upper Paleolithic thus far known.

> Being of eliptical shape, with the longer axis toward the northeast, the grave covered a space 4 m long and 2.5 m wide. It was covered by sharp-edged limestone blocks of various sizes, crossing the boundaries of the features to the north and the east, and not reaching its southern part. This stone coverage was up to 40 cm thick. The base of the grave was 2.6 m deep, and the human remains reached 30 cm higher. An important circumstance should be mentioned: single human remains continued quite frequently to the south and the southeast, outside the grave, together with mammoth, reindeer, and fox bones. (Maška, 1895b:5)
>
> On the basis of a preliminary classification of this rich material, I may state that the discovered specimens belong to at least 20 individuals, 15 of which are represented by more-or-less complete skeletons, while single parts only are preserved of the remaining five. Among the 20 individuals, there are 8 adults and 12 young people, mostly children, the youngest of them only half a year old. The skeletons were found usually in a contracted position next to each other, sometimes over each other. (Maška, 1895b:5)
>
> Immediately by the human bones lay remains of the following diluvial fauna: mammoth, polar fox, wolf, wolverine, hare, beaver, and reindeer. A fox skull was placed on one of the human skeletons. Two left shoulder bones of mammoths of various sizes, one of them scratched by a flint on the lower face, bounded the grave at the northwest and the northeast. Some flint splitters and burnt bone fragments lay in the grave as well. (Maška 1895b:6)

CATALOG OF PRINCIPAL SITES 227

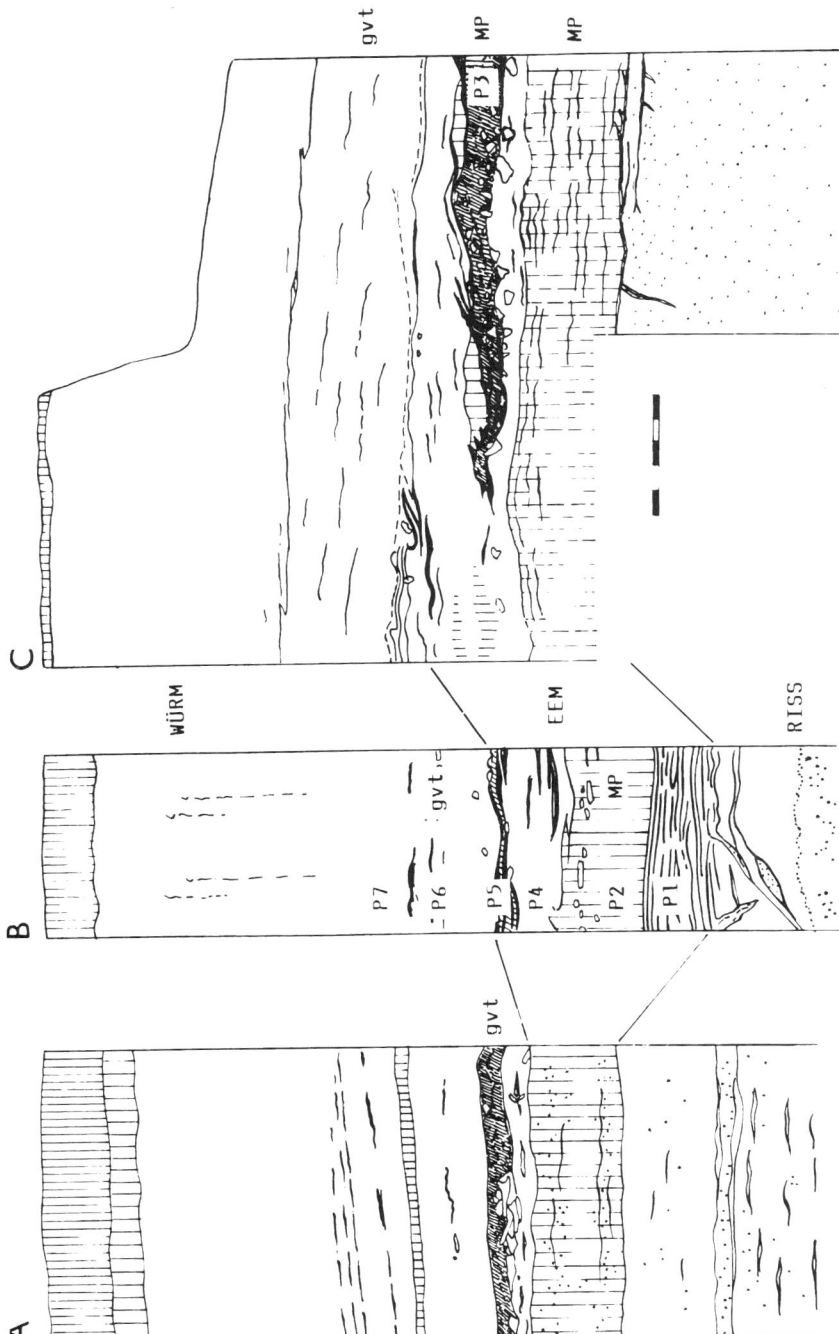

Figure 9.11. Předmostí I and II: Comparative stratigraphy: excavation, 1989–1991. MP—Middle Paleolithic; gvt—Gravettian; P1–7—pollen analysis samples. A–C: sections (for locations see Figure 9.10).

Besides this authentic published description, Maška left sketches showing the position of the individual skeletons in his diaries. The latest effort to reconstruct the burial was published by B. Klíma (1991, Figure 6.24).

Maška's discoveries attracted another Moravian researcher, M. Kříž (1894, 1896, 1903), to start his own excavation at the same site. Kříž was the first and the only one to report some data on structures such as hearths and related concentrations of objects. These features obviously formed separate settlement units, as known from later excavations at Dolní Věstonice and Pavlov.

> The hearths use to be in depressions artificially hollowed into the loess, and measuring 1–1.5 m in diameter. Such a place is covered by ash, mostly of bones, with a gray, dark gray, and black coloration. In the ash and around it, there lies a number of larger, burnt bone fragments. A number of splintering bones of mammoths or of smaller herbivores (reindeer, horse), of stones (for splinting the bones), flint knives, and flakes is concentrated around a hearth. We observe a deposit of accumulated bones, not far from or directly on a hearth; here lie the backbones and shoulder bones, there the ribs and femurs, skulls and jaws, tusks, etc., intentionally deposited in one place by prehistoric man, together with numerous carnivore remains. (Kříž, 1896:91)

In 1895, Kříž discovered a human skull, two fragments of jaws, and other human bones. He also found several important objects of art (a mammoth statue of ivory and a female engraving on a tusk), but their correct interpretation is due to Maška (1912).

In 1926, K. Absolon discovered another mammoth-bone deposit and a radiolarite workshop, Aurignacian in his view, further to the west of Skalka, near the village cemetery (point A). He immediately started to excavate systematically in regular zones, and in 1928, he succeeded in finding another human postcranial skeleton. With this last find, the minimal number of individuals at Předmostí reached 25 (according to Vlček, 1991b). As late as the 1970s, B. Klíma (1973a) turned back to the main cultural layer at the edge of the cemetery. By now, the cultural contents had been classified as Gravettian or Pavlovian, with a hypothetical Aurignacian horizon below. Finally, in 1982–1983, building activities at margins of the city of Přerov extended as far as Předmostí. New salvage excavations at the southeast boundary of the Gravettian site were carried out by B. Klíma and J. Svoboda (Klíma, 1984c, 1985b).

In conclusion, the Gravettian forms the most important, dense, and extended occupation stage (Zotz and Freund, 1951; Absolon and Klíma, 1977; Klíma, 1990a; Svoboda et al., 1994). The two C-14 dates from B. Klíma's excavation place it between 26,000 and 27,000 B.P. As is the case at Dolní Věstonice and Pavlov, the Předmostí site may in fact be a horizontal cluster of separate settlement units, extending over fairly large areas. One of the characteristic typological patterns observed in the lithics is the continual lateral, steep, and even scalariform retouch along the edges of the artifacts. This pattern is observed on blades, pointed blades, and sidescrapers (Absolon and Klíma, 1977:Tables 8–10, 14, 18, 36, and 41). Microliths are very rare, perhaps because of the absence of sediment floating during the earlier excavations. The retouch, together with a few Aurignacioid types, led various researchers to suspect an Aurignacian intrusion. On the basis of recent analyses, the "Předmostí style" may instead be compared to the middle, Pavlovian part of the Willendorf sequence. Furthermore, the Předmostí materials include at least one shouldered point (Valoch, 1981a: Figure 1, Number 25) and a series of less morphologically standard points; it is probable that these implements, together with some of the leaf-points, are comparable to the upper (Willedorfian-Kostenkian) part of the Willendorf sequence.

Site II (Hradisko)

During the 1920s and 1930s, with the progress of loess exploitation, the thick loess deposit attached to the limestone outcrop of Hradisko started to attract attention. In 1923, J. Knies (1929) described a section with thick reddish soil below the Upper Paleolithic horizon. At a total depth of 6 m, in the lower loess, there was a charcoal lense with two artifacts recalling Acheulian bifaces and mammoth bones. Further "Acheulioid" objects are recorded among the finds of K. Absolon between 1929 and 1931 (Absolon, 1945a; Absolon and Klíma, 1977). In 1943, the geologist J. Pelíšek found some Middle Paleolithic artifacts in a brown soil in the southern loess wall of Hradisko. In 1952–1953, K. Žebera, V. Ložek, O. Fejfar, and a group of geologists excavated larger Middle Paleolithic assemblages in the northeast part of the same elevation (Žebera, Ložek, Kneblová, Fejfar, and Mazálek 1955). The artifacts formed two horizons within redeposited soil sediments, dated, at that time, to the Würmian (the so-called section Žebera).

As a part of the present research project, new excavations were undertaken in 1989–1992 (points B and C). At the base, there is Rissian loess and a stripped solifluction layer, overlaid by reddish brown soil remains of the last interglacial (this age is confirmed by thermoluminiscence dating). In the northeast part of Hradisko, two larger and several smaller lenses of dark humus soil sediment with limestone blocks appeared in the upper part or above this deposit. The Middle Paleolithic artifacts appeared scattered in the reddish brown soil remains (at the lower level) and concentrated in one of the dark lenses (at the upper level). Few isolated artifacts lay in the other lenses. The two main Middle Paleolithic assemblages are formed by the groups of pebble tools, debitage (cores, flakes, and fragments), and small retouched tools. While the number of retouched tools remains the same in both layers (about 15%), the lower layer is generally more rich in pebbles and pebble tools (37%). Besides simple techniques of raw material percussion, some elements of Levalloisian technique appear in a small-dimensional variety (Svoboda, 1991d; Svoboda et al., 1994). A few Gravettian artifacts were dispersed in the overlying loess, and dated to 25,040 ± 320 B.P. (OxA 5971), i.e., later than site I.

The environmental analyses suggests that both the Middle and the Upper Paleolithic occupations of Předmostí II took place in temperate conditions, with extended forest (Arboreal pollen = 30%–67% of the total sum). The data for the Gravettian occupation are very comparable to evidence from Dolní Věstonice (Svobodová, 1991a,b), suggesting relatively mild conditions in the Würmian interpleniglacial, but also their gradual deterioration in the overlying layer at Předmostí.

STRÁNSKÁ SKÁLA (BRNO, FIGURE 4.1, NUMBER 1; FIGURE 5.1, NUMBER 1; FIGURE 5.2, NUMBER 1; FIGURE 7.1, NUMBER 1)

Stránská skála is a Jurassic limestone cliff located in the eastern vicinity of Brno (Figure 9.12). The limestone contains layers of chert, which was used for the production of lithic tools throughout the Paleolithic and the Neolithic (the Stránská skála exploitation area). Steep rock slopes at the northwest margins of the site are flanked by Lower to Middle Pleistocene slope deposits (site I) and by Upper Pleistocene loess at the northern margin (site IV). The upper part of the elevation is covered by the remains of terraces, deposits of Pleistocene soil sediments, limestone debris, and loess (sites II and III).

Site I has been excavated since 1910 by J. Woldřich, K. Absolon, R. Musil, and others, as an important paleontological site of the Biharian age (Musil and Valoch, 1968). Surface collections of Upper Paleolithic artifacts have been made there since the 1930s (Schirmeisen, 1933b; Valoch, 1954, 1974b). Systematic archaeological investigations of the various Upper Paleolithic occupations were begun in 1982 (Svoboda, 1985, 1987d,f, 1991e).

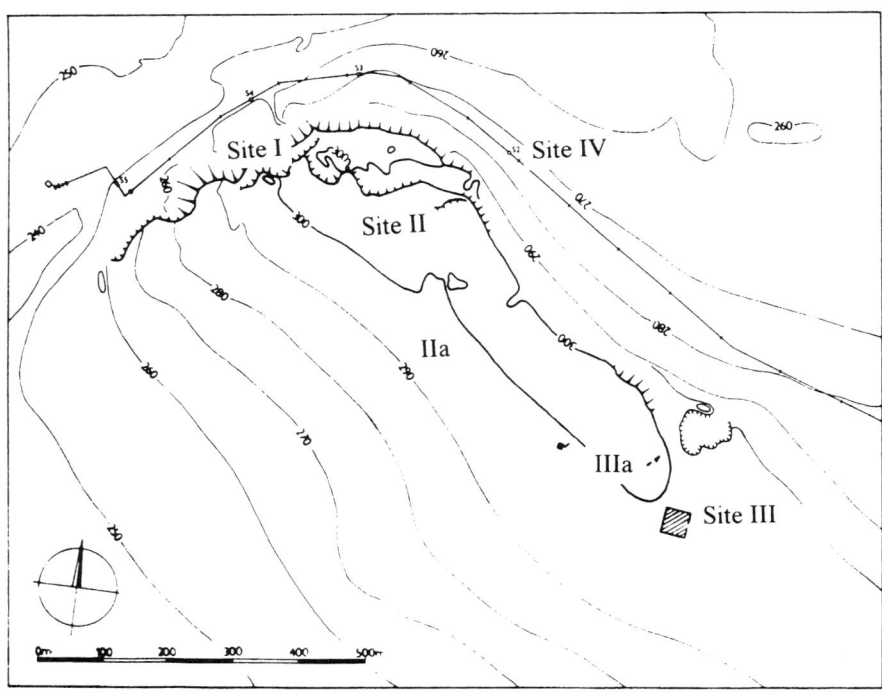

Figure 9.12. Stránská skála: General plan showing the position of sites I–IV.

Site I

Stratigraphically, the finds at this site were located in slope sediments and in small caves (Musil and Valoch, 1968). The Matuyama–Brunhes boundary was found inside the slope sediments, while the fauna dates generally to the Upper Biharian stage (Musil, 1982). The associated lithics are fragments of local chert which show no clear traces of working, except for a few possible flakes from the small cave number 8. Valoch (1987b) argues that some specimens were made of a chert which is slightly different from that available at the site, or of fluviatile pebbles. However, there are several types of chert at different levels of the Stránská skála rock (Přichystal, 1987), and our own excavation on its top revealed a river terrace as a possible source of pebbles. Valoch's arguments also take into account the indication of burning on three bones and a piece of chert, the state of fragmentation of the animal bones, and a possible engraving on one of them.

Site II

This site, located at the top of the Stránská skála rock and thus only partly covered by the loess, was discovered by surface survey by Schirmeisen, and the collected industries were subsequently studied and published by Valoch (1954) as an Aurignacian site.

In 1985, an industrial trenching exposed the Aurignacian layer in a soil covered by loess, deposited directly on the limestone subsoil (Svoboda, 1987f). This industry contains about 40% endscrapers, including typical Aurignacian types. This small assemblage is completed by a burin, a splintered piece, two retouched blades, a sidescraper, notches, and denticulates.

Site IIa

Site IIa (Figure 9.13; Svoboda, 1991e; Czudek et al., 1991) revealed a section with rubble redeposited by solifluction under extremely cold conditions at the base (layer 6), overlaid by earth with Bohunician industry (layer 5). This is followed by a phase of erosion and a phase of loess sedimentation and pedogenesis, related to a Middle Aurignacian industry (layer 4, about 32,500 B.P.). The upper part of the section is formed by the last Würmian loess with an Upper Aurignacian industry at the base (layer 3).

All the lithic assemblages recovered are made of the local chert. The Bohunician assemblage is relatively small, while the Middle Aurignacian is the largest assemblage of this culture thus far excavated in Moravia: it is a blade industry characterized by the dominance of endscrapers (Figure 5.7). The smaller Upper Aurignacian assemblage differs in that burins became more frequent and the artifacts are generally smaller.

Site III

Site III (cf. Figures 5.9 and 5.10; Svoboda, 1987d) yielded a different section, with a Bohunician industry within one of the interpleniglacial soils (soil 1, layer 5).

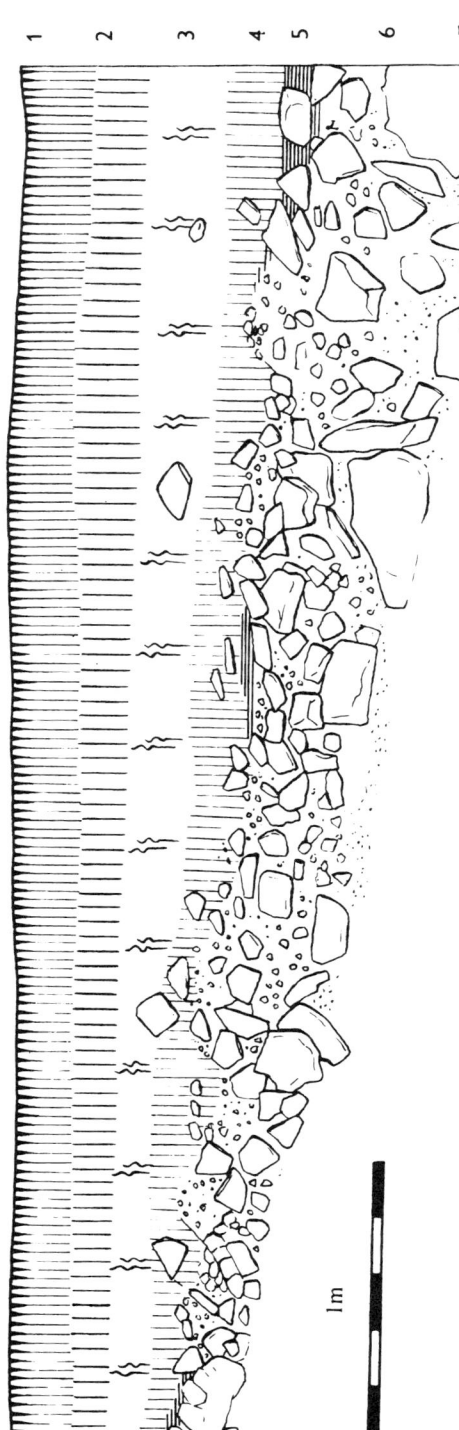

Figure 9.13. Stránská skála IIa: Section. From top to bottom, two Holocene soil horizons (1 and 2), loess (3, Upper Aurignacian), interpleniglacial soil (4, Middle Aurignacian), redeposited earth (5, Bohunician), redeposited debris layer (6), and weathered subsoil (7).

The artifacts formed separate clusters, with places that may be interpreted as hearths (dated around 38,000 B.P.). They were accompanied by a number of red and yellow ocher pellets. The pollen analysis indicates a steppe landscape with arboreal elements (*Pinus*, *Betula*, *Picea*, and *Alnus*).

Most of the retouched tools are made of foreign rocks (radiolarite, various cherts). The rest of the industry, made of the local chert, documents a primary workshop specialized in Levalloisian points, blades, and precores. The endscrapers dominate (including one thick Aurignacioid piece), while burins are absent. A flat ventroterminal retouch was applied on the extremity of a Levalloisian point. Sidescrapers, notches, and denticulates complete the toolkit (Figure 5.5).

Site IIIa

Stránská skála IIIa (cf. Figure 5.11; Svoboda, 1987d), again, is a multilayer archaeological site comparable to site IIa (Czudek et al., 1991). The first pleniglacial is demonstrated by a redeposited sequence of paleosoils, calcareous earths, and small gravel removed by solifluction. According to T. Czudek, the character of the redeposit was influenced by increasing humidity, increasing temperature, and a deep thaw of the permafrost. The pollen spectrum is poor and documents a cold climate (Svobodová, 1987d). The Bohunician industry lies in the uppermost part of the redeposited sequence (layer 4), overlaid by the second interpleniglacial soil with an Aurignacian industry (layer 3) (Figure 5.4).

The original position of the Bohunician layer seems widely affected by soliflucition around 40,000 B.P. With few exceptions (quartz, radiolarite, etc.), the bulk of the Bohunician material is made of local cherts of the Stránská skála type. Levalloisian points, sidescrapers, notches, and denticulates appear frequently. An endscraper or a burin may even be made on the extremity of Levalloisian points. Compared to Bohunice, the endscrapers predominate over the burins, and the thick Aurignacioid form is more frequently used. Of importance is an atypical point with a ventroterminal retouch.

The Aurignacian industry is dispersed in a relatively regular pattern around a circular hearth, cut a few centimeters deep (dated around 31,000 B.P.). The artifacts, still predominantly made of the local chert, is endscraper-dominated, with Aurignacian forms composing the greater part of this group. The burins are less common. Sidescrapers, notches, denticulates, and truncated blades complete the toolkit.

Site IIIb

This site holds another superposition of Bohunician and Aurignacian layers in a comparable stratigraphic situation. The lower, Bohunician layer is important in yielding the largest faunal (horse) assemblage. The upper, Middle Aurignacian layer is dated to 32,600 B.P. (Svoboda, 1993c).

Site IV

This site was found downslope of the limestone cliff. The finds lie in the uppermost part of the basal loess (Figure 6.12; Svoboda, 1991e). Dated to about

18,000 B.P., it offers the only well-dated evidence of pleniglacial occupation in Moravia.

The finds were localized in two accumulations found about 5 m from each other. The western accumulation consisted of a circular cluster of limestone blocks, horse bones (predominantly), and lithics. A cluster of horse bones redeposited longitudinally along the slope lay in clear association with this accumulation. The eastern accumulation consisted primarily of large blocks, the largest of which measured up to 0.75 m in length. Horse bones predominated in the cluster as well, but other species were also represented. Lithics were less numerous in this cluster, and neither of the clusters contained any charcoal or evidence of domestic activities. Local raw materials were less frequently used, and about half of the artifacts were made of exotic materials (various cherts, radiolarite, flint, porcelanite, rock crystal, and obsidian; Figure 6.4). Unretouched blades and a few retouched tools, as well as a possible whistle made from a reindeer phalange, are of Epigravettian character (further surface surveys in the vicinity were published by Škrdla and Plch, 1993b).

Archaeozoological research on the faunal remains is currently in progress. Preliminary results obtained by Peške reveal the presence of minimal percentages of humeri and skull fragments and the absence of femora. A broader comparative study by D. West (1996) correlates this assemblage with contemporary settlements of Central Europe, confirming differences in the bone composition. It appears that site IV was a specialized hunting site, where the terrain morphology, with the dominant rock cliff, may have played a role in the hunting strategies.

ŠIPKA AND ČERTOVA DÍRA CAVES (ŠTRAMBERK, FIGURE 4.1, NUMBER 10; FIGURE 7.1, NUMBER 26)

The two caves had mostly been explored by the end of the last century (Figure 4.7; Maška, 1882, 1885, 1886). Later work was based mainly on a reconstruction or revision of the sections (Bayer, 1925; Kukla, 1954), presentation of the lithic industries (Absolon, 1932; Valoch, 1957, 1965c), and publication of the Neanderthal fossil from Šipka (Jelínek, 1965; Vlček, 1969). Actually, Čertova díra Cave has been destroyed, while Šipka still exists (440 m above sea level), but the Würmian sediments have mostly been removed.

The stratigraphic reconstructions show that, located below the Holocene layers of both caves, was a loessic layer with limestone rubble, with a Magdalenian layer in the upper part and a culturally undeterminable Upper Paleolithic layer in the lower part. Below lay a complex of loams with the Mousterian, which may be separated into two or three layers. The subsoil is formed by silts, sands, sterile loams, and limestone rock.

The Mousterian industry is made mostly of local chert, with few implements of flint, quartz, and radiolarite (Figure 4.5).

The most important discovery is the Neanderthal child mandible, found on 26 August 1880. K. J. Maška (1884: 21–22) described the discovery:

In a very protected place, in a corner in front of the side gallery called "Jezevčí díra," 12 m from the main entrance, I found the remains of a large, mostly well-conserved hearth with burned stones scattered around. The diameter was about 2 m. At the cave wall on the left side, in a layer of ash and coal, there were almost 2000 pieces of sharp quartzite in all degrees of manufacture: simple flakes; rejected pieces; cores or nuclei, of which the flakes were made; misused or broken tools; and several fine used tools. Among these remains of antediluvial lithic workshop, burnt or partly burnt bones of cave bear, rhinoceros, aurochs, and mammoth were found, together with chipped bones and teeth of these same animals, as well as of cave lion, hyena, wolf, horse, and deer.... Behind this hearth, at the entrance of "Jezevčí díra," the fragment of human mandible was found.

ŠVÉDŮV STŮL CAVE (OCHOZ, FIGURE 4.1, NUMBER 12; FIGURE 7.1, NUMBER 14)

The filling of this large cave of the southern part of the Moravian karst (at 335 m above sea level; Figure 4.8) and the numerous remains of Pleistocene fauna were studied primarily by M. Kříž (1903). However, the site became famous after the discovery of a Neanderthal mandible by K. Kubásek (Rzehak, 1906, 1909). It was found in the cave filling with animal bones, but no human artifacts were recovered at that time. Later, the meaning of this find was discussed several times in the literature (Kříž, 1909; Skutil, 1927a; Schirmeisen, 1929), until a systematic excavation of the remaining cave fillings by B. Klíma (1962a) and the following exploration by J. Vaňura (1965a,b).

The sections (Figure 9.14) are mostly composed of Holocene loams and travertines, followed by Würmian loess with Upper Paleolithic (Magdalenian and probably earlier Upper Paleolithic [layers 6–9]). Below lies a complex of brown loams, soils, and limestone fragments (layers 11–13) with Mousterian artifacts in the uppermost part. The base is formed by ocherous loam, probably of the last interglacial. The Middle Paleolithic artifacts are rare (layer 11). They are mostly made of cherts and quartz. The Early Würmian fauna, on the other hand, is very rich, but only partly associated with the artifacts.

VEDROVICE (FIGURE 5.1, NUMBER 8; FIGURE 5.2, NUMBER 6)

The sites at Vedrovice are located at the margins of the Krumlovský les highland, with rich sources of redeposited chert pebbles emerging from the Tertiary marine sediments (the Krumlovian exploitation area). This material may have been exploited from the Middle Paleolithic (Valoch, 1990a), but especially in the EUP (e.g., Valoch, 1985a, 1993b), to the Neolithic and the Bronze Age.

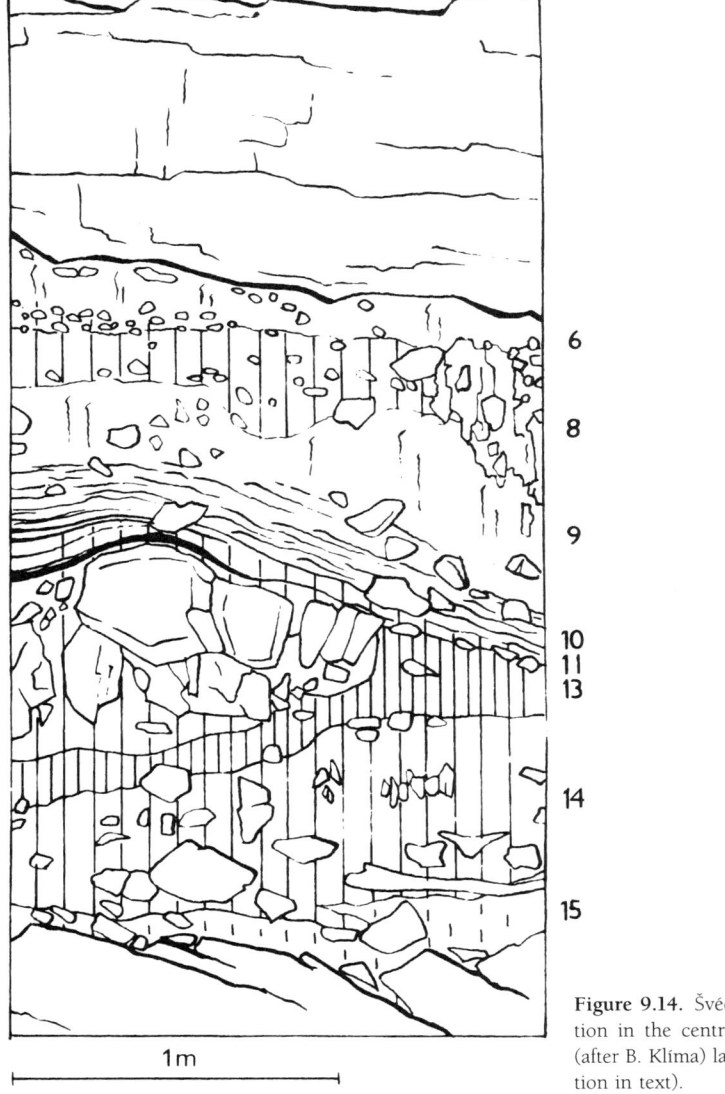

Figure 9.14. Švédův stůl Cave: Section in the central part of the cave (after B. Klíma) layers 6–15 (description in text).

Site I

Excavations have been in progress at this site since 1992 by M. Oliva (1993b). Aurignacian artifacts appear in at least two stratigraphic horizons, and an earlier (Bohunician or Middle Paleolithic) occupation may be suspected in the subsoil.

Site II

This surface Aurignacian site and its dating evoked vivid literary discussions in the 1980s. The main question was whether the "archaic" appearance of the artifacts was due to their great age (estimated at before 40,000 B.P. by Valoch, 1976b:14, and Oliva, 1980:53) or to the workshop character of the lithic production (Svoboda, 1983, 1984b). In a section near the site, K. Valoch discovered nine artifacts in loess covered by a paleosoil classified by Smolíková as belonging to the basis of PK II, that is, to the beginning of the Würmian glaciation (Valoch, 1985a). It is certainly difficult to use this section to date the surface Aurignacian finds in the vicinity.

Site V

This assemblage, the most important, well-stratified, and well-dated Szeletian in Moravia (Valoch, 1984b, 1993b), demonstrates by stratigraphy and C-14 datings that the Szeletian existed in Moravia during the first pedogenic process of the interpleniglacial (about 38,000 B.P.). The artifacts are concentrated (in scatters) but no features were recovered (Figure 5.8). The conditions were not favorable for bone preservation.

Again, the lithic artifacts are made of local cherts of the Krumlovský les type, very rarely radiolarite, by using non-Levalloisian flake and blade technologies. An important part of the retouched implements (leaf-points and sidescrapers) are covered by flat retouches. Sidescrapers, notches, and denticulates are common; endscrapers and burins are also present. Only a few pieces witness that core preparation techniques were known (Figure 5.6).

Comparable EUP surface sites, mostly made from local cherts, and with a more-or-less pronounced workshop character, are located along the margins of the Krumlovský les Highland in the vicinity (e.g., Jezeřany, Maršovice, and Dolní Kounice).

ŽITNÉHO CAVE (BŘEZINA, FIGURE 7.1, NUMBER 19)

The most important Magdalenian site in the eastern part of the Křtiny valley (in the middle part of the Moravian karst) lies at 414 m above seal level. Both the first excavation by Szombathy (1884a,b) and the last one by Dvořák, Pelíšek, Musil, and Valoch (1957) located the archaeological layer in a brown earth at the base of the Holocene sequence. According to Szombathy, the subsoil was formed by limestone rock; according to Dvořák et al. by loess. The lithic assemblage originates from various excavations (Skutil, 1927b). According to Valoch (1960c), the burins predominate slightly over the endscrapers. Both groups are accompanied by borers, numerous backed blades, ventrally retouched microblades, and single truncated blades or trapezoids. Very unusual is the high percentage (24%) of lithic tools made of rock crystal: endscrapers, burins, borers, and small cores. The most typical find among the bone industry is a 13-cm-long needle, accompanied by fragments of further needles, and of antler points.

Appendix B

List of Sites

Compiling a complete evidence from the Paleolithic sites in Moravia and the Czech part of Silesia is a long-term task that would call for the collaboration of all interested professionals and amateur collectors. The site list is based on the Register Book by Svoboda et al. (1994); it is intended to be a part of these two synthesis only, and it centers on sites that are culturally identifiable. For more complete regional reviews, including nondistinctive solitary finds and a discussion of dubious sites, see Hrubý (1951—distr. U. Hradiště), Mazálek (1960—reg. Bučovice), Jisl (1971—Czech Silesia), Podborský and Vildomec (1972–distr. Znojmo), Klíma (1986—distr. Břeclav), Oliva (1986—distr. Třebíč), Oliva (1989c—distr. Brno-venkov), and Grepl (1991—distr. N. Jičín).

The localities listed here correspond to modern site cadastres, some of which actually cover clusters of several prehistoric sites: large excavated areas (Dolní Věstonice and Předmostí) and extended surface-site agglomerations (Bořitov, Dolní Kounice, Drnovice, Nová Dědina, Ondratice, Žlutava, and many others). This list does not go into more detail than these site numeration systems.

KEY: LwP—Lower Paleolithic; MP—Middle Paleolithic; EUP—Early Upper Paleolithic; UP—undetermined Upper Paleolithic; LtP—Late Paleolithic

A

Adlerova Cave, Ochoz, distr. Brno-venkov: Magdalenian. Ref.: Klíma, 1953a; Valoch, 1960b; Svoboda, 1987c.
Alojzov, Určice, distr. Prostějov: EUP.

B

Babice, distr. Brno-venkov: Magdalenian? See also Jáchymka.
Bačov, distr. Blansko: MP/EUP. Ref.: Oliva and Štrof, 1985.
Balcarova Cave, Ostrov u Macochy, distr. Blansko: Magdalenian. Ref: Knies, 1990, 1901b; Musil, 1958; Valoch, 1960c.
Banín, distr. Svitavy: EUP? Ref.: Mackerle, 1948.
Barová Cave, Habrůvka, distr. Blansko: Magdalenian, Epimagdalenian. Ref.: Svoboda and Seitl, 1985; Seitl et al., 1986; Svobodová and Svoboda, 1988.
Bělov, distr. Kroměříž: Aurignacian. Ref.: Oliva, 1983.
Bílovec, distr. N. Jičín: UP. Ref.: Jisl, 1971; Grepl, 1991.
Blansko: EUP?
Blatec, distr. Olomouc: Gravettian. Ref.: Skutil, 1959; Svoboda et al., 1994.
Blazice, distr. Kroměříž: UP. Ref.: Skutil, 1959.
Blažovice, distr. Brno-venkov: Aurignacian/Epigravettian. Ref.: Oliva, 1989c.
Bohaté Málkovice, distr. Vyškov: LtP. Ref.: Mazálek, 1960; Valoch, 1966c.
Bohunice, Brno-město: Bohunician. Ref.: Makowsky, 1888, 1897; Maška, 1889; Skutil, 1936; Valoch, 1965b, 1974a, 1976a, 1982c; Allsworth-Jones, 1986; Oliva, 1984b; Svoboda, 1987e.
Bohuslavice, distr. Opava: Acheulean. Ref.: Svoboda et al., 1991.
Bojanovice, distr. Znojmo: EUP.
Boleradice, distr. Břeclav: UP. Ref.: Klíma, 1986.
Bořetice, distr. Břeclav: Gravettian? stone discs.
Bořitov, distr. Blansko: MP/Szeletian. Ref.: Valoch, 1977b, 1978c, 1993a; Svoboda, 1983; Oliva, 1987c; Oliva and Štrof, 1985.
Boršice, distr. U. Hradiště: Aurignacian, Gravettian. Ref.: Skutil, 1940b; Hrubý, 1951; Klíma, 1965b.
Boskovice, distr. Blansko: MP/EUP. Ref.: Oliva and Štrof, 1985.
Bratčice, distr. Brno-venkov: Szeletian. Ref.: Skutil, 1962d, 1963a; Valoch, 1965b, 1974a; Oliva, 1989c.
Brno: See also Bohunice, Červený kopec, Hády, Jundrov, Kohoutovice, Líšeň, Maloměřice, Modřice, Nová hora, Podstránská, Stránská skála, Švédské Šance, Žabovřesky, Žlutý kopec
Brno—Francouzská Street (Brno II); Gravettian burial. Ref.: Makowsky, 1892; Jelínek et al., 1959.
Brno—Kamenná Street: Epigravettian. Ref.: Skutil, 1930.
Brno—Malá Klajdovka: MP. Ref.: Musil, Valoch, and Nečesaný, 1955; Valoch, 1962a, 1977a.
Brno—Růženin dvůr: LwP. Ref.: Musil et al., 1955; Valoch, 1977a; Smolíková and Kovanda, 1983.
Brno—Vídeňská (former Koněvova) Street: Epigravettian. Ref.: Valoch, 1975b, 1980b.
Brodek, distr. Prostějov: Aurignacian.
Brumovice, distr. Břeclav: UP. Ref.: Klíma, 1986.
Březina: See Drátenická Cave, Nová Drátenická Cave, Výpustek Cave, Žitného Cave.

LIST OF SITES

Buchlovice, distr. U. Hradiště: Aurignacian, Gravettian. Ref.: Hrubý, 1951.
Bučovice, distr. Vyškov: Tišnovian. Ref.: Mazálek, 1960; Valoch, 1966c.
Bukovany, distr. Olomouc: UP.
Bulhary, distr. Břeclav: UP. Ref.: Klíma, 1986.
Býčí skála Cave, Habrůvka, distr. Blansko: Magdalenian. Ref.: Wankel, 1871a, 1882, 1884; Maška, 1886; Bayer, 1925; Schirmeisen, 1929; Absolon, 1945a; Valoch, 1960c, 1961a, 1966b, 1978a; Sobczyk, 1984; Svoboda, 1987g; Allsworth-Jones, 1986.
Býkovice, distr. Blansko: Szeletian. Ref.: Valoch, 1977b; Oliva and Štrof, 1985.
Bystrovany, distr. Olomouc: UP.

C

Charváty, distr. Olomouc: UP.
Chuchelná, distr. Opava: EUP, Epigravettian. Ref.: Svoboda et al., 1994.
Cvrčovice, distr. Kroměříž: UP.
Čebín, distr. Brno-venkov: Szeletian. Ref.: Skutil, 1932; Oliva and Doležel, 1985.
Čechovice-Domamyslice, distr. Prostějov: Epigravettian.
Černá Hora, distr. Blansko: Szeletian. Ref.: Valoch, 1977b; Oliva and Štrof, 1985.
Čertova díra Cave, Štramberk, distr. N. Jičín; Mousterian, Magdalenian. Ref.: Maška, 1882, 1884, 1886; Bayer, 1925; Valoch, 1957, 1965c.
Červený kopec, Brno-město: LwP. Ref.: Kukla, 1975; Smolíková, 1982; Zeman, 1983; Klíma, 1963a; Valoch, 1977a; Musil, 1982; Svoboda et al., 1994.

D

Dědice, Vyškov: MP. Ref.: Musil and Valoch, 1956; Svoboda, 1994c.
Diváky, distr. Břeclav: Aurignacian. Ref.: Oliva, 1984a; Svoboda and Havlíček, 1987.
Dobrochov, distr. Prostějov: Aurignacian. Ref.: Kopecký, 1938; Svoboda and Přichystal, 1990.
Dobronice, Tavíkovice, distr. Znojmo: UP. Ref.: Podborský and Vildomec, 1972.
Dobrotice, distr. Kroměříž: UP.
Dolany, distr. Olomouc: UP.
Dolní Kounice, distr. Brno-venkov: LwP?, MP, Bohunician, Szeletian. Ref.: Skutil, 1962d, 1963a; Oliva, 1989c; Valoch, 1990a, 1991.
Dolní Lutyně, distr. Karviná: LwP? Ref.: Svoboda et al., 1994.
Dolní Věstonice, distr. Břeclav, site I: Gravettian. Ref.: Absolon, 1938a,b, 1945b; Bayer, 1931; Knor et al., 1953; Klíma, 1950a,b, 1952a, 1963b, 1969a, 1979b, 1981b,c, 1983a,d, 1990c; Musil, 1959a; Svoboda, 1993d; Soffer et al., 1993. Site II: Gravettian. Ref.: Absolon et al., 1933; Klíma et al., 1962; Havlíček and Kovanda, 1985; Havlíček, 1991; Klíma, 1987b,d, 1990a,c, 1995; Svoboda, 1989a,d, 1990b, 1991b; Svoboda et al., 1993. Site III: Aurignacian, Gravettian. Ref.: Svoboda et al., 1995.
Domaželice, distr. Přerov: UP.

Doubravice, distr. Blansko: Szeletian. Ref.: Valoch, 1977b; Oliva and Štrof, 1985.
Drahanovice, distr. Olomouc: Aurignacian. Ref.: Oliva, 1987a.
Drahotuše, distr. Přerov: UP.
Drásov, distr. Brno-venkov: UP. Ref.: Oliva, 1989c.
Drátenická Cave, Březina, distr. Brno-venkov: Micoquian? Ref.: Bayer, 1925.
Drnovice, distr. Vyškov: Szeletian, Epigravettian? Ref.: Svoboda, 1989c, 1994c.
Droždín, Olomouc: Szeletian. Ref.: Trňáčková, 1967.
Drysice, distr. Vyškov: EUP.
Dubicko, distr. Šumperk: EUP. Ref.: Schirmeisen, 1933a.
Dukovany, distr. Třebíč: Szeletian. Ref.: Skutil and Oulehla, 1961; Oliva, 1986.

G

Gottwaldov: See Zlín.
Grygov, distr. Olomouc: UP.

H

Habrovany-Olšany, distr. Vyškov: Szeletian. Ref.: Klíma, 1971a; Svoboda, 1994c.
Habrůvka: See Barová Cave, Býčí skála Cave, Vinckova Cave.
Hadí Cave, Mokrá, distr. Brno-venkov: Magdalenian. Ref.: Klíma, 1961a.
Hády, distr. Brno-město: Magdalenian? Ref.: Valoch, 1977b.
Hajany, distr. Brno-venkov: Szeletian. Ref.: Klíma, 1963e; Oliva, 1989c.
Hanušovická Cave, Hanušovice, distr. Šumperk: Magdalenian? Ref.: Skutil, 1955a.
Hlavicova Cave, Hranice, distr. Přerov: Magdalenian? Ref.: Skutil, 1955b.
Hluchov, distr. Prostějov: Aurignacian. Ref.: Oliva, 1987a.
Hněvošice, distr. Opava: Szeletian. Ref.: Svoboda et al., 1994: Figure 50.
Hodonice, distr. Znojmo: Gravettian? Ref.: Skutil, 1936; Podborský and Vildomec, 1972.
Horákov, distr. Brno-venkov: EUP, LUP. Ref.: Skutil, 1937a; Oliva, 1989c.
Horní Moštěnice, distr. Přerov: Gravettian?
Horní Sukolom, distr. Olomouc: UP.
Horní Věstonice, distr. Břeclav: Szeletian? LtP. Ref.: Klíma, 1986; Ložek, 1985.
Hostějov, distr. U. Hradiště: EUP. Ref.: Valoch, 1985b.
Hošťálkovice, distr. Opava: EUP.
Hovorany, distr. Hodonín: UP.
Hradčany, distr. Brno-venkov: Szeletian, LtP. Ref.: Skutil, 1932; Oliva, 1989c; Oliva and Doležel, 1985.
Hranice, distr. Přerov: Epigravettian. Ref.: Klíma, 1947, 1951b, 1958a; Dvořák and Valoch, 1962. See also Hlavicova j.
Hrubšice, distr. Brno-venkov: EUP.
Hrušovany, distr. Znojmo: Gravettian. Ref.: Skutil, 1936; Podborský and Vildomec, 1972.

LIST OF SITES

I

Ivančice, distr. Brno-venkov: EUP. Ref.: Oliva, 1989c.
Ivaň, distr. Břeclav: LwP?, UP. Ref.: Valoch, 1982a.

J

Jabloňany, distr. Blansko: Tišnovian. Ref.: Klíma, 1971b.
Jáchymka and Evina Caves, Babice, distr. Brno-venkov: UP. Ref.: Wankel, 1871b, 1884; Szombathy, 1884a; Skutil, 1940a.
Jalubí, distr. U. Hradiště: UP.
Jamolice, distr. Znojmo: MP/EUP. Ref.: Oliva, personal communication.
Jaroměřice nad Rokytnou, Třebíč: UP, LtP. Ref.: Oliva, 1986.
Jaroslavice, distr. Znojmo: Gravettian. Ref.: Wurmbrand, 1873, 1879; Knies, 1897; Makowsky, 1899b; Bayer, 1925; Podborský and Vildomec, 1972.
Jarošov, U. Hradiště: Gravettian. Ref.: Hrubý, 1951; Procházka, 1983.
Javoříčko: See Zkamenělý zámek.
Jedovnice: See Kolíbky.
Jeskyně 184 (Cave), Vavřinec, distr. Blansko: EUP. Ref.: Svoboda et al., 1983.
Jevišovice, distr. Znojmo: EUP.
Jezeřany, distr. Znojmo: Szeletian. Ref.: Valoch, 1965d, 1966a; Oliva 1979a; Allsworth-Jones, 1986.
Ježkovice, distr. Vyškov: EUP. Ref.: Svoboda, 1994c.
Jiřice, distr. Znojmo: EUP.
Jiříkovice, distr. Brno-vekov: UP.
Jundrov, Brno-město: Epigravettian. Ref.: Skutil, 1937a; Oliva, 1991b.

K

Kadov, distr. Znojmo: Acheulean. Ref.: Skutil, 1946b.
Kanice, distr. Brno-venkov: UP. See also Pod vyhlídkou Cave.
Karolín, distr. Kroměříž: Acheulean?, Aurignacian. Ref.: Oliva, 1981b, 1987a.
Kateřinská Cave, Vavřinec, distr. Blansko: Magdalenian. Ref.: Wankel, 1871b; Skutil, 1929a; Svoboda et al., 1983; Svoboda, 1987g).
Klentnice, distr. Břeclav: Gravettian? Ref.: Klíma, 1986.
Klobouky, distr. Břeclav: Aurignacian. Ref.: Skutil, 1936, 1939.
Kněžice, distr. Třebíč: LtP. Ref.: Diviš and Grepl, 1984.
Kobylí, distr. Břeclav: EUP.
Kohoutovice, distr. Brno-město: Aurignacian. Ref.: Valoch, 1968b; Allsworth-Jones, 1986.
Kojetín, distr. N. Jičín: UP.

Kolíbky Caves, Jedovnice, distr. Blansko: Magdalenian. Ref.: Knies, 1907; Skutil, 1929b; Svoboda, 1987c; Svoboda et al., 1996.
Količín, distr. Kroměříž: UP.
Koňská Cave, Vavřinec, distr. Blansko: Magdalenian. Ref.: Skutil, 1962b.
Kosíř: See Slatinice, Drahanovice.
Kostelec, distr. Kroměříž: UP. Ref.: Skutil, 1931b.
Kozmice, distr. Opava: UP.
Kožichovice, distr. Třebíč: Gravettian. Ref.: Oliva, 1986.
Krhov, distr. Blansko: EUP. Ref.: Oliva and Štrof, 1985.
Krumvíř, distr. Břeclav: EUP. Ref.: Klíma, 1986.
Křepice, distr. Břeclav: Aurignacian. Ref.: Klíma, 1959b, 1969b; Allsworth-Jones, 1986.
Křižanovice, distr. Vyškov: Swiderian?
Křížova Cave, Ochoz, distr. Brno-venkov: EUP, Magdalenian. Ref.: Klíma, 1951a; Valoch, 1960b,c; Allsworth-Jones, 1986.
Kubšice, distr. Znojmo: Aurignacian. Ref.: Valoch, 1965d; Oliva, 1987a.
Kůlna Cave, Sloup, distr. Blansko: Early Middle Paleolithic, Taubachian, Micoquian, Gravettian?, Magdalenian, Epimagdalenian. Ref.: Kříž, 1891; Knies, 1913; Valoch, 1981b, 1988.
Kůlnička Cave, Morká, distr. Brno-venkov: Magdalenian. Ref.: Skutil, 1941; Klíma, 1960b; Svoboda and Seitl, 1987; Oliva, 1989c.
Kupařovice, distr. Brno-venkov: Szeletian?, Aurignacian. Ref.: Valoch, 1985a; Oliva, 1989c; Allsworth-Jones, 1986.
Kvasice, distr. Kroměříž: Aurignacian. Ref.: Klíma, 1952b; Žebera, 1958; Oliva, 1987a.
Kyjov, distr. Hodonín: Gravettian.

L

Lažánky; See Rytířská Cave.
Lechotice, distr. Kroměříž: UP. Ref.: Skutil, 1931b.
Lednice, distr. Břeclav: Acheulean. Ref.: Chlachula, personal communication, 1991.
Letonice, distr. Vyškov: LtP. Ref.: Mazálek, 1960.
Lhánice, distr. Třebíč: Bohunician. Ref.: Oliva, 1986.
Lhota, distr. Přerov: Aurignacian. Ref.: Klíma, 1979a.
Lhota Rapotina, distr. Blansko: Szeletian. Ref.: Oliva and Štrof, 1985.
Lhotka, distr. Kroměříž: Aurignacian. Ref.: Oliva, 1979b; Valoch, 1979b.
Lipovec: See Michalova skála Cave.
Liščí Cave, Ochoz, distr. Brno-venkov: Magdalenian. Ref.: Klíma, 1960c.
Líšeň, Brno-město: MP, Bohunician, UP. Ref.: Klíma, 1959a; Valoch, 1962b; Svoboda, 1987d. Eastern part called "Podolí": Bohunician. Ref.: Oliva, 1981a, 1984b.
Loučany, distr. Olomouc: UP.
Lubná, distr. Kroměříž: Aurignacian. Ref.: Skutil, 1937a.
Ludmírov-Milkov: See Průchodnice Caves.

LIST OF SITES

Ludslavice, distr. Kroměříž: UP. Ref.: Klíma, 1983b.
Luhačovice, distr. Zlín: Swiderian?
Luleč, distr. Vyškov: Szeletian.
Lutín, distr. Olomouc: UP

M

Malhostovice, distr. Brno-venkov: EUP. Ref.: Oliva, 1989c; Oliva and Doležel, 1985.
Maloměřice, distr. Brno-město: MP, Aurignacian, Magdalenian. Ref.: Schirmeisen, 1933b; Valoch, 1955a, 1963, 1964, 1969c, 1979a; Allsworth-Jones, 1986.
Marefy, distr. Vyškov: LtP. Ref.: Mazálek, 1960; Valoch, 1966c.
Maršovice, distr. Znojmo: MP?, Szeletian. Ref.: Valoch, 1965d, 1971, 1976d; Valoch and Seitl, 1988.
Medlov, distr. Brno-venkov: EUP. Ref.: Oliva, 1989c.
Medlov-Zadní Újezd, distr. Olomouc: EUP. Ref.: Skutil, 1959.
Mělčany, distr. Brno-venkov: Szeletian. Ref.: Valoch, 1974a; Oliva, 1989c.
Měnín, distr. Brno-venkov: Gravettian? stone disk.
Michalova skála Cave, Lipovec, distr. Blansko: Magdalenian. Ref.: Knies, 1897.
Mikulov, distr. Břeclav: UP. See also Turold Cave.
Milovice, distr. Břeclav: Aurignacian, Gravettian. Ref.: Klíma, 1987a; Oliva, 1988, 1989a.
Milovice, distr. Kroměříž: Aurignacian. Ref.: Oliva, 1979b.
Miroslav-Kašenec, distr. Znojmo: LwP?
Míškovice, distr. Kroměříž: Aurignacian. Ref.: Skutil, 1960, 1962c; Klíma, 1983b.
Mladeč, Mladečské Caves, distr. Olomouc: Aurignacian. Ref.: Szombathy, 1884a,b, 1925; Knies, 1906; Maška, 1886, 1905; Bayer, 1925; Smyčka, 1904, 1922; Skutil, 1938b; Jelínek, 1987; Oliva, 1989b. See also Podkova Cave.
Mladeč, Plavatisko, distr. Olomouc: Gravettian. Ref.: Skutil, 1938b; Valoch, 1981a.
Mladoňovice, distr. Třebíč: LtP. Ref.: Oliva, 1986.
Modřice, Brno-město: MP, Szeletian. Ref.: Musil et al., 1955; Valoch, 1974a, 1977a; Oliva, 1989c.
Mohelno, distr. Třebíč: Bohunician. Ref.: Oliva, 1986; Škrdla and Plch, 1993a.
Mokrá, distr. Brno-venkov: EUP, Magdalenian. Ref.: Škrdla, personal communication, 1995. See also Hadí Cave, Pekárna Cave, Kůlnička Cave.
Moravany, distr. Brno-venkov: EUP. Ref.: Oliva, 1989c.
Moravské Bránice, distr. Brno-venkov: EUP, UP. Ref.: Oliva, 1989c.
Moravské Knínice, distr. Brno-venkov: UP. Ref.: Oliva and Doležel, 1985; Oliva, 1989c.
Moravský Krumlov, distr. Znojmo: MP, UP. Ref.: Valoch and Dvořák, 1956; Valoch, 1962a; Klíma, 1960a.
Morkůvky, distr. Břeclav: EUP. Ref.: Klíma, 1986.
Mořice, distr. Prostějov: EUP. Ref.: Skutil, 1934.
Mostkovice, distr. Prostějov: EUP. Ref.: Skutil, 1931a.

Mušov, distr. Břeclav: LwP? Ref.: Valoch, 1982a.
Mutěnice, distr. Hodonín: MP.
Myslejovice, distr. Prostějov: Szeletian. Ref.: Skutil, 1937b, 1938a; Valoch, 1983.

N

Napajedla, distr. Zlín: UP.
Násedlovice, distr. Hodonín: Gravettian?
Nebovidy, distr. Brno-venkov: UP. Ref.: Oliva, 1989c.
Němčičky, distr. Brno-venkov: Szeletian. Ref.: Oliva, 1989c.
Neslovice, distr. Brno-venkov: Szeletian. Ref.: Valoch, 1973; Allsworth-Jones, 1986.
Nevojice, distr. Vyškov: LtP. Ref.: Mazálek, 1960.
Nikolčice, distr. Břeclav: EUP. Ref.: Klíma, 1986.
Nová Dědina, distr. Kroměříž: Aurignacian. Ref.: Skutil, 1924; Klíma, 1977a; Allsworth-Jones, 1986; Oliva, 1987a.
Nová Drátenická Cave, Březina, distr. Brno-venkov: Magdalenian. Ref.: Klíma, 1949, 1951c.
Nová hora, Brno-město: MP, Bohunician. Ref.: Svoboda, 1985, 1991d; Valoch, 1987c.
Nová Ves, distr. Brno-venkov: UP. Ref.: Oliva, 1989c.
Nová Ves, distr. Břeclav: LwP?, UP. Ref.: Valoch, 1982a; Klíma, 1986.
Nové Bránice, distr. Brno-venkov: EUP. Ref.: Oliva, 1989c.
Nuzířov, distr. Brno-venkov: Szeletian, LtP. Ref.: Skutil, 1932; Oliva, 1989c.

O

Obora, distr. Blansko: Szeletian. Ref.: Oliva and Štrof, 1985.
Ochoz distr. Brno-venkov: UP. Ref.: Oliva, 1989c. See also Adlerova Cave, Křížova Cave, Liščí Cave, Ochozská Cave, Švédův stůl.
Ochozská Cave, Ochoz, distr. Brno-venkov: Magdalenian. Ref.: Klíma, 1970a, 1984a; Valoch, 1953, 1960c.
Ohrozim, distr. Prostějov: UP. Ref.: Skutil, 1931a.
Olbramovice, distr. Znojmo: EUP. Ref.: Podborský and Vildomec, 1972; Oliva, 1987a.
Oldřišov, distr. Opava: LtP.
Omice, distr. Brno-venkov: EUP. Ref.: Klíma, 1962b.
Ondratice, distr. Prostějov: Bohunician, Szeletian, Aurignacian. Ref.: Absolon, 1936; Skutil, 1954; Prosche, 1960; Valoch, 1967, 1975d, 1983; Svoboda, 1980, 1983; Allsworth-Jones, 1986.
Opatovice, distr. Vyškov: Szeletian. Ref.: Svoboda, 1990c, 1994c.
Opava: Epigravettian. Ref.: Bayer and Stumpf, 1929; Brenner, 1949; Jisl, 1971; Svoboda, 1995c.
Ořechov, distr. Brno-venkov: Bohunician. Ref.: Valoch, 1956, 1961b, 1973.
Oslavany, distr. Brno-venkov: EUP, Gravettian/Epigravettian. Ref.: Oliva, 1989c.

LIST OF SITES

Ostopovice, distr. Brno-venkov: EUP. Ref.: Valoch, 1974a; Oliva, 1989c.
Ostrava: See Petřkovice, Přívoz.
Ostrov u Macochy., distr. Blansko: Aurignacian. Ref.: Skutil, 1962a; Valoch, 1977b. See also Balcarova Cave.
Ostrožská Nová Ves, distr. U. Hradiště: Epigravettian. Ref.: Hrubý, 1951; Valoch, 1979b.
Otaslavice, distr. Prostějov: EUP, Epigravettian. Ref.: Absolon, 1935c.
Otice, distr. Opava: Szeletian. Ref.: Klíma, 1974c.

P

Pasohlávky, distr. Břeclav: LwP?, UP. Ref.: Valoch, 1982a; Klíma, 1986.
Pavlov, distr. Břeclav, site I: Gravettian (Pavlovian). Ref.: Klíma, 1954, 1955a, 1957b, 1959c, 1962d, 1963f, 1964b, 1973b, 1977b, 1984b, 1987c, 1988, 1989; Musil, 1955, 1959b; Vlček, 1961; Svoboda, 1994a,b. Site II: Gravettian. Ref.: Klíma, 1961b, 1976. Site III: Gravettian. Ref.: Klíma, 1981a, 1983e; Havlíček and Kovanda, 1985.
Pavlovice, distr. Přerov: Aurignacian. Ref.: Klíma, 1980.
Pekárna Cave. Mokrá, distr. Brno-venkov: Micoquian, EUP, Magdalenian. Ref.: Wankel, 1881, 1882; Kříž, 1891, 1897–1998, 1898; Absolon and Czižek, 1926–1932; Absolon, 1943; Musil, 1958; Valoch, 1961a; Klíma, 1974a; Svoboda, 1991c; Musil, 1974.
Petřkovice, Ostrava: Gravettian (Willendorfian-Kostenkian). Ref.: Folprecht and Skutil, 1931; Klíma, 1955b, 1958a, 1969d; Svoboda et al., 1995.
Pístovice, distr. Vyškov: Epigravettian. Ref.: Svoboda, 1994c.
Pod hradem Cave, Vavřinec, distr. Blansko: Szeletian. UP. Ref.: Knies, 1901a; Skutil, 1941, 1946a; Valoch, 1965a, 1969c; Allsworth-Jones, 1986; Gargett, 1994.
Podivice, distr. Vyškov: EUP.
Pod Koňským spádem, caves, Vavřinec, distr. Blansko: UP.
Podkova Cave, Mladeč, distr. Olomouc: UP. Ref.: Skutil, 1938b.
Pod vyhlídkou Cave, Kanice, distr. Brno-venkov: Magdalenian. Ref.: Klíma, 1958b.
Podstránská, Brno-město: Bohunician. Aurignacian. Ref.: Valoch, 1974b.
Pohořelice, distr. Zlín: EUP. Ref.: Skutil, 1931b, 1936.
Polánka, distr. Znojmo: EUP.
Polanka nad Odrou, distr. N. Jičín: Acheulean. Ref.: Svoboda et al., 1991.
Popice, distr. Břeclav: UP. Ref.: Skutil, 1936.
Popovice, distr. Brno-venkov: Szeletian, LtP?. Ref.: Oliva, 1989c.
Poustevna Cave, Sloup, distr. Blansko: Magdalenian? Ref.: Maška, 1886.
Pouzdřany, distr. Břeclav: LwP?, Gravettian? Ref.: Makowsky, 1899a,b; Skutil, 1936; Valoch, 1982a.
Pozořice, distr. Brno-venkov: UP. Ref.: Oliva, 1989c.
Pravlov, distr. Brno-venkov: LwP?, Szeletian,. Ref.: Oliva, 1989c.
Prštice, distr. Brno-venkov: UP. Ref.: Oliva, 1989c.
Průchodnice Caves, Ludmírov-Milkov, distr. Prostějov: Magdalenian? Ref.: Knies, 1905; Skutil and Stehlík, 1939; Svoboda and Ložek, 1993.

Prusínovice, distr. Kroměříž: MP. Ref.: Valoch, 1979b.
Předmostí, Přerov: Acheulean?, Taubachian, Gravettian. Ref.: Wankel, 1884, 1890; Maška, 1886, 1894, 1895a,b, 1912; Kříž, 1894, 1896, 1903; Absolon, 1918; Absolon and Klíma, 1977; Knies, 1929; Breuil, 1925; Zotz and Freund, 1951; Žebera, 1954; Žebera et al., 1955; Valoch, 1960a, 1969a, 1975a, 1981a, 1982b, 1987a; Klíma, 1962c, 1973a, 1974b, 1984c, 1985b, 1990b, 1991; Macoun, 1982; Svoboda, 1991d; Svoboda et al. 1994; Musil, 1968.
Přestavlky, distr. Přerov: Aurignacian. Ref.: Klíma, 1978.
Přibice, distr. Břeclav: LwP, UP. Ref.: Valoch, Smolíková, and Zeman, 1978.
Přívoz, Ostrava: MP? Ref.: Žebera, 1946; Lindner, 1956.

R

Radkova Lhota, distr. Přerov: UP. Ref.: Skutil, 1931b, 1936.
Radostice, distr. Brno-venkov: EUP. Ref.: Valoch, 1965b; Oliva, 1989c.
Radslavice, distr. Vyškov: EUP. Ref.: Skutil, 1936.
Rájec, distr. Blansko: EUP. Ref.: Oliva and Štrof, 1985.
Ráječko, distr. Blansko: MP, EUP. Ref.: Oliva and Štrof, 1985; Oliva, 1991a.
Rakvice, distr. Břeclav: UP.
Rašov, distr. Blansko: EUP. Ref.: Doležel, 1993.
Rostěnice, distr. Vyškov: EUP. Ref.: Svoboda, 1989c.
Rozdrojovice, distr. Brno-venkov: Szeletian. Ref.: Valoch, 1955b; Allsworth-Jones, 1986.
Rudice, distr. Blansko: Aurignacian? Ref.: Oliva, 1987a.
Rychtářov, distr. Vyškov: EUP. Ref.: Skutil, 1936.
Rychvald, distr. Karviná: LtP.
Rytířská Cave, Lažánky, distr. Blansko: Szeletian, Magdalenian. Ref.: Skutil, 1946a, 1963b; Valoch, 1965e; Allsworth-Jones, 1986.
Říčky, Domašov, distr. Brno-venkov: UP.
Řimice, distr. Olomouc: UP.

S

Sady, U. Hradiště: LtP. Ref.: Valoch, 1974c, 1979b.
Samotíšky, dist. Olomouc: UP.
Sebranice, distr. Blansko: EUP. Ref.: Oliva and Štrof, 1985.
Sedlec, distr. Břeclav: UP. Ref.: Klíma, 1986.
Sedlešovice, Znojmo: LwP. Ref.: Smolíková and Zeman, 1979; Valoch, 1981c.
Seloutky, Určice, distr. Prostějov: Aurignacian.
Senorady, distr. Třebíč: UP.
Silůvky, distr. Brno-venkov: EUP. Ref.: Oliva, 1989c.
Sivice, distr. Brno-venkov: EUP. Ref.: Oliva, 1989c.

Skalice, distr. Blansko: EUP. Ref.: Oliva and Štrof, 1985.
Sklep Cave, Vratíkov, distr. Blansko: MP, Magdalenian. Ref.: Knies, 1903; Bayer, 1925; Valoch, 1977a.
Skřečoň, distr. Karviná: LwP? Ref.: Svoboda et al., 1991.
Slatinice, distr. Olomouc: Aurignacian. Ref.: Janásek and Skutil, 1956; Přichystal, 1975; Oliva, 1987a.
Slatinky, distr. Prostějov: Aurignacian.
Slavkov, distr. U. Hradiště: UP.
Sloup, distr. Blansko: See Kůlna Cave, Poustevna Cave.
Smrtní Cave, Vilémovice, distr. Blansko: Magdalenian? Ref.: Skutil, 1961.
Sněhotice, distr. Prostějov: EUP. Ref.: Valoch, 1983.
Spytihněv, distr. Zlín: Gravettian? (strong Neolithic admixture). Ref.: Hrubý, 1951.
Srnčí Cave, Vilémovice, distr. Blansko: Magdalenian. Ref.: Skutil, 1961.
Staré Město, U. Hradiště: LtP. Ref.: Hrubý, 1951; Jelínek, 1956.
Strahovice, distr. Opava: UP.
Stránská skála, Brno-město: LwP, Bohunician, Aurignacian, Epigravettian. Ref.: Woldřich, 1916; Schirmeisen, 1926; Musil, 1965a, 1982; Musil and Valoch, 1968; Valoch, 1954, 1972, 1987b; Svoboda, 1984c, 1985, 1987d,f, 1991e, 1993a,c; Svoboda and Škrdla, 1995; Czudek et al. 1991; Škrdla and Plch, 1993b; Škrdla, 1996.
Strážná u Hostišové, distr. Zlín: Aurignacian.
Střelice, distr. Brno-venkov: UP. Ref.: Klíma, 1962b.
Stříbrnice, distr. U. Hradiště: Aurignacian. Ref.: Klíma, 1972.
Suchohrdly u Znojma, distr. Znojmo: Szeletian.
Svitávka, distr. Blansko: EUP, burial. Ref.: Klíma, 1963c; Smolíková and Ložek, 1963; Vlček, 1968a.
Syrovice, distr. Brno-venkov: EUP.

Š

Šatov, distr. Znojmo: UP. Ref.: Podborský and Vildomec, 1972.
Šipka Cave, Štramberk, distr. N. Jičín: Mousterian, Magdalenian. Ref.: Maška, 1882, 1884, 1885, 1886; Bayer, 1925; Absolon, 1932; Kukla, 1954; Valoch, 1957, 1965c; Vlček, 1969; Musil, 1965b.
Šlapanice, distr. Brno-venkov: UP.
Šošůvské Caves, Šošůvka, distr. Blansko: Magdalenian? Ref.: Valoch, 1960c.
Štěpánovice, distr. Brno-venkov: UP.
Šternberk, distr. Olomouc: EUP.
Štramberk, distr. N. Jičín: See Čertova díra Cave, Šipka Cave.
Šumice, distr. Znojmo: Szeletian. Ref.: Podborský and Vildomec, 1972.
Švédské šance, Brno-město: LwP?
Švédův stůl Cave, Ochoz, distr. Brno-venkov: Mousterian, EUP?, Magdalenian. Ref.: Kříž, 1903, 1909; Rzehak, 1906, 1909; Skutil, 1927a; Schirmeisen, 1929; Klíma, 1962a; Vlček, 1969.

T

Těšnovice, distr. Kroměříž: UP.
Tišnov, distr. Brno-venkov: EUP, Tišnovian. Ref.: Skutil, 1937a; Klíma, 1963d; Kos, 1971.
Trboušany, distr. Brno-venkov: MP?, Szeletian. Ref.: Skutil, 1962d, 1963a; Valoch, 1974a; Oliva, 1989c.
Troubky, distr. Kroměříž: Aurignacian. Ref.: Valoch, 1986.
Troubsko, distr. Brno-venkov: EUP. Ref.: Valoch, 1969c.
Třebářov, distr. Svitavy: EUP? Ref.: Skutil, 1946b; Mackerle, 1948.
Třebčín, distr. Olomouc: Szeletian.
Třebíč, distr. Třebíč: Tišnovian. Ref.: Klíma, 1970b.
Třebom, distr. Opava: Szeletian. Ref.: Svoboda et al., 1994: Figure 50.
Tučapy, distr. U. Hradiště: UP. Ref.: Hrubý, 1951.
Turold Cave, Mikulov, distr. Břeclav: Szeletian?
Tvarožná, distr. Brno-venkov: Aurignacian. Ref.: Valoch, 1976b; Oliva, 1987a; Blades, 1993.

U

Uherské Hradiště distr. Uherské Hradiště: UP. See also Jarošov, Sady, Staré Město.
Újezd u Brna, distr. Brno-venkov: UP. Ref.: Musil and Valoch, 1956.
Újezd u Černé Hory, distr. Blansko: EUP. Ref.: Oliva and Doležel, 1985.
Určice, distr. Prostějov: Acheulean, Aurignacian, Epigravettian? Ref.: Skutil, 1925, 1931a, 1933; Valoch, 1980a; Oliva, 1987a.

V

Vávrovice-Palhanec, Opava: EUP. Ref.: Jisl, 1971.
Vavřinec: See Jeskyně (Cave) Number 184, Kateřinská Cave, Koňská Cave, Pod hradem Cave, Pod Koňským spádem.
Vážany-Vítovice, distr. Vyškov: EUP.
Vedrovice, distr. Znojmo: MP?, Szeletian, Aurignacian. Ref.: Valoch, 1965d, 1976d, 1984b, 1985a, 1993b; Allsworth-Jones, 1986.
Velatice, distr. Brno-venkov: UP.
Velké Pavlovice, distr. Břeclav: EUP, Epigravettian. Ref.: Svoboda, 1987b; Svoboda et al., 1994:156.
Velký Týnec, distr. Olomouc: UP. Ref.: Skutil, 1959.
Verunčina Cave, Vilémovice, distr. Blansko: Magdalenian. Ref.: Skuti, 1928b, 1961; Svoboda et al., 1994: Figure 84.
Veverská Bitýška, distr. Brno-venkov: EUP. Ref.: Oliva, 1989c.
Věžky, distr. Kroměříž: Aurignacian. Ref.: Skutil, 1937a; Valoch, 1979b.

Vícemilice, distr. Vyškov: LtP. Ref.: Mazálek, 1960; Valoch, 1966c.
Vilémovice: See Smrtní Cave, Srnčí Cave, Verunčina Cave.
Vincencov, Otaslavice, distr. Prostějov: Szeletian. Ref.: Kopecký, 1937; Svoboda and Přichystal, 1987.
Vinckova Cave, Habrůvka, distr. Blansko: UP.
Vojkovice, distr. Brno-venkov: Aurignacian. Ref.: Valoch, 1977b.
Vratíkov: See Sklep Cave.
Výpustek Cave, Březina, distr. Brno-venkov: MP?, Magdalenian. Ref.: Wankel, 1871b; Szombathy, 1882a,b; Bayer, 1925; Skutil, 1927c; Valoch, 1965b.
Vyškov, distr. Vyškov: MP?, UP. Ref.: Musil and Valoch, 1956; Svoboda, 1994c. See also Dědice.

Z

Záblatí, distr. Karviná: Epigravettian. Ref.: Svoboda and Wodecki, 1981.
Zahnašovice, distr. Kroměříž: EUP. Ref.: Skutil, 1931b.
Závišice, distr. N. Jičín: LtP. Ref: Grepl, 1991.
Zdislavice, distr. Kroměříž: Aurignacian. Ref.: Valoch, 1979b, 1986.
Zdounky, distr. Kroměříž: Aurignacian. Ref.: Valoch, 1979b, 1986.
Zelená Hora, distr. Vyškov: Epigravettian. Ref.: Klíma, 1983c.
Zkamenělý zámek Rock, Javoříčko, distr. Olomouc: Magdalenian? Ref.: Svoboda et al., 1994:174.
Zlín-Louky, distr. Zlín: Epigavettian. Ref.: Klíma, 1956a; Allsworth-Jones, 1986.
Zlín-Tečovice, distr. Zlín: Epigravettian?
Znojmo, distr. Znojmo: Gravettian? Ref.: Podborský and Vildomec, 1972. See also Sedlešovice.

Ž

Žabovřesky, distr. Brno-město (Brno III): Gravettian burial. Ref.: Absolon, 1929; Absolon et al., 1933.
Ždánice, distr. Hodonín: UP.
Želešice, distr. Brno-venkov: EUP (Szeletian/Bohunician). Ref.: Valoch, 1956; Oliva, 1989c.
Žernovník, distr. Blansko: UP. Ref.: Oliva and Štrof, 1985.
Židlochovice, distr. Brno-venkov: EUP, Gravettian? stone disc. Ref.: Oliva, 1989c.
Žilina, distr. N. Jičín: UP. Ref.: Jisl, 1971; Grepl, 1991.
Žitného Cave, Březina, distr. Brno-venkov: Magdalenian. Ref.: Szombathy, 1884a,b; Skutil, 1927b; Dvořák et al., 1957.
Žlutava, distr. Zlín: Aurignacian. Ref.: Klíma, 1952b; Oliva, 1987a; Allsworth-Jones, 1986.

References

Absolon, K.
  1918   Předmost. Eine Mammutjäger-Station in Mähren. In H. Klaatsch-Heilborn (ed.), *Der Werdegang der Menschheit und die Entstehung der Kultur* (pp. 357–373). Berlin: Bong.
Absolon, K.
  1926   Bericht über die paleolithische Abteilung am mährischen Landes-Museum und die paleolithische Forschung in Mähren. *Časopis Moravského zemského muzea*, 24 (reprint) 1–11.
Absolon, K.
  1929   New finds of fossil human skeletons in Moravia. *Anthropologie*, 7, 79–89.
Absolon, K.
  1932   O pravé podstatě paleolithických industrií ze Šipky a Čertovy díry na Moravě. *Anthropologie*, 10 (reprint) 1–19.
Absolon, K.
  1935a   L'Aurignacien trés ancien (quartzitique) dans l'Europe centrale, avec ses industries osseuses. *Congrès préhistorique de France, XIe session* (reprint) 1–6.
Absolon, K.
  1935b   Ein Anhängsel aus einem fossilen Menschenzahn. *Zeitschrift für Rassenkunde*, 1, 317.
Absolon, K.
  1935c   *Ottaslawitz, eine neue paläolithische Station in Mähren mit Quarzit Aurignacien. Versuch einer systematisch-typologischen Bestimmung der Artefakte.* Brünn: Polygrafia.
Absolon, K.
  1936   *Über Grossformen des quarzitischen Aurignaciens der paläolithischen Station Ondratitz in Mähren: Typologie der sogenannten "Gigantolithen."* Brünn: Polygrafia.
Absolon, K.
  1937   Les résultats des nouvelles recherches paléolithiques en Moravie. *XVIe Congrès international d'Anthropologie, Bruxelles* (reprint) 1–10.
Absolon, K.
  1938a   *Die Erforschung der diluvialen Mammutjäger-Station von Unter-Wisternitz in Mähren: Arbeitsbericht über das zweite Jahr 1925.* Brünn: Polygrafia.

Absolon, K.
1938b *Výzkum diluviální stanice lovců mamutů v Dolních Věstonicích na Pavlovských kopcích na Moravě: Pracovní zpráva ze první rok 1924*. Brno: Polygrafia.

Absolon, K.
1943 Výzkum jeskyně Pekárny na Moravě. *Pestrý týden 18/31*, 4–9; *18/32*, 4–9.

Absolon, K.
1945a *Die praehistorische Erforschung der Býčí skála-Höhle in Mähren vergleichend dargestellt: 3. kritischer Beitrag zur Kenntnis des Uraurignaciens*. Brno: Polygrafia.

Absolon, K.
1945b *Výzkum diluviální stanice lovců mamutů v Dolních Věstonicích na Pavlovských kopcích na Moravě: Pracovní zpráva za třetí rok 1926*. Brno: Polygrafia.

Absolon, K.
1957 Dokumente und Beweise der Fähigkeiten des fossilen Menschen zu zählen im mährischen Paleolithikum. *Artibus Asiae, 20*, 123–150.

Absolon, K., and Czižek, R.
1926–1932 Paleolitický výzkum jeskyně Pekárny na Moravě. *Časopis Moravského zemského muzea, 24*, 1–59; *25*, 112–201; *26–27*, 479–598.

Absolon, K., and Klíma, B.
1977 *Předmostí: Ein Mammutjägerplatz in Mähren*, Praha: Academia.

Absolon, K., Zapletal, K., Skutil, J., and Stehlík, A.
1933 *Bericht der čechoslovakischen Subkommission der "The International Commission for the Study of the Fossil Man" bei den Internationalen geologischen Kongressen*. Brünn: Polygrafia.

Adloff, P.
1911 Über das Alter des menschlichen Molaren von Taubach. *Deutscher Monatschrift der Zahnheilkunde, 29*, 804–817.

Adloff, P.
1920 Der Molar von Taubach. *Prähistorische Zeitschrift, 11/12*, 203–204.

Allsworth-Jones, P.
1986 *The Szeletian and the Transition from Middle to Upper Palaeolithic in Central Europe*. Oxford: Clarendon Press.

Allsworth-Jones, P.
1990 Les industries à pointes foliacées d Europe Centrale: Questions de définitions et relations avec les autres technocomplexes. In C. Farizy, ed., *Paléolithique moyen récent et Paléolithique supérieur ancien en Europe* (pp. 79–95). Nemours: Musée de Préhistoire d'Ile-de-France.

Angeli, W.
1953 Der Mammutjägerhalt von Langmannersdorf an der Perschling. *Mitteilungen der Prähistorischen Kommission, 6*, 1952–1953.

Bach, H.
1974 Menschliche Skelettreste aus Kniegrotte und Urdhöhle. In R. Feustel (ed.), *Die Kniegrotte* (pp. 202–206). Weimar: Böhlaus Nachfolger.

Bánesz, L.
1991 Die Entwicklung der Travertine in den Nordkarpaten im Lichte archäologischer Funde. *Quartär, 41/42*, 45–62.

Bárta, J.
1980 *Významné paleolitické lokality na strednom a západnom Slovensku*. Nitra: Institute of Archaeology.

Bárta, J.
　1987　Prínos nových poznatkov slovenskej archeológie ku stratigrafi pleistocénu a starého holocénu. *Anthropozoikum N.S.*, *18*, 202–228.

Bárta, J.
　1988　Trenčianské Bohuslavice. Un habitat gravettien en Slovaquie occidentale. *L'Anthropologie*, *92*, 173–182.

Bartucz, L., and Szabo, J.
　1940　Der Urmensch der Mussolini-Höhle. *Geologica hungarica*, *14*, 47–112.

Baumann, W., and Mania, D.
　1983　*Die paläolithischen Neufunde von Markkleeberg bei Leipzig*, Berlin: DVW.

Bayer, J.
　1925　Die ältere Steinzeit in den Sudetenländern. *Sudeta*, *1*, 21–120.

Bayer, J.
　1931　*Die falsche Venus von Wisternitz und ihre Geschichte*. Brünn-Prag-Leipzig-Wien: M. Rohrer.

Bayer, J., and Stumpf, G.
　1929　Die eiszeitlichen Stationen auf dem Gilschwitzer Berg in Troppau. *Eiszeit und Urgeschichte*, *6*, 109–137.

de Beaune, S. A.
　1987　*Lampes et godets au Paléolithique*. Paris: CNRS.

Behm-Blancke, H.
　1960　Altsteinzeitliche Rastplätze im Travertingebiet Taubach, Weimar, Ehringsdorf. *Alt-Thüringen*, *4*, 1–246.

Benecke, N.
　1995　Mensch-Tier-Beziehungen im Jung- und Spätpalaolithikum. In H. Ullrich (ed.), *Man and environment in the Paleolithic, ERAUL 62* (pp. 77–87). Liege: Université de Liege.

Berckhemmer, F.
　1933　Ein Mensch-Schädel aus den diluvialen Schottern von Steinheim a.d. Murr. *Anthropologischer Anzeiger*, *10*, 318–321.

Berckhemmer, F.
　1936　Der Urmenschschädel aus den zwischeneiszeitlichen Fluss-Schottern von Steinheim an der Murr. *Forschungen und Fortschrite*, *12*, 349–350.

Berke, H.
　1989　Archaeology and site catchment in the Magdalenian: Solutré, Petersfels, Pekárna Cave, Kniegrotte. *Early Man News*, *14*, 15–31.

Binford, L. R.
　1981　*Bones: Ancient men and modern myths*. New York: Academic Press.

Binford, L. R.
　1989　Isolating the transition to cultural adaptations: An organisational approach. In L. R. Binford, *Debating archaeology* (pp. 464–481). San Diego: Academic Press.

Binford, L. R.
　1993　Bones for stones: Consideration of analogies for features found on Central Russian Plain. In O. Soffer and N. D. Praslov (eds.), *From Kostenki to Clovis* (pp. 101–124). New York-London: Plenum Press.

Blades, B.
　1993　Lithic utilization and the organization of mobility in Early Upper Paleolithic Moravia. Paper presented at the 58th annual meeting, Society for American Archaeology, St. Louis, 1–9.

Bluszcz, A., Kozlowski, J. K., and Foltyn, E.
  1994 New sequence of EUP leaf point industries in southern Poland. *Préhistoire européene*, 6, 197–222.
Bosinski, G.
  1967 Die mittelpaläolithischen Funde im westlichen Mitteleuropa. Köln-Graz: Bohlau.
Bosinski, G.
  1981 *Gönnersdorf: Eiszeitjäger am Mittelrhein*. Koblenz: Rhenania.
Bosinski, G.
  1982a *Die Kunst der Eiszeit in Deutschland und in der Schweiz*. Bonn: R. Habelt.
Bosinski, G.
  1982b The transition Lower/Middle Paleolithic in northwestern Germany. In A. Ronen (ed.), *The transition from Lower to Middle Paleolithic and the origin of modern man* (pp. 165–175). Oxford, England: British Archaeological Reports.
Brandtner, F.
  1990 Die Paläolithstation "Grubgraben" bei Kammern: Vorläufige Ergebnisse neuerer Grabungen. *Fundberichte aus Österreich*, 28, 17–26.
Breitinger, E.
  1955 Das Schädelfragment von Swanscombe und das "Praesapiensproblem." *Mitteilungen der Anthropologischen Gesellschaft Wien*, 84/85, 1–45.
Brenner, F.
  1949 Několik nálezů v posledním zbytku býv. Lundwallovy pískovny u Opavy. *Přírodovědný sborník Ostravského kraje*, 10/1, 76–77.
Breuil, H.
  1925 Notes de voyage paléolithique en Europe Centrale. *L'Anthropologie*, 34, 515–552.
Burdukiewicz, J. M.
  1993 Osadnictwo dolnopaleolityczne w Trzebnicy. Acta Universitatis Wratislaviensis. *Studia archaeologiczne*, 24, 5–31.
Chase, P. G., and Dibble, H.
  1987 Middle Paleolithic symbolism: A review of current evidence and interpretation. *Journal of Anthropological Archaeology*, 6, 263–296.
Chase, P. G., and Dibble, H.
  1990 On the emergence of modern humans. *Current Anthropology*, 31, 58–59.
Chmielewski, W., Schild, R., and Wieckowska, H.
  1975 *Prahistoria ziem polskich, tom I, Paleolit i mezolit*. Wroclaw-Warszawa-Kraków-Gdansk: PWN.
Clark Le Gros, W. E., and Morant, G. M.
  1938 *Report on the Swanscombe skull*. London: Royal Anthropological Institute of Great Britain and Ireland.
Conkey, M. W.
  1987 New approaches in the search for meaning? A review of research in "Paleolithic art." *Journal of Field Archaeology*, 14, 413–430.
Czudek, T.
  1994 Reliéf Moravy a Slezska. In J. Svoboda et al., *Paleolit Moravy a Slezska* (pp. 11–16). Brno: Institute of Archaeology.
Czudek, T., Smolíková, L., and Svoboda, J.
  1991 Profil IIIa na Stránské skále v Brně. *Anthropozoikum*, N.S., 20, 203–223.
Červinka, I. L.
  1902 *Morava za pravěku*. Brno: Vlastivěda moravská.

Červinka, I. L.
 1927 *Pravěk zemí čekých.* Brno: J. Slovák.
Dančo, J.
 1966 O stratenej lebke z Drevenika. *Vlastivedný bulletin, príloha Podtatranských novín, 18/19,* 13.5.
Delporte, H.
 1959 Notes de voyage leptolithique en Europe Centrale. *Rivista di scienze preistoriche, 14,* 18–57.
Demek, J., and Kukla, J., eds.
 1969 *Periglazialzone, Löss und Paläolithikum der Tschechoslowakei.* Brno: Institute of Geography.
Diviš, J., and Grepl, E.
 1984 Nálezy křišťálové a pazourkové industrie z Kněžic (okr. Třebíč). *Přehled výzkumů, 1982,* 14.
Dohnal, Z.
 1961 Die Steinkerne des Zürgelbaumes (Celtis) im tschechoslowakischen Quartär, *Anthropozoikum, 9,* 203–239.
Doležel, J.
 1993 Paleolitický úštěp z Rašova (okr. Blansko). *Přehled výzkumů, 1993,* 43.
Dvořák, J., Pelíšek, J., Musil, K., and Valoch, K.
 1957 Komplexní výzkum Žitného jeskyně v Moravském krasu. *Práce brněnské základny ČSAV, 29/12,* 541–600.
Dvořák, J., and Valoch, K.
 1962 Příspěvek k poznání kvartéru v okolí Hranic na Moravě. *Anthropozoikum, 11,* 153–162.
Ehgartner, W.
 1959 Menschliche Knochenreste aus Willendorf. *Mitteilungen der Prähistorischen Kommission Wien, 8/9,* 79–80.
Emmerling, E., Geer, H., and Klíma, B.
 1993 Ein Mondkalenderstab aus Dolní Věstonice. *Quartär, 43/44,* 151–162.
Feblot-Augustins, J.
 1993 Mobility strategies in the late Middle Paleolithic of central Europe and western Europe. *Journal of Anthropological Archaeology, 12,* 211–265.
Fejfar, O.
 1969 Human remains from the Early Pleistocene in Czechoslovakia. *Current Anthropology, 10,* 170–173.
Fejfar, O.
 1976 Recent research at Přezletice. *Current Anthropology, 17,* 343–344.
Felgenhauer, F.
 1951 Aggsbach, ein Fundplatz des späten Paläolithikums in Niederösterreich. *Mitteilungen der Prähistorischen Kommission Wien, 5,* 160–266.
Felgenhauer, F.
 1959 Willendorf in der Wachau. *Mitteilungen der Prähistorischen Kommission Wien, 8/9,* 1–217.
Feustel, R. (ed.)
 1971 Die Urdhöhle bei Döbritz. *Alt-Thüringen,* 11.
Feustel, R.
 1974 *Die Kniegrotte.* Weimar: Bohlaus Nachfolger.

Feustel, R.
  1983 Zur zeitlichen und kulturellen Stellung des Paläolithikums von Weimar-Ehringsdorf. *Alt-Thüringen*, 19, 16–42.
Fink, J.
  1956 Zur Korrelation der Terrassen und Lösse in Österreich. *Eiszeitalter und Gegenwart*, 7, 49–77.
Fink, J., and Kukla, G. J.
  1977 Pleistocene climates in Central Europe: At least 17 interglacials after the Olduvai event. *Quarternary Research*, 7, 363–371.
Folprecht, J., and Skutil, J.
  1931 Palaeolithická industrie z Petřkovic z výkopů 1929. *Věstník Matice opavské*, 36, 15–18.
Frenzel, B.
  1964 Zur Pollenanalyse von Lössen (Untersuchungen der Lössprofile von Oberfellabrunn und Stillfried/Niederösterreich). *Eiszeitalter und Gegenwart*, 15, 5–39.
Frenzel, B.
  1968 *Grundzüge der Pleistozänen Vegetationsgeschichte Nord-Eurasiens*. Wiesbaden: Erdwissenschaftliche Forschungen.
Fridrich, J.
  1973 Počátky mladopaleolitického osídlení Čech. *Archeologické rozhledy*, 25, 392–442.
Fridrich, J.
  1976a The first industries of eastern and south-eastern Central Europe. In *UISPP, IXe Congrès, Colloque VIII* (pp. 8–23). Nice: Louis-Jean.
Fridrich, J.
  1976b Příspěvek k problematice počátků uměleckého a estetického cítění u paleantropů. *Památky archeologické*, 67, 5–27.
Fridrich, J.
  1982 *Středopaleolitické osídlení Čech*. Praha: Institute of Archaeology.
Fridrich, J.
  1989 *Přezletice: A Lower Palaeolithic site in Central Bohemia (Excavations 1969–1985)*. Praha: Národní muzeum.
Fürst, J.
  1922 Nálezy diluviálních kostí lidských u Litovle. *Příroda*, 15, 266.
Gábori-Csánk, V.
  1968 *La station du paléolithique moyen d Érd, Hongrie*, Budapest: Akadémiai Kiadó.
Gamble, C.
  1986 *The Palaeolithic settlement of Europe*. Cambridge, England: Cambridge University Press.
Gargett, R. H.
  1994 *Taphonomy and spatial analysis of a cave bear (Ursus spelaeus) fauna from Pod hradem Cave, Czech Republic: Implications for the archaeology of modern human origins*. Ph.D. Dissertation, University of California, Berkeley.
Ginter, B.
  1974 Wydobywanie, przetwórstwo i dystrybucja surowców i wyrobów krzemiennych w schylkowym paleolicie pólnocznej czesci Europy srodkowej. *Przeglad Archeologiczny*, 22, 5–122.
Ginter, B., Kozlowski, J. K., and Sobczyk, K.
  1987 The Late Glacial environment and Paleolithic cultures in the Upper Vistula Basin. In

J. M. Burdukiewicz and M. Kobusiewicz (eds.), *Late glacial in Central Europe* (pp. 255–266). Wroclaw-Warszawa-Kraków-Gdansk-Lódz: Wydawnictwo PAN.

Grepl, E.
1991 Paleolitické osídlení okresu Nový Jičín. *Informační zpravodaj členů SM pobočky ČSSA, březen 1991,* 1–13.

Grimm, H., and Ullrich, H.
1965 Ein jungpaläolitischer Schädel und Skelettreste aus Döbritz, Kr. Pöneck. *Alt-Thüringen,* 7, 50–89.

Haesaerts, P.
1990 Nouvelles recherches au gisement de Willendorf (Basse Autriche). *Bulletin de l'Institut Royal des Sciences naturelles de Belgique,* 60, 203–218.

Hahn, J.
1977 *Aurignacien—Das ältere Jungpaläolithikum in Mittel- und Osteuropa.* Koln-Graz: Bohlaus.

Hahn, J.
1986 *Kraft und Agression: Die Botschaft der Eiszeitkunst im Aurignaciean Süddeutschlands.* Tübingen: Archaeologia Venatoria.

Hahn, J.
1987 Aurignacian and Gravettian settlement patterns in Central Europe. In O. Soffer (ed.), *The Pleistocene Old World: Regional perspectives* (pp. 251–261). New York–London: Plenum Press.

Hahn, J. (ed.)
1988 *Die Geissenklösterle-Höhle im Achtal bei Blaubeuren I.* Stuttgart: Fundberichte Baden-Würtemberg.

Hausmann, R., and Brunnacker, K.
1986 U-series dating of Middle European travertines. In M. Otte (ed.), *L'homme de Néandertal, Edition anticipée* (pp. 20–27). Liège: Université de Liège.

Havlíček, P.
1991 Dolní Věstonice II—Nová významná kvartérně—geologická lokalita. *Acta Universitalis Carolinae-geologica,* Kettner volume, 283–288.

Havlíček, P., and Kovanda, J.
1985 Nové výzkumy kvartéru v okolí Pavlovských vrchů. *Anthropozoikum 16,* 21–59.

Havlíček, P., and Macoun, J.
1994 Paleogeografický a stratigrafický vývoj Moravy a Slezska v pleistocénu. In J. Svoboda (ed.), *Paleolit Moravy a Slezska* (pp. 26–39). Brno: Institute of Archaeology.

Hillebrand, J.
1911 Die diluvialen Knochenreste eines Kindes aus der Ballahöhle bei Répáshuta in Ungarn. *Földtani Közleketi,* 41, 518–531.

Hillebrand, J.
1914 Az 1913 évi barlangkutatasaim ereményei. *Barlangkutatás,* 2, 115–124.

Horáček, I., and Ložek, V.
1990 Biostratigrafický výzkum výplně rozsedliny na Martince. *Československý kras,* 41, 83–99.

Hrubý, V.
1951 Paleolitické nálezy z Uh.–Hradištska. *Časopis Moravského muzea,* 36, 65–101.

Hülle, W.
1939 Vorläufige Mitteilung über die altsteinzeitliche Fundstelle Ilsenhöhle unter Brug Ranis, Kr. Ziegerück. In J. Andrée (ed.), *Der eiszeitliche Mensch in Deutschland und seine Kulturen* (pp. 105–114). Stuttgart.

J. J.
    1937   Hynie Drevenik pri Spišskom hrade. *Szepessi Lapok*, 1937.
Janásek, J., and Skutil, J.
    1956   Paleolitické stanice na Malém Kosíři. *Archeologické rozhledy*, 8, 86–89.
Jelínek, J.
    1953   Nálezy zubů fosilního člověka v Dolních Věstonicích. *Časopis Moravského muzea*, 38, 180–190.
Jelínek, J.
    1954   Nález fosilního člověka Dolní Věstonice III. *Anthropozoikum*, 3, 37–92.
Jelínek, J.
    1956   Homo sapiens fossilis ze Starého Města u Uh. Hradiště. *Časopis Moravského muzea*, 41, 139–196.
Jelínek, J.
    1962   Der Unterkiefer von Ochoz. *Anthropos*, 13, 261–284.
Jelínek, J.
    1965   Srovnávací studium šipecké čelisti. *Anthropos*, 17, 135–179.
Jelínek, J.
    1966   Jaw of an intermediate type Neanderthal man from Czechoslovakia. *Nature 5063*, 701–702.
Jelínek, J.
    1967   Der Fund eines Neandertaler Kiefers aus der Kůlna-Höhle in Mähren. *Anthropologie*, 5, 3–19.
Jelínek, J.
    1969   Neanderthal man and Homo sapiens in Central and Eastern Europe. *Current Anthropology*, 10, 475–503.
Jelínek, J.
    1981   Neanderthal parietal bone from Kůlna Cave, Czechoslovakia. *Anthropologie N.S.*, 19, 195–196.
Jelínek, J.
    1987   Historie, identifikace a výzkum mladečských antropologických nálezů z počátku mladého paleolitu. In *25 let pavilonu Anthropos 1961–1986* (pp. 57–70). Brno: Moravské Muzeum.
Jélinek, J.
    1988   Anthropologische Funde aus der Kůlna-Höhle. *Anthropos*, 24, 261–283.
Jelínek, J., Pelíšek, J., and Valoch, K.
    1959   Der fossile Mensch Brno II, Anthropos 9. Brno: Moravské Muzeum.
Jisl, L.
    1971   Poznámky k poznání paleolitu ve Slezsku. *Časopis Slezského muzea*, B/20, 1–9.
Jochim, M.
    1983   Paleolithic cave art: Some ecological speculations. In G. Bailey (ed.), *Hunter-gatherer economy in prehistory: A European perspective* (pp. 212–219). Cambridge, England: Cambridge University Press.
Jochim, M.
    1987   Late Pleistocene refugia in Europe. In O. Soffer (ed.), *The Pleistocene Old World* (pp. 317–331). New York: Plenum Press.
Kaminská, L., Kovanda, J., Ložek, V., and Smolíková, L.
    1993   Die Travertinfundstelle Horka-Ondrej bei Poprad, Slowakei. *Quartär*, 43/44, 95–112.

REFERENCES

Kehoe, A.
1991   No possible, probable shadow of doubt. *Antiquity*, 246, 129–131.

Kleinschmidt, O.
1931   *Der Urmensch*. Leipzig.

Klíma, B.
1947   Nová paleolitická stanice u Hranic. *Časopis Vlastivědného spolku musejního Olomouc*, 56, 75–79.

Klíma, B.
1949   Výzkum jeskyně "Nové Drátenické" u Křtin. *Časopis Moravského muzea*, 34, 123–137.

Klíma, B.
1950a   Objev diluviálního hrobu v Dolních Věstonicích. *Časopis Moravského muzea*, 35, 216–232.

Klíma, B.
1950b   Sídelní objekt na tábořišti lovců mamutů v Dolních Věstonicích. *Časopis Moravského muzea*, 35, 261–273.

Klíma, B.
1951a   Křížova jeskyně v Moravském krasu. *Archeologické rozhledy*, 3, 109–130.

Klíma, B.
1951b   Nové nálezy na paleolitické stanici u Hranic. *Časopis Moravského muzea*, 36, 102–118.

Klíma, B.
1951c   Nové nálezy z jeskyně Nové Drátenické. *Československý kras*, 5, 107–108.

Klíma, B.
1952a   Druhý sídelní objekt a paleolitická keramická pec v Dolních Věstonicích. *Archeologické rozhledy*, 4, 193–197.

Klíma, B.
1952b   Zjišťovací výzkum výšinných stanic u Napajedel. *Archeologické rozhledy*, 4, 385–388.

Klíma, B.
1953a   Archeologický výzkum jeskyně Adlerovy. *Československý kras*, 6, 94–102.

Klíma, B.
1953b   Nejstarší použití ostravského uhlí. *Archeologické rozhledy*, 5, 441–443.

Klíma, B.
1954   Pavlov, nové paleolitické sídliště na jižní Moravě. *Archeologické rozhledy*, 6, 137–142.

Klíma, B.
1955a   Přínos nové paleolitické stanice v Pavlově k problematice nejstarších zemědělských nástrojů. *Památky archeologické*, 46, 7–29.

Klíma, B.
1955b   Výsledky archeologického výzkumu na tábořišti lovců mamutů v Ostravě-Petřkovicích v roce 1952 a 1953. *Časopis Slezského muzea*, 4, 1–35.

Klíma, B.
1956a   Nová paleolitická stanice v Gottwaldově-Loukách. *Anthropozoikum*, 5, 425–438.

Klíma, B.
1956b   Statistická metoda—Pomůcka při hodnocení paleolitických kamenných industrií: Návrh české terminologie mladopaleolitických kamenných nástrojů. *Památky archaeologické*, 47, 193–209.

Klíma, B.
1957a   Übersicht über die jüngsten paläolithischen Forschungen in Mähren. *Quartär*, 9, 85–130.

Klíma, B.
1957b Výzkum paleolitického sídliště u Pavlova v roce 1954. *Archeologické rozhledy*, 9, 145–151.

Klíma, B.
1958a Příspěvek k stratigrafii nejmladšího sprašového pokryvu. *Anthropozoikum*, 7, 111–143.

Klíma, B.
1958b Zjišťovací výzkum v jeskyních Moravského krasu. *Přehled výzkumů*, 1958, 9–10.

Klíma, B.
1959a *Brno-Líšeň, nálezová zpráva 2731/59*. Brno: Institute of Archaeology.

Klíma, B.
1959b Křepice, nová stanice aurignacienu na Moravě. *Anthropozoikum*, 8, 139–157.

Klíma, B.
1959c Objev paleolitického pohřbu v Pavlově. *Archeologické rozhledy*, 11, 305–316.

Klíma, B.
1959d Výzkum paleolitického sídliště u Pavlova v roce 1956. *Archeologické rozhledy*, 11, 3–15.

Klíma, B.
1959e Zur Problematik des Aurignacien und Gravettien in Mittel-Europa. *Archaeologia Austriaca*, 26, 35–51.

Klíma, B.
1960a Paleolitický nález v Mor. Krumlově. *Přehled výzkumů*, 1959, 14.

Klíma, B.
1960b Zahajovací výzkum v jeskyni Kůlničce (Mokrá u Brna). *Přehled výzkumů*, 1959, 13.

Klíma, B.
1960c Zjišťovací výzkum v jeskyni "Liščí díra" u Hoštěnic. *Přehled výzkumů*, 1959, 11–12.

Klíma, B.
1961a Archeologický výzkum jeskyně Hadí (Mokrá u Brna). *Anthropozoikum*, 9, 277–289.

Klíma, B.
1961b Paleolitická stanice Pavlov II. *Archeologické rozhledy*, 13, 461–464.

Klíma, B.
1961c Současný stav problematiky aurignacienu a gravettienu. *Archeologické rozhledy*, 13, 84–121.

Klíma, B.
1962a *Die archäologische Erforschung der Höhle "Švédův stůl" in Mähren, Athropos 13*. Brno: Moravské Muzeum.

Klíma, B.
1962b Nová paleolitická stanoviště u Brna. *Sborník Československé společnosti archeologické*, 2, 193–199.

Klíma, B.
1962c Příspěvek k poznání paleolitických industrií z Předmostí u Přerova. *Anthropozoikum*, 11, 29–47.

Klíma, B.
1962d Výzkum paleolitického sídliště Pavlov I. *Přehled výzkumů*, 1961, 16–19.

Klíma, B.
1963a Altpaläolitischer Fund auf Červený kopec (Roter Berg) bei Brno. *Přehled výzkumů*, 1962, 1–2.

Klíma, B.
1963b *Dolní Věstonice, výsledky výzkumu tábořiště lovců mamutů v letech 1947–1952*. Praha: Nakladatelstvím Československé Akademie Věd.

REFERENCES

Klíma, B.
  1963c Die Entdeckung eines pleistozänen Menschen bei Svitávka. *Přehled výzkumů*, 1962, 2–3.
Klíma, B.
  1963d Epipaleolitická kamenná industrie z Tišnova. *Anthropozoikum*, 1, 127–164.
Klíma, B.
  1963e Paleolitický nález v Hajanech. *Přehled výzkumů*, 1962, 8.
Klíma, B.
  1963f Výzkum paleolitického sídliště Pavlov I. *Přehled výzkumů*, 1962, 4–6.
Klíma, B.
  1964a Paleolitická reliéfní plastika lvice ze sídliště u Pavlova. *Památky archeologické*, 55, 82–90.
Klíma, B.
  1964b Výzkum paleolitického sídlisětě Pavlov I. *Přehled výzkumů*, 1963, 5–8.
Klíma, B.
  1965a Eine neue paläolithische Ritzzeichung aus der Pekárna-Höhle in Mähren. *Quartär*, 15/16, 167–172.
Klíma, B.
  1965b Výzkum na paleolitické stanici v Boršicích v r. 1964. *Archeologické rozhledy*, 17, 469–482.
Klíma, B.
  1969a *Die grosse Anhäufung von Mammutknochen in Dolní Věstonice, Přírodovědné práce ústavů ČSAV v Brně 3/6*. Praha: Academia.
Klíma, B.
  1969b Nové nálezy na paleolitické stanici u Křepic. *Časopis Moravského muzea*, 53/54, 31–50.
Klíma, B.
  1969c Das Paläolithikum der Tschechoslowakei. In. J. Demek and J. Kukla (eds.), *Periglazialzone, Löss und Paläolithikum der Tschechoslowakei* (pp. 109–117).
Klíma, B.
  1969d Petřkovice II: Nová paleolitická stanice v Ostravě. *Archeologické rozhledy*, 21, 583–595.
Klíma, B.
  1970a Eine jungpaläolithische Behausung im Mährischen Karst. *Anthropologie*, 8, 31–34.
Klíma, B.
  1970b Pozdně paleolitická kamenná industrie z Třebíče. *Archeologické rozhledy*, 22, 85–89.
Klíma, B.
  1971a Paleolitické a mesolitické nálezy od Olšan. *Sborník prací Filozofické fakulty Brněnské univerzity*, E 16, 51–58.
Klíma, B.
  1971b Die spätpaläolithische Steinidustrie aus Jabloňany in Mähren (ČSSR). *Proceedings of the Prehistoric Society*, 37, 118–130.
Klíma, B.
  1972 Nová paleolitická stanice u Stříbrnic. *Časopis Moravského muzea*, 57, 17–25.
Klíma, B.
  1973a Archeologický výzkum paleolitické stanice v Předmostí u Přerova v r. 1971. *Památky archeologické*, 64, 1–23.
Klíma, B.
  1973b Závěr výzkumu paleolitické stanice Pavlov I (okr. Břeclav). *Přehled výzkumů*, 1972, 15.

Klíma, B.
1974a Archeologický výzkum plošiny před jeskyní Pekárnou. Praha: Academia.

Klíma, B.
1974b Mladopaleolitická keramika z Předmostí. Památky archeologické, 65, 229–240.

Klíma, B.
1974c Paleolitické nálezy z Otic u Opavy. Archeologický sborník, 1, 9–21.

Klíma, B.
1976 Die paläolithische Station Pavlov II, Přírodovědné práce ústavů ČSAV v Brně 10/4. Praha: Academia.

Klíma, B.
1977a Křišťálová paleolitická industrie z Nové Dědiny. Anthropozoikum, 11, 113–133.

Klíma, B.
1977b Malaja poluzemljanka na paleolitičeskoj stojanke Pavlov v Čechoslovakiji. In Problemy paleolita Vostočnoj i Centralnoj Jevropy (pp. 144–148). Leningrad: Nauka.

Klíma, B.
1978 Paleolitická stanice u Přestavlk, okr. Přerov. Archeologické rozhledy, 30, 5–13.

Klíma, B.
1979a Nová stanice aurignacienu v Moravské bráně. Archeologické rozhledy, 31, 361–369.

Klíma, B.
1979b Les représantations animales du Paléolithique supérieur de Dolní Věstonice. In La contribution de la zoologie et de l'ethnologie á l'interprétation de l'art des peuples chasseurs préhistoriques (pp. 323–332). Fribourg: Université Fribourg.

Klíma, B.
1980 Nová paleolitická stanice s křemencovou industrií od Pavlovic u Přerova. Anthropozoikum, 13, 149–170.

Klíma, B.
1981a Další doklady paleolitického osídlení u Pavlova (okr. Břeclav). Přehled výzkumů, 1979, 8.

Klíma, B.
1981b Střední část paleolitické stanice u Dolních Věstonic. Památky archeologické, 72, 5–92.

Klíma, B.
1981c Výzkum paleolitické stanice u Dolních Věstonic (o. Břeclav). Přehled výzkumů, 1979, 7–8.

Klíma, B.
1983a Dolní Věstonice, tábořiště lovců mamutů. Praha: Academia.

Klíma, B.
1983b Dvě nové stanice aurignacienu u Holešova (okr. Kroměříž). Přehled výzkumů, 1981, 16.

Klíma, B.
1983c Mladopaleolitická kamenná industrie ze Zelené hory. Archeologické rozhledy, 35, 601–605.

Klíma, B.
1983d Une nouvelle statuette paléolithique á Dolní Věstonice. Boulletin de la Société préhistorique française, 80, 176–178.

Klíma, B.
1983e Zachraňovací výzkum v hliníku u Pavlova (okr. Břeclav). Přehled výzkumů, 1981, 14–15.

REFERENCES

Klíma, B.
1984a Grundrisse ganzer jungpaläolithischer Siedlungen aus Mähren. In *Jungpaläolithische Siedlungsstrukturen in Europa* (pp. 257–263). Tübingen: Archaeologica Venatoria.

Klíma, B.
1984b Sonderbare Rohstoffe der paläolithischen Steinindustrie aus Pavlov (ČSSR). In *IIIrd Seminar in Petroarchaeology: Reports* (pp. 201–213). Plovdiv: Bulgarian Academy of Sciences.

Klíma, B.
1984c Zachraňovací výzkum v Přerově-Předmostí (okr. Přerov). *Přehled výzkumů, 1982,* 9.

Klíma, B.
1985a Gravierte Tierbilder aus der Děravá-Höhle in Böhmen. In *Jagen und Sammeln: Festschrift für H.-G. Bandi zum 65. Geburstag* (pp. 199–209). Bern: Stampfli & Cie.

Klíma, b.
1985b Pokračování zachraňovací akce v Přerově-Předmostí (okr. Přerov). *Přehled výzkumů, 1983,* 8.

Klíma, B.
1986 *Nejstarší osídlení Břeclavska.* Mikulov: Regionální Muzeum.

Klíma, B.
1987a Další stopy paleolitického osídlení pod Pavlovskými kopci (okr. Břeclav). *Přehled výzkumů, 1984,* 9.

Klíma, B.
1987b Mladopaleolitický trojhrob z Dolních Věstonic. *Archeologické rozhledy, 39,* 241–254.

Klíma, B.
1987c Paleolitická parohová industrie z Pavlova. *Památky archeologické, 78,* 289–370.

Klíma, B.
1987d Zachraňovací výzkum nad cihelnou u Dolních Věstonic. *Přehled výzkumů, 1985,* 16–18.

Klíma, B.
1988 Nejstarší moravská mapa. In V. Frolec (ed.), *Rodná země* (pp. 110–121). Brno: Muzejní a vlastivědná spol.

Klíma, B.
1989 Figürliche Plastiken aus der paläolithischen Siedlung von Pavlov (ČSSR). In *Religion und Kult* (pp. 81–90). Berlin: Deutscher Verlag der Wissenschaften.

Klíma, B.
1990a Dřevěné zbytky z paleolitické stanice Dolní Věstonice 2. In *Pravěké a slovanské osídlení Moravy* (pp. 7–14). Brno: Muzejní a vlastivědná spolećnost.

Klíma, B.
1990b *Lovci mamutů z Předmostí.* Praha: Academia.

Klíma, B.
1990c Der pleistozäne Mensch aus Dolní Věstonice. *Památky archeologické,, 81,* 5–16.

Klíma, B.
1991 Der Paläolithische Massengrab von Předmostí, Versuch einer Rekonstruktion. *Quartär, 41/42,* 187–194.

Klíma, B.
1994a Cadre stratigraphique du paléolithique supérieur en Moravie. In *El cadro geochronologico del paleolitico superior inicial* (pp. 67–71). Madrid: Museo y Centro de Investigacion Altamira.

Klíma, B.
1994b Die Knochenindustrie, Zier- und Kunsgegenstande. In J. Svoboda (ed.), *Pavlov I, Excavations 1952–53, ERAUL 66* (pp. 87–150). Liège: Université de Liège.

Klíma, B.
1995 *Dolní Věstonice II: Ein Mammutjägerplatz und seine Bestattungen*, ERAUL 73 Liège: Université de Liège.

Klíma, B., Kukla, J., Ložek, V., and de Vries, H.
1962 Stratigraphie des Pleistozäns und Alter des paläolithischen Rastplatzes in der Ziegelei von Dolní Věstonice (Unter-Wisternitz). *Anthropozoikum*, 11, 93–145.

Kneblová, V.
1960 Entwicklung der Vegetation im Elster/Saale-Interglazial im Suchá-Stonava Gebiet. *Anthropozoikum*, 9, 129–174.

Knies, J.
1897 Příspěvky k poznání diluviálního člověka a savectva na Moravě. *Časopis Vlastivědného spolku musejního Olomouc*, 14, 61–81.

Knies, J.
1900 Pravěké nálezy jeskyní Balcarovy skály u Ostrova na vysočině drahanské. *Věstník Klubu přírodovědeckého Prostějov*, 3, 31–81.

Knies, J.
1901a Čtvrtohorní zvířena jeskyně pod hradem u Suchdola na Moravě. *Časopis Vlastivědného spolku musejního Olomouc*, 18, 5–12, 50–56.

Knies, J.
1901b Druhá zpráva o pravěkých nálezech v Balcarově skále u Ostrova. *Věstník Klubu přírodovědeckého Prostějov*, 4, 126–127.

Knies, J.
1903 Soupis palaeontologicko-archaeologických sbírek konservátora Moravského zemského muzea Jana Kniese. *Časopis Moravského zemského muzea*, 3, 60–78.

Knies, J.
1905 Stopy diluviálního člověka a fossilní zvířena jeskyň Ludmírovských. *Časopis Moravského zemského muzea*, 5 (reprint) 1–42.

Knies, J.
1906 Nový nález diluviálního člověka u Mladče na Moravě. *Věstník Klubu přírovědeckého Prostějov*, 9, 3–19.

Knies, J.
1907 Nové sídliště diluviálního člověka u Jedovnic na Moravě. *Lidové noviny*, 15, No. 344, 13 December.

Knies, J.
1913 Nové doklady přítomnosti palaeolithického člověka v Kůlně u Sloupu. *Časopis Moravského zemského muzea*, 11, 199–221.

Knies, J.
1925 Přehled moravského paleolitu. *Obzor prehistorický*, 4, 89–116.

Knies, J.
1929 První stopy lidské na Moravě *Sborník přírodovědného spolku v Ostravě*, 4, 1–4.

Knor, A., Ložek, V., Pelíšek, J., and Žebera, K.
1953 *Dolní Věstonice: Výzkum tábořiště lovců mamutů v letech 1945–1947*. Praha: Nakladatelství Českoslovanské akademie věd.

Königswald, v. W.
1987 The problematics of the find of a "human molar." In J. Fridrich (ed.), *Přezletice: A Lower Palaeolithic site in Central Bohemia* (p. 29). Praha: Národní Muzeum.

Kopecký, J.
1937 Paleolitická stanice u Vincencova na Prostějovsku. *Ročenka Národopisného a průmyslového muzea Prostějov*, 14, 85–92.

Kopecký, J.
1938 Předina na Prostějovsku—sídliště siluviálního lovce. *Ročenka Národopisného a průmyslového muzea Prostějov*, 15, 13–20.

Kos, O.
1971 Die Grabung auf der spätpaläolithischen Station Tišnov in den Jahren 1966 und 1967. *Časopis Moravského muzea*, 54, 9–52.

Kovanda, J.
1991 Molluscs from the section with the skeleton of Upper Paleolithic man at Dolní Věstonice. In J. Svoboda (ed.), *Dolní Věstonice II, Western slope, ERAUL 54* (pp. 89–95). Liège: Université de Liège.

Kozlowski, J. K.
1966 Zagadnienie górnopaleolitycznych pracowni krzemieniarskich. *Prace archeologiczne*, 8, 7–22.

Kozlowski, J. K. (ed.)
1974 *Upper Paleolithic site with dwellings of mammoth bones—Cracow, Spadzista Street B, Folia Quaternaria 44*, Kraków.

Kozlowski, J. K.
1986 The Gravettian in Central and Eastern Europe. *Advances in world archaeology*, 5, 131–200.

Kozlowski, J. K., Manecki, A., Rydlewski, J., Valde-Nowak, P., and Wrzak, J.
1981 Mineralogigo-geochemical characteristic of radiolarites used in the Stone Age in Poland and Slovakia. *Acta Archaeologica Carpatica*, 21, 171–210.

Kozlowski, J. K., and Sobczyk, K.
1987 *The Upper Paleolithic site Kraków-Spadzista Street C2: Excavations 1980*. Warszawa-Kraków: *Prace archeologiczne 42*.

Kretzoi, M., and Vértés, L.
1965 Upper Biharian (Intermindel) pebble-industry occupation site in Western Hungary. *Current Anthropology*, 6, 74–87.

Kříž, M.
1891 *Kůlna a Kostelík: Dvě jeskyně v útvaru devonského vápence na Moravě*. Brno: Musejní spolek.

Kříž, M.
1894 Die Lösslager in Předmostí bei Prerau. *Mitteilungen der Anthropologischen Gesellschaft Wien*, 24, 40–50.

Kříž, M.
1896 Mé výzkumné práce v Předmostí a jich hlavní výsledky. *Časopis Vlastivědného spolku musejního Olomouc*, 13, 1–9, 51–61, 87–102.

Kříž, M.
1897–1898 O jeskyni Kostelíku na Moravě. *Časopis Vlastivědného spolku musejního Olomouc*, 14, 49–61, 15, 19–41.

Kříž, M.
1898 L'époque quaternaire en Moravie, II: La caverne "Kostelik." *L'Anthropologie*, 1898, 257–280.

Kříž, M.
1903 *Beiträge zur Kenntnis der Quartärzeit in Mähren*. Steinitz: Selbstverlag.

Kříž, M.
1909 Die Schwedentischgrotte bei Ochoz in Mähren und Rzehaks Bericht über Homo primigenius wilseri. *Verhandlungen der Geologischen Reichsanstalt 10*, reprint.

Kukla, J.
1954 Složení pleistocenních sedimentů v kontrolním profilu v Šipce z r. 1950. *Přírodovědný sborník Ostravského kraje*, 15, 105–124.

Kukla, J.
1961 Survey of Czechoslovak Quaternary: Quaternary sedimentation cycle. *Institut geologiczny, Prace* 34:1, 145–154.

Kukla, J.
1975 Loess stratigraphy of Central Europe. In K. Butzer and G. Isaac (eds.), *After the Australopithecines* (pp. 99–188). The Hague–Paris: Mouton.

Kukla, J., and Ložek, V.
1961 Survey of Czechoslovak Quaternary: Loesses and related deposits. *Institut geologiczny, Prace*, 34:1, 11–28.

Lieberman, D. E., and Shea, J. J.
1994 Behavioral difference between archaic and modern humans in the Levantine Mousterian. *American Anthropologist*, 96, 300–332.

Linding, K.
1934 *Der Altsteinzeitmensch des Ilmtals: Skeletreste aus dem Travertine von Weimar-Ehringsdorf*. Weimar.

Lindner, H.
1956 Die geologische Datierung des Schildkerns von Oderfurt. *Quartär*, 7/8, 188–193.

Lorenc-Römer
1957 Ergebnisse einer Roentgenuntersuchung des magdalénienzeitlichen Kinderunterkiefers aus der Ilsenhöhle bei Ranis. *Ausgrabungen und Funde*, 2, 8–15.

Ložek, V.
1961 Nález interglaciálních sedimentů v Pavlově. *Věstník Ústředního ústavu geologického*, 36, 365–368.

Ložek, V.
1965a Das Problem der Lössbildung und die Lössmollusken. *Eiszeitalter und Gegenwart*, 16, 61–75.

Ložek, V.
1965b The relationship between the development of soils and faunas in the warm Quarternary phase. *Anthropozoikum*, 3, 7–33.

Ložek, V.
1966a Die quartäre Klimaentwicklung in der Tschechoslowakei. *Quartär*, 17, 1–19.

Ložek, V.
1966b Sprašová série se třemi interglaciály u Dolních Kounic. *Věstník Ústředního ústavu geologického*, 41, 203–207.

Ložek, V.
1968 Bedeutung des tschechoslowakischen Raumes für die Quartärstratigraphie. In *Twenty-third International Geological Congress, Proceedings of Section 10* (pp. 79–88). Praha: Institute of Geology.

Ložek, V.
1976 *Klimaabhängige Zyklen der Sedimentation und Bodenbildung während des Quartärs im Lichte malakozoologischer Untersuchungen*. Praha: Academia.

Ložek, V.
1980a Altersstellung und Umwelt des Aurigniaciens. In L. Bánesz and J. K. Kozlowski (eds.), *L'aurignacien et le gravettien (périgordien) dans leur cadre écologique* (pp. 139–151). Nitra: Institute of Archaeology.

Ložek, V.
1980b Chronological position of the last phase of slope retreat in Czechoslovak karst areas. *Československý kras*, 31, 7–17.

Ložek, V.
1980c Quaternary molluscs and stratigraphy of the Mažarná Cave. *Československý kras*, 30 67–80.

Ložek, V.
1981 Zur Altersstellung der jüngsten Tieferosion in den Tälern der innerböhmischen Hügelländer. *Biuletyn Instytutu Geologicznego*, 321/23, 239–248.

Ložek, V.
1982 *Faunengeschichtliche Grundlinien zur spät- und nacheiszeitlichen Entwicklung der Molluskenbestände in Mitteleuropa. Rozpravy*. Praha: Academia.

Ložek, V.
1985 The site of Soutěska and its significance for Holocene climatic development. *Československý kras*, 36, 7–22.

Ložek, V.
1988 Slope depositions in karst environments of Central Europe, *Československý kras*, 39, 15–33.

Ložek, V.
1991 Molluscs in loess, their paleoecological significance and role in geochronology—Principles and methods. *Quaternary International*, 7–8, 71–79.

Ložek, V., and Šibrava, V.
1968 Zur Altersstellung der jüngsten Labe-Terrassen. *Anthropozoikum*, 5, 7–31.

Ložek, V., Tyráček, J., and Fejfar, O.
1959 Die quartären Sedimente der Felsnische auf der Velká Kobylanka bei Hranice. *Anthropozoikum*, 8, 177–203.

Lumley, M. A.
1982 L'Homme de Tautavel. In *Congrès international de Paléontologie humaine, prétirage* (pp. 19–136). Nice: Louis-Jean.

Mackerle, J.
1948 *Pravěk Malé Hané* Jevíčko: Nákladem vlastním.

Macoun, J.
1982 Stellung des paläolithischen Standorts Předmostí im Quartär Mitteleuropas. *Věstník Ústředního úst. geologického*, 57, 17–36.

Macoun, J.
1985 Stratigraphie des Mittelpleistozäns in Mähren in Bezug auf das Quartär Europas. *Časopis Slezského muzea*, A/34, 125–143, 219–237.

Macoun, J.
1989 Die kontinentale Vereisung in der Mährischen Pforte. *Anthropozoikum*, 19, 75–104.

Macoun, J., Šibrava, V., Tyráček, J., and Kneblová-Vodičková, V.
1965 *Kvartér Ostravska a Moravské brány*. Praha: Ústřední ústav geologický.

Makowsky, A.
1888 Der Löss von Brünn und seine Einschlüsse an diluvialen Thieren und Menschen. *Verhandlungen des Naturforschenden Vereines Brünn*, 26, 207–243.

Makowsky, A.
1890 Ueber die Anwesenheit des Menschen währed der Lössperiode in der Umgebung von Brünn. *Mitteilungen der Anthropologischen Gesellschaft Wien*, 20, 60–65.

Makowsky, A.
1892   Der diluviale Mensch im Löss von Brün. *Mitteilungen der Anthropologischen Gesellschaft Wien*, 22, 73–84.

Makowsky, A.
1897   Das Rhinoceros der Diluvialzeit Mährens als Jagdthier des paläolithischen Menschen. *Mitteilungen der Anthropologischen Gesellschaft Wien*, 27, 73–79.

Makowsky, A.
1899a   Bearbeitete Mammutknochen aus dem Löss von Mähren. *Mitteilungen der Anthropologischen Gesellschaft Wien*, 29, 53–57.

Makowsky, A.
1899b   Der Mensch der Diluvialzeit Mährens. In *Festschrift d.K.k. technischen Hochschule in Brünn* (pp. 25–26, 39–41). Brünn: Technische Hochschule.

Malán, M.
1955   Zahnkeim aus der zweiten Aurignacien Schicht der Höhle Istállóskö. *Acta archaeologica hungarica*, 5, 145–148.

Malina, J.
1970   Die jungpaläolithische Steinindustrie aus Mähren, ihre Rostoffe und ihre Patina. *Acta Praehistorica et Archaeologica*, 1, 157–173.

Malý, J.
1939   Lebky fosilního člověka v Dolních Věstonicích. *Anthropologie*, 17, 171–190.

Mania, D.
1979   Zur technologie der Knochen- und Geweihartefakte von Bilzingsleben. *Ethnographisch-archäologische Zeitschrift*, 20, 708–722.

Mania, D.
1983   Zue Jagd des Homo erectus von Bilzingsleben. *Ethnographisch-archäologische Zeitschrift*, 24, 326–337.

Mania, D.
1984   Zur Geochronologie des Mittelpleistozäns und einiger paläolithischen Fundstellen im Saale- und mittleren Elbegebiet. *Arbeits- und Forschungbserichte Dresden*, 27/28, 13–58.

Mania, D., Mania, U., and Vlček, E.
1994   Latest finds of the skull remains of Homo erectus from Bilzingsleben (Thuringia). *Naturwissenschaften*, 81, 123–127.

Mania, D., Thomae, M., Litt, T., and Weber, T.
1990   *Neumark-Grobern: Beitrage zur Jagd des mittelpaläolithischen Menschen.* Berlin: Deutschen Verlag der Wissenschaften.

Mania, D., and Toepfer, V.
1973   *Königsaue: Gliederung, Ökologie und mittelpaläolithische Funde der letzten Eiszeit.* Berlin: Deutscher Verlag der Wissenschaften.

Mania, D., Toepfer, V., and Vlček, E.
1980   *Bilzingsleben I: Homo erectus—seine Kultur und seine Umwelt.* Berlin: Deutscher Verlag der Wissenschaften.

Mania, D., and Vlček, E.
1981   Homo erectus in Middle Europe: The discovery from Bilzingsleben. In B. A. Sigmon and J. S. Cybulski (eds.), *Homo erectus papers in honour of Davidson Black* (pp. 133–151). Toronto: University of Toronto Press.

Mania, D., and Vlček, E.
1987   Homo erectus from Bilzingsleben (GDR)—His culture and his environment. *Anthropologie*, 25, 1–45.

Mania, D., and Weber, T.
1986 Bilzingsleben III: Homo erectus—Seine Kultur und seine Umwelt. Berlin: Deutscher Verlag der Wissenschaften.

Marshack, A.
1972 The roots of civilization. New York: McGraw-Hill.

Marshack, A.
1981 On Paleolithic ochre and the early uses of colours and symbol. *Current Anthropology*, 22, 188–191.

Marshack, A.
1988 The Neanderthals and the human capacity for symbolic thought: Cognitive and problem-solving aspects of Mousterian symbols. In O. Bar-Yosef (ed.), *L'Homme de Néandertal: Vol. 5. ERAUL 32* (pp. 57–91). Liège: Université de Liège.

Marshack, A.
1991 The female image: A "time-factored" symbol. A study in style and aspects of image use in the Upper Paleolithic. *Proceedings of the Prehistoric Society*, 57, 17–31.

Marshack, A.
1992 The analytical problem of subjectivity in the maker and user. In T. Shay and J. Clottes (eds.), *The limitations of archaeological knowledge, ERAUL 49* (pp. 181–210). Liège: Université de Liège.

Mason, S. L., Hather, J. G., and Hillman, G. C.
1994 Preliminary investigation of the plant macro-remains from Dolní Věstonice II, and its implications for the role of plant foods in Palaeolithic and Mesolithic Europe. *Antiquity*, 68, 48–57.

Maška, K.
1882 Über den diluvialen Menschen in Stramberg. *Mitteilungen der Anthropologischen Gesellschaft Wien*, 12, 32–38.

Maška, K.
1884 Pravěké nálezy ve Štramberku. *Časopis Vlastivědného spolku musejního Olomouc*, 1, 15–24, 64–69, 152–159.

Maška, K.
1885 Čelist' předpotopního člověka nalezená v Šipce u Štramberka. *Časopis Vlastivědného spolku musejního Olomouc*, 2, 27–35.

Maška, K.
1886 Der diluviale Mensch in Mähren: Ein Beitrag zur Urgeschichte für das Schuljahr 1885/86. Neutitschen.

Maška, K.
1889 Lössfunde bei Brünn und der diluviale Mensch: Eine kritische Studie. *Mitteilungen der Anthropologischen Gesellschaft Wien*, 19, 46–64.

Maška, K.
1894 Nové nálezy v Předmostí. *Časopis Vlastivědného spolku musejního Olomouc*, 11 (separata), 1–3.

Maška, K.
1895a Ausgrabungen aus dem Mammutjägernlager im Předmostí im Jahr 1893. *Bulletin international de l'Académie tchéque*, Sc. mat.-nat. 1, 29–30.

Maška, K.
1895b Diluviální člověk v Předmostí. *Časopis Vlastivědného spolku musejního Olomouc*, 12, 4–7.

Maška, K.
1905 Poznámky k diluviálním nálezům v jeskyních mladečských a stopám glaciálním na severovýchodní Moravě. *Časopis Moravského zemského muzea*, 5 (reprint), 1–3.

Maška, K.
  1912 Soška mamutí z Předmostí. *Pravěk, 8,* 5–12.
Maška, K.
  1913 Lidské figurky z Předmostí. *Pravěk, 9,* 24.
Matiegka, J.
  1929 The skull of fossil man Brno III and the cast of its interior. *Anthropologie, 7,* 90–107.
Matiegka, J.
  1934 *Homo předmostensis, fosilní člověk z Předmostí na Moravě: I. Lebky.* Praha: Česká akademie věd a umění.
Matiegka, J.
  1938 *Homo předmostensis, fosilní člověk z Předmostí na Moravě: II. Ostatní části kostrové.* Praha: Česká akademie věd a umění.
Mazálek, M.
  1960 Paleolitický výzkum Bučovska na Moravě. *Časopis Moravského muzea, 45,* 27–68.
Mellars, P.
  1989 Major issues in the emergence of modern humans. *Current Anthropology, 30,* 349–385.
Mithen, S.
  1993 Simulating mammoth hunting and extinction: Implications for the Late Pleistocene of the Central Russian Plain. In *Hunting and animal exploitation in the Late Paleolithic* (pp. 163–178). New York: American Anthropological Association.
Montet-White, A. (ed.)
  1990 *The Epigravettian site of Grubgraben, Lower Austria: The 1986–1987 excavations, ERAUL 40.* Liège: Université de Liège.
Morawski, W.
  1992 Komplex stanowisk paleolitycznych w Piekarach. In J. Lech and J. Partyka (eds.), *Prof. Stefan Krukowski (1890–1982)* (pp. 163–172). Ojców: Ojcówski park narodowy.
Much, M.
  1878 Noch ein Wort über Höhlenwohnungen im Löss. *Mitteilungen der Anthropologischen Gesellschaft Wien, 8,* 131–134.
Murrill, R.
  1980 New measurements of the face of the Petralona fossil hominid skull. *Anthropos (Athens), 7,* 40–41.
Murrill, R.
  1981 *Petralona man.* Springfield, IL: Charles C Thomas.
Musil, R.
  1955 Osteologický materiál z paleolitického sídliště v Pavlově. *Práce brněnské základny ČSAV, 27,* 279–319.
Musil, R.
  1958 Fauna moravských magdalénských stanic. *Anthropozoikum, 7,* 7–26.
Musil, R.
  1959a Bemerkungen zum paläontologischen Material aus Dolní Věstonice. *Anthropozoikum, 8,* 73–82.
Musil, R.
  1959b Das osteologische Material aus der paläolithischen Siedlungsstätte in Pavlov. *Anthropozoikum, 8,* 83–106.
Musil, R.
  1962 Die Höhle "Švédův stůl," ein typischer Höhlenhyänenhorst. *Anthropos, 13,* 97–260.

Musil, R.
 1965a Aus der Geschichte der Stránská skála. *Časopis Moravského muzea*, 50, 75–106.
Musil, R.
 1965b Zhodnocení dřívějších paleontologických nálezů ze Šipky. *Anthropos*, 17, 127–134.
Musil, R.
 1968 Die Mammutmolaren von Předmostí (ČSSR). *Paläontologische Abhandlungen*, 3/1, 1–192.
Musil, R.
 1974 Faunistické společenstvo z výkopů před jeskyní Pekárnou. In B. Klíma (ed.), *Archeologický výzkum plošiny před jeskyní Pekárnou* (pp. 19–20). Praha: Academia.
Musil, R. (ed.)
 1982 *Kvartér brněnské kotliny: Stránská skála IV. Studia geographica 80*. Brno: Institute of Geography.
Musil, R.
 1988 Ökostratigraphie der Sedimente in der Kůlna-Höhle. *Anthropos*, 24, 215–255.
Musil, R.
 1994 Hunting game of the culture layer of Pavlov. In J. Svoboda (ed.), *Pavlov I, Excavations 1952–53, ERAUL 66* (pp. 170–196). Liège: Université de liège.
Musil, R., and Valoch, K.
 1956 Spraše Vyškovského úvalu. *Práce brněnské základny ČSAV*, 28/6, 263–315.
Musil, R., and Valoch, K.
 1968 Stránská skála: Its meaning for Pleistocene studies. *Current Anthropology*, 9, 534–539.
Musil, R., Valoch, K., and Nečesaný, V.
 1955 Pleistocenní sedimenty okolí Brna. *Anthropozoikum*, 4, 107–168.
Nehring, A.
 1895a Über einen menschlichen Molar aus dem Diluvium von Taubach bei Weimar. *Zeitschrift für Ethnologie*, 27, 573–577.
Nehring, A.
 1895b Über fossile Menschenzähne aus dem Diluvium von Taubach bei Weimar. *Naturwissenschaftliche Wochenschrift*, 10, 369–372.
Neugebauer-Maresch, Ch.
 (1988) Vorbericht über die Rettungsgrabung an der Aurignacien-Station Stratzing/Krems-Rehberg in den Jahren 1985–1988: Zum Neufund einer weiblichen Statuette. *Fundberichte aus Österreich*, 26, 73–84.
Neugebauer-Maresch, Ch.
 1993 Alsteinzeit im Osten Österreichs. *Wissenschaftliche Schriftenreihe Niederösterreichs*, 95–97, 7–96.
Noble, W., and Davidson, I.
 1993 Tracing the emergence of modern human behavior: Methodological pitfalls and theoretical path. *Journal of Anthropological Archaeology*, 12, 121–149.
Oakley, K. P., Campbell, B. G., and Molleson, T. I.
 1971 *Catalogue of fossil hominids. Part 2. Europe*. London: British Museum, National History.
Oliva, M.
 1979a Die Herkunft des Szeletiens im Lichte neuer Funde von Jezeřany. *Časopis Moravského muzea*, 64, 45–78.
Oliva, M.
 1979b Nové paleolitické stanice Milovice a Lhotka, okr. Kroměříž. *Studie Muzea Kroměřížska*, 79, 36–42.

Oliva, M.
1980   Význam moravských lokalit pro koncepci aurignacienu. *Archeologické rozhledy*, 32, 48–71.

Oliva, M.
1981a   Die Bohunicien-Station bei Podolí (Bez. Brno-Land) und ihre Stellung im beginnenden Jungpaläolithikum. *Časopis Moravského muzea*, 66, 7–45.

Oliva, M.
1981b   Acheulian finds from Karolín, District of Kroměříž (Czechoslovakia). *Anthropologie*, 19, 27–32.

Oliva, M.
1983   Paleolitická stanice u Bělova (okr. Kroměříž): Příspěvek k otázce homogenity celků moravského aurignacienu. *Časopis Moravského muzea*, 68, 21–41.

Oliva, M.
1984a   Aurignacká stanice u Divák (okr. Břeclav): Příspěvek k problematice stability osídlení v aurignacienu. *Sborník prací Filozofické fakulty Brněnské univerzity*, E 29, 7–26.

Oliva, M.
1984b   Le Bohunicien, un nouveau groupe culturel en Moravia: Quelques aspects psychotechnologiques du development des industries paléolithiques. *L'Anthropologie*, 88, 209–220.

Oliva, M.
1984c   Technologie výroby a použité suroviny štípané industrie moravského aurignacienu. *Archeologické rozhledy*, 36, 601–628.

Oliva, M.
1986   Starší doba kamenná (paleolit). In P. Koštuřík (ed.), *Pravěk Třebíčska* (pp. 31–56). Brno: Muzejní a vlastivědná společnost.

Oliva, M.
1987a   Aurignacien na Moravě. *Studie Muzea Kroměřížska*, 87, 5–128.

Oliva, M.
1987b   Drobné lokality micoquienu v okolí Brna. *Sborník prací Filozofické fakulty Brněnské univerzity*, E 32, 7–18.

Oliva, M.
1987c   Vyvinutý micoquien z návrší "Horky" u Bořitova-prvé výsledky. Příspěvek k otázce stanic dílenského charakteru. *Časopis Moravského muzea*, 72, 21–44.

Oliva, M.
1988   A Gravettian site with mammoth-bone dwelling in Milovice (Southern Moravia). *Anthropologie*, 26, 105–112.

Oliva, M.
1989a   Excavations in the Palaeolithic site of Milovice I (Southern Moravia) in the year 1988. *Anthropologie*, 27, 265–271.

Oliva, M.
1989b   Mladopaleolitické nálezy z Mladečských jeskyní. *Časopis Moravského muzea*, 74, 35–54.

Oliva, M.
1989c   Paleolit. In L. Belcredi (ed.), *Archeologické lokality a nálezy okresu Brno-venkov* (pp. 8–32). Brno: Okresní muzeum.

Oliva, M.
1990   La signification des pointes foliacées dans l' Aurignacien morave et dans le type de Míškovice. In J. K. Kozlowski (ed.), *Les feuilles de pierre*, ERAUL 42 (pp. 223–232). Liège: Université de Liège.

Oliva, M.
1991a The Micoquian open-air site of Ráječko 1. *Anthropologie*, 29, 45–61.
Oliva, M.
1991b Mladopaleolitická stanice s radiolaritovou industrií v Brně-Jundrově. *Časopis Moravského muzea*, 76, 19–29.
Oliva, M.
1991c The Szeletian in Czechoslovakia. *Antiquity*, 65, 318–325.
Oliva, M.
1993a The Aurignacian in Moravia. In H. Knecht et al. (eds.), *Before Lascaux* (pp. 37–55). Boca Raton, FL: CRC Press.
Oliva, M.
1993b Zahájení výzkumu paleolitické lokality Vedrovice Ia (okr. Znojmo). *Časopis Moravského muzea*, 78, 11–22.
Oliva, M., and Doležel, J.
1985 Nové paleolitické lokality z Tišnovska (okr. Brno-venkov, Blansko, Žďár n.S.). *Přehled výzkumů*, 1983, 17–19.
Oliva, M., and Štrof, A.
1985 Přehled paleolitického osídlení Lysické sníženiny a blízkého okolí (okr. Blansko). *Přehled výzkumů*, 1983, 10–17.
Opravil, E.
1976 Ergebnisse der Holzkohlenanalyse von Brno-Bohunice. In K. Valoch (ed.), *Die altsteinzeitliche Fundstelle in Brno-Bohunice* (pp. 72–74). Praha: Academia.
Opravil, E.
1988 Ergebnisse der Holzkohlenanlyse aus der Kůlna-Höhle. *Anthropos*, 24, 211–214.
Opravil, E.
1994 The vegetation. In J. Svoboda (ed.), *Pavlov I, Excavations 1952–1953*, ERAUL 66 (pp. 163–167). Liège: Université de Liège.
Otte, M.
1981 *Le gravettien en Europe centrale: Disertationes archaeologicae Gandenses 20*. Brugge: Tempel.
Otte, M.
1990 Les industries aux pointes foliacées du nord-ouest européen. In J. K. Kozlowski (ed.), *Les feuilles de pierre*, ERAUL 42 (pp. 247–269). Liège: Université de Liège.
Otte, M.
1991 Révision de la séquence de Willendorf. In A. Montet-White (ed.), *Les Bassins du Rhin et du Danube au Palélithique supérieur*, ERAUL 43 (pp. 45–59). Liège: Université de Liège.
Podborský, V., and Vildomec, V.
1972 *Pravěk Znojemska*. Brno: Musejní spolek.
Procházka, R.
1983 Záchranný výzkum paleolitické stanice v Uherském Hradišti-Jarošově, okr. Uherské Hradiště. *Archeologické rozhledy*, 35, 552–554.
Prosche, K.
1960 Das Jungpaläolithikum von Ondratice (Mähren) nach der Sammlung des Landesmuseums fur Vorgeschichte Halle. *Wissenschaftliche Zeitschrift der Martin-Luther-Universität Halle-Wittenberg*, 9, 333–364.
Prošek, F. (ed.)
1952 Výzkum jeskyně Zlatého koně u Koněprus. *Československý kras*, 5, 161–179.

Prošek, F.
1953   Szeletien na Slovensku. *Slovenská archeológia*, 1, 133–164.
Prošek, F., and Ložek, V.
1954   Stratigrafické otázky československého paleolitu. *Památky archeologické*, 45, 35–74.
Přichystal, A.
1975   Příspěvek k charakteristice paleolitických nalezišť v oblasti Kosíře (okr. Olomouc, Prostějov). *Folia Facultatis Scientiae Naturalis 16, Geologica*, 27 117–124.
Přichystal, A.
1978   K původu hematitových barviv z paleolitických stanic Brzoskwinia u Krakova a Dolní Věstonice na Moravě. Manuscript. Faculty of Science, Brno.
Přichystal, A.
1979   Suroviny štípaných artefaktů na Moravě a metody jejich výzkumu. In *Aplikace geofyzikálních metod v archeologii a moderní metody terénního výzkumu a dokumentace* (pp. 175–179). Brno: Institue of Achaeology.
Přichystal, A.
1987   Geologie a petrografie rohovců ze Stránské skály. Barvivo. In J. Svoboda (ed.), *Stránská skála: Bohunický typ v brněnské kotlině* (pp. 28–32). Praha: Academia.
Přichystal, A.
1989   Zdroje křišťálové suroviny v pravěku na Moravě. *Geologický průzkum*, 31, 86–87.
Přichystal, A.
1994a Geochemical analysis of the lithic materials. In J. Svoboda (ed.), *Pavlov I, Excavations 1952–53, ERAUL 66* (pp. 18–22). Liège: Université de Liège.
Přichystal, A.
1994b Zdroje kamenných surovin. In J. Svoboda (ed.), *Paleolit Moravy a Slezska* (pp. 43–49). Brno: Institute of Archaeology.
Richter, R. M.
1955   Die jüngere Altsteinzeit im Ostthürigen Orlaugau. *Alt-Thürigen*, 1, 11–42.
Roebroeks, W., and van Kolfschoten, T.
1994   The earliest occupation of Europe: A short chronology. *Antiquity*, 68, 489–503.
Rybníčková, E., and Rybníček, K.
1972   Erste Ergebnisse paläogeobotanischer Untersuchungen des Moores bei Vracov, Südmähren. *Folia Geobotanica et Phytotaxonomica*, 7, 285–308.
Rybníčková, E., and Rybníček, K.
1992   The environment of the Pavlovian—Palaeoecological results from Bulhary, South Moravia. In J. Kovar-Eder (ed.), *Palaeovegetational development in Europe and the regions relevant to its palaeofloristic evolution* (pp. 73–79). Wien: Naturhistorisches Museum.
Rzehak, A.
1906   Der Unterkiefer von Ochos. *Verhandlungen des Naturforschenden Vereines Brünn*, 44, 91–114.
Rzehak, A.
1909   Das Alter des Unterkiefers von Ochos. *Časopis Moravského zemského muzea*, 9, 277–313.
Saban, R.
1982   Les emprintes endocraniennes des veines méningées moyennes et les étapes de l'évolution humaine. *Annales de Paléontologie*, 68, 171– 220.
Schild, R., and Sulgostowska, Z.
1988   The Middle Paleolithic of the Northern European Plain at Zwolen: Preliminary results. In J. K. Kozlowski (ed.), *L'Homme de Néandertal*, Vol. 8, *ERAUL 35* (pp. 149–167). Liège: Université de Liège.

Schirmeisen, K.
1926 Altdiluviale Mahlzeitreste auf dem Lateiner Berge bei Brünn. *Verhandlungen des Naturforschenden Vereines Brünn*, 60, 29–51.
Schirmeisen, K.
1929 Beiträge zur mährischen Vorgeschichte. *Sudeta*, 5, 1–14.
Schirmeisen, K.
1933a Beiträge zur Vorgeschichte des Mähr.-Neustadter Gebietes. *Verhandlungen des Naturforschenden Vereines Brünn*, 64, 115–143.
Schirmeisen, K.
1933b Jungeiszeitliche Funde bei Brünn. *Sudeta*, 9, 78–81.
Schonhals, E., Rohdenburg, H., and Semmel, A.
1964 Ergebnisse neuerer Untersuchungen zur Würm-Loss-Gliederung in Hessen. *Eiszeitalter und Gegenwart*, 15, 199–206.
Schwabedissen, H.
1943 Stand und Aufgaben der Alt- und Mittelsteinzeitforschung im mährischen Raum. *Zeitschrift des Mährischen Landesmuseums, Neue Folge* (reprint), 1–31.
Seitl, L., Svoboda, J., Ložek, V., Přichystal, A., and Svobodová, H.
1986 Das Spätglazial in der Barová-Höhle im Mährischen Karst. *Archäologisches Korrespondenzblatt*, 16, 393–398.
Skutil, J.
1924 Paleolitická stanice u Nové Dědiny. *Obzor prehistorický*, 3, 133–137.
Skutil, J.
1925 Paleolitická stanice na Golštýně u Určic (Prostějovsko). *Obzor prehistorický*, 4, 194–197.
Skutil, J.
1927a Archäologisches zur Altersbestimmung des Ochoskiefers. *Die Eiszeit*, 4, 117.
Skutil, J.
1927b Miscelanea k moravskému paleolithu: Žitného jeskyně. *Památky archeologické*, 35, 202–206.
Skutil, J.
1927c Paleolitická stanice ve Výpustku. *Obzor prehistorický*, 5–6,47–58.
Skutil, J.
1928a Geografické rozšíření solutréenu. *Bratislava*, 2/1, 166–180.
Skutil, J.
1928b Paleolithická stanice ve Verunčině díře. *Časopis Vlastivědného spolku musejního Olomouc*, 40, 149–152.
Skutil, J.
1929a Palaeolithická stanice v Kateřinské jeskyni. *Časopis Vlastivědného spolku musejního Olomouc*, 41–42, 294–295.
Skutil, J.
1929b Paleolitická stanice u Kolíbkách u Jedovnic. *Časopis Vlastivědného Spolku musejniko Olomouc*, 41–42, 105–108.
Skutil, J.
1930 Zpráva o nové paleolithické stanici v Brně, objevené v r. 1929. *Časopis Moravského zemského muzea*, 26–27, 436–440.
Skutil, J.
1931a Paleolithické nálezy A. Gottwaldovy. *Ročenka Národopisného a průmyslového muzea Prostějov*, 8, 47–57.

Skutil, J.
1931b   Rud. Janovského palaeolithické nálezy z Holešovska. *Naše Valašsko*, 3, 77–89.

Skutil, J.
1932   Hradčany, Nuzířov a Čebín, palaeolithické staice na Tišnovsku. *Časopis Moravského zemského muzea*, 29 (reprint), 1–11.

Skutil, J.
1933   Nové příspěvky k poznání paleolitika drahanského. *Ročenka Národopisného a průmyslového muzea Prostějov*, 10, 5–11.

Skutil, J.
1934   Ojedinělý paleolitický nález z Mořic (okr. Kojetín). *Ročenka Národopisného a průmyslového muzea Prostějov*, 11, 5.

Skutil, J.
1935   Věžky, paleolitická stanice na Zdounecku. *Vlastivědný sborník střední a severní Moravy*, 13, 43–44.

Skutil, J.
1936   Übersicht der mährischen paläolithischen Funde. *Swiatowit*, 16, 47–78.

Skutil, J.
1937a   Některé dosud blíže neznámé paleolitické nálezy na Moravě. *Obzor prehistorický*, 10, 259–280.

Skutil, J.
1937b   Paleolitické stanice u Myslejovic, Krumsína, Vícova. *Ročenka Národopisného a průmyslového muzea Prostějov*, 14, 72–84.

Skutil, J.
1938a   Nové paleolitické nálezy z Myslejovic. *Ročenka Národopisného a průmyslového muzea Prostějov*, 15, 5–12.

Skutil, J.
1938b   *Pravěké nálezy v Mladči u Litovle na Moravě*. Litovel: Krajinská musejní společnost.

Skutil, J.
1939   *Pravěké nálezy na Kloboucku*. Klubouky u Brna.

Skutil, J.
1940a   K paleolitické stanici v jeskyni "Jáchymce" v Josefovském údolí u Adamova. *Časopis Vlastivědného spolku musejního Olomouc*, 53, 1–4.

Skutil, J.
1940b   Paleolitické nálezy z Hradišťska a přilehlého Pomoraví. *Sborník velehradský*, 11, 50–69.

Skutil, J.
1940c   Paleolitikum v bývalém Československu. *Obzor prehistorický*, 12, 5–99.

Skutil, J.
1941   Tři drobné příspěvky paleolitické z Moravského krasu. *Časopis Vlastivědného spolku musejního Olomouc*, 54, 1–9.

Skutil, J.
1946a   Moravské prehistorické výkopy a nálezy—oddělení moravského pravěku Zemského muzea 1937–1945. *Časopis Moravského zemského muzea*, 33, 45–134.

Skutil, J.
1946b   Staropaleolitické nálezy z Moravy. *Památky archeologické*, 42, 2–9.

Skutil, J.
1954   Ondratické nálezy prostějovského musea. *Sborník Krajského vlastivědného muzea Olomouc*, B 2, 3–24.

Skutil, J.
  1955a Paleolitická stanice v Hanušovicích na severní Moravě. *Sborník Krajského vlastivědného muzea Olomouc*, B 3, 243–250.
Skutil, J.
  1955b Příspěvek k poznání paleolitika Moravské brány. *Anthropozoikum*, 4, 447–468.
Skutil, J.
  1959 Některé paleolitické nálezy z olomouckého a přerovského muzea. *Sborník Krajského vlastivědného muzea Olomouc*, B 4, 423–460.
Skutil, J.
  1960 Paleolitická stanice v Míškovicích na Holešovsku. *Přehled výzkumů*, 1959, 15–17.
Skutil, J.
  1961 Předběžná zpráva o výzkumu Verunčiny díry a některých jiných jeskyní v Suchém žlebu v Moravském krasu. *Přehled výzkumů*, 1960, 29–36.
Skutil, J.
  1962a Dolina, první otevřená paleolitická stanice v Ostrově u Macochy. *Archeologické rozhledy*, 14, 564–566.
Skutil, J.
  1962b Nález figurální plastiky na volutové keramice z jeskyně Koňské jámy v Moravském krase. *Přehled výzkumů*, 1961, 33–37.
Skutil, J.
  1962c Nové akvisice z paleolitické stanice v Míškovicích na Holešovsku. *Přehled výzkumů*, 1961, 31–32.
Skutil, J.
  1962d Předběžná zpráva o skupině nových 24 paleolitických lokalit na Kounicku na Jihlavě. *Přehled výzkumů*, 1961, 22–30.
Skutil, J.
  1963a Další paleolitické nálezy z Kounicka na Jihlavě. *Přehled výzkumů*, 1962, 9–10.
Skutil, J.
  1963b Předběžná zpráva o hlavních výsledcích výzkumu Rytířské jeskyně (Lažánky, okr. Blansko) v Mor. Krase. *Přehled výzkumů*, 1962, 12–14.
Skutil, J., and Oulehla, V.
  1961 Solutrénská stanice v Dukovanech na Moravě. *Archeologické rozhledy*, 13, 8–12.
Skutil, J., and Stehlík, A.
  1932a Druhá paleolitická stanice "Šanova díra" v Ludmírově (okr. Konice) na Moravě. *Ročenka Národopisného a průmyslového musea Prostějov*, 9, 73–80.
Skutil, J., and Stehlík, A.
  1932b Moraviae fauna diluvialis, A. Mammalia. *Sborník Klubu přírodovědeckého v Brně*, 14, 102–178.
Skutil, J., and Stehlík, A.
  1939 Nové paleolitické nálezy z Konického krasu. *Ročenka Národopisného a průmyslového musea Prostějov*, 16, 96–106.
Smith, F.
  1982 Upper Pleistocene hominid evolution in South-Central Europe: A review of the evidence and analysis of trends. *Current Anthropology*, 23, 667–686.
Smolíková, L.
  1967 Mikromorphologie der altpleistozänen Fossilböden von Červený kopec bei Brno (Brünn). *Věstník Ústředního ústavu geologického*, 42, 369–373.

Smolíková, L.
1982 Zur Genese mittelpleistozäner Böden auf Hügel Červený kopec bei Brno. *Věstník Ústředního ústavu geologického*, 57, 169–178.

Smolíková, L.
1984 On the development of Pleistocene soils in Czechoslovakia. In M. Pécsi (ed.), *Lithology and stratigraphy of loess and paleosoils* (pp. 33–38). Budapest: Geographical Research Institute.

Smolíková, L.
1988 Mikromorphologische Charakteristik des Profils vor dem Eingang in die Kůlna-Höhle. *Anthropos*, 24, 201–203 (Brno).

Smolíková, L.
1991 Soil micromorphologic investigation of the section at Dolní Věstonice II. In J. Svoboda (ed.), *Dolní Věstonice II—Western slope, ERAUL 54* (pp. 65–74). Liège: Université de Liège.

Smolíková, L., and Kovanda, J.
1983 Die Bedeutung der pleistozänen Sedimente des Fundortes Růženin dvůr (Brno—Židenice II) für die Stratigraphie des Brno-Beckens. *Anthropozoikum*, 15, 9–38.

Smolíková, L., and Ložek, V.
1963 Interglaciál a nález pleistocénního člověka u Svitávky. *Časopis pro mineralogii a geologii*, 8, 189–197.

Smolíková, L., and Zeman, A.
1979 Fossilböden im Profil von Sedlešovice und ihre Beziehung zu den Flussablagerungen. *Věstník Ústředního ústavu geologického*, 54, 215–224.

Smyčka, J.
1904 Neue diluviale Funde von Lautsch in Mähren. *Jahrbuch der K.k. Zentral-Kommission für Erforschung*, 1, Wien.

Smyčka, J.
1922 Nálezy diluviálního člověka v Mladči u Litovle na Moravě. *Obzor prehistorický*, 1, 111–120.

Sobczyk, K.
1984 Modes de débitage dans le magdalénien d'Europe centrale. *L'Anthropologie*, 88, 309–326.

Sobczyk, K.
1993 The Late Paleolithic flint workshop at Brzoskwinia-Krzemionki near Krakow. Krakow: *Prace archeologiczne*, 55.

Soergel, W.
1922 *Die Jagd der Vorzeit*. Jena.

Soergel, W.
1925 Die Gliederung und absolute Zeitrechnung des Eiszeitalters. *Fortschritte der Geologie und Paläeontologie*, 13, 125–251.

Soffer, O.
1985 *The Upper Paleolithic of the central Russian Plain*. Orlando, FL: Academic Press.

Soffer, O.
1987 Upper Paleolithic connubia, refugia, and the archaeological record from Eastern Europe. In O. Soffer (ed.), *The Pleistocene Old World* (pp. 333–348). New York: Plenum Press.

Soffer, O.
1989 Storage, sedentism and the Eurasian Palaeolithic record. *Antiquity*, 63, 719–732.

Soffer, O.
  1993 Upper Paleolithic adaptations in Central and Eastern Europe and man–mammoth interactions. In O. Soffer and N. D. Praslov (eds.), *From Kostenki to Clovis* (pp. 31–49). New York–London: Plenum Press.
Soffer, O., and Gamble, C. (eds.)
  1990 *The world at 18,000 B.P.: High latitudes*. London: Unwin Hyman.
Soffer, O., and Vandiver, P.
  1994 The ceramics. In J. Svoboda (ed.), *Pavlov I, Excavations 1952–53, ERAUL 66* (pp. 151–162). Liège: Université de Liège.
Soffer, O., Vandiver, P., Klíma, B., and Svoboda, J.
  1993 The pyrotechnology of performance art: Moravian Venuses and wolverines. In H. Knecht et al. (eds.), *Before Lascaux* (pp. 259–275). Boca Raton, FL: CRC Press.
Steenstrup, J.
  1890 Die Mammuthjäger-Station bei Předmostí im österreichischen Kronlande Mähren. *Mitteilungen der Anthropologischen Gesellschaft Wien*, 20, 1–31.
Stringer, C. B., and Andrews, P.
  1988 Genetic and fossil evidence for the origin of modern humans. *Science*, 239, 1263–1268.
Stringer, C. B., Howell, F. C., and Melentis, J. K.
  1979 The significance of the fossil hominid skull from Petralona, Greece. *Journal of Archaeology*, 6, 235–253.
Sturdy, D. A.
  1975 Some reindeer economies in prehistoric Europe. In E. S. Higgs (ed.), *Palaeoeconomy* (pp. 55–95). Cambridge, England: Cambridge University Press.
Svoboda, J.
  1976 Zur Problematik der magdalénienzeitlichen Kunst Mitteleuropas. *Anthropologie*, 14, 163–193.
Svoboda, J.
  1980 *Křemencová industrie z Ondratic. K problému počátků mladého paleolitu*. Praha: Academia.
Svoboda, J.
  1982 Stone industries of Early Man: Some aspects of the instrumental adaptation process. In J. Jelínek (ed.), *Man and his origins, Anthropos 21* (pp. 223–228). Brno: Moravian Museum.
Svoboda, J.
  1983 Raw material sources in Early Upper Paleolithic Moravia: The concept of lithic exploitation areas. *Anthropologie*, 21, 147–158.
Svoboda, J.
  1984a Cadre chronologique et tendances évolutives du Paléolithique tchécoslovaque: Essai du synthése. *L'Anthropologie*, 88, 169–192.
Svoboda, J.
  1984b K některým aspektům studia exploatačních oblastí kamenných surovin. *Archeologické rozhledy*, 36, 361–369.
Svoboda, J.
  1984c Stránská skála: Study of a lithic exploitation area. In *Third Seminar in Petroarchaeology, Reports* (pp. 153–167). Plovdiv: Bulgarian Academy of Sciences.
Svoboda, J.
  1985 Průzkum v okolí Stránské skály (okr. Brno-město). *Přehled výzkumů*, 1983, 21–22.

Svoboda, J.
1986 Mistři kamenného dláta. Praha: Panorama.
Svoboda, J.
1987a Lithic industries of the Arago, Vértésszölös and Bilzingsleben hominids: comparison and evolutionary interpretation. *Current Anthropology*, 28, 219–227.
Svoboda, J.
1987b Paleolitické nálezy z Velkých Pavlovic (okr. Břeclav). *Přehled výzkumů*, 1985, 15.
Svoboda, J.
1987c Present state of the Late Upper Paleolithic studies in Moravia. In J. M. Burdukiewicz and M. Kobusiewicz (eds.), *Late glacial in Central Europe* (pp. 131–141). Wroclaw-Warszawa-Kraków-Gdansk-Lódz: Wydawnictwo PAN.
Svoboda, J.
1987d *Stránská skála. Bohunický typ v brněnskekotlině*. Praha: Academia.
Svoboda, J.
1987e Stratigrafická dokumentace na Červeném kopci (okr. Brno-město). *Přehled výzkumů*, 1985, 14.
Svoboda, J.
1987f Výzkum aurignacké stanice Stránská skála II. *Archeologické rozhledy*, 39, 376–383.
Svoboda, J.
1987g Výzkumy v Moravském krasu v roce 1984 (okr. Blansko). *Přehled výzkumů*, 1984, 12–13.
Svoboda, J.
1988 Early Upper Paleolithic industries in Moravia: A review of recent evidence. In J. K. Kozlowski (ed.), *L'Homme de Néandertal, Vol. 8, ERAUL 35* (pp. 169–192). Liège: Université de Liège.
Svoboda, J.
1989a Další objev paleolitického hrobu v Dolních Věstonicích. *Archeologické rozhledy*, 41, 233–242.
Svoboda, J.
1989b Middle Pleistocene adaptations in central Europe. *Journal of World Prehistory*, 3, 33–70.
Svoboda, J.
1989c Průzkum paleolitu na Vyškovsku v roce 1986 (okr. Vyškov). *Přehled výzkumů*, 1986, 4–5.
Svoboda, J.
1989d Výzkum mamutí skládky u Dolních Věstonic (okr. Břeclav). *Přehled výzkumů*, 1986, 7–8.
Svoboda, J.
1990a The Bohunician. In J. K. Kozlowski (ed.), *Les feuilles de pierre, ERAUL 42* (pp. 199–211). Liège: Université de Liège.
Svoboda, J.
1990b Moravia during the Upper Pleniglacial. In O. Soffer and C. Gamble (eds.), *World at 18,000 B.P., High Latitudes* (pp. 193–203). London: Unwin Hyman.
Svoboda, J.
1990c Průzkum paleolitu na Vyškovsku v roce 1987 (okr. Vyškov). *Přehled výzkumů*, 1987, 13–15.
Svoboda, J.
1990d Sídelní celek LP/1-4 v Dolních Věstonicích. In *Pravěké a slovanské osídlení Moravy* (pp. 15–25). Brno: Muzejní a vlastivědna společnost.

Svoboda, J.
1991a Beendigung der Untersuchungen der Anhäufung von Mammutknochen bei Dolní Věstonice. *Přehled výzkumů, 1988*, 9–10.
Svoboda J. (ed.)
1991b *Dolní Věstonice II, Western slope, ERAUL 54*. Liège: Université de Liège.
Svoboda, J.
1991c Neue Erkentnisse zur Pekárna Höhle im Mährischen Karst. *Archäologisches Korrespondenzblatt, 21*, 39–43.
Svoboda, J.
1991d Das Mittelpaläolithikum von Předmostí in Mähren: Ausgrabungen 1989–1991. *Archaeologica Austriaca, 75*, 1–10.
Svoboda, J.
1991e Stránská skála: Výsledky výzkumu v letech 1985–1987. *Památky archeologické, 82*, 5–47.
Svoboda, J.
1993a The Aurignacian of Stránská skála. In *Union Internationale des sciences pre- et protohistoriques, 12th Congres, Vol. 2* (pp. 216–223). Bratislava: Institute of Archaeology.
Svoboda, J.
1993b The complex origin of the Upper Paleolithic in the Czech and Slovak republics. In H. Knecht et al. (eds.), *Before Lascaux* (pp. 23–36). Boca Raton, FL: CRC Press.
Svoboda, J.
1993c Výzkum na Stránské skále v letech 1988–1989 (k.o. Slatina, okr. Brno-město). *Přehled výzkumů, 1989*, 14–16.
Svoboda, J.
1993d Erforschung der paläolithischen Station Dolní Věstonice I (Bez Břeclav). *Přehled výzkumů, 1990*, 67, 152–153.
Svoboda, J. (ed.)
1994a *Pavlov I, Excavations 1952–53, ERAUL 66*. Liège: Université de Liège.
Svoboda, J.
1994b The Pavlov site, Czech Republic: Lithic evidence from the Upper Paleolithic. *Journal of Field Archaeology, 21*, 69–81.
Svoboda, J.
1994c The Upper Paleolithic settlement of the Vyškov Gate: Regional survey, 1988–1992. *Památky archeologické, 85*, 18–34.
Svoboda, J.
1995a L'art gravettien en Moravie: Contexte, dates et styles. *L'Anthropologie, 100*, 258–272.
Svoboda, J.
1995b Environment and Upper Paleolithic adaptations in Moravia. In H. Ullrich (ed.), *Man and environment in the Palaeolithic, ERAUL 62* (pp. 291–295). Liège: Université de Liège.
Svoboda, J.
1995c Wedge-shaped microblade cores from Moravia and Silesia. *Archeologické rozhledy, 47*, 651–656.
Svoboda, J.
1996 Gravettian and Epigravettian chronologies in the Middle Danube area. In *Chronologies géophysiques et archéologiques du Paléolithique supérieur*. Ravello: in press.
Svoboda, J., Czudek, T., Havlíček, P., Ložek, V., Macoun, J., Přichystal, A., Svobodová, H., and Vlček, E.
1994 *Paleolit Moravy a Slezska*. Brno: Institute of Archaeology.

Svoboda, J., and Havlíček, P.
1987 Paleolitické nálezy a stratigrafická pozorování v Divákách (okr. Břeclav). Přehled výzkumů, 1985, 15.

Svoboda, J., and Ložek, V.
1993 Nález mezolitu a sled malakofauny v Průchodnicích. Bulletin České geologické společnosti, 1, 39–40.

Svoboda, J., Klíma, B., and Škrdla, P.
1995 The Gravettian project: Activities in the 1991–1994 period. Archeologické rozhledy, 47, 279–300.

Svoboda, J., Ložek, V., Přichystal, A., Svobodová, H., and Toul, J.
1996 Kolíbky: A Magdalenian site in the Moravian Karst. Quartär, 45/46, in press.

Svoboda, J., Ložek, V., Svobodová, H., and Škrdla, P.
1994 Předmostí after 110 years. Journal of Field Archaeology, 21, 457–472.

Svoboda, J., Macoun, J., and Přichystal, A.
1991 Acheulian finds from Silesia. Archeologické rozhledy, 43, 371–375.

Svoboda, J., and Přichystal, A.
1987 Szeletská industrie z Vincencova (Otaslavice, okr. Prostějov). Časopis Moravského muzea, 72, 5–19.

Svoboda, J., and Přichystal, A.
1990 Aurignacká industie z Prediny u Dobrochova (okr. Prostějov). Archeologické rozhledy, 42, 475–491.

Svoboda, J., and Seitl, L.
1985 Výzkum v Moravském krasu (okr. Blansko). Přehled výzkumů, 1983, 8–9.

Svoboda, J., and Seitl, L.
1987 Výzkumy v Moravském krasu v roce 1985 (okr. Blansko, Brno-venkov). Přehled výzkumů, 1985, 18.

Svoboda, J., Seitl, L., and Štrof, A.
1983 Výzkumy jeskynních výplní v severní části Moravského krasu (zpráva za rok 1981). Přehled výzkumů, 1981, 9–13.

Svoboda, J., and Simán, K.
1989 The Middle-Upper Paleolithic transition in Southeastern Central Europe (Czechoslovakia, Hungary). Journal of World Prehistory, 3, 283–322.

Svoboda, J., and Svobodová, H.
1985 Les industries du type Bohunice dans leur cadre stratigraphique et écologique. L'Anthropologie, 89, 505–514.

Svoboda, J., and Škrdla, P.
1995 The Bohunician technology. In H. Dibble and O. Bar-Yosef (eds.), The definition and interpretation of Levallois technology (pp. 279–300). Madison: Prehistory Press.

Svoboda, J., Škrdla, P., and Jarošová, L.
1993 Analyse einer Siedlungsfläche von Dolní Věstonice. Archäologisches Korrespondenzblatt, 23, 393–404.

Svoboda, J., and Vlček, E.
1991 La nouvelle sépulture de Dolní Věstonice (DV XVI), Tchécoslovaquie. L'Anthropologie, 95, 323–328.

Svoboda, J., and Wodecki, P.
1981 Paleolitická stanice v Záblatí, okr. Karviná. Archeologické rozhledy, 33, 676–679.

Svobodová, H.
1987a Přírodní prostředí. In J. Svoboda (ed.), Stránská skála, Bohunický typ v brněnské kotlině (pp. 18–21). Praha: Academia.

Svobodová, H.
1987b Pylová analýza půdního horizontu ze Stránské skály II. *Archeologické rozhledy*, 39, 383–385.

Svobodová, H.
1988 Pollenanalytische Untersuchung aus der Kůlna-Höhle. In K. Valoch (ed.), *Die Erforschung der Kůlna-Hohle 1961–1976, Anthropos 24* (pp. 209–214). Brno: Moravské Muzeum.

Svobodová, H.
1991a The pollen analysis of Dolní Věstonice II, section No. 1. In J. Svoboda (ed.), *Dolní Věstonice II, Western Slope, ERAUL 54* (pp. 75–88). Liège: Université de Liège.

Svobodová, H.
1991b Pollen analysis of the Upper Palaeolithic triple burial at Dolní Věstonice. *Archeologické rozhledy*, 43, 505–510.

Svobodová, H.
1991c *Vývoj vegetace jižní Moravy v pozdním glaciálu a holocénu v závislosti na osídlení (palynologická studie)*. C.Sc. dissertation, Institute of Systematic and Ecological Biology, Brno.

Svobodová, H.
1992 Palaeobotanical evidence on the Late Glacial in the Moravian Karst. In J. Eder-Kovar (ed.), *Palaeovegetational development in Europe and the regions relevant to its palaeofloristic evolution* (pp. 81–85). Wien: Naturhistorisches Museum.

Svobodová, H., and Svoboda, J.
1988 Chronostratigraphie et paléoécologie du Paléolithique supérieur morave d'aprés les fouilles récentes. In A. Tuffreau (ed.), *Cultures et industries paléolithiques en milieu loessique* (pp. 11–15). Amiens: Printex.

Szilvássy, J.
1983 Hautleistenbefunde aus der jungpaläolithischen Station Pavlov (Südmähren, ČSSR). *Mitteilungen der Anthropologischen Gesellschaft Wien*, 113, 61–64.

Szombathy, J.
1884a Ausgrabungen in den mährischen Höhlen im Jahre 1883. *Sitzungsberichte der Kaiserlichen Akademie der Wissenschaften*, 89, 1 Abteilung, 353–358.

Szombathy, J.
1884b Über Ausgrabungen in den mährischen Höhlen im Jahre 1881. *Sitzungsberichte der Kaiserlichen Akademie der Wissenschaften*, 85, 1 Abeitelung, 90–107.

Szombathy, J.
1910 Die diluvialen Kulturschichten von Willendorf. *Mitteilungen der Anthropologischen Gesellschaft Wien*, 40, 4–9.

Szombathy, J.
1925 Die diluvialen Menschenreste aus der Fürst-Johanns-Höhle bei Lautsch in Mähren. *Die Eiszeit*, 2, 1–34, 73–95.

Šibrava, V. (ed.)
1979 Erforschung der Pleistozänablagerungen auf dem Hügel Zlatý kopec bei Přezletice (NO–Rand von Prag), Teil 1. *Anthropozoikum*, 12, 57–146.

Škrdla, P.
1994 Refitting. In J. Svoboda (ed.), *Pavlov I, Excavations 1952–53, ERAUL 66* (pp. 27–28). Liège: Université de Liège.

Škrdla, P.
1996 Rekonstrukce pravěkých technologií na Stránské skále. *Pravěk*, 4.

Škrdla, P., and Plch, M.
1993a Nová mladopaleolitická kolekce z lokality Mohelno (okr. Třebíč). *Přehled výzkumů, 1990*, 67–70, 154–156.

Škrdla, P., and Plch, M.
1993b Osídlení epigravettienu v okolí Stránské skály (okr. Brno-Město). *Archeologické rozhledy*, 45, 429–435.
Štelcl, J., and Malina, J.
1975 *Základy petroarcheologie*. Brno: Faculty of Science.
Thieme, H., and Veil, S.
1985 Neue Untersuchungen zum eemzeitlichen Elefanten-Jagdpatz Lehringen, Ldkr. Verde. *Die Kunde, Neue Folge*, 36, 11–58.
Thoma, S.
1957 Un fragment d'occipital d'Homo sapiens fossilis provenant de l'abri de Tapolca: *Hermann Otto Muzeum, Miskolcz*, 1, 60–69.
Thoma, S.
1966 L'occipital de l'Homo mindelien de Vértészöllös. *L'Anthropologie*, 70, 495–534.
Thoma, S.
1967 Human teeth from the Lower Paleolithic of Hungary. *Zeitschrift für Morphologie und Anthropologie*, 58, 152–180.
Thoma, S.
1969 Biometrische Studie über das Occipitale von Vértészöllös. *Zeitschrift für Morphologie und Anthropologie*, 60, 229–241.
Tode, A., Preul, F., Richter, K., Selle, W., Pfaffenberg, K., Kleinschmidt, A., and Guenther, E.
1953 Die Untersuchung der paläolithischen Freilandstation von Salzgitter-Lebenstedt. *Eiszeitalter und Gegenwart*, 3, 144–215.
Tomášková, S.
1994 Use-wear analysis and its spatial interpretation. In J. Svoboda (ed.), *Pavlov I, Excavations 1952–53, ERAUL 66* (pp. 28–40). Liège: Université de Liège.
Trnka, G.
1990 Ein neuer paläolithischer Blattspitzenfund aus Schletz in Niederösterreich. *Archäologie Österreichs*, 1, 20–27.
Trnka, G.
1992 Eine Station des Epiaurignaciens in Alberndorf. *Archäologie Österreichs*, 3, 30–31.
Trňáčková, Z.
1967 Paleolitické nálezy z Droždína u Olomouce. *Práce odboru společenských věd Vlastivědného ústavu v Olomouci*, 16, 1–31.
Ullrich, H.
1979 Bemerkungen zu den Defekten an jungpaläolithischen Kinderunterkiefer von Ranis. *Zeitschrift für Archäologie*, 13, 153–161.
Urban, B.
1984 Palynology of Central European loess-soil sequences. In M. Pécsi (ed.), *Lithology and stratigraphy of loess and paleosoils* (pp. 229–248). Budapest: Geographical Research Institute.
Valoch, K.
1953 Paleolitické sídliště u Ochozské jeskyně v Moravském krasu. *Časopis Moravského muzea*, 38, 11–26.
Valoch, K.
1954 Paleolitická stanice na Stránské skále u Brna. *Časopis Moravského muzea*, 39, 5–30.
Valoch, K.
1955a Spodní aurignacien v Maloměřicích u Brna. *Práce brněnské základny ČSAV*, 27/6, 321–340.

Valoch, K.
1955b Výzkum paleolitického naleziště v Rozdrojovicích u Brna. *Časopis Moravského muzea*, 40, 5–32.

Valoch, K.
1956 Paleolitické stanice s listovitými hroty nad údolím Bobravy. *Časopis Moravského muzea*, 41, 5–44.

Valoch, K.
1957 Jeskyně Šipka a Čertova díra u Štramberku I. Mladší paleolit. *Časopis Moravského muzea*, 42, 5–24.

Valoch, K.
1959 Lösse und paläolithische Kulturen in der Tschechoslowakei. *Quartär*, 10–11, 115–149.

Valoch, K.
1960a Bemerkenswerte jungpaläolithische Steingeräte aus Předmostí in Mähren. *Časopis Moravského muzea*, 45, 21–26.

Valoch, K.
1960b K otázce předmagdalénského osídlení jeskyní Adlerovy a Křížovy na Říčkách u Brna. *Časopis Moravského muzea*, 45, 5–20.

Valoch, K.
1960c *Magdalénien na Moravě, Anthropos 12*. Brno: Moravské Muzeum.

Valoch, K.
1961a Benützte und gravierte Schiefergerölle im Magdalénien Mährens. *Časopis Moravského muzea*, 46, 5–18.

Valoch, K.
1961b Die Blattspitzenindustrie von Ořechov II bei Brno (Brünn). *Anthropozoikum*, 10, 35–47.

Valoch, K.
1961c K chronologii paleolitických kultur v Československu. *Anthropozoikum*, 9, 15–20.

Valoch, K.
1962a Altpaläolithische Steingeräte aus der Umgebung von Brno. *Anthropozoikum*, 11, 163–184.

Valoch, K.
1962b Archaické industrie mladšího paleolitu v okolí Brna. *Časopis Moravského muzea*, 47, 5–34.

Valoch, K.
1963 Borky I, eine Freilandstation des Magdaléniens in Brno-Maloměřice. *Časopis Moravského muzea*, 48, 5–30.

Valoch, K.
1964 Borky II, eine Freilandstation des Aurignaciens in Brno-Maloměřice. *Časopis Moravského muzea*, 49, 5–48.

Valoch, K.
1965a Die altsteinzetlichen Begehungen der Höhle Pod hradem. *Anthropos*, 18, 93–106.

Valoch, K.
1965b Altsteinzeitliche Funde aus Brno und Umgebung. *Časopis Moravského muzea*, 50, 21–30.

Valoch, K.
1965c *Jeskyně Šipka a Čertova díra u Štramberku, Anthropos 17*. Brno: Moravské Muzeum.

Valoch, K.
1965d Industrien des Szeletiens im Raume des Kromauer Waldes in Südmähren. *Časopis Moravského muzea*, 50, 5–20.

Valoch, K.
  1965e Paleolitické nálezy z Rytířské jeskyně v Moravském krasu. *Anthropozoikum*, 3, 141–155.
Valoch, K.
  1966a Die altertümlichen Blattspitzenindustrien von Jezeřany (Südmähren). *Časopis Moravského muzea*, 51, 5–60.
Valoch, K.
  1966b Die Quarzitindustrie aus Býči skála in Mähren. *Quartär*, 17, 51–89.
Valoch, K.
  1966c Spätpaläolithische Stationen im Raum von Bučovice in Mähren. *Sborník prací Filosofické fakulty Brněnské university*, 15, 5–14.
Valoch, K.
  1967 Die altsteinzetlichen Stationen im Raum von Ondratice in Mähren. *Časopis Moravského muzea*, 52, 5–46.
Valoch, K.
  1968a Evolution of the Palaeolithic in Central and Eastern Europe. *Current Anthropology*, 9, 351–390.
Valoch, K.
  1968b Eine jungpaläolithische Station in Brno-Kohoutovice. *Sborník prací Filosofické fakulty Brněnské university*, 17, 63–80.
Valoch, K.
  1969a Darstellung von Mensch und Tier in Předmostí in Mähren. *Jahrbuch für prähistorische und ethnographische Kunst*, 22, 1–9.
Valoch, K.
  1969b Das Mittelpaläolithikum mit Blattspitzen aus der Höhle Kůlna im Mährischen Karst. *Časopis Moravského muzea*, 43/54, 5–30.
Valoch, K.
  1969c Das Paläolithikum in der Tschechoslowakei. In *Quarternary in Czechoslovakia* (pp. 69–149). Prague: Ústřední ústav geologický.
Valoch, K.
  1971 Eine mittelpaläolithische Industrie von Maršovice I in Südmähren (ČSSR). *Anthropologie*, 9, 29–47.
Valoch, K.
  1972 Gab es eine altpaläolitische Besiedlung der Stránská skála? *Anthropos*, 20, 199–204.
Valoch, K.
  1973 Neslovice, eine bedeutende Oberflächenfundstelle des Szeletiens in Mähren. *Časopis Moravského muzea*, 58, 5–76.
Valoch, K.
  1974a Nové kolekce ve sbírkách ústavu Anthropos Moravského muzea. *Přehled výzkumů*, 1973, 9–14.
Valoch, K.
  1974b Podstránská, eine Oberflächenfundstation des Aurignaciens in Brno-Židenice. *Časopis Moravského muzea*, 59, 5–42.
Valoch, K.
  1974c Eine spätpaläolitische Industrie aus Sady bei Uherské Hradiště. *Sborník prací Filosofické fakulty Brněnské university*, 20, 111–124.
Valoch, K.
  1975a Ornamentale Gravierungen und Ziergegenstände von Předmostí bei Přerov in Mähren. *Anthropologie N.S.*, 13, 81–91.

REFERENCES

Valoch, K.
1975b Paleolitická stanice v Koněvově ulici v Brně. *Archeologické rozhledy*, 27, 3–17.

Valoch, F.
1975c Příspěvek k otázce provenience surovin v moravském paleolitu. *Folia Facultatis Scientiae naturalis*, 16, Geologica, 27, 83–87.

Valoch, K.
1975d Ein spätes Aurignacien in Mähren. *Časopis Moravského muzea*, 60, 23–44.

Valoch, K.
1976a *Die altsteinzeitliche Fundstelle in Brno-Bohunice*. Praha: Academia.

Valoch, K.
1976b Das entwickelte Aurignacien von Tvarožná bei Brno. *Časopis Moravského muzea*, 61, 7–30.

Valoch, K.
1976c Un groupe spécifique du paléolithique ancien et moyen d'Europe Centrale. In *Union internationale des sciences pré- et protohistoriques, 9th Congrès, Collogue X* (pp. 86–91). Nice: Louis-Jean.

Valoch, K.
1976d Neue mittelpaläolithische Industrien in Südmahren. *Anthropologie*, 14, 55–64.

Valoch, K.
1977a Neue alt- und mittelpaläolithische Funde aus der Umgebung von Brno. *Anthropozoikum*, 11, 93–112.

Valoch, K.
1977b Neue frühjungpaläolithische Fundstellen in der Umgebung von Brno. *Časopis Moravského muzea*, 62, 7–27.

Valoch, K.
1978a Eine gravierte Frauendarstellung aus Býčí skála-Höhle in Mähren. *Anthropologie*, 16, 31–33.

Valoch, K.
1978b Nové poznatky o paleolitu v Československu. *Sborník prací Filosofické fakulty Brněnské university*, 22/23, E, 7–25.

Valoch, K.
1978c Die paläolithische Fundstelle Bořitov I (Bez. Blansko). *Časopis Moravského muzea*, 63, 7–24.

Valoch, K.
1979a Paleolitický nález z Brna-Maloměřic. *Archeologické rozhledy*, 31, 290–291.

Valoch, K.
1979b Paleolit středního Pomoraví. *Studie Muzea Kroměřížska*, 79, 22–35.

Valoch, K.
1980a Ein Faustkeil aus Mittelmähren. *Anthropologie*, 18, 287–289.

Valoch, K.
1980b La fin des temps glaciaires en Moravie (Tchécoslovaquie). *L'Anthropologie*, 84, 380–390.

Valoch, K.
1981a Beitrag zur Kenntnis des Pavloviens. *Archeologické rozhledy*, 33, 279–298.

Valoch, K.
1981b Einige mittelpaläolithische Industrien aus der Höhle Kůlna im Mährischen Karst. *Časopis Moravského muzea*, 66, 47–67.

Valoch, K.
1981c Stratifikovaný valounový nástroj ze Sedlešovic u Znojma. *Archeologické rozhledy*, 33, 92–94.

Valoch, K.
1982a Altpaläolithische Geröllgeräte in Südmähren. *Anthropozoikum*, 14, 127–139.

Valoch, K.
1982b Die Beingeräte von Předmostí in Mähren. *Anthropologie*, 20, 57–69.

Valoch, K.
1982c Neue paläolithische Funde von Brno-Bohunice. *Časopis Moravského muzea*, 67, 31–48.

Valoch, K.
1983 Příspěvek k paleolitickému osídlení Prostějovska. *Časopis Moravského muzea*, 68, 5–19.

Valoch, K.
1984a Le Taubachien, sa géochronologie, paléontologie et paléoethnologie. *L'Anthropologie*, 88, 193–208.

Valoch, K.
1984b Výzkum paleolitu ve Vedrovicích V (okr. Znojmo). *Časopis Moravského muzea*, 69, 5–22.

Valoch, K. (ed.)
1985a Das Frühaurignacien von Vedrovice II und Kupařovice I in Südmähren. *Anthropozoikum*, 16, 107–203.

Valoch, K.
1985b Paleolitická stanice v Hostějově (o. Uh. Hradiště). *Časopis Moravského muzea*, 70, 5–16.

Valoch, K.
1986 Příspěvek k poznání zdrojů surovin v mladém paleolitu na Moravě. *Časopis Moravského muzea*, 71, 5–18.

Valoch, K.
1987a Contribution to the architecture of Upper Paleolithic dwellings. *Anthropologie*, 25, 115–116.

Valoch, K.
1987b The Early Palaeolithic site Stránská skála I near Brno (Czechoslovakia). *Anthropologie*, 25, 125–142.

Valoch, K.
1987c Eine neue frühjungpaläolithische Fundstelle in Brno-Židenice. *Časopis Moravského muzea*, 72, 45–51.

Valoch, K.
1987d Raw materials used in Moravian Middle and Upper Paleolithic. In *International Conference on Prehistoric Flint Mining and Lithic Raw Material Identification* (pp. 263–268). Budapest-Sümeg: Magyar Nemzeti Muzeum.

Valoch, K. (ed.)
1988 *Die Erforschung der Kůlna Höhle 1961–1976, Anthropos 24*. Brno: Moravské Muzeum.

Valoch, K.
1990a Mittelpaläolithische Fundstellen in der Umgebung von Dolní Kounice in Südmähren. *Časopis Moravského muzea*, 75, 3–15.

Valoch, K.
1990b La Moravie il y a 40.000 ans. In C. Farizy (ed.), *Paléolithique moyen récent et paléolithique supérieur ancien* (pp. 115–124). Nemours: Musée de Préhistoire d'Ile-de-France.

Valoch, K.
1991 Altpaläolithische Geröllgeräte aus der Umgebung von Dolní Kounice in Südmähren. *Časopis Moravského muzea*, 76, 3–17.

Valoch, K.
   1993a V záři ohňů nejstarších lovců. In V. Podborský (ed.), *Pravěké dějiny Moravy* (pp. 11–70). Brno: Muzejní a vlastivědná spol.
Valoch, K. (ed.)
   1993b Vedrovice V, eine Siedlung des Szeletiens in Sudmahren. *Quartär, 43/44*, 7–93.
Valoch, K., and Dvořák, J.
   1956 Staropaleolitické nálezy z okolí Moravského Krumlova. *Archeologické rozhledy, 8*, 145–149.
Valoch, K., and Seitl, L.
   1988 Grabung auf der paläolithischen Fundstelle Maršovice II (Bez. Znojmo) in Südmähren. *Časopis Moravského muzea, 73*, 15–28.
Valoch, K., Smolíková, L., and Zeman, A.
   1978 The Middle Pleistocene site Přibice I in South Moravia. *Anthropologie, 14*, 229–241.
Vandiver, P., Soffer, O., Klíma, B., and Svoboda, J.
   1990 Venuses and wolverines: The origins of ceramic technology ca 26,000 B.P. In W. D. Kingery (ed.), *The changing roles of ceramics in society* (pp. 13–81). Westerville, OH: American Ceramic Society.
Vaňura, J.
   1965a Nález moláru neandrtálského člověka na haldě před jeskyní Švédův stůl v Moravském krasu. *Časopis pro mineralogii a geologii, 10*, 337–341.
Vaňura, J.
   1965b *Nové nálezy zbytků neandrtálského člověka v jeskyni Švédův stůl v Moravském krasu*. Manuscript, Brno.
Vértés, L.
   1964 *Tata, eine mittelpaläolithische Travertinsiedlung in Ungarn*. Budapest: Akadémiai Kiadó.
Vértés, L.
   1965 Discovery of Homo erectus in Hungary. *Antiquity, 29*, 303.
Verworn, M., Bonnet, R., and Steinmann, G.
   1919 *Der diluviale Menschenfund von Oberkassel bei Bonn*. Wiesbaden.
Virchow, H.
   1917 Der Taubacher Zahn des prähistorischen Museums der Universität Jena. *Prähistorische Zeitschrift, 9*, 1–18.
Vlček, E.
   1949 Travertinový výlitek neandertaloidního typu z Gánovců u Popradu. *Archeologické rozhledy, 1*, 156–161.
Vlček, E.
   1951a Otisky papilárních linií mladodiluviálního člověka z Dolních Věstonic. *Zprávy Anthropologické společnosti Brno, 4*, 90–94.
Vlček, E.
   1951b Pleistocenní člověk z jeskyně sv. Prokopa. *Anthropozoikum 1*, 213–226
Vlček, E.
   1952a Empreintes papillaires d'un homme paléolithique. *L'Anthropologie, 56*, 557–558.
Vlček, E.
   1952b Nález pleistocenního člověka v jeskyních Zlatého koně. *Československý kras, 5*, 180–191.
Vlček, E.
   1952c První nález pleistocenního člověka v Českém krasu. *Československý kras, 5*, 2–9.

Vlček, E.
1953   Nález neandrtálského člověka na Slovensku. *Slovenská archeológia*, 1, 5–132.
Vlček, E.
1955   The fossil man of Gánovce, Czechoslovakia. *Journal of the Royal Anthropological Institute*, 85, 163–171.
Vlček, E.
1957a Další nálezy pozůstatků pleistocenního člověka na Zlatém koni u Koněprus. *Archeologické rozhledy*, 9, 305–310.
Vlček, E.
1957b Lidský zub pleistocenního stáří ze Silické Brezové. *Anthropozoikum*, 6, 397–405.
Vlček, E.
1957c Pleistocenní člověk z jeskyně na Zlatém Koni u Koněprus. *Anthropozoikum*, 6, 283–311.
Vlček, E.
1958a Neandertálský člověk na Spiši. *Przeglad antropologiczny*, 24, 138–158.
Vlček, E.
1958b Die Reste des Neanderthalmenschen aus dem Gebiete der Tschechoslowakei. In *Hundert Jahre Neanderthaler* (pp. 107–120). Utrecht: Utrecht University.
Vlček, E.
1961   Pozůstatky mladopleistocenního člověka z Pavlova. *Památky archeologické*, 52, 46–56.
Vlček, E.
1964   Neuer Fund eines Neandertalers in der Tschechoslowakei. *Anthropologischer Anzeiger*, 27, 162–166.
Vlček, E.
1967   Morphological relations of the fossil human types Brno and Cro-Magnon in the European Late Pleistocene. *Folia Morphologica*, 15, 214–221.
Vlček, E.
1968a Der jungpleistozäne Menschenfund aus Svitávka in Mähren. *Anthropos*, 19, 262–270.
Vlček, E.
1968b Nález pozůstatků neandrtálce v Šali na Slovensku. *Anthropozoikum*, 5, 105–124.
Vlček, E.
1969   *Neandertaler der Tschechoslowakei*. Praha: Academia.
Vlček, E.
1970   Relations morphologiques des types humains fossiles de Brno et Cro-Magnon au Pleistocéne supérieur d'Europe. In G. Camp and G. Olivier (eds.), *L'Homme de Cro-Magnon* (pp. 59–72). Paris.
Vlček. E.
1978a Diagnosis of a fragment of the "hominid molar" from Přezletice, Czechoslovakia. *Current Anthropology*, 19, 145–146.
Vlček, E.
1978b A new discovery of Homo erectus in Central Europe. *Journal of Human Evolution*, 7, 239–251.
Vlček, E.
1979   "Homo erectus bilzingslebensis"—Eine neue Form des mittelpleistozänen Menschen Europas. *Ethnographisch-archäologische Zeitschrift*, 20, 634–661.
Vlček, E.
1983   Über einen weiteren Schädelrest des Homo erectus von Bilzingsleben. *Ethnographisch-archäologische Zeitschrift*, 24, 321–325.

Vlček, E.
1985 Der fossile Mensch aus Weimar-Ehringsdorf. In J Herrmann and H Ullrich (eds.), *Menschwerdung—Biotischer und gesellschaftlicher Entwicklungsprozess* (pp. 111–117). Berlin: Deutscher Verlag der Wissenschaften.

Vlček, E.
1986a Les Antenéandertaliens en Europe centrale et leur comparaison avec L'Homme de Tautavel. *L'Anthropologie*, 90, 143–153.

Vlček, E.
1986b Die ontophylogenetische Entwicklung des Gebisses des Neandertalers. *Verhandlungen der Anatomischen Gesellschaft*, 80, 295–296.

Vlček, E.
1987 Funde von Zähnen des Homo erectus aus dem Travertin bei Bilzingsleben. *Jahreschrift für mitteldeutsche Vorgeschichte*, 70, 83–94.

Vlček, E.
1988 Gánovecký nález v CT–počítačové tomografii. *Slovenská archeológia*, 36, 353–362.

Vlček, E.
1989a Die hominidenreste von Bilzingsleben: Über Neufunde von 1981–1987. *Ethnographisch-archäologische Zeitschrift*, 30, 270–286.

Vlček, E.
1989b Homo erectus in Europe. *Ethnographisch-archäologische Zeitschrift*, 30, 287–305.

Vlček, E.
1990 Nové nálezy lovců mamutů v Dolních Věstonicích. *Sborník Československé společnosti antropologické*, 1989, 1–9.

Vlček, E.
1991a L'homme fossile en Europe centrale. *L'Anthropologie*, 95, 409–472.

Vlček, E.
1991b *Die Mammutjäger von Dolní Věstonice: Archäologie und Museum, Heft 22*, Liestal: Amt für Museen und Archäologie.

Vlček, E.
1993a *Fossile Menschenfunde von Weimar-Ehringsdorf*, Stuttgart: K. Theiss Verlag.

Vlček, E. (ed.)
1993b *Lovci mamutů z Dolních Věstonic*. Praha: Národní Museum.

Vlček, E., and Kysela, B.
1979 Zur Diagnose des Molars von Přezletice. *Anthropozoikum*, 12, 111–115.

Wankel, H.
1871a Der Menschenknochenfund in der Býčí skála Höhle. *Mitteilungen der Anthropologischen Gesellschaft Wien*, 1, 101.

Wankel, H.
1871b Prähistorische Alterthümer in den mährischen Höhlen. *Mitteilungen der Anthropologischen Gesellschaft Wien*, 1, 266–282, 309–314, 329–343.

Wankel, H.
1881 Prähistorische Funde in der Pekárna-Höhle in Mähren. *Mitteilungen der Anthropologischen Gesellschaft Wien*, 10, 347–348.

Wankel, H.
1882 *Bilder aus der Mährischen Schweiz*. Wien.

Wankel, H.
1884 První stopy lidské na Moravě. *Časopis Vlastivědného musejního spolku Olomouc*, 1, 2–7, 41–49, 89–100, 137–147.

Wankel, H.
1890 Ložiska mamutí v Předmostí. *Časopis Vlastivědného spolku musejního Olomouc*, 7, 1–10, 53–64.
Wankel, H.
1892 *Die prähistorische Jagd in Mähren*. Olmütz: Kramář & Procházka.
Weidenreich, F.
1928 *Der Schädelfund von Weimar-Ehringsdorf*. Jena.
Weinert, H.
1936 Der Urmenschschädel von Steinheim. *Zeitschrift für Morphologie und Anthropologie*, 25, 463–518.
Weniger, G. C.
1987 Magdalenian settlement pattern and subsistence in Central Europe: The Southwestern and Central German cases. In O. Soffer (ed.), *The Pleistocene Old World* (pp. 201–215). New York–London: Plenum Press.
Weniger, G. C.
1989 The Magdalenian in Western Central Europe: Settlement pattern and regionality. *Journal of World Prehistory*, 3, 323–372.
West, D.
1996 Horse hunting, processing, and transport in the Middle Danube. In J. Svoboda (ed.), *Paleolithic in the Middle Danube Region*. Brno: Institute of Archaeology.
White, R.
1993 Technological and social dimensions of the "Aurignacian age": Body ornaments across Europe. In H. Knecht et al. (eds.), *Before Lascaux* (pp. 277–299). Boca Raton, FL: CRC Press.
Woldřich, J.
1916 První nálezy Machaeorodů v jeskynním diluviu moravském a dolnorakouském. *Rozpravy České akademie*, 25, třída 2/12, 1–8.
Wurmbrand, G. V.
1873 Gleichzeitigkeit des Menschen mit dem Mammuth. *Mitteilungen der Anthropologischen Gesellschaft Wien*, 3, 123–135.
Wurmbrand, G. V.
1878 Über behauptete Höhlenwohnungen im Löss bei Joslowitz. *Mitteilungen der Anthropologischen Gesellschaft Wien*, 8, 128–130.
Wurmbrand, G. V.
1879 Über die Anwesenheit des Menschen zur Zeit der Lössbildung. *Denkschrift der mathematisch-naturwissenschaftlichen Classe der kaiserlichen Akademie der Wissenschaften*, 39, (Wien).
Xirotiris, N., and Vlček, E.
1982 Arago et Petralona: Compraison de l'endocrane. *Congrès international de Paléontologie humaine*, communication 21 October, Nice.
Zeman, A.
1982 Fluviální a fluviolakustrinní sedimenty brněnské kotliny. *Studia geographica*, 80, 55–84.
Zeman, A.
1983 Morphostratigraphical levels of the nonglaciated region between the northern and Alpine glaciations in Czechoslovalia. *Project 73/1/24, Report 9* (pp. 171–175) (Paris).
Zotz, L., and Freund, G.
1951 Die paläolithische und mesolithische Kulturentwicklung in Böhmen und Mähren. *Quartär*, 5, 7–40.

Žebera, K.
1946   Nálezová zpráva o úštěpovém pěstním klínu z Přívozu u Moravské Ostravy. *Věstník Královské české společnosti nauk*, 1945 (reprint) 1–6.
Žebera, K.
1954   Výsledky výzkumu kvartérních sedimentů v Předmostí u Přerova na Moravě za rok 1952. *Anthropozoikum*, 3, 139–170.
Žebera, K.
1958   Československo ve starší době kamenné. Praha: Nakladatelství Československé Akademie Věd.
Žebera, K., Ložek, V., Kneblová, V., Fejfar, O., and Mazálek, M.
1955   Zpráva o II. etapě geologického výzkumu kvartéru v Předmostí u Přerova na Moravě. *Anthropozoikum*, 4, 291–362.

Index

Abri Tapolca (Hungary), 56
Acheulean (hand-axe) culture, 7, 44, 81–82, 90, 195
Adlerova Cave, Ochoz, 181, 186, 223, 239
Aggsbachian culture, 131
Alberndorf (Austria), 115
Alojzov, 239
Andernach (Germany), 181
Antler. See Bone and antler industries
Arago (France), hominid remains from, 39, 45
Art. See Rituals; Symbolism (art)
Aurignacian culture, 7, 8, 10, 11, 56, 103, 105, 114–118, 195

Babice, 239. See also Jáchymka
Bachokirian culture, 107
Bačo Kiro (Bulgaria), 103
Bačov, 240
Balcarova Cave, 174, 194, 205, 240
Balla Cave (Hungary), human remains from, 69
Banín, 240
Barová Cave, 240
  description of, 208, 209
  excavations at, 11
  Magdalenian occupation at, 175–176, 185
  Pleistocene deposits at, 22, 23
  Upper Paleolithic fauna at, 174
  Upper Pleistocene deposits at, 32
Beauty, Gravettian view of, 72–73

Bečov (Bohemia)
  Acheulian industry at, 82
  Lower Paleolithic occupation at, 77, 80, 93
  Lower Pleistocene deposits at, 37
  powdered ocher found at, 96
Bečov Mousterian industry, 82, 84
Bečov quartzite, 186
Bělov, 240
Beroun (Bohemia), 77
Bílovec, 240
Bilzingsleben (Germany)
  hominid remains from, 39–43
  incised animal bones from, 96
  Lower Paleolithic occupation at, 77, 81, 92–93, 95
Black Venus of Dolní Věstonice, 157
Blansko, 240
Blatec, 240
Blazice, 240
Blažovice, 240
Bohaté Málkovice, 240
Bohemian culture, 77
Bohunice, Brno–město, 240
Bohunice–Červený kopec (Red Hill)
  description of, 206–207
  Lower and Middle Paleolithic stratigraphy of, 78–79
  Lower Paleolithic artifacts from, 80
  Lower Paleolithic deposits at, 77
  Pleistocene deposits at, 16, 21
  Upper Paleolithic occupation at, 102

297

Bohunician culture, 11, 102, 105, 107–110, 123, 195, 206–207
Bohuslavice, 82, 240
Bojanovice, 240
Boleradice, 240
Bone and antler industries
  Aurignacian, 115
  Epigravettian, 145
  Gravettian, 168
  Magdalenian, 179, 188–190, 192
Bořetice, 240
Bořitov, 111, 240
Bořitov chert, 123, 199, 201, 207
Boršice, 207, 240
Boskovice, 240
Bratčice, 240
Brillenhohle (Germany), 179
Brno, 77–78. See also Bohunice; Červený kopec; Hády; Jundrov; Kohoutovice; Líšeň; Maloměřice; Modřice; Nová hora; Podstránská; Stránska skála; Švédské Šance
Brno I (fossil human remains), 60–62
Brno–Francouzská Street (Brno II), 240
  burial at, 170
  description of, 207–208
  ivory statue from, 167
  Upper Paleolithic human remains from, 60, 62, 72
Brno–Kamenná Street, 240
Brno–Malá Klajdovka, 240
Brno–Růženin dvůr, 79, 80, 81, 240
Brno–Svitava River terraces, 75
Brno–Vídeňská Koněvova, 135, 240
Brodek, 240
Brumovice, 240
Březina. See Drátenická Cave; Nová Drátenická Cave; Výpustek Cave; Žitného Cave
Buchlovice, 240
Bučovice, 240
Bukovany, 241
Bulhary, 26, 28, 137, 241
Burials
  Gravettian, 72–73, 169–170
  Magdalenian, 194
Býčí skála (Bull Rock) Cave, Habrůvka, 241
  description of, 208–209

Býčí skála (Bull Rock) Cave, Habrůvka (cont.)
  Magdalenian occupation at, 181, 182, 185, 186, 187
Býčí skála chert, 200
Býkovice, 241
Bystrovany, 241

Cave Bear Age, 5
Caves
  early research in, 4, 197
  fossil hominid remains from, 47–56
  Magdalenian occupation of, 171, 179–185, 187
  Middle Paleolithic occupation of, 90
Central Europe, geography of, 1–4, 195–196
Ceramics, Gravettian, 164, 168
Charváty, 241
Chronology, Moravian, 4–8
Chuchelná, 241
Clay figurines, Gravettian, 168
Climate, during Pleistocene, 16–19, 33–36
Cretaceous chert, 93, 110, 153, 187
Cro-Magnon fossil human remains, 59, 101
Cryomeres (glaciations), 1, 10, 11, 16–19, 21–25, 34–35
Cvrčovice, 241
Čebín, 241
Čechovice–Domamyslice, 241
Černá Hora, 241
Čertova díra Cave, Štramberk, 5, 6, 7, 234–235, 241
Čertova pec Cave (Slovakia), 102
Červený kopec, 241. See also Bohunice–Červený kopec (Red Hill)

Danube River, 195–196
Death, Gravettian view of, 72–73
Dědice, 241
Diváky, 241
Döbritz (Germany), 73
Dobrochov, 241
Dobronice, 241
Dobrotice, 241
Dolany, 241
Dolní Kounice, 20, 21, 79, 237
Dolní Věstonice
  excavations at, 7, 8, 11

Dolní Věstonice (cont.)
 Gravettian occupation at, 133, 137, 141, 147, 157
 Lower and Middle Pleistocene stratigraphy of, 79
 meeting in 1995 at, 13
 Pleistocene deposits at, 21
 relationship to Russian Central Plain sites, 10
Dolní Věstonice, Site I, 241
 burials at, 170
 description of, 209–212
 Gravettian occupation at, 141, 147, 168
 human remains from, 60, 64–66, 71–72
Dolní Věstonice, Site II, 241
 burials at, 170
 description of, 212–214
 Gravettian occupation at, 141, 147–151, 153, 156, 168
 human remains from, 60, 64–66, 71–72
 soils at, 105
 Upper Pleistocene sequence at, 26
Dolní Věstonice, Site III, 214, 241
Domaželice, 241
Doubravice, 241
Drahanovice, 242
Drahany quartzite, 187
Drahotuše, 242
Drásov, 242
Drátenická Cave, Březina, 85, 219, 242
Dreveník Hill (Slovakia), 38
Drnovice, 242
Droždín, Olomouc, 242
Drysice, 242
Dubicko, 242
Dukovany, 242
Dzeravá skála Cave (Slovakia), 56

Ehringsdorf (Germany)
 hominid remains from, 43–44
 Paleolithic fauna of, 95
 red ocher found at, 96
Ehringsdorf Mousterian industry, 82, 84
Ehringsdorf travertine, 21
Engraved pebbles, 96, 190
Environment. *See* Paleoenvironment
Eolian sediments, 22
Epiaurignacian culture, 115

Epigravettian culture, 135, 138, 143–145, 146, 151, 153, 155, 164–165, 195
Epimagdalenian culture, 176, 179, 185
Erd (Hungary), 96
Exchange networks, 125–127

Felsställe (Germany), 179
Flint, imported, 176, 186, 201
Fossil human remains. *See* Human remains

Gánovce (Slovakia)
 hominid remains from, 46–47, 101
 Paleolithic fauna of, 95
 Taubachian industry at, 84
Geissenklösterle Cave (Germany), 114, 179
Geochronology, development of, 8–11
Geography, 1–4, 195–196
Glaciations (cryomeres), 1, 10, 11, 16–19, 21–25, 34–35
Gönnersdorf (Germany), 181, 190
Gottwaldov. *See* Zlín
Gravettian culture
 description of, 10, 11, 31, 56, 103, 131–170 passim, 196
 fossil human remains associated with, 59–74
Graywacke lamps, 182, 185, 187
Grèzes litées, 22, 23
Grossweikersdorf (Austria), 114, 128
Grubgraben (Austria), 143, 145, 151, 165, 179
Grygov, 242
Gudenus Cave (Austria), 179

Habrovany–Olšany, 242
Habrůvka. *See* Barová Cave; Býčí skála Cave; Vinckova Cave
Hadí Cave, Mokrá, 181, 223, 242
Hády, 242
Hajany, 242
Hanušovická Cave, Hanušovice, 242
Heidelbergian culture, 76
Hematite figurines, 164
Hlavicova Cave, Hranice, 242
Hluchov, 115, 242
Hněvošice, 242
Hodonice, 242
Holocene fauna and vegetation, 33
Holstein period, hominids during, 44–46

Hominids. *See* Human remains
Homo erectus, 38–43, 44–46
　bilzingslebensis, 45
Homo mousteriensis Hauseri, 99
Homo (erectus seu sapiens) palaeohungaricus, 39
Homo primigenius, 99
Homo sapiens, 43–46, 102
　neanderthalensis, 46–56, 101–102
　sapiens, 56–74, 99, 101–102
　sapiens "Brno type," 62, 71–72, 101
　steinheimensis, 45, 47
Horákov, 242
Horky, 76
Horní Moštěnice, 242
Horní Sukolom, 242
Horní Věstonice, 242
Hostějov, 242
Hostim (Bohemia), 181
Hošťálkovice, 242
Hovorany, 242
Hradčany, 242
Hranice, 145, 242. *See also* Hlavicova Cave, Hranice
Hrubšice, 242
Hrušovany, 242
Human evolution. *See* Human remains
Human remains
　of Lower Pleistocene, 37–38
　of Middle Pleistocene period, 38–46
　of Upper Paleolithic period, 56–74
　of Upper Pleistocene period, 46–56
Hunting. *See* Subsistence
Hunting cults, Gravettian, 168
Hunting magic, 133, 168, 192

Interdisciplinary collaborations, 8, 13
Interglacials (thermomeres), 19–21, 34
Interpleniglacial, 34–35, 103, 133, 135
Interstadials, 34–35
Istállóskö Cave (Hungary), 56, 114
Ivančice, 243
Ivaň, 243
Ivory, carved, 157, 160, 164, 167, 188. *See also* Bone and antler industries

Jabloňany, 243
Jáchymka and Evina Caves, Babice, 243
Jalubí, 243
Jamolice, 243
Jaroměřice nad Rokytnou, 243
Jaroslavice, 5, 131, 243
Jarošov, U. Hradiště, 214, 243
Javoříčko. *See* Zkamenělý zámek Rock, Javoříčko
Jedovnice. *See* Kolíbky Caves, Jedovnice
Jenerálka (Bohemia), 26
Jerzmanowician culture, 113–114, 139
Jevišovice, 243
Jezeřany, 111, 237, 243
Ježkovice, 243
Jiřice, 243
Jiříkovice, 243
Jundrov, 243

Kadov, 82, 243
Kanice, 243. *See also* Pod vyhlídkou Cave
Karlštejn (Bohemia), 76
Karolín, 243
Karst areas, Pleistocene sediments in, 16
Kateřinská Cave, Vavřinec, 94, 243
Kaufertsberg (Germany), 179
Kesslerloch (Switzerland), 181, 192
Klausen Caves (Germany), 179
Kleine Ofnet (Germany), 179
Klementowice (Poland), 181
Klentnice, 243
Klobouky, 243
Kněžice, 243
Kniegrotte Cave (Germany), 73
Kobylí, 243
Kohoutovice, 243
Kojetín, 243
Kolíbky Caves, Jedovnice, 244
　excavations at, 11
　description of, 215
　Magdalenian occupation at, 182, 187
Količín, 244
Koněprusy Cave, Zlatý kůň Hill
　archaeological evidence, 129
　human remains from, 56, 58–59
Königsaue (Germany), hominid remains from, 47, 48
Koňská Cave, Vavřinec, 244
Kosíř. *See* Drahanovice; Slatinice
Kostelec, 244

Kostenkian culture, 131–132, 139
Kostěnki (Russia), 72
Kozmice, 244
Kožichovice, 244
Krapina, hominid remains from, 54
Krems-Hundsteig (Austria), 114
Krhov, 244
Krumlov (Krumlovský les) chert, 110, 123, 125, 153, 199, 201, 207, 213
Krumlovian culture, 103
Krumvíř, 244
Křepice, 244
Křižanovice, 244
Křižova Cave, Ochoz, 181, 223, 244
Kubšice, 244
Kůlna Cave, Sloup, 244
  dating of, 5, 6
  description of, 215–218
  Magdalenian occupation at, 172, 174–175, 181, 182, 194
  Micoquian industry at, 85, 111
  Middle Paleolithic occupation at, 77, 79, 93
  Mousterian industry at, 82
  Taubachian industry at, 84–85
  Upper Paleolithic fauna at, 174
  Upper Paleolithic human remains from, 73, 194
  Upper Pleistocene hominid remains from, 47, 50–52, 97
Kůlnička Cave, Mokrá, 181, 223, 244
Kupařovice, 115, 244
Kutná Hora (Bohemia), 26
Kvasice, 244
Kyjov, 244

La Madeleine (France), 5, 171
Langmannnersdorf (Austria), 114, 115
Lažánky. See Rytířská Cave
Lebenstedt (Germany), 95
Lechotice, 244
Lechovice, 26
Lednice, 82, 244
Le Moustier (France), 5, 171
Letky (Bohemia), 26, 76
Letonice, 244
Lhánice, 244
Lhota, 244
Lhota Rapotina, 244

Lhotka, 244
Lindenthaler Hyänenhöhle (Germany), 192
Lipovec. See Michalova skála Cave, Lipovec
Liščí Cave, Ochoz, 20, 244
Líšeň, Brno-město, 123, 244
Lithics
  development of typology for, 10
  exploitation areas, 93, 127, 199
  Lower and Middle Paleolithic industries, 80–88
  Lower Paleolithic raw material acquisition, 93–94
  research focus on, 199–200
  technology of, 11
  Upper Paleolithic exploitation of, 120–127, 153, 186–187
Litoměřice (Bohemia)
  site I, 26
  site II, 26
Loess series, 15–16, 22–23, 26–27, 30–32, 79
Loučany, 244
Lower Paleolithic period
  cultural development in, 80–88
  evidence of, 75–77
  raw material acquisition in, 93–94
  settlement pattern of, 88–93
  stratigraphy of, 77–79
  subsistence in, 94–96
  symbolism (art) and rituals in, 96–97
Lower Pleistocene hominids, 37–38
Lubná, 244
Ludmírov-Milkov. See Průchodnice Caves
Ludslavice, 245
Luhačovice, 245
Luleč, 245
Lutín, 245

Magdalenian culture
  description of, 7, 8, 27, 171–194 passim, 195, 196
  fossil human remains associated with, 73–74
Malhostovice, 245
Maloměřice, 245
Maloměřice-Borky I, 181, 186, 223
Mammoth Age, 5
Marefy, 245

Markkleeberg (Germany), 82
Maršovice, 237, 245
Martinka, 22
Maszycka Cave (Poland), 174, 179, 194
Mauer (Germany), hominid remains from, 39
Mažarná Cave (Slovakia), 23
Medlov, 245
Medlov-Zadní Újezd, 245
Mělčany, 245
Měnín, 245
Michalova skála Cave, Lipovec, 194, 245
Micoquian culture, 79, 85, 90, 103, 111
Microblades
  Gravettian, 139, 145, 151
  Magdalenian, 176
Middle Paleolithic period
  cultural development in, 80–88
  evidence of, 75
  raw material acquisition in, 93–94
  settlement pattern of, 88–93
  stratigraphy of, 77–79
  subsistence in, 94–96
  symbolism and rituals in, 96–97
Middle Pleistocene hominids, 38–46
Mikulov, 245. *See also* Turold
Mikulov Castle, fire at, 8, 101
Milovice (distr. Břeclav), 245
  Aurignacian occupation at, 114, 115
  description of, 218
  excavations at, 11
  soils at, 105
Milovice (distr. Kroměříž), 245
Miroslav-Kašenec, 245
Míškovice, 245
Mladeč, Plavatisko, 245
Mladeč Caves, 245. *See also* Podkova Cave
  dating of, 6
  evidence of personal adornment at, 128–130
  Pleistocene fauna in, 20
Mladeč Caves, Site I
  bone and antler industry at, 115
  description of, 218–219
  human remains from, 56–57, 59
Mladeč Caves, Site II
  bone and antler industry at, 115
  description of, 219

Mladeč Caves, Site II (*cont.*)
  human remains from, 56, 57–58, 59
Mladoňovice, 245
Mlazice (Bohemia), 76
Modřice, Brno-město, 10, 26, 245
Mohelno, 245
Mokrá, 223, 245. *See also* Hadí Cave; Kůlnička Cave; Pekárna Cave
Molodova (Ukraine), 133, 143
Moravany (Slovakia), 141–143, 164, 245
Moravany (distr. Brno-venkov), 245
Moravia
  early development of chronology for, 4–8
  geochronology of, 8–11
  geography of, 1–4
  glaciations in, 1, 10, 11, 16–19, 21–25, 34–35
  human remains from, 37–74 passim
  interglacials in, 19–21, 34
  Lower and Middle Paleolithic stratigraphy of, 77–79
  microregions in, 197–204
  past archaeological research in, 4–13
  present state of research in, 13–14
  Upper Pleistocene sequence in, 25–33
  Western scholars in, 11–13
Moravian Gate
  as communication axis, 90, 196
  glaciation to, 15, 24
  glacigenic deposits in, 16
Moravian Museum, destruction of collections of, 8, 101
Moravské Bránice, 245
Moravské Knínice, 245
Moravský Krumlov, 245
Morkůvky, 245
Mořice, 245
Mostkovice, 245
Mousterian culture
  evidence of, 75
  fossil human remains associated with, 43, 44
  lithic industry associated with, 82–84
  Mušov sites associated with, 79, 90
  paleoenvironment of, 7
Mutěnice, 246
Myslejovice, 246

INDEX

Napajedla, 246
Násedlovice, 246
Neanderthals. *See* Homo sapiens neanderthalensis
Nebovidy, 246
Nebra (Germany), 181
Neslovice, 246
Neumark-Gröbern (Germany), 95
Nevojice, 246
Němčičky, 246
Nietoperzowa Cave (Poland), 114
Nikolčice, 246
Nitra-Čermáň (Slovakia), 143
Nová Dědina, 125, 246
Nová Drátenická Cave, 174, 219–220, 246
Nová Hora, Brno-město, 85, 246
Nová Ves (distr. Břeclav), 246
Nová Ves (distr. Brno-venkov), 246
Nové Bránice, 246
Nuzířov, 246

Oberkassel (Germany), 194
Obora, 246
Ocher. *See* Red ocher
Ochoz, 246. *See also* Adlerova Cave; Křížova Cave; Liščí Cave; Ochozská Cave; Švédův stůl
Ochoz jawbone. *See* Švédův stůl Cave, Ochoz: hominid remains from
Ochozská Cave, Ochoz, 181, 223, 246
Oelknitz (Germany), 181
Ohrozim, 246
Olbramovice, 246
Oldřišov, 246
Olduvai, hominid remains from, 43, 45
Olomučany chert, 200
Omice, 246
Ondratice, 6, 102, 246
Ondratice quartzite, 108, 123, 199, 201
Ondrej-Horka (Slovakia), 84
Opatovice, 246
Opava, 246
Ořechov, 246
Oslavany, 246
Ostopovice, 246
Ostrava. *See* Petřkovice; Přívoz
Ostrava Glacial Basin, 24
Ostrov u Macochy, 247. *See also* Balcarova Cave

Ostrožská Nová Ves, 247
Otaslavice, 247
Otice, 247

Paleoenvironment
 of Pleistocene period, 15–36 passim
 of Upper Paleolithic period, 103–107, 133–138
Paleolithic hominids, 56–74
Pasohlávky, 247
Paudorf (Austria), 30n
Pavlov, Pleistocene deposits at, 21
Pavlov, Site I, 247
 analysis of, 13–14
 burials at, 170
 description of, 220–221
 Gravettian occupation at, 141, 147, 151–153, 157–160, 168
 human remains from, 60, 66–67, 72
Pavlov, Site II, 221, 247
Pavlov, Site III, 221, 247
Pavlovian culture, 11, 60, 131–132
Pavlovian stage, 141
Pavlovice, 247
Pavlovské Hills-Soutěska, 22, 23, 32, 34
Peat bogs, pollen from, 176
Pedocomplexes, 15, 19
Pekárna Cave, Mokrá, 247
 dating of, 5, 6, 7
 description of, 221–223
 Magdalenian occupation at, 172, 174, 176, 179, 181, 185, 186, 187, 192
 Micoquian industry at, 85
 Middle Paleolithic occupation at, 79
 stratigraphy of, 172
 Upper Paleolithic fauna at, 174
Pellet sands, 27, 29–30, 79
Petersfels (Germany), 179, 192
Petralona (Greece), hominid remains from, 39, 45
Petřkovice, Ostrava, 141, 164, 223, 247
Piekary IIb (Poland), 82
Pístovice, 247
Plastosols, 21
Pleistocene period
 hominids remains of, 37–56
 paleoenvironment of, 15–36 passim
 sediments of, 15–16, 22–23, 26–27, 30–32

Pod hradem Cave, Vavřinec, 127–128, 247
Podivice, 247
Pod Koňským spádem Caves, Vavřinec, 247
Podkova Cave, Mladeč, 219, 247
Podstránská, Brno-ěsto, 247
Pod vyhlídkou Cave, Kanice, 247
Pohořelice, 247
Polánka, 247
Polanka nad Odrou, 82, 247
Popice, 247
Popovice, 247
Pottery. See Ceramics
Poustevna Cave, Sloup, 5, 247
Pouzdřany, 247
Pozořice, 247
Prague, Cave of St. Prokop (Bohemia), 56, 59
Pravlov, 247
Pre-Aurignacian period, 8
Prštice, 247
Průchodnice Caves, Ludmírov-Milkov, 31, 247
Prusínovice, 248
Předmostí, Přerov, 248
  analysis of, 8
  burials at, 170
  dating of, 5, 7
  description of, 223–226
  flat pebbles found at, 96
  Gravettian occupation at, 131, 137, 138, 154, 160–165, 168
  human remains from, 60, 62–64, 70, 72
  lithic raw materials at, 93
  Lower and Middle Paleolithic stratigraphy of, 79
  Pleistocene deposits at, 24
  Taubachian industry at, 85
Předmostí, Site I (Skalka), 226–229
Předmostí, Site II (Hradisko), 21, 229
Přestavlky, 248
Prezletice Zlatý kopec (Bohemia)
  hominid remains from, 37–38
  Lower Paleolithic occupation at, 77, 80, 92, 94
  Lower Pleistocene deposits at, 37
Přibice, 248
Přívoz, Ostrava, 248
Pustožlebská Zazděná Cave, 22, 23

Quaternary climatic cycle, 16–19, 33–36

Radiolarite, 93, 125, 141, 153, 186, 199, 233
Radkova Lhota, 248
Radostice, 248
Radošiná Cave, 111
Radslavice, 248
Rájec, 248
Ráječko, 248
Rakvice, 248
Ranis (Germany), human remains from, 73
Rašov, 248
Raw material acquisition. See Lithics
Red ocher, 96, 128, 153, 166, 187
Regional surveys, 197
Reindeer Age, 5, 154
Rheindahlen Mousterian industry, 82, 84
Rituals, of Upper Paleolithic period, 73, 128–130, 157–170, 181, 188–194. See also Death; Symbolism
Rock crystal, imported, 176, 185, 200, 203
Rostěnice, 248
Rozdrojovice, 248
Rudice, 248
Rudice chert, 187
Rychtářov, 248
Rychvald, 248
Rytířská Cave, Lažánky, 188, 248
Říčky, Domašov, 248
Řimice, 248

Sady, U. Hradiště, 248
Samotíšky, 248
Sandstone, 187, 200
Schweizersbild (Switzerland), 179, 192
Sebranice, 248
Sedlec (Bohemia), 26
Sedlec (distr. Břeclav), 248
Sedlešovice, Znojmo, 80, 248
Seloutky, Určice, 248
Senftenberg (Austria), 114
Senorady, 248
Settlement patterns
  of Lower and Middle Paleolithic periods, 88–93
  of Upper Paleolithic period, 118–120, 145–153, 179–186
Settlement units, 120, 146, 147
Shale, 187
Shells, imported, 153

Silická Brezová, human remains from, 56
Silůvky, 248
Sinanthropus, 41, 45
Sivice, 248
Skalice, 249
Skhul, hominid remains from, 54
Sklep Cave, Vratíkov, 85, 249
Skřečoň, 249
Slate plaques, Magdalenian, 168, 181, 190–192, 194
Slatinice, 115, 249
Slavkov, 249
Sloup. *See* Kůlna Cave; Poustevna Cave
Sloupské Caves, 94
Smrtní Cave, Vilémovice, 249
Sněhotice, 249
Spadzista (Poland), 143
Spytihněv, 249
Srnči Cave, Vilémovice, 23, 249
Staré Město, Uherské Hradiště, 74, 249
Steinheim, hominid remains from, 43, 44
Stillfied Complex, 26–27
Strahovice, 249
Stránská skála, Brno-město, 249
  description of, 230
  excavations at, 11, 103
  incised animal bones from, 96
  settlement patterns at, 120
  soils at, 105
  Upper Paleolithic occupation at, 102
Stránská skála, Site I
  description of, 230, 231
  Lower and Middle Pleistocene stratigraphy of, 79
  Lower Paleolithic artifacts from, 80
  Paleolithic depositis at, 75–76
  Pleistocene deposits at, 22, 75
  slope deposits at, 20
Stránská skála, Site II-III
  Aurignacian occupations at, 114, 115
  Bohunician occupations at, 108–110, 123–124
  description of, 231–233
  red ocher at, 128
Stránská skála, Site IV
  description of, 233–234
  Epigravettian occupation at, 135, 138, 143, 153, 155, 165

Stránská skála chert, 108, 123–125, 199, 201, 207, 231
Stratigraphy
  of Lower and Middle Paleolithic period, 77–79
  of Upper Paleolithic period, 103–107, 133–138, 173–176
Stratzing (Austria), 114, 120, 128
Strážná u Hostišové, 249
Střelice, 249
Střébrnice, 249
Stvolínky (Bohemia), 82
Subalyuk Cave (Hungary), 48, 54–56
Subsistence
  of Lower and Middle Paleolithic periods, 94–96
  of Upper Paleolithic period, 127–128, 154–157, 187–188
Suchdol (Bohemia), 37
Suchohrdly u Znojma, 249
Sungir, human remains from, 72
Svitávka, 60, 72, 249
Swanscombe, hominid remains from, 43, 44
Symbolism (art)
  of Lower and Middle Paleolithic periods, 96–97
  of Upper Paleolithic period, 72–73, 99, 118, 128–130, 157–170, 188–194
Syrovice, 249
Szeleta Cave (Hungary), 102, 132
Szeletian culture, 8, 10, 11, 56, 102, 103, 105, 107, 110–113, 119, 132, 139, 195, 204
Šala nad Váhom, hominid remains from, 47, 48
Šatov, 249
Šipka Cave, Štramberk, 249
  dating of, 5, 6
  description of, 234–235
  geochronology of, 10
  Paleolithic fauna of, 95
  Middle Paleolithic occupation of, 79
  Mousterian industry in, 88
  Upper Pleistocene hominid remains from, 48, 52–54, 97, 100
Šlapanice, 249
Šošůvské Caves, Šošůvka, 249
Štěpánovice, 249
Šternberk, 249

Štramberk. *See* Čertova díra Cave; Šipka Cave
Štramberk flysch sandstone, 200
Šumice, 249
Švédské Šance, Brno-město, 249
Švédův stůl Cave, Ochoz, 249
 description of, 223, 235
 hominid remains from, 48, 54, 97
 Magdalenian occupation at, 181
 Middle Paleolithic occupation of, 79
 Mousterian industry in, 88

Tata (Hungary), 84, 95, 96
Taubach (Germany), 47, 95
Taubachian culture, 79, 84–85, 90, 94
Těšnovice, 250
Territorial types, 200–204
Thermomeres (interglacials), 19–21, 34
Tišnov, 182, 250
Tišnovian culture, 179, 185, 204
Trboušany, 250
Trenčianské Bohuslavice (Slovakia), 143
Troubky, 250
Troubsko, 250
Trzebnica (Poland), 81
Třebářov, 250
Třebčín, 250
Třebíč, 250
Třebom, 250
Tučapy, 250
Turold, Mikulov, 20, 250
Tvarožná, 125, 250
Typology, of lithics, 10

Uherské Hradiště, 250. *See also* Jarošov; Sady; Staré Město
Újezd u Brna, 250
Újezd u Černé Hory, 250
Upper Paleolithic period
 cultural development in, 107–118, 138–145, 176–179
 environment and stratigraphy of, 103–107, 133–138, 173–176
 fossil hominid remains of, 56–74
 lithic exploitation in, 120–127, 153, 186–187
 migrations during, 99–100, 171–172, 185, 186

Upper Paleolithic period (*cont.*)
 settlement patterns in, 118–120, 145–153, 179–186
 subsistence in, 127–128, 154–157, 187–188
 symbolism (art) and ritual in, 128–130, 157–170, 188–194
 symbolism of, 72–73, 99
Upper Pleistocene period
 fossil hominid remains from, 46–56
 sequence for, 25–33
Určice, 82, 250

Vávrovice-Palhanec, Opava, 250
Vavřinec. *See* Jeskyně Number 184 (Cave); Kateřinská Cave; Koňská Cave; Pod hradem Cave; Pod Koňským spádem
Vážany-Vítovice, 250
Vedrovice, 11, 120, 235, 250
 Site I, 114, 237
 Site II, 115, 237
 Site V, 111, 237
Velatice, 250
Velké Pavlovice, 26, 135, 250
Velký Špunt, 23
Velký Týnec, 250
Venus figurines, 72, 143, 157
Vértesszölös locality (Hungary)
 Lower Paleolithic occupation at, 77, 81, 94
 Middle Pleistocene hominid remains from, 38–39, 43, 46
Verunčina Cave, Vilémovice, 250
Veverská Bitýška, 250
Věžky, 250
Vícemilice, 251
Vilémovice. *See* Smrtní Cave; Srnčí Cave; Verunčina Cave
Vincencov, Otaslavice, 111, 251
Vinckova Cave, Habrůvka, 251
Vogelherd (Germany), 179
Vojkovice, 251
Vracov Lake, 176
Vratíkov. *See* Sklep Cave
Výpustek Cave, Březina, 85, 251
Vyškov, 251. *See also* Dědice

Willendorf (Austria)
 Aurignacian occupation at, 103, 114

Willendorf (Austria) (*cont.*)
  chronological sequence at, 133
  Gravettian occupation at, 138, 141, 164
  human remains from, 68–69
  soils at, 105–107
  Upper Paleolithic tool industry at, 107
Willendorfian-Kostenkian stage. *See* Gravettian culture

Záblatí, 251
Žabovřesky–Brno (Brno III), 60, 62, 78, 208
Zahnašovice, 251
Záviïce, 251
Zdislavice, 251
Zdounky, 251
Zelená Hora, 251
Zkamenělý zámek Rock, Javoříčko, 251

Zlatý kopec locality, hominid remains from, 37–38
Zlatý kůn Hill. *See* Koněprusy Cave, Zlatý kůn Hill
Zlín-Louky, 251
Zlín-Tečovice, 251
Znojmo, 26, 251. *See also* Sedlešovice
Zwolen (Poland), 95
Žabovřesky, 251
Ždánice, 26, 28, 31, 251
Želešice, 251
Žernovník, 251
Židlohovice, 251
Žilina, 251
Žitného Cave, Březina, 179, 237–238, 251
Žitný Cave. *See* Žitného Cave, Březina
Žlutava, 251
Zuttiyeh, hominid remains from, 48, 54

INTERDISCIPLINARY CONTRIBUTIONS TO ARCHAEOLOGY
Chronological Listing of Volumes

THE PLEISTOCENE OLD WORLD
Regional Perspectives
Edited by Olga Soffer

HOLOCENE HUMAN ECOLOGY IN NORTHEASTERN NORTH AMERICA
Edited by George P. Nicholas

ECOLOGY AND HUMAN ORGANIZATION ON THE GREAT PLAINS
Douglas B. Bamforth

THE INTERPRETATION OF ARCHAEOLOGICAL SPATIAL PATTERNING
Edited by Ellen M. Kroll and T. Douglas Price

HUNTER–GATHERERS
Archaeological and Evolutionary Theory
Robert L. Bettinger

RESOURCES, POWER, AND INTERREGIONAL INTERACTION
Edited by Edward M. Schortman and Patricia A. Urban

POTTERY FUNCTION
A Use-Alteration Perspective
James M. Skibo

SPACE, TIME, AND ARCHAEOLOGICAL LANDSCAPES
Edited by Jacqueline Rossignol and LuAnn Wandsnider

ETHNOHISTORY AND ARCHAEOLOGY
Approaches to Postcontact Change in the Americas
Edited by J. Daniel Rogers and Samuel M. Wilson

THE AMERICAN SOUTHWEST AND MESOAMERICA
Systems of Prehistoric Exchange
Edited by Jonathon E. Ericson and Timothy G. Baugh

FROM KOSTENKI TO CLOVIS
Upper Paleolithic–Paleo-Indian Adaptations
Edited by Olga Soffer and N. D. Praslov

EARLY HUNTER–GATHERERS OF THE CALIFORNIA COAST
Jon M. Erlandson

HOUSES AND HOUSEHOLDS
A Comparative Study
Richard E. Blanton

THE ARCHAEOLOGY OF GENDER
Separating the Spheres in Urban America
Diana diZerega Wall

ORIGINS OF ANATOMICALLY MODERN HUMANS
Edited by Matthew H. Nitecki and Doris V. Nitecki

PREHISTORIC EXCHANGE SYSTEMS IN NORTH AMERICA
Edited by Timothy G. Baugh and Jonathon E. Ericson

STYLE, SOCIETY, AND PERSON
Archaeological and Ethnological Perspectives
Edited by Christopher Carr and Jill E. Neitzel

REGIONAL APPROACHES TO MORTUARY ANALYSIS
Edited by Lane Anderson Beck

DIVERSITY AND COMPLEXITY IN PREHISTORIC MARITIME SOCIETIES
A Gulf of Maine Perspective
Bruce J. Bourque

CHESAPEAKE PREHISTORY
Old Traditions, New Directions
Richard J. Dent, Jr.

PREHISTORIC CULTURAL ECOLOGY AND EVOLUTION
Insights from Southern Jordan
Donald O. Henry

STONE TOOLS
Theoretical Insights into Human Prehistory
Edited by George H. Odell

THE ARCHAEOLOGY OF WEALTH
Consumer Behavior in English America
James G. Gibb

STATISTICS FOR ARCHAEOLOGISTS
A Commonsense Approach
Robert D. Drennan

DARWINIAN ARCHAEOLOGIES
Edited by Herbert Donald Graham Maschner

CASE STUDIES IN ENVIRONMENTAL ARCHAEOLOGY
Edited by Elizabeth J. Reitz, Lee A. Newsom, and Sylvia J. Scudder

HUMANS AT THE END OF THE ICE AGE
The Archaeology of the Pleistocene–Holocene Transition
Edited by Lawrence Guy Straus, Berit Valentin Eriksen, Jon M. Erlandson, and David R. Yesner

VILLAGERS OF THE MAROS
A Portrait of an Early Bronze Age Society
John M. O'Shea

HUNTERS BETWEEN EAST AND WEST
The Paleolithic of Moravia
Jiří Svoboda, Vojen Ložek, and Emanuel Vlček

DATE DUE

DEC 0 8 2001			

HIGHSMITH #45230

Printed in USA